Politicians and Rhe

MW00778791

Politicians and Rhetoric

The Persuasive Power of Metaphor

Second edition

Jonathan Charteris-Black
University of the West of England, UK

First published 2005
Second edition published 2011 by
PALGRAVE MACMILLAN

Palgrave Macmillan in the UK is an imprint of Macmillan Publishers Limited, registered in England, company number 785998, of Houndmills, Basingstoke, Hampshire RG21 6XS.

Palgrave Macmillan in the US is a division of St Martin's Press LLC, 175 Fifth Avenue, New York, NY 10010.

Palgrave Macmillan is the global academic imprint of the above companies and has companies and representatives throughout the world.

Palgrave® and Macmillan® are registered trademarks in the United States, the United Kingdom, Europe and other countries.

ISBN 978–0–230–25164–9 hardback
ISBN 978–0–230–25165–6 paperback

A catalogue record for this book is available from the British Library.

Library of Congress Cataloging-in-Publication Data
Charteris-Black, Jonathan, 1955–
   Politicians and rhetoric : the persuasive power of metaphor /
Jonathan Charteris-Black. — 2nd ed.
      p.   cm.
   Includes index.
   ISBN 978–0–230–25165–6 (alk. paper)
   1. Metaphor.   2. Rhetoric—Political aspects.   I. Title.
P301.5.M48C486 2011
825'.9109—dc22

2011013740

10   9   8   7   6   5   4   3   2   1
20   19   18   17   16   15   14   13   12   11

Transferred to Digital Printing in 2013

Speech was given to man to enable him to conceal his thoughts.
(Fournier – *L'Esprit dans l'Histoire*)

The task will be hard. There may be dark days ahead, and war can no longer be confined to the battlefield. But we can only do the right as we see the right, and reverently commit our cause to God.
(George VI – Speech on outbreak of war)

Make sure that we are talking with each other in a way that heals, not a way that wounds.
(Barack Obama – Memorial Service for the victims of the shooting in Tucson, University of Arizona, January 2011)

Contents

List of Figures   xii

List of Tables   xiii

Preface   xiv

1 Persuasion, Speech Making and Rhetoric   1
  1.1   Language and politics   1
  1.2   The art of speech making   5
        1.2.1   'Spin', manipulation and trust   5
        1.2.2   Classical speech making   6
        1.2.3   Contemporary rhetoric   9
  1.3   Persuasion and rhetoric   13
        1.3.1   Persuasion   13
        1.3.2   Rhetoric and dialect   15
        1.3.3   The psychology of persuasion   17
        1.3.4   Media influences   20
  1.4   Ideology and myth   21
        1.4.1   Ideology   21
        1.4.2   Myth   22
        1.4.3   Political myth   24
  1.5   Summary   26

2 Metaphor in Political Discourse   28
  2.1   Metaphor and political thinking   28
        2.1.1   Introduction – Gordon Brown's 'moral
                compass'   28
        2.1.2   What is metaphor?   31
        2.1.3   The purpose of metaphor – conventional
                metaphor   32
  2.2   Metaphor in political persuasion   35
        2.2.1   Right thinking   35
        2.2.2   Myth making: telling the right story   38
        2.2.3   Evaluating metaphor in political persuasion   43
  2.3   Critical metaphor analysis and cognitive semantics   45
  2.4   Summary   50

3   Winston Churchill: Metaphor and Heroic Myth   52
    3.1   Background   52
    3.2   The rhetoric of Winston Churchill   54
    3.3   Metaphor analysis   58
    3.4   Personification   61
    3.5   Journey metaphors   66
    3.6   Metaphors of light and darkness   71
    3.7   Nested metaphors   74
    3.8   Summary   77

4   Martin Luther King: Messianic Myth   79
    4.1   Background   79
    4.2   Messianic myth   81
    4.3   The rhetoric of Martin Luther King   83
    4.4   Metaphor analysis: source domains   87
        4.4.1   Introduction to findings   87
        4.4.2   Journey metaphors   88
        4.4.3   Landscape metaphors   96
    4.5   Metaphor analysis: target domains   100
        4.5.1   Segregation metaphors   100
        4.5.2   Metaphors for non-violence   104
    4.6   Metaphor interaction   104
    4.7   Summary   107

5   Enoch Powell: the Myth of the Oracle   109
    5.1   Background   109
    5.2   The rhetoric of Enoch Powell   111
    5.3   Rhetorical strategies   116
        5.3.1   Popular phrases: sounding right   116
        5.3.2   Reported dialogue with interlocutors:
                thinking right   117
        5.3.3   Narrative: telling the right story   120
    5.4   Metaphor analysis   123
    5.5   Summary   136

**6   Ronald Reagan and Romantic Myth: 'From the Swamp
    to the Stars'**   138
    6.1   Background – romantic myth   138
    6.2   The rhetoric of Ronald Reagan – the actor
          politician   142
    6.3   Sports metaphors and the broadcaster politician   146
    6.4   Reaching for the stars: intergalactic myth   149

6.5		Intergalactic metaphors and light metaphors	155
6.6		Conclusion	163

7 Margaret Thatcher and the Myth of Boudicca   **165**

7.1		Background – the Iron Lady	165
7.2		The rhetoric of Margaret Thatcher	168
	7.2.1	SOCIAL AND ECONOMIC PROBLEMS ARE ENEMIES	170
	7.2.2	INDUSTRIAL RELATIONS IS A BATTLE	171
	7.2.3	POLITICAL OPPONENTS ARE ENEMIES	173
	7.2.4	Summary of Margaret Thatcher's rhetoric	176
7.3		Metaphor analysis	178
	7.3.1	Journey metaphors	178
	7.3.2	Health metaphors	180
	7.3.3	Metaphors for religion and morality	182
	7.3.4	Metaphors of life and death	187
	7.3.5	Animal metaphors	189
	7.3.6	Master–servant metaphors	190
	7.3.7	Other metaphors	191
7.4		Summary	192

8 Clinton and the Rhetoric of Image Restoration   **195**

8.1		Background	195
8.2		The rhetoric of Bill Clinton: metaphor and image presentation	196
8.3		Metaphor analysis	200
	8.3.1	Creation metaphors	202
	8.3.2	Destruction metaphors	205
	8.3.3	Metaphors for life, rebirth and death	208
	8.3.4	Journey metaphors	211
	8.3.5	Religious metaphors	217
8.4		Metaphor diversity and everyday heroes	219
8.5		Summary	221

9 Tony Blair and Conviction Rhetoric   **223**

9.1		Background	223
9.2		Blair, communication and leadership	225
9.3		Blair and the rhetoric of legitimisation: the epic battle between good and evil	228
9.4		Metaphor analysis	234
	9.4.1	Journey metaphors	234
	9.4.2	Blair and reification	236

9.4.3	Personification	243
9.4.4	Neutral reification and the use of phraseology	245
9.5	Summary	246

10   George Bush and the Rhetoric of Moral Accounting   **251**
10.1   Introduction   251
10.2   The rhetoric of George W. Bush: the moral accounting metaphor   253
10.3   Metaphor analysis   256
   10.3.1   Personifications and telling the right story   256
   10.3.2   Depersonifications   264
   10.3.3   Finance metaphors   266
   10.3.4   Crime and punishment metaphors   270
10.4   Summary   278

11   Barack Obama and the Myth of the American Dream   **280**
11.1   Introduction   280
11.2   Obama and the American Dream   281
11.3   Classical rhetoric   288
11.4   Metaphor analysis   295
   11.4.1   Overview   295
   11.4.2   Metaphor and speech structure   301
11.5   Blending of rhetorical traditions   305
11.6   Conclusion   309

12   Myth, Metaphor and Leadership   **311**
12.1   Politicians and metaphor   311
12.2   Overview of metaphor types in political speeches   313
12.3   Metaphor and political communication   318
   12.3.1   Establishing the politician's ethos: having the right intentions   318
   12.3.2   Heightening the pathos: sounding right   320
   12.3.3   Communicating and explaining political policies: thinking right   321
   12.3.4   Communication of ideology by political myth: telling the right story   323
12.4   Summary: myth, magic and power   326

Appendix 1   Churchill Corpus (25 speeches)   330

Appendix 2   Churchill's Metaphors Classified by Type/Source Domain   331

Appendix 3   Luther King Corpus (14 speeches)   332

Appendix 4   Luther King's Metaphors Classified by Type/Source Domain   333

Appendix 5   Powell Corpus (24 speeches)   335

Appendix 6   Powell's Metaphors Classified by Type/Source Domain   336

Appendix 7   Reagan Corpus (13 speeches)   338

Appendix 8   Reagan's Metaphors Classified by Type/Source Domain   339

Appendix 9   Thatcher Corpus (11 speeches)   341

Appendix 10   Thatcher's Metaphors Classified by Type/Source Domain   342

Appendix 11   Clinton Corpus (9 speeches)   344

Appendix 12   Clinton's Metaphors Classified by Type/Source Domain   345

Appendix 13   Blair Corpus (14 speeches)   347

Appendix 14   Blair's Metaphors Classified by Type/Source Domain   348

Appendix 15   Bush Corpus (19 speeches)   350
(i) George Bush Senior corpus (4 speeches)   350
(ii) George Bush Junior corpus (15 speeches)   350

Appendix 16   Metaphors of George Bush Junior and Senior   351

Appendix 17   Obama Corpus (19 speeches)   353

Appendix 18   Obama's Metaphors Classified by Type/Source Domain   354

Bibliography   356

Index of Conceptual Metaphors   362

General Index   365

List of Figures

1.1 Rhetorical means for persuasion in political
communication   14

3.1 Summary of conceptual metaphors for Churchill's
heroic myth   78

4.1 Stages of the messianic myth   91

5.1 Analysis of 'toad beneath the harrow' using blending
theory   127

5.2 Analysis of 'immigration' metaphor using blending
theory   129

6.1 Analysis of 'intergalactic metaphor' using blending
theory   157

6.2 Analysis of 'reach for the stars' using blending theory   158

11.1 Blending analysis of 'bending the arc of history'   300

List of Tables

1.1	'Sound bites' in political rhetoric	10
3.1	Summary of metaphor targets in Churchill's personifications	65
3.2	Evaluation in light and dark metaphors	72
4.1	Rhetorical and narrative stages in messianic myth	91
4.2	The conceptual metaphors of Martin Luther King	107
7.1	Margaret Thatcher's political myths	193
12.1	Overview of metaphor types by source domain – British politicians	314
12.2	Overview of metaphor types by source domain – American politicians	315

Preface

It has always been preferable for the governed to be ruled by the spoken word rather than by the whip, the chain or the gun. For this reason we should be happy when power is based – at least to some extent – upon language; at least when our leaders are taking the trouble to persuade us, we have the choice of accepting or rejecting their arguments. Leadership is a social act which requires two parties: individuals who are gifted in the arts of self-representation and others who are ready to follow when they are convinced by rhetoric. The language of persuasion looks both outwards and inwards: it promises a better future – often based on what is wrong with the present; but it communicates this vision by activating deep-seated ideas, values and feelings that are hidden within the audience. Successful politicians are those who have credible stories to tell, who can involve us with the drama of the present by explaining in simple terms what is right and wrong and who can convince us that they are better than their opponents.

In this second edition I have analysed the rhetorical use of language of three additional politicians to produce a study of nine politicians – four British and five North American – who have demonstrated great success in their ability to persuade. I hope to explain how their use of language created credible and consistent stories about themselves and the social world they inhabit. I hope to explore their use of metaphors, the nature of their myths and show how language analysis helps us to understand how politicians are able to persuade.

1
Persuasion, Speech Making and Rhetoric

1.1 Language and politics

Within all types of political system leaders have relied on the spoken word to contrast the benefits that arise from their leadership with the dangers that will arise from that of their opponents. The more democratic societies become, the greater the onus on leaders to convince potential followers that they and their policies can be trusted. As Burns (1978: 18) explains: 'Leadership over human beings is exercised when persons with certain motives and purposes mobilize, in competition or conflict with others, institutional, political, psychological, and other resources so as to arouse, engage, and satisfy the motives of followers.' In this book I illustrate how, in democracies, those who aspire to political leadership persuade their followers through their command of rhetoric and their skill in using metaphor.

Voters make decisions based on their judgements of the honesty, morality and integrity of politicians. These views arise from considerations such as the consistency of actions with words and the efficacy of political arguments. However, they are also influenced by impressions arising from a politician's style and self-presentation. Presentation is gauged through eyes, hair, height, body shape, dress and through a range of bodily mannerisms, such as gaze and gesture. Politicians 'design' their own style of leadership through the cumulative effect of characteristics over which they have some control. For example, they undertake symbolic actions – displays of health, vigour and physical prowess, such as engaging in a sport – that convey a symbolic meaning to followers. With the growth of media, appearance and visually based verbal methods, such as metaphor, are increasingly persuasive. We are only partially conscious of how a bundle of interacting attributes influence our judgements of a candidate's credibility as a leader. The purpose

1

of this second edition of *Politicians and Rhetoric* is to raise further our awareness of these persuasive methods to guide us towards where our trust might best be placed.

The spoken language is the primary mode of communication in the gentle arts of persuasion and impression management because it projects shared social beliefs about what is right and wrong so that alliances can be formed around these beliefs. Spoken strategies include humour, metaphor and the telling of myth. I investigate the rhetoric of four British and five American politicians who are recognised as the most persuasive exponents of these arts. I will argue that their choice of metaphor is essential to their persuasiveness. I will demonstrate the cognitive and affective appeal of metaphor and illustrate how it contributes to persuasion. This, I suggest, is because it exploits subliminal resources that are aroused non-verbally and then developed through language. The subliminal potential of metaphor is central to the performance of leadership.

I employ an empirical method to investigate the relation between rhetoric, metaphor and leadership; in each chapter I first identify a range of rhetorical features used by the politician concerned. I then identify a number of metaphors and organise these according to their original or 'literal' sense; I consider in what sense they are metaphors – inevitably this requires some attention to the contexts in which they are used. Following conceptual metaphor theory as first proposed by Lakoff and Johnson (1980), I then look for patterns that account for the correspondences between the literal senses of words and how they are used as metaphors. In practice this means inferring from a group of metaphors an underlying or 'conceptual' metaphor that explains what is *systematic* in the correspondence between the literal and metaphoric uses. A conceptual metaphor is one that identifies a pattern of thought from a number of actual instances of metaphor. An example may serve to make this approach clearer. The following metaphors (in italics) were chosen from the speeches of Margaret Thatcher and concern different areas of policy such as inflation, home ownership and schools:

> *Inflation threatens democracy* itself. We've always *put its victory* at the top of our agenda. For *it's a battle which never ends*. It means keeping your budget on a *sound financial footing*.
>
> Home ownership too has soared. And to extend the right to council tenants, *we had to fight the battle* as you know, *the battle in Parliament every inch of the way*. Against Labour opposition. And against Liberal opposition.

A new battle for Britain is under way in our schools. *Labour's tattered flag* is there for all to see. *Limp in the stale breeze of sixties ideology.*

In each case the word 'battle' and other conflict words are metaphors because their basic, literal sense refers to physical combat whereas here they refer to abstract political actions such as trying to control inflation or allowing council tenants to buy their houses. So the metaphoric senses could be summarised as:

OPPOSING INFLATION IS A BATTLE

GETTING POLICIES ACCEPTED IS A BATTLE

In each case the metaphor 'battle' describes different political actions. The basis for these separate metaphors can then be represented by a general statement that shows this systematic pattern of correspondence between them; so here a 'conceptual metaphor' might be: POLITICS IS CONFLICT. As Burns argues in his classic study:

> Leadership as conceptualized here is grounded in the seedbed of conflict. Conflict is intrinsically compelling; it galvanizes, prods, motivates people ... Leadership acts as an inciting and triggering force in the conversion of conflicting demands, values, and goals into significant behaviour. (Burns 1978: 38)

There is also evidence in words such as 'victory' and 'tattered' of strong evaluations associated with political actions. This value system is described with the language of war – of victory and defeat – and so linguistic choices communicate how Thatcher placed a positive value on conflict and competitiveness. This value system reflected a general view of human and social relations that informed her use of language. In cognitive terms we can say that the conceptual metaphor POLITICS IS CONFLICT describes a cognitive frame, or schema, underlying Margaret Thatcher's conflict metaphors; it might be used to explain her thinking to others – even though it may not be one that she was aware of when using these metaphors. Understanding the systematic nature of metaphor choices is therefore necessary if we are to understand *how* political language becomes persuasive.

But as already mentioned, it is not language *alone* that is persuasive; increasingly other media are exploited in successful political communication. Dress and gesture are important in face-to-face communication, voice quality in radio and eye and mouth movements are important in television because of close-up frames. A politician needs to know how to use a particular medium for maximum effect. Contemporary concern with the influence of the media reflects in the choice of the pejorative word 'spin' – to refer broadly to manipulation using *any* channel of communication. Although the public were not aware of it at the time, the preoccupation with media effect commenced with John F. Kennedy's election campaign in 1960. His advisers concealed his diagnosis with Addison's disease and Kennedy's self-administered injections were not public knowledge; the public witnessed images of a stylish and vigorous leader who played golf and went yachting. Those who listened to the radio debates with his Republican rival thought that Nixon had won, whereas those who watched on television *knew* that Kennedy had won. Nixon was visibly suffering from the discomfort of an injured leg and had a tense facial expression, perspired heavily and had a 'five-o'clock shadow' that matched his car salesman's suit. By contrast, Kennedy was relaxed and the effect of his make-up and suntan made him look like a Greek god. The media exploited his wartime injury to portray him as a valiant and heroic leader and he spoke like one too: it was the correspondence between his rhetoric, especially his metaphors, and the subliminal impressions he gave off – between what was heard and what was felt – that was so convincing.

Politics is concerned with acquiring, maintaining and sustaining power: it is about how resources are allocated and how social actions are harmonised to predetermined purposes. Language is the lifeblood of politics: it is debatable whether language would have developed in the first place without politics and certain that politics would never have developed without language. But the more skilled politicians become in self-representation, the greater the pressure on them to convince followers that they and their policies can be trusted. Politics is about building trust, but, with an increasing awareness of the potential for manipulation of public opinion and the 'massaging' of consent through focus groups, trust has become a rare commodity in democracies. We live in an era of scepticism in an age of conspiracy theories, believing – probably correctly – that we only ever know even half the story.

In this chapter I will first discuss some central issues in political speeches – such as their authenticity, the role of speech writers and the need for trust; I will then discuss the origins of speech making in classical rhetoric and the different perspective of our own media-driven culture. I then explain what I mean by 'persuasion', its relationship to rhetoric and how persuasion works in political communication. In the last section of the chapter I explain how ideology and myth contribute to persuasion. In the second chapter I will demonstrate how metaphor contributes to political communication. In the remaining chapters I illustrate how some of the most rhetorically successful of British and American political leaders in modern times have exploited metaphor and myth for the persuasive communication of their ideas.

1.2 The art of speech making

1.2.1 'Spin', manipulation and trust

I will first consider a key question that has vexed rhetoricians since the origins of political reflection: is the purpose of rhetoric to arrive at a single commonly agreed truth or can we only ever arrive at a version of the truth? The way this question is often raised in the contemporary period is over the authorship of political speeches: since it is known that political advisers and speech-writers are involved in the creation of these texts, to what extent can we trust the politician who delivers them? Do the words convey the speaker's 'real' beliefs, a political substance, or is his[1] authenticity to be doubted because the words are chosen by others and their speaker is therefore both manipulative and manipulated? Is rhetoric a means to truth or is it only 'spin'?

With the growth of digital communication the words of others have become increasingly available, so how can we be sure that anyone is any longer the author of their own words? Social network sites and the blogosphere have led to language itself becoming socialised to the extent that it challenges and even threatens our sense of individual identity: how can we be sure that we are hearing *our own voice* within a virtual cacophony of language, sound and image? Although politicians have, to varying extents, always relied on others to provide their scripts, there has been an increased reliance on speech-writers in modern times; soon after his election Barack Obama publicly recognised the contribution of his speech-writer Jon Favreau by appointing him 'Director of Speech Writing'. The use of speech-writers and the associated rise of political marketing raise important issues of authenticity, interest and authorship.

---

[1] Throughout this work the pronouns 'he' and 'his' are used generically to refer equally to men and women. This is not intended to place greater value on male politicians, but as all of the politicians except one are men, it is preferable to use 'he' and 'his' rather than 'she' and 'her'.

It may be seen as part of a wider process of media management 'whereby political actors may seek to control, manipulate or influence media organizations in ways which correspond with their political objectives' (Jones 1996: 135). The role of a team of speech-writers is to utilise a full range of rhetorical resources to contribute to a politician's image. But speech-writers can only choose words that fit a politician's image; his or her beliefs and unique political identity must be mirrored in the 'voice' we hear in their speeches and this necessarily constrains the options available to the speech-writer. Although authorship relies on the collaborative endeavour of a team of skilled individuals, speeches can *only* succeed rhetorically when they comply with a distinct political image that is 'owned' by the politician. The politician has the power to appoint speech-writers and dismiss them when their services are no longer required. Contrary to popular belief, the politician is usually the puppet master pulling the strings rather than the other way around. But knowledge of how the media are used to 'spin' messages has contributed to an increasing difficulty in *trusting* leaders. Yet for democracy to work, individuals need to have their own thoughts rather than rely on those of others and 'seeing' trust is a precondition.

Modern political speeches are usually multi-authored texts with a shared rhetorical purpose of legitimising the speech maker. The political speaker is more than a mere mouthpiece in this process because ultimately he has the opportunity to edit the content of the speech and to improvise in its delivery. Though the words he utters may originate in the minds of invisible others, the politician is ultimately accountable for them. Words said by someone who has an official status – such as a Member of Parliament – are recorded in official sources (Hansard) and are considered to be in the public domain so they can no longer be denied or disowned. This is why a politician's own words may be quoted back to him to query his consistency and moral integrity. The role of speech-writers is, then, to contribute to the marketing of a political 'brand', but the brand is *owned by the politician* who should therefore be treated as the author of his speeches. We need to be able to believe in the possibility of a leader who can be trusted – while seeing with sceptical eyes – when there is evidence for it, as for example when a rhetorical style is inconsistent with a politician's image.

1.2.2   Classical speech making

The origins of speech making as an art are closely related to the origins of democracy, since if power was to be negotiated and distributed to the people then there would need to be those who were skilled in persuasion. Socrates resisted the idea of persuasive appeals to interest groups because he believed in a permanent and abstract truth – one that would be to the benefit of all – rather than in the fickle concept of persuasion. But rhetoricians such as Aristotle and Quintilian recognised that different contexts required different methods of persuasion: influencing political decisions would not require the same methods as arguing legal cases or commemorating fallen heroes. Even philosophers would need to understand when language was being used to discover universal truth and when it was being used to manipulate or misrepresent: the development of rhetorical theory in Ancient Greece was therefore motivated by the idea of a truth that varied according to time, place and situation.

Audiences are only persuaded when the speaker's rhetoric is successful. In classical antiquity the definition of rhetoric was *ars bene dicendi*, the art of speaking well in public (Nash 1989). As Sauer (1997) notes, this definition requires a *comparative* judgement because it assumes that some people speak better than others – this is evident from speech events such as debating competitions and parliamentary debates that are concerned with deciding on future actions. The most rhetorically successful speech performance is the most persuasive one as measured by audience responses. Rhetoric may be said to have failed when an audience expresses opposition to the speaker's underlying purposes.

In the classical tradition Aristotle's views on rhetoric were based on the three artistic proofs of ethos, logos and pathos. He argued that in addition to taking a stance that was morally worthy (ethos) and proofs to support argument (logos), the successful rhetorician should also be able to arouse the feelings (pathos). Rhetoric went beyond the orator's verbal communication alone to his moral credibility, or *ethos*. A model orator was necessarily morally virtuous (*vir bonus*) and could only persuade if his behaviour met with social approval. As we will see later, there is a potential tension between evaluation of the *linguistic choices* made in a text and evaluation of the *behaviour* of the speaker. In addition to ethos, successful rhetoric also required a combination of an effective heuristic or *logos* (the rational content) with pathos (the emotional content); for example, feelings could be aroused by considering fundamental human experiences such as life and death. We will see that these three artistic proofs are still relevant to how persuasion is achieved in contemporary political rhetoric and are integrated into Figure 1.1 (section 1.3.1) where my views on political persuasion are summarised.

Classical rhetoricians identified three main contexts where speeches could occur (Sauer 1997). The first was the deliberative, or political, speech that deals with an important controversial topic and is addressed to a public assembly; it required a decision to be made about a future action such as, for example, whether to make peace or go to war. Next was the forensic or judicial speech that was addressed to a judge and jury and was concerned with the evaluation of a past action such as a crime. Finally, there was the epideictic or 'display' speech that was addressed to an audience whose role was passive; the purpose of this type of speech was either to praise (as in eulogies) or to blame. Because of its focus on politicians, this book will mainly concentrate on deliberative speeches though I include some epideictic speeches as well. The three speech types varied in terms of the types of response they expected of the audience, such as voting or applauding, and in terms of their purpose – for example whether they were concerned with influencing future actions or evaluating past ones. It therefore followed that the methods of persuasion were not something unchanging – based on an abstract or idealised situation – but analysed what was most likely to be effective in the specific speech context. Consideration of effect or impact in the world of lawyers, politicians and flatterers made speech making an art rather than an exercise in philosophical enquiry; speech making was about creating a reputation for the speaker *and* making the world: about words and action.

Classical rhetoric distinguished between issues of structure and style. Structure was concerned with how the sequencing of a speech could influence an audience. Initially there is a need to gain hold of the audience's attention through *heurisis* 'discovery' and then to continue according to a plan (*taxis*). The planning stages of a speech focused on considerations of *heuresis, taxis* and *lexis*,[2] but equally important were factors that influenced the performance or delivery of a speech. Persuasive rhetoric is characterised by the ability to conceal the presence of the pre-existent text (formed by *heurisis, taxis* and *lexis*) through skilful use of the techniques of memorising and gesture through which a speech is enacted.

The *taxis* or structure of an argument contained five stages: the first was an introduction (*exordium*) in which the speaker aims to ingratiate the audience. Some techniques, such as flattery or an appeal to goodwill, could be orientated towards the audience; others, such as a confession of inadequacy, were orientated towards the speaker. Alternatively, they could appeal to the *sharing* of interests between speaker and audience – as in the use of first person plural pronoun 'we'. The next stage was

---

[2] Compared with its present sense of word choice, *lexis* referred more broadly to 'style' in classical rhetoric.

the outline of the argument (*narratio*); the following stage was support of the argument with examples, precedents or analogies (*confirmatio*). There was then anticipation of counter-arguments (*refutatio*) and finally the *conclusio* in which there would be some form of appeal to the better instincts of the audience. We will find that many of these features continue to be used in contemporary political speeches.

1.2.3 Contemporary rhetoric

Early modern studies of speech making were concerned with the management of the interaction between leaders and followers; for example, Atkinson (1984) uses the term 'claptrap' to refer to a range of strategies that could be investigated by measuring audience applause. Atkinson identified linguistic strategies such as – when introducing a politician – saying a few words about the speaker before actually naming him; he also identified strategies such as three-part lists and the use of contrastive pairs. While his approach was admirable, I will argue that it largely overlooked the significance of metaphor in contributing to persuasive effect. This is especially the case when these other rhetorical strategies interact with metaphor since it is the combined effect of various strategies that can often be most effective in political speeches. The interplay between overlapping rhetorical strategies ensures political communication is persuasive because it conceals the contribution of any single strategy, and this avoids alerting the audience to the fact that they are being persuaded. For persuasion to become an art, its artifice should not be apparent.

I would like to illustrate some of these overlapping rhetorical strategies first with reference to some well-known political utterances. Short memorable and quotable phrases have become known in media communication as 'sound bites'. They are effective because they encapsulate arguments by compressing a large idea into a small number of words, thereby taking up less media time. They can be used in headlines and gain the 'viral' effect of being constantly recycled through various media including of course the Internet. In communicative terms they are therefore highly efficient. Table 1.1 summarises a few of these.

These much-quoted phrases share a number of features: they all state an argument very succinctly since any paraphrase would require many more words, and yet the argument is not jeopardised by this economy of style. As speech action they share a rhetorical purpose of exhorting an audience to do something (as indicated in some cases by use of the imperative verb form) and they all communicate the impression that there is absolutely no doubt in the mind of the speaker. In linguistic

Table 1.1   'Sound bites' in political rhetoric

---

1. And so, my fellow Americans: ask not what your country can do for you –
    ask what you can do for your country. (J.F. Kennedy, Inaugural
    Address, 1961)
2. Tough on crime, tough on the causes of crime. (T. Blair, Labour Party
    Conference, 1992)
3. The only thing we have to fear is fear itself. (F.D. Roosevelt, Inaugural
    Address, 1933)
4. Mr. Gorbachev, tear down this wall. (R. Reagan, Berlin, 1987)

---

terms this is because they are expressed with a very high degree of
modality: the more convinced a politician sounds about his or her own
ideas and beliefs, the more convincing he is likely to be. The discourse
of leadership necessarily provides a sense of purpose by using conviction rhetoric to express self-belief. The first three all contain at least one
word that is repeated: repetition communicates a sense of conviction –
think of how in traditional political rhetoric a point is 'drummed' home
by repeating an up and down gesture of the hand with finger pointed.

Conviction rhetoric is grounded in ethical appeal and arouses emotions. In each of these phrases there is a contrast between negative and
positive entities that are either explicit or implied: these are respectively:
selfishness v. self-sacrifice; crime v. the cause of crime; fear v. courage
(i.e. over fear); imprisonment (implied by 'wall') v. freedom. The first
uses a rhetorical figure of two parts in which the word order of the second part is the reverse of the word order in the first part; this is known
as 'chiasmus'[3] and the reversal of word order changes the meaning by
reversing subject and object positions. The second demonstrates parallelism in which a grammatical pattern is repeated. The third shifts 'fear'
from a verb to a 'noun' and implies that we do not have to fear anything.
The fourth makes a very direct appeal by *naming* an addressee – although
expressed as a command, the personalisation of TITLE + NAME is a
form of appeal. What I have hoped to show by this brief analysis is that
it is the *combined effect* of a range of linguistic and rhetorical features
that explains *why* these expressions caught media attention and became
'sound bites'.

I would now like to show how Margaret Thatcher used a range of
such strategies in her 1987 Party Conference speech. A favoured strategy

---

[3] The most well-known example of chiasmus is J.F. Kennedy's 'Think not what
your country can do for you, but what you can do for your country'.

for Margaret Thatcher is the rhetorical question responded to by a three-part list:

> Just why did we win? I think it is because we knew what we stood for, we said what we stood for. And we stuck by what we stood for.

Here the third element summarises and reinforces what has gone before. Without the third element the comparison would be incomplete – with it there is a clear signal to the audience that this is an optional (and optimal) point for applause.

Various research into conversation (Tsui 1994), and other forms of spoken interaction such as classroom discourse (Sinclair and Coulthard 1975), have indicated that spoken discourse is typically organised in terms of three parts. A first part, or initiation, a response and then, a required third part; the role of the third part varies according to the discourse setting. The motivation of the third element is not so much to convey information (as with the first and second parts) but to make the interaction socially acceptable and well formed in terms of the social relations that exist between the participants. In political speaking I suggest that the function of the third part is to reinforce the meaning of the first two parts by repetition and to indicate completion. This type of signalling of discourse structure is important in speech making because it indicates a transitional point, where there is the option of applause. As Atkinson argues:

> In the first place, the speaker must make it quite clear to them that he has launched into the final stages of delivering an applaudable message. Secondly, he has to supply enough information for them to be able to anticipate the precise point at which the message will be completed. (Atkinson 1984: 48)

Margaret Thatcher's speech contains an example of *antithesis* in which sequencing and comparison are combined to contrast the period of the last Labour government prior to 1979 with the period after the third Conservative victory. The contrast between the 'then' of Labour and the 'now' of Conservatism forms a leitmotif running through the speech – as in the following:

> The old Britain of the 1970s, with its strikes, poor productivity, low investment, winters of discontent, above all its gloom, its pessimism, its sheer defeatism – that Britain is gone.

And we now have a new Britain, confident, optimistic, sure of its economic strength – a Britain to which foreigners come to admire, to invest, yes, and to imitate.

Here the contrast between old Labour that is associated with disharmonious industrial relations and low productivity is achieved through pairs with a new efficient and productive Conservative Britain.

Apart from figures that exploit sequencing and comparison Margaret Thatcher employed other rhetorical resources such as biblical allusion:

Far be it from me to deride the sinner that repenteth. The trouble with Labour is they want the benefit of repentance without renouncing the original sin. No way!

Sarcasm:

I have a feeling that, if Dr Owen didn't know it before, he knows now: six inches of fraternal steel beneath the shoulder blades.

Sarcasm and irony are stylistic choices that communicate the attitudes of the speaker towards the topic.

What is important, though, about discursive modes and figures of speech is that they *act in combination with one another* rather than in isolation; indeed we often isolate them only for the purpose of identifying communication strategies. Atkinson (1984: 48) wishes to

. . . stress from the outset that the successful claptrap always involves the use of more than one technique at a time. This is because of the difficulties involved in co-ordinating the activities of a large number of individuals, not all of whom can be relied on to be paying full attention to what a speaker is saying.

Biblical allusions, modes of discourse such as irony and sarcasm, recounting anecdotes and rhetorical questions are all ways of arousing audience interest and retaining the attention of the hearer. Successful leaders do not take audience attention for granted but hail their potential followers through a rich and varied range of rhetorical strategies: it is the combined effect of a variety of rhetorical strategies that constitutes the language of leadership.

1.3 Persuasion and rhetoric

1.3.1 Persuasion

Persuasion refers generally to the use of language by one party to encourage another to accept a point of view. Rhetoric is the range of methods for persuading others, and while rhetoric and persuasion are inseparable, since any definition of rhetoric necessarily includes the idea of persuasion, they are not identical. Persuasion assumes the existence of a prior intention on the part of one participant before this participant acts upon another passive participant that I will refer to – using a theatre metaphor – as an 'audience'. When we think of 'persuading', we imagine two parties: one acting upon the other, and we assume there was an *intention* that came prior to the act of persuading. But when we think of an audience as being 'persuaded' (note the use of a 'passive' verb) we are highlighting the *effect* of persuasion because it refers to a change in the point of view of the passive party. We are also probably assuming that language caused this change – since it is rare in political contexts to be persuaded by appearance alone. 'Persuasion' therefore refers to the intention, act and effect of changing an audience's thinking. So persuasion should be considered a *speech act*; this means that it is a type of language that *changes* cognition, rather than simply describes it or how such a change is achieved. By contrast, the term 'rhetoric' is used when we want to focus on *how* persuasion is undertaken: it refers specifically to the *methods* that the speaker uses to persuade, rather than to the whole gestalt of intention, action and effect.

Usually the audience will not be fully aware of a premeditated point of view until it is revealed by the speaker – though there may be some expectations based on prior knowledge of this speaker's beliefs and the setting. For example, a speaker at a right-wing meeting is likely to represent 'the nation' positively and 'immigrants' negatively by reinforcing pre-existing stereotypes through dehumanising metaphors; these may include referring to immigration as if it were the movement of water, using metaphors such as 'flood' and 'tide'. The unfurling of a premeditated point of view by a speaker that either reinforces or changes how an audience thinks – their cognition as a group – is how I understand 'persuasion' in political contexts.

As I have suggested above, it is important to distinguish two roles in persuasion. An active role for the speaker is characterised by deliberate intentions: persuasion does not occur by chance but because of a speaker's underlying purposes and ability to communicate this intention effectively through rhetoric. The purpose will be to change the audience's mind about something, because unless there is a change of opinion, the audience cannot be said to have been persuaded. The audience's role is primarily passive; however, social cognition must have occurred if we are to say that an audience thinks differently after the act of persuasion. In democratic political contexts we will know initially when a politician has persuaded an audience through its response – for example by clapping, chanting or cheering in face-to-face settings. In non-interactive situations we will know through opinion polls, then by voting behaviour at elections; finally, in an elected legislature we will know that persuasion has occurred when politicians vote for policies so that they become law.

I would now like to summarise my own views on the rhetorical means for persuading in political communication; Figure 1.1 is based on Aristotle's three artistic proofs that I have introduced in section 1.2.2 but also takes into account psychological and cognitive factors that influence persuasion.

Persuasion is about being right and only once the speaker has convinced the audience that he is right can the audience be said to have been persuaded. A prerequisite for being right is that the speaker gains trust by establishing his ethical integrity: when the people no longer trust their leader, any arguments or narratives that he offers will not be persuasive. The way that trust is established is by convincing the audience that the leader has the right intentions for the group and that he has their interests at heart. This is why corruption scandals are so

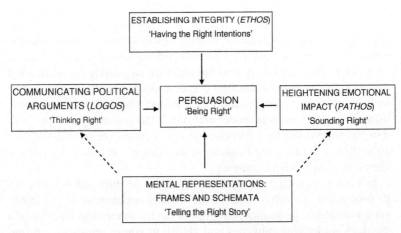

Figure 1.1   Rhetorical means for persuasion in political communication

damaging for politicians since they imply that the leader has the wrong intentions because he has entered politics for self-interest rather than for the interests of the group. Integrity is therefore a general concept that includes both language and behaviour and is one where political actors contest to establish legitimacy. I have put it at the top of the diagram to represent it as a prerequisite of persuasion.

Another rhetorical means for persuading an audience that the speaker is right is through political arguments demonstrating that policies are based on rationality; this is what I describe as 'thinking right' because reasonable arguments are inherently persuasive. I elaborate in the contribution of metaphor to thinking right in section 2.2.1. As well as having the right intentions and thinking right, the speaker also needs to persuade by heightening the emotional impact through 'sounding right': this is the ability to engage emotionally with an audience through empathy, humour or arousing feelings such as fear or hate. 'Sounding right' is also achieved by a display of rhetorical competence since this demonstrates the ability to engage with an audience through command of political discourse; a command of traditional rhetoric therefore contributes to creating the right emotional climate for persuasion to occur.

From a psychological perspective a political leader also needs to convince that he is right by creating mental representations that influence the audience's ways of understanding situations; 'telling the right story' means providing a set of frames or schemata that make political actions and agents intelligible by providing an explanation that fits with the audience's previous experience and assumptions about how the world works. I discuss how metaphor contributes significantly to forming these mental representations in section 2.2.2. Another dimension that I referred to at the start of this chapter as being relevant to persuasion is appearance and manner; this might be summarised as 'looking right'. I have not included it in the figure and the non-verbal aspects of persuasion are examined in more detail in a study of non-Western leaders (Charteris-Black 2007); however, the focus on metaphor in this work prevents a detailed exploration of appearance and other non-verbal communication modes, though I comment on appearance when discussing the influence of the media (section 1.3.4).

1.3.2 Rhetoric and dialect

We find a negative evaluation of rhetoric in phrases such as 'empty rhetoric' or 'rhetorical ploy' that refer to language use as if it were independent of values. It is because of the negative semantic associations that have emerged for the term 'rhetoric' that it has now often been replaced by 'persuasion' which does not evoke the same opposition between what is said and what is done – between word and deed. It is failure to understand this tension that has historically led to the emergence of a negative sense of rhetoric as over-decorative use of language; this sense assumes that rhetoric is *style alone* and not also the values and credibility, the *ethos*, of the speaker. However 'persuasion', though largely positive in connotation, does not identify clearly the methods by which it is achieved. Concern with outcome alone can lead us to overlook the methods used to influence opinion and establishing these was the purpose of both rhetoric and dialect.

Suspicion of rhetoric can in fact be traced to antiquity as Socrates and Plato had both criticised rhetoric because of its lack of concern with a truth that was independent of the speaker's interests: it did not therefore fit with the purpose of philosophy which was to discover a truth that was independent of calculation of interest. In the classical period an opposition therefore developed between rhetoric and dialect: dialect gave equal weight to *both sides of* an argument as they emerged in debate; in dialect there were *two active* participants who engaged on equal terms and in a balanced way for a common purpose. However, rhetoric was concerned with presenting a case *from only one side* and therefore assumed only a single *active* participant and a mainly passive 'audience'.

Differences in attitudes towards interest-based advocacy led to differences between rhetoric and dialect in speaker and audience roles, and patterns of language use, that corresponded with differences of purpose between a rhetorician and dialectician. Dialect required a question and answer procedure from which truth emerged after presentation of both points of view, whereas

> In traditional rhetorical argumentation, a speaker is seen as making a presentation to an audience, typically a mass audience, they listen to and/or watch the performance, the speaker is active. He is an arguer who makes claims and supports them with arguments, but the audience is relatively passive with respect to advancing argumentation. (Walton 2007: 17)

In dialect the purpose is a collaborative engagement between speaker and audience to *discover* or establish *what is true* and what action should be taken; in rhetoric the speaker *already knows what is true* and has the purpose of enabling an audience to discover his point of view. While the effectiveness of dialect can be evaluated by the quality of argumentation, the effectiveness of rhetoric may be evaluated by how successfully a speaker influences an audience. This is more measurable in certain types of speech event than others; for example, the effect of a speech given in Parliament can be measured by the number of people voting in favour of a proposition; however, the impact of, for example, a funeral eulogy is less measurable because the contribution made to historical memory will only be known over time. In both cases the speaker will only employ arguments, or figures of speech, in so far as they contribute to realising the underlying purpose of persuading the audience.

1.3.3 The psychology of persuasion

Jowett and O'Donnell (1992) argue that there are three ways in which the persuader may seek to influence the receiver of a persuasive message; these are response shaping, response reinforcing and response changing. In all cases a persuasive message needs to comply with the audience's wants and needs, since arousing their desires and imagination involves exploiting *existing* beliefs, attitudes and values rather than introducing completely new ones. As they put it:

> People are reluctant to change; thus, in order to convince them to do so, the persuader has to relate change to something in which the persuadee already believes. This is called an 'anchor' because it is already accepted by the persuadee and will be used to tie down new attitudes or behaviors. An anchor is a starting point for a change because it represents something that is already widely accepted by the potential persuadees. (Jowett and O'Donnell 1992: 22–3)

This is particularly true in political contexts where the majority is often unsure or uncommitted to the detailed content of policy. They respond more effectively to messages that explain proposed actions with reference to familiar experiences; successful politicians are those who can develop their arguments with evidence taken from beliefs about the world around them. In a discussion of propaganda Walton (2007) makes a similar point about the importance of a fit between existing commitments and the new propositions for which the speaker seeks to gain acceptance:

> In persuasion dialogue, the proponent's goal is to use the commitments of the respondent as premises in order to persuade the

respondent to also become committed to some particular proposition he previously had doubts about accepting. (Walton 2007: 106–7)

Messages become persuasive when they evoke things that are already known or at least familiar. As Jowett and O'Donnell go on to say (1992: 25–6):

> A persuader analyses an audience in order to be able to express its needs, desires, personal and social beliefs, attitudes, and values as well as its attitudes and concerns about the social outcome of the persuasive situation. The persuader is a voice from without speaking the language of the audiences' voice within.

In the following chapter I will argue that metaphor is an effective rhetorical means for persuading because metaphors work by transferring what is already known to understand things that are less well known and therefore activates pre-existing knowledge. Metaphor provides a frame through which words from a literal source domain are used to interpret a lesser known, abstract target domain. Metaphor is therefore a crucial means for accessing the 'voice within'.

As we have seen, central to classical rhetoric were the notions of ethos, logos and pathos and I have integrated these into the model for persuasion presented in Figure 1.1. I would like to illustrate how Tony Blair activates the artistic proofs in his October 2002 conference speech. This was a difficult speech because of his stance in relation to the evolving crisis in Iraq where he was proposing a largely unpopular policy of support for, and involvement with, direct military intervention by the USA and Britain. He is believed to have dispensed with the services of New Labour speech-writers and authored most of the text himself. Consider first the sections of the speech that establish his ethos:

> The value of progressive politics – solidarity, justice for all – have never been more relevant: and their application never more in need of modernisation.

One of the goals of the speech was to integrate the international issue of Iraq with domestic issues such as reform of the public services and this explains the selection of broad notions such as 'solidarity, justice for all' that could apply equally to foreign and home policy. He exhorts followers to ally themselves with him on the basis of a Latin adage that if you want peace prepare for war:

> Let us lay down the ultimatum. Let Saddam comply with the will of the UN. So far most of you are with me. But here is the hard part. If he doesn't comply then consider … Sometimes and in particular when dealing with a dictator, the only chance of peace is readiness for war.

He contrasts the difficulty that he faced as a leader in making the decision, but also his high level of commitment to a position made on the basis of moral legitimacy – to demonstrate that he has the right intentions. This is made explicit later on when anticipating the counter-argument that the decision goes against popular opinion:

> The right decision is usually the hardest one. And the hardest decisions are often the least popular at the time.

The rhetorical goal is to establish his ethos by convincing the audience that though difficult decisions may not be popular, they are, nevertheless, 'right' – and leads to a sound bite summarizing his main argument:

> We are at our best when we are boldest.

The slogan is introduced at the beginning of the speech and repeated at the end. It demonstrates what van Dijk describes as 'positive self-representation', in this case by attributing virtue and courage – both of which are emotionally appealing – to the audience. This short alliterative statement introduced by 'we' indicates high commitment and reluctance to compromise on ethical issues. The essence of legitimisation by political leaders is to identify a set of values regarding what is good and bad because shared beliefs about right and wrong form the basis for political action. The speech was well received because it appeared to be ethically motivated – although it entailed following the foreign policy of a right-wing government in the USA and involved the country in an unpopular war with long after-effects.

1.3.4   Media influences

Impressions originating from the media were clearly demonstrated in the televised debates that were held for the first time in the United Kingdom in April 2010. After the first debate all the polls showed that Nick Clegg, the leader of the smallest party (the Liberal Democrats) had won. This was partly because he commanded a particular media skill: to come over forcefully television requires looking directly into the camera. Normally in television news and chat programmes it is only the presenter or host who has the authority to do this, but the rules were less clear in a new political genre. By looking into the camera Nick Clegg gave himself an influence over and beyond that of his position because viewers were unconsciously attributing to him a privileged position that is normally reserved for media professionals; his rivals, David Cameron and Gordon Brown, were relegated to the status of guests at the show. Successful political leadership requires physical attributes, but it also requires skill in performance as the success of professional actors such as Ronald Reagan and Arnold Schwarzenegger has demonstrated. Knowing how to use the media effectively therefore contributes significantly to sounding right.

Politicians are now encountered primarily in the home through the media and therefore the tone and style of delivery need to be intimate and domesticated. Through a ubiquitous presence on television or radio the speaker becomes an intimate voice and while politicians may no longer need to kiss a baby, they must at least look like people who would be welcome at the hearth. In spite of his superior intellectual abilities, it was precisely the absence of this easy affability, of human warmth, that is widely held to have been responsible for the failure of Gordon Brown to win over the British public; in particular television highlighted his manner of inadvertently dropping his jaw when speaking and gave a rather downbeat impression. In addition to having the right intentions, thinking and sounding right, it is vital that in modern media contexts a politician also looks right. The eventual leaders of the Coalition, Nick Clegg and David Cameron, both looked better than Gordon Brown and also had a more relaxed and informal style that contributed to them sounding right.

Exposure is also crucial to politicians working with the media in mind: political speeches are now, as I have illustrated above, designed to contain brief, topical 'sound bites' to be recycled through various media. Political slogans must necessarily be creative, appealing and readily repeatable as they are competing for attention with the multimodal appeal of advertisements. It was perhaps this search for creativity that explains – at the time of writing – David Cameron's espousing of 'The Big Society', although it has not as yet evoked any strong positive response – even at the Conservative Party conference. In a small country that values local community life, the sound bite 'The Small Society' may have been more successful. This would have appealed to environmentalists because of the positive association of smallness originating in the title of a book *Small is Beautiful* by the economist E.F. Schumacher. The reason 'The Small Society' was avoided was because it would have been associated with Reagan's notion of 'Small Government' that would in turn be linked to the harsh outcomes of Thatcher's free market economics. It may also not have fitted with the associations of 'big' with traditional values for masculinity – important for a party that had been out of power for 17 years and had few women MPs. One of the characteristics of persuasive politicians in the twenty-first century will be the ability to adapt their rhetorical choices so that they correspond with pre-existing interpretative frames so that they sound right.

Although the media may be novel there is nothing inherently novel about the classical notion of pathos – the ability of the speaker to arouse human emotions – it has become more influential in an age that has started to reject the rationalism of the Enlightenment; an age that though it wants science, still wants to keep humanity at the centre of its world view. Aristotle's important development of Plato's thinking on rhetoric is that he clarified the relationship between cognition and emotional response; prior to Aristotle, emotion was seen as *opposed to* reason and as likely to *impair* judgements. However, Aristotle identified that – just as emotional responses could be influenced by reasoned persuasion – so reasoned persuasion could be influenced by the emotions: sounding right was therefore in a dynamic relation with thinking right. The media provide insight into the interdependency of emotion and cognition and modern cultures of consumption have enhanced the appeal of metaphor as a rhetorical means for arousing emotions of which we are rarely fully conscious.

1.4 Ideology and myth

1.4.1 Ideology

An ideology is a coherent set of ideas and beliefs adhered to by a group of people that provides an organised and systematic representation of the world about which they can agree. Because 'ideology' refers to ideas rather than the individuals who hold those ideas, discussion of ideology often seems to take place as if it existed apart from society. It is important not to forget that ideology is an inherently social phenomenon because it contributes to the formation of a group identity and provides the basis for communicating a world view to others. If an ideology were not social, then we would simply refer to someone's 'ideas' rather than their 'ideology'. As Seliger (1976: 14) proposes, ideologies are:

> Sets of ideas by which men posit, explain and justify ends and means of organized social action, and specifically political action, irrespective of whether such action aims to preserve, amend, uproot or rebuild a given social order.

So, once articulated, an ideology serves to bring individuals together for the purpose of some form of *social action*. An ideology may either confirm or resist existing beliefs but it will always claim authority over its members. An ideology is therefore a precondition for establishing certain actions as legitimate – in the sense that they follow a set of established ideas – irrespective of whether these ideas are as yet encoded in a particular legal system. An ideology is based on a set of intentions that are claimed to be 'right' and combines right thinking, having the right intentions and telling the right story because a group that is united for social purposes needs to have a story to tell.

1.4.2   Myth

A myth is another type of story that provides an explanation of all the things for which explanations are felt to be necessary. These could be the origins of the universe, the causes of good and evil, life and death or anything else that is believed to be mysterious. Myth therefore shares with ideology a persuasive purpose and engages the hearer by providing stories that express aspects of the unconscious. It provides a narrative-based representation of intangible experiences that are evocative because they are unconsciously linked to emotions such as sadness, happiness and fear. Its function in political communication is to create positive or negative representations and it contributes significantly to telling the right story. Myth gains its power by distinguishing between angels and demons and creating drama out of the struggle between them.

Myth originates in emotions such as fear of danger, the dark, or death; these emotions require an expressive medium to accommodate them into a social narrative that enables them to be accepted and understood. The medium is not necessarily language since dance, music and other expressive mediums also express myth. Myth may be translated into language but, unlike ideology, does not originate in language – and is not therefore text-bound in the way that an ideology is. We are more conscious of the effect of an ideology than a myth; myth is only partly conveyed in language and its origins are often not in language at all; when myth does draw on language it will rely more heavily on metaphors and other rhetorical strategies directed to creating mythic thinking – this is a type of thought that deals with the difficult emotions for which myth provides the answers and it contributes to telling the right story.

Cassirer (1946: 49) proposes that the origin of religious myth is in a desire to provide a rational answer to the problem of death using a language that was understandable to the primitive mind. Myth was a way in which death could be explained as a change in the form of life. He quotes Euripides: 'Who knows if life here be not really death, and death be turned into life?' Thatcher's use of metaphors and oratory provides extensive evidence that a subliminal use of metaphor can activate two of the deepest human emotions: love of life and fear of death. It is hard therefore to deny that success as a leader is based on sophisticated handling of myth. Basing her metaphors on the lexicon of war – employing words such as 'battle' and 'fight' – gave her the power to arouse emotions that are associated with physical combat such as pride, anger and resentment. These emotions then evoke feelings of antipathy towards an implied or named 'enemy' – or 'villain' – and feelings of loyalty and affection towards a 'hero' figure with whom they identify. Myth becomes a way of articulating ideology because it relates abstract notions to our experience of reality; it is an effective way of making abstract ideas seem accessible.

Before explaining in more detail how myth works in political rhetoric, it is important that we understand the relationship between ideology and myth because this is essential in understanding their rhetorical effect. Ideology and myth are similar in that they share the common purpose of persuasion, but they vary in how aware we are likely to be of how they achieve their effect. Ideology needs language to formulate a belief system and requires language to express them: *ideology originates in a text*, and though the origin of the text is usually in the spoken language, it does not become an ideology until it is in the form of a written text – this may be a religious text such as the Bible, or the Koran or a political text such as Mao Zedong's 'Little Red Book' or Gaddafi's 'The Green Book'.

Ideology and myth are similar in that they need language to contribute to what van Dijk refers to as 'social cognition'. This is 'the system of mental representations and processes of group members' (van Dijk 1995: 18) and is characterised by long-term mental representations that emerge through *how* language is typically and conventionally used. Ideology and myth arise from, and contribute to, the typical shared mental representations of a social group and they both contribute to the impression that a leader is telling the right story. As we will see in the next chapter, metaphor provides a linguistic means for mediating between conscious and unconscious mental activities, between cognition and emotion, between ideology and myth. When a metaphor corresponds with a pattern of correspondence I have referred to it as a schema, or conceptual metaphor, such as POLITICS IS CONFLICT; it contributes to a neural connection between short- and long-term memory, and in doing so contributes to the formation of a covert ideology through myth.

1.4.3   Political myth

Flood (1996: 44) describes a political myth as 'An ideologically marked narrative which purports to give a true account of a set of past, present, or predicted political events and which is accepted as valid in its essentials by a social group'. As Geiss (1987: 29) notes, 'a political myth is an empirical, but usually not verifiable, explanatory thesis that presupposes a simple causal theory of political events and enjoys wide public support'. Words such as 'purport', 'not verifiable' and 'simple' imply a perspective that is *independent* of those who accept myths and the presence of others who challenge the easy explanations they offer. Critical evaluation is necessary to determine whether an explanation should be classified as a 'myth' rather than a 'truth' and I propose that analysis of politicians' metaphors contributes to identifying how it is that they tell the right story.

An example of a political myth is the attitude to immigration conveyed by Norman Tebbit in the now famous claim that Britain was in danger of being 'swamped' by immigrants – clearly the association of being overwhelmed by something unpleasant, as if in a swamp, has a strong negative force. The myth is that immigrants will outnumber natives and eventually overwhelm them numerically; in reality it is often the immigrants that are absorbed into the native 'swamp' in multicultural societies. The 'swamp' metaphor arouses feelings of fear and was revived in connection with asylum seekers who some politicians claimed to be swamping the country. Analysis of metaphor reveals that evaluations implied by political myths are positive or negative and is a method for understanding *how* political myths communicate ideology.

Margaret Thatcher drew extensively on political myth when describing socialism with a range of metaphors that contributed to negative representations. These were anything from an unreliable person, a second-hand car, to an illness or even original sin: the metaphors differ but they all draw on negatively evaluated cultural stereotypes. Second-hand cars are associated with unreliability (in British culture) and their salesmen have a low social status. The narrative theme of this political myth is that socialism is bad and will cause some form of social damage unless it is stopped; her argument assumes an associative relation is a causal one. What is remarkable is the consistency and regularity with which Thatcher reiterated this narrative in her conference speeches. There is no room for compromise with anything that is represented as a form of social menace and the myth arouses fears for self and the family.

It is interesting how in the 1990s and the decline of socialism as a political force, other political myths related to paedophilia, terrorism and Islam have emerged. The banking crisis of 2008 demonstrated the power of myths to influence international money markets. Emotionally charged fears could wipe billions off share values in the twinkling of an eye. There has been no shortage of demand for easy explanations of phenomena that are both threatening and difficult to understand in the increasingly complex world that has arisen from a convergence of the growth of world trade, mass migration, travel and technologically driven globalisation.

Successful leaders rely on the recurrent power of imagery to activate mental representations, or schemata, relating to fear and social menace; the ostensible aim of government is to eliminate fear but political power is usually enhanced by heightening it. Fear is, of course, very closely related to control, since the more cause there is for fear of certain social groups (Muslims, terrorists, paedophiles, etc.), the greater the rationale for all forms of social control. These include, for example, monitoring the contents of blogs and all-pervasive digital surveillance through the use of cheap visual technology. The construction of political myth impinges very closely on the freedoms with which people live their lives. Creating simple causal explanations before the real causes are known leads to solutions being imposed that may not deal with genuine causes. As Jowett and O'Donnell (1992: 215) suggest, a myth is a story in which meaning is embodied in recurrent symbols and events, but it is also an idea to which people already subscribe; therefore, it is a predisposition to act.

Edelman (in Geiss 1987) identifies three particular political myths as follows:

1. The myth of the Conspiratorial Enemy is a myth in which a hostile out-group is plotting to commit some harmful acts against an in-group. I illustrate this in Chapter 10 when Reagan's representation of the Soviet Union as 'an evil empire whose leaders are the focus of evil in the modern world'[4] was reinvented in George W. Bush's 'an axis of evil'.[5] In my research I have found that conspiratorial myths are more characteristic of the rhetoric of the political right.
2. The second myth is the Valiant Leader myth, where the political leader is benevolent and effective in saving people from danger by displaying qualities of courage, aggression and the ability to overcome difficulties. Geiss (1987) illustrates this with reference to John F. Kennedy and Lyndon Johnson.
3. The United We Stand myth is a belief that a group can achieve victory over its enemies by obeying and making sacrifices for its leader. This myth is more characteristic of the political left.

Edelman's myths show how in rhetorical terms legitimisation involves the identification of some form of threat, of some form of response to that threat and the emergence of a valiant leader. In a discourse-historical analysis of four 'calls to arms' speeches by leaders, Graham et al. (2004) identify four legitimisation strategies. These are appeals to a 'good' legitimate power source ('God', 'the people', 'the nation', etc.), appeals to history or historical mythology, the construction of a thoroughly Evil Other (infidels, terrorists, etc.), and appeals for uniting behind a legitimate power source. While these correspond well with the first and third of Edelman's myths, they omit to mention that successful legitimisation also makes claims for the heroic leadership qualities of specific individuals.

1.5 Summary

In this chapter I have explained what I mean by 'persuasion', its relationship to rhetoric and how persuasion works in political communication.

---

[4] Quoted in Geiss (1987: 54).
[5] This was made in the State of the Union Address in January 2002 and referred specifically to the development of weapons of mass destruction in North Korea, Iran and Iraq.

Drawing on theories of speech making that were developed in classical antiquity, I have argued that rhetorically they first need to establish trust; they do this by showing that they have the audience's interests at heart and are therefore ethically credible. I have then suggested that they need to integrate the right political arguments, right thinking, with an appeal to empathy by sounding right. Part of sounding right in the contemporary period is utilising the full resources of the media, which also place demands on looking right. In the last section of the chapter I explained how ideology and myth contribute to persuasion by giving the impression of telling the right story.

Political power is based in the flesh and blood presence of a leader who can charm and inspire followers. Ultimately, because many people do not understand ideas or ideologies, they are more likely to trust their instincts when evaluating individual politicians. People will be attracted to an individual who offers them a future that is better than the past and who gives them hope by making anything seem possible. This is why it is especially appealing when a male political leader becomes a father when in power since, as Christianity has found, the birth of a child symbolises the hope for a better future. In the next chapter I will explain a methodology for exploring further how myths are systematically created in political speeches and will propose that this is primarily through the analysis of their metaphors.

2
Metaphor in Political Discourse

2.1 Metaphor and political thinking

2.1.1 Introduction – Gordon Brown's 'moral compass'

In this chapter I will develop the argument that in political contexts metaphor can be, and often is, used for ideological purposes because it activates unconscious emotional associations and thereby contributes to myth creation: politicians use metaphor to tell the right story. I explain my understanding of the term 'metaphor' and provide a number of illustrations of the everyday, conventional metaphors that are the bread and butter of political language. I hope to demonstrate how, rhetorically, metaphors contribute to mental representations of political issues, making alternative ways of understanding these issues more difficult and in so doing 'occupy' the mind. However, I will also explain how metaphors are contested by illustrating how the same type of metaphor may be used by a politician's critics to convey a completely different evaluation from the one that was originally intended. In doing this I hope to show – both in this chapter and the remainder of the book – how analysis of metaphors contributes to our knowledge of political rhetoric by enabling us to understand how world views are communicated persuasively in language.

In this section I will illustrate how metaphor becomes persuasive through establishing moral credibility (ethos). When announcing his successful candidacy for leadership of the Labour Party in May 2007 at a critical point near the beginning of the speech leading up to the announcement, Gordon Brown used the expression 'moral compass':

> For me, my parents were – and their inspiration still is – *my moral compass*. The *compass* which has guided me through each stage of my

life. They taught me the importance of integrity and decency, treating people fairly, and duty to others. And now the sheer joy of being a father myself – seeing young children develop, grow and flourish – like for all parents, has changed my life. Alongside millions juggling the pressures of work, I struggle too to be what I want to be – a good parent.

The moral compass metaphor makes an appeal based on ethos as he describes himself as struggling to pass on a legacy of good parenting that he has inherited from his parents. By referring to 'like for all parents', he is broadening the metaphor frame to imply that he is a benevolent and typical 'parent' of Britain; he is activating a highly pervasive conceptual metaphor in politics: THE NATION IS A FAMILY. Ideas of the national family (as in 'motherland' and 'fatherland') are persuasive because the family symbolises a source of security, and the desire to protect the family is at the basis of moral systems and therefore contributes to the impression that a politician has the right intentions. The metaphor fitted with a political image based on high morals that had gained credence as he was already well known to the British public – having been Chancellor of the Exchequer for a number of years. Lakoff sees 'family' metaphors as central in political discourse and argues that different projections of the metaphor distinguish between left- and right-wing world views:

I believe that the Nation As Family metaphor is what links conservative and liberal worldviews to the family-based moralities we have been discussing. I believe that this metaphor projects the Strict Father and Nurturant Parent moral systems onto politics to form the conservative and liberal political worldviews. (Lakoff 2002: 154)

When referring to 'his moral compass' Brown may have been drawing on THE NATION IS A FAMILY metaphor, although it was not entirely clear what type of parent he considered himself as he goes on to say: 'These are for me the best of British values: responsibilities required in return for rights; fairness not just for some but all who earn it.' The idea of 'earning' fairness is a point of view associated with a 'strict father' as it implies a frame of 'moral accounting'; this is the idea that moral issues are discussed as if they were financial ones, as in expressions such as 'incurring a moral debt', the 'cost' of war, or 'paying the price' for a belief. Brown was successful in his bid for leadership of the party but it may be that his rhetoric contributed to an uncertainty as to whether he would be a 'strict father' or 'nurturant parent'; this uncertainty may have contributed to his lack of success in the General Election.

The 'moral compass' metaphor was taken up extensively by Brown's critics; for example, it occurred over 200 times in the Conservative newspaper *The Daily Mail*, to question whether or not he did have the right intentions. These counter-representations portray Brown as a hypocrite, for example: 'He always kept his head down when the going got rough for Blair but we knew all along he was in there, plotting his next career move with the aid of his "moral compass".'[1] Other right-wing newspapers also used the metaphor for negative counter-representation, for example *The Sunday Times* wrote: 'Brown's moral compass seems to have lost its bearings; instead of pointing true north, it now seems to be jittering in the direction of ravening ambition.'[2] An aspect of the source domain – here the instability of a compass – were exploited to argue that Brown's moral values were also likely to change. Mio (1997) provides evidence that metaphors extending an opponent's metaphor are more effective than those that introduce a new source domain. Analysing the source domain of a metaphor is therefore a way of exploiting it persuasively in political discourse.

Linguists describe the interacting effect between some words and their associated senses as semantic prosody (Louw 1993). These do not always fit with our expectations; for example, while we may expect words associated with the family to be positive, we might be surprised to find that words associated with 'conflict' also have a positive association in the British press – such senses do not usually appear under the definition of 'conflict' in a dictionary. In an analysis of press sports reporting I discovered that they were ubiquitous and invariably associated with attributes that appealed to positive emotions such as strength, courage and determination in notions such as a 'relegation battle' or to 'surrender' (Charteris-Black 2004). By this association such metaphors have ideological potential because they evoke ideas based on having the right intentions because protecting the nation from invasion is morally justified. In British culture it seems that conflict metaphors activate mental representations of the evacuation of the British Expeditionary Force from Dunkirk in 1940 that was associated with national survival and these associations are then exploited in sports reporting. The

---

[1] 'Is Gordon any Better than Tony?', *Daily Mail*, 11 September 2006.
[2] 'Gordon Brown Betrays us all to Deliver his Diana Moment', Minette Marrin, 14 February 2010.

ideological potential of metaphor works by accessing powerful underlying cultural evaluations that originate in personal, social and national struggle.

2.1.2   What is metaphor?

What, given its ideological and myth-forming effect, is a metaphor? Aristotle (in *Poetics* [Ross 1952]: 1457b) defined metaphor as 'giving the thing a name that belongs to something else'. The etymological origin of the word 'metaphor' is from the Greek *metapherein* 'to transfer'; clearly, the central notion of metaphor is one in which meanings are transferred, the question is what they are transferred from and to – given that word senses are not stable over time. I will define a metaphor as a word or phrase that is used with a sense that differs from another more common or more basic sense that this word or phrase has. The sense that a word commonly has is its literal meaning; when analysing the conceptual basis of metaphor, we use the term 'source domain' to refer to this common-sense, literal meaning. The metaphoric sense differs from the common or basic sense and is known as the 'target domain' of the metaphor. So a metaphor is a shift in the use of a word or phrase by giving it a new sense. If the innovative sense is taken up, it will eventually change the meaning of a word that is used metaphorically. It is the shift in meaning that enables metaphors to evoke emotional responses and we should recall that 'motion' and 'emotion' have the same etymological source and so we may think of metaphors as bearers of affective meaning.

Metaphors arise from how language is used: *any* word can be a metaphor if the way that it is used makes it so. So metaphors come into being when there is a *change* in how a word is *used*: this is why metaphor is a feature of language use or 'discourse'. We understand the 'common' sense of a word as it appears in a dictionary, and so when it is not being used in this way we know that it is a metaphor. So, crucially, metaphor arises from our *expectations* about meaning that are based on our knowledge of how words have previously been used. So a pure metaphor is a word or phrase that undergoes a change of use from a common or basic sense to another sense that is contrary to the common use. Metaphor therefore arises *only* from discourse knowledge (or knowledge of language in use).

Expectations of the common senses of words vary between individuals according to their differing experiences of language and what for one speaker is novel may be familiar for another because experience of language is unique and personal. However expectations may be socially influenced. A hearer may not initially experience a word as a metaphor, because he or she does not recognise the sense as differing in any way from the common, basic use, however, on knowing more about the earlier sense(s) of a word, the hearer may accept it as a metaphor when used in a new discourse context. Not to have this broader interpretation would otherwise exclude many political metaphors because – especially with rapid recycling in the media – they are often of this conventional type: we do not immediately recognise them as metaphors in the way that we might when encountering the same words in a poem.

For example, when a British politician refers to achievements on the way to an objective as 'milestones' a hearer who knows the literal meaning of 'a milestone' may consider this a metaphor, whereas someone who only ever comes across the word in political contexts may not consider it a metaphor because this hearer does not know the basic sense of 'milestone' – it is simply the conventional way of talking about political 'progress'. This is why people vary in how many instances of metaphor they find a particular text: this should not surprise us, nor should it be a problem. At any one instance in time a word may be *more* or *less* metaphoric for an individual speaker because judgements of what is normal, or conventional, depend on language users' unique experiences of discourse. Fortunately, much current metaphor research relies on multiple instances of language use stored on computers: these corpora as they are known give us the context necessary for disambiguation – allowing us to see how people use words as metaphors by giving them new senses. Not all individuals – because of their different experience of language – will agree on which words are metaphors, however they will hopefully be tolerant of what are metaphors for others. Waves of novel metaphors exist in an ocean of conventional metaphors. Metaphors change how we understand and think about politics by influencing our feelings and thoughts and the question I would like to answer in the next section is how do they do this?

2.1.3   The purpose of metaphor – conventional metaphor

In political rhetoric the primary purpose of metaphors is to frame how we view or understand political issues by eliminating alternative points of view. Politicians use metaphors for negative representations of states of affairs that are construed as problematic and positive representations of future scenarios that are construed as solutions to problems; they also use them for negative and positive representations of out-groups (i.e. opponents) and of in-groups (i.e. supporters) respectively.

So they combine the rhetoric of right thinking with sounding right and having the right intentions. Chilton (2004) summarises the legitimising purpose of political discourse as follows:

> ...political discourse involves, among other things, the promotion of representations, and a pervasive feature of representation is the evident need for political speakers to imbue their utterances with evidence, authority and truth, a process that we shall refer to in broad terms, in the context of political discourse, as 'legitimisation'. Political speakers have to guard against the operation of their audience's 'cheater detectors' and provide guarantees for the truth of their sayings. (Chilton 2004: 23)

An important purpose of much metaphor use in political rhetoric is to establish the speaker as a legitimate source of authority by 'sounding right', and part of this in the democratic tradition is to attack political opponents and their ideas, not with weapons but with words – as Chilton explains:

> Delegitimisation can manifest itself in acts of negative other-presentation, acts of blaming, scape-goating, marginalising, excluding attacking the moral character of some individual or group, attacking the communicative cooperation of the other, attacking the rationality and sanity of the other. The extreme is to deny the humanness of the other. (Chilton 2004: 47)

I identified these delegitimising strategies in Chapter 1 where Margaret Thatcher framed political opponents as the enemy by using metaphors from the source domain of war. Many political issues are complicated and abstract – about which the majority of people have only a partial understanding (and often for example in the case of financial matters, none at all), so it is valuable to political audiences when abstract issues are explained by image-based metaphors that make them more intelligible by representing them as visual and tangible. Over time it is often such cognitively accessible metaphors that become conventionalised. As Mio (1997: 130) explains that: 'Because of information-processing demands, people cannot pay attention to all aspects of political evidence. Therefore, something is needed to simplify decision making, and metaphor and other shortcut devices (e.g. cognitive heuristics) address this need', so a metaphor like 'the winds of change' is more accessible than a concept such as 'decolonization'. Metaphor therefore provides the mental means of accessing a concept by for example referring to something that is abstract such as 'immovability', 'justice' or 'victory' using a word or phrase that in other contexts refers to something material such as 'path' or 'road' or 'iron'. Part of right thinking is then to simplify abstract issues by activating pre-existing knowledge so as to comprehend them.

The metaphors most commonly used by politicians lie between new and familiar uses of language; politicians are not poets and so their language is characterised by *conventional* metaphors such as 'the path of justice' or 'the road to victory'. In a study I undertook comparing the use of metaphor by male and female politicians I interpreted the greater use of conventional metaphors by male politicians as arising from their longer experience of political discourse (Charteris-Black 2009b) – metaphors contribute to sounding right. Though occasionally they may speak of 'an iron curtain descending across Europe' (Churchill), 'the winds of change' (Macmillan) or 'a river of blood' (Powell), and these expressions were originally creative, they gradually became conventionalised to become the quickest way of referring respectively to the Cold War, decolonisation and immigration anxieties. But this will happen to varying degrees: compare 'the Iron Curtain' with the 'Iron Lady' – the first became highly conventional quite rapidly whereas the second retained its status as an innovative metaphor much longer, perhaps because of the greater unlikelihood of a woman made of metal as compared with curtains made of metal.

The sorts of words that are used metaphorically are influenced by the values placed on what these words refer to when used literally in different cultures. For example, some cultures place a negative value on physical conflict and so avoid metaphoric uses of 'fight' and 'battle' in leisure and entertainment contexts such as sport. In Asia the expression 'Bamboo Curtain' was used in place of 'Iron Curtain' to refer to the boundary between Communist China and its non-Communist neighbours because bamboo is more part of everyday experience than iron. Words readily become used as conventional metaphors when they transfer a set of readily available cultural knowledge associations.

To be persuaded, the audience should initially be aware of some mild difference between an original or common sense of a word or phrase, and a novel sense: otherwise classification as a 'metaphor' would be a purely academic exercise only possible for linguists who knew earlier senses of a word. However, over time, repeated use erodes the status of a word or phrase as a metaphor, so, for example, once the 'Iron

Curtain had descended across Europe' it became the *only* way of talking about Soviet–Western relations. When metaphors displace other ways of talking about the same thing, language has acted upon the world by colonising rival ways of thinking about it, and in doing so frames our understanding of the political world.

My thinking about metaphor owes a huge debt to extensive work of others, some of which I will mention at this point. Conceptual metaphor theory owes its birth to Lakoff and Johnson (1980) and the field of research continues to take its inspiration from Lakoff (1991, 1993, 2002). More recent work such as Ahrens (2009), Musolff and Zinken (2009) and Semino (2008) all provide overviews of various aspects of metaphor in political discourse. Beer and de Landtsheer (2004) offer a valuable collection of empirical studies into metaphor and politics in diverse national settings. Other earlier research that formed a platform for this more recent work includes Cameron and Low (1999), Charteris-Black (2004, 2006, 2007, 2009a, b), Chilton (1996, 2004), Chilton and Ilyin (1993), Chilton and Schaffner (2002), Howe (1988), Jansen and Sabo (1994), Koller (2004), Musolff (2004, 2006), Semino and Masci (1996), Straehle et al. (1999), Thornborrow (1993) and Voss et al. (1992). All the research has contributed to a burgeoning and rich tradition of research into various aspects of metaphor and political discourse.

2.2 Metaphor in political persuasion

2.2.1 Right thinking

Metaphor is an effective means for politicians to develop persuasive arguments by applying what is familiar, and already experienced, to new topics to demonstrate that they are thinking rationally about political issues. For example, both Margaret Thatcher, and the current Chancellor of the Exchequer, George Osborne, have used metaphors based on ordinary household budgeting to argue about how to manage a nation's economy – for example the need not to spend more than one earns. People understand more about their personal finances than they do about national finances. Thatcher often used a metaphor based on this understanding:

> Protecting the taxpayer's purse, protecting the public services – these are our two great tasks, and their demands have to be reconciled. How very pleasant it would be, how very popular it would be, to say 'spend more on this, expand more on that'. We all have our favourite

causes – I know I do. But someone has to add up the figures. Every business has to do it, every housewife has to do it, every Government should do it, and this one will. (14 October 1983)

Here public expenditure is discussed in terms of the family budget: the principles of a housewife managing a household budget are used to argue by analogy a case for how the government should manage the national budget. It implied that a nation should avoid living beyond its means just as a family should 'cut its coat according to its cloth'. Personal debt arising from domestic expenditure was likened to the national debt caused by government overspending. The reactivation of the historical sense of economics as 'household management'[3] creates a metaphor concept based on personification by which abstract financial decisions of government are described as if they were the more familiar financial decisions made by families. The metaphor extends the knowledge that the audience already has to new situations that are more complex and leads them to make inferences on the basis of this extended meaning – even though in reality personal and national finances work in rather different ways.

In political argumentation metaphors frequently become dialogical as they are employed by different political interests for their own purposes. It is part of right thinking that metaphor scenarios are employed to frame arguments in a way that is favourable to the case being proposed by the speaker; they do this through a process of foregrounding and revealing some aspects of a political issue and at the same time concealing other aspects by putting them into the background. I will illustrate this by examining a few well-known metaphors that have been used in relation to British foreign policy since the Second World War, one of which I have already mentioned. When Churchill spoke of 'an Iron Curtain descending across Europe' this brought to the fore the idea that Europe would be divided by a solid barrier that would not be easily moved, it predicted and contributed to reality, but it concealed any human agency for the descent of the Curtain: as if it were wound down by an invisible hand in a theatre. The idea of irreversibility and permanence would have been different had a term such as 'silk curtain' been used.

Similarly, when Harold Macmillan spoke of a 'wind of change blowing through this continent' it again concealed agency and represented

---

[3] 'Economics' originates from the Greek *oikonomikos*, 'household management'.

change as if it were inevitable because of the limits of control we have over natural processes: we may harvest the wind, or find the answer in it, but we cannot stop it blowing. It concealed the fact that the Conservative government of the time was not prepared to fight to retain what remained of the British Empire and this was a way of facilitating decolonisation by representing it as beyond the control of politicians. Most would agree that it fitted with new political realities but it did so rhetorically in a way that would escape blame falling on the government of the day!

Metaphors provide the ammunition for debate – since nowhere is Lakoff and Johnson's (1980) conceptual metaphor ARGUMENT IS WAR more appropriate than in political debates. Once a particular metaphor scenario has entered political discourse it becomes difficult to displace and demonstrates its rhetorical success; as Semino (2008: 117) puts it: 'once a particular metaphor occupies a prominent position in the public domain, it can be alluded to and exploited in different ways by different participants in political debates'. Typically, skilled debaters will not reject a particular metaphor outright but will draw on different aspects of the source domain to extend the metaphor to generate a different inference from the one intended by the person who first used it, as we saw when the press media picked up on and exploited Gordon Brown's use of the 'moral compass' metaphor.

Musolff (2006) employs the term 'metaphor scenario' to refer to the explanatory but also potentially argumentative role for metaphor that combines what I refer to as 'right thinking' and 'telling the right story'. A scenario provides details of the scenes and plot and therefore turns a series of political events such as the negotiations between European states over EU membership into a narrative about marriage and relationships that is accessible – because – like a televised soap opera – it involves love and sex. In the classic scenario countries joining the EU are described as 'getting engaged', 'marrying', 'flirting' and 'getting into bed' with each other. However, our knowledge of the problematic nature of human relationships also has the potential to be used in political debates to construe other representations so they might also 'fall out of love with', or 'divorce' each other. Another European example was the discussion of European monetary union as 'a train' in which all the cars of the train – representing the economies of each of the separate nations – needed to travel at the same speed (Semino 2008: 94) which argued for convergence and against late arrivals joining the euro.

Metaphor can be used to legitimise and to delegitimise political actors; for example, Sandikcioglu (2000) contrasts positive self-representations of the West as the centre of Civilisation, Power, Maturity, Rationality and Stability with negative frames of Other representation: Barbarism Weakness, Immaturity, Irrationality and Instability. Such contrasting evaluations were also found in press reporting of political ideas, as Musolff (2003) identifies how even the same metaphor of 'a two-speed Europe' can be positively evaluated by the German press while negatively evaluated in the British press. Similarly, Tony Blair was mocked in the House of Commons for having reversed an earlier decision on whether to have a referendum over the proposed EU constitution; this is because he claimed in his September 2003 Conference speech to 'have no reverse gear',[4] and his positive self-representation was explicitly challenged. In this way metaphors may be turned against their authors and a rhetorical strategy that was intended to legitimise may be used to undermine this. Skill in debate depends on speed and versatility in extending a particular metaphor to the speaker's own goals.

2.2.2   Myth making: telling the right story

In this section, I will illustrate how one of the main rhetorical purposes of metaphor is to contribute to developing political myths that I have referred to as telling the right story. One of the major advantages of metaphor is that, because it is not too specific or precise, it is open to multiple interpretations and like many persuasive mental representations, allows hearers to bring their own meanings to a text. I would like to illustrate this first with reference to the central and all-pervasive myth of American politics: 'the American Dream' and then with reference to what I suggest is an equivalent 'British Dream' proposed by Margaret Thatcher (although this metaphor is never actually used and is only implied). I will first briefly illustrate the 'American Dream' metaphor:

> I came to this hallowed chamber two years ago on a mission: *To restore the American dream* for all our people and to make sure that we move into the 21st century still the strongest force for freedom and democracy in the entire world. (Bill Clinton, 24 January 1995)

> This is our time – to put our people back to work and open doors of opportunity for our kids; to restore prosperity and promote the cause of peace; *to reclaim the American dream* and reaffirm that fundamental truth – that out of many, we are one; that while we breathe, we hope,

---

[4] Semino (2008: 81ff.) provides an analysis of this metaphor and I discuss it further in section 2.3.

and where we are met with cynicism and doubt, and those who tell us that we can't, we will respond with that timeless creed that sums up the spirit of a people: yes, we can. (Barack Obama, 15 June 2008)

Like all myths, the American Dream serves as a narrative that spans geographical space and historical time and is therefore expressed with a high level of certainty. The narrative activates a set of positive associations and may broadly be paraphrased as 'hopes for a future that is better than the present'; but the nature of these hopes varies according to the individual and the groups with whom he or she identifies. The metaphoric use of 'dream' therefore creates a very flexible myth of an imagined ideal future that accommodates to personal desires. The narrative is based on aspirations for the future that are based on a golden age of the past – notice the use of 'restore' and 'reclaim' in the extracts above. Most versions of this myth are historically rooted in the notion of an ideal community based on religious values that have been lost. The myth originates in the historical memory of many present-day Americans that they came to North America to build a better life that was free from the persecution, poverty or famine that they had experienced elsewhere. However, it does not have ubiquitous appeal since there are those whose lives are very far from what they had hoped for and others, such as first nation ('native') Americans, who never felt part of the narrative in the first place – since their dream time pre-dated the arrival of the white man.

But the flexibility of the 'dream' metaphor enables it to be used to refer either to personal hopes – since real dreams are only experienced individually – or, more metaphorically, to social hopes, as when people unite to understand and realise a shared social purpose. Although the narrative appears simple, drawing on bodily experience of sleep, it is its very flexibility (since really we can dream or imagine anything we want) that allows it to be ideologically exploited in political debate. There is no single 'right story' and an attractive myth is one that can tell many different stories. It is this versatility that activates what has been described as a logico-rhetorical module (Sperber 2001). The interpretation of a 'dream' as private or personal is a right-wing republican myth, while the idea that a dream being social is a left-wing democratic myth, the fact it can be either activates the logico-rhetorical module. Such variation in interpretation led to different political arguments as to who exactly would have access to the American Dream. The anti-Vietnam War, post-war baby boom generation claimed that *all* were 'entitled' to the American Dream, whereas supporters of an American global hegemony based on capitalism held that the American Dream had to be earned and there-fore, by implication, was only available to those who worked hard. This interpretation appealed to the work ethic value system associated with Protestantism and was the basis of the moral accounting myth that I have summarised in section 2.1.1 (Lakoff 2002).

What both versions of the narrative share is that although the dream is in the future, they imply action or experience in the present. Some of the most common verbs that precede the expression in the Corpus of Contemporary American English (COCA)[5] are: the verbs 'chase' and 'pursue' (32 and 27 occurrences respectively) which imply a future orien-tation. However, there are also those who are 'living' or have 'achieved' the American Dream (74 and 31 occurrences respectively) – meaning that their past efforts have already realised the dream. The rhetorical effect of metaphor originates in the connotations aroused by words from their basic, literal senses. When 'dream' means 'hope', we experience positive connotations that are not fully explicit in the everyday sense of 'dream'. Yet, like a nebula, these positive associations of hope, and the value placed on optimism in American culture, circulate around the word 'dream' and provide the potential for its use in mythic nar-rative. Equally, the creative extensions of the metaphor can express a sense of disillusionment and deep pessimism by using its antonym 'The American Nightmare'– as for example in a CBS debate on the topic of the global credit crisis:

> It would have been illegal during most of the 20th century, but eight years ago Congress gave Wall Street an exemption. And it's turned to have been a very bad idea. Unidentified Man 1: 'The term "derivative" is almost becoming a household word.' Unidentified Woman 1: 'The cat's kind of out of the bag here.' Senator Richard Lugar: 'This is not the American dream. It's an American nightmare.' (COCA)

It is the opportunity for multiple interpretations that has enabled the metaphor 'The American Dream' to be used in political argumentation to express contesting versions of the myth.

I would now like to illustrate how on other occasions politicians may express contested myths within their own discourse by offering one myth that provides a positive representation of their own party and an alternative counter-myth about the opposing party. Margaret Thatcher

---

[5] Available at http://www.americancorpus.org/

employed metaphor in combination with other rhetorical strategies in developing a political myth that was a British version of the American Dream: Britain could, like America, become a successful free enterprise economy. In her 1987 Conference address at Blackpool (after her third consecutive election victory), a relation of contrast, or antithesis, underlay Thatcher's representation of the policies of the Labour Party when they were in power with current Conservative policies. The basic contrast can be summarised by two conceptual metaphors that account for a range of actual metaphors that she used to represent each party's position: CONSERVATIVE POLICY IS A LIFE FORCE and LABOUR POLICY IS A DEATH FORCE. These conceptual metaphors interact with the other rhetorical strategies such as three-part lists and contrasting pairs to legitimise the free market. I will indicate metaphors using italics:

All too often, the planners *cut the heart* out of our cities. They *swept aside* the familiar city centres that had grown up over the centuries. They replaced them with a wedge of tower blocks and linking expressways, interspersed with token patches of grass and a few windswept piazzas, where pedestrians fear to tread.

Oh! the schemes won a number of architectural awards. But they were *a nightmare* for the people. They *snuffed out* any *spark* of local enterprise. And they made people entirely dependent on the local authorities and the services they chose to provide. ...

So *dying* industries, *soulless* planning, municipal socialism – these deprived the people of the most precious things in life: hope, confidence and belief in themselves. And that *sapping* of the spirit is at the very *heart of urban decay*.

Mr President, to *give back heart* to our cities we must give back hope to the people.
And it's beginning to happen.

Because today Britain has a strong and *growing* economy. Oh yes, *recovery* has come faster in some parts of the country than others. But now it is *taking root* in our most depressed urban landscapes. We all applaud the organisation 'Business in the Community' – it is over 300 major firms that have come together to assist in reviving the urban communities from which so many of them *sprang*.

Each of the first three paragraphs contains a three-part list that identifies three negative characteristics of Labour policy (the context shows that Labour is equated with urban planners). The creation of a scape-goat for negative social phenomena is an important way of pre-empting criticism of the effect of Conservative policies. The fourth paragraph highlights the positive results of Conservative policy that will legitimise free enterprise by offering it as a British version of the American Dream.

An evaluative framework is created by the contrast that is set up between two interacting chains of metaphor. The first is associated with the negative feelings aroused by death images and includes: *cut the heart, snuff out, dying, sapping, decay*; the other is associated with the positive feelings aroused by life images: *spark, give back heart, growing, recovery, take root, sprang*. The first chain associates Labour policy with death while the contrasting chain associates Conservative policies with life. These two interacting metaphor chains are employed in a set of contrastive pairs – both at level of the individual paragraph but also over larger units of text because death metaphors are employed throughout the first three paragraphs, while life metaphors occur only in the last paragraph. The use of the address term 'Mr President' serves to draw attention to the switch from the chain of death metaphors to the chain of life metaphors. Inevitably, these associations are likely to arouse powerful feelings. So here metaphor – both in terms of individual metaphor choices and the conceptual level – combines with other rhetorical strategies such as three-part lists and contrasting pairs to tell a story about free enterprise as a British version of the 'Dream'.

Further evidence occurs in the conclusion to the speech, where she returns to the life–death theme:

> But the philosophy of enterprise and opportunity, which *has put the spark back into* our national economy – that is the way – and the only way – to *rejuvenate* our cities and restore their confidence and pride.

The two italicised phrases are life images – one is based on an inanimate notion (fire) while the other is based on an animate one (youth). Both animate and inanimate images serve to reinforce each other and the use of transitive verbs implies the positive effect of the free enterprise that characterised the British version of the Dream. Leadership is based on such imaginative rhetoric because even though the evidence from reality may be limited, metaphor assists in the creation of a reality by a politically motivated representation that is based on fundamental knowledge that death is to be avoided and life embraced.

There is extensive evidence in the speeches of Margaret Thatcher that she is able to draw on life images to convey very strong and potent political evaluations. Further evidence of the role of language in leadership occurs in her first conference address after Britain's victory against Argentina in the Falklands War:

> This is not going to be a speech about the Falklands campaign, though I would be proud to make one. But I want to say just this, because it is true for all our people. The spirit of the South Atlantic was the spirit of Britain at her best. It has been said that we surprised the world, that British patriotism was rediscovered in those spring days. (October 1982)

Here 'patriotism' is associated with 'spirit' which is, in turn, associated with 'those spring days'. Had Thatcher simply used an expression such as 'earlier in the year', the emotional impact of her oratory would have been reduced: 'spring' is an iconographic choice that activates the same underlying conceptualisation CONSERVATIVE POLICY IS A LIFE FORCE that contributed to the British version of the American Dream; this was a persuasive story because it assumed that Britain still had imperial aspirations.

2.2.3 Evaluating metaphor in political persuasion

We may think of metaphor as intellectually seductive in argument precisely because it gains the hearer's submission, and eventual compliance, by taking as a premise something that the hearer already believes in and so avoids arousing Chilton's 'cheat detectors'. A crucial issue in evaluating the act of persuasion is the question of the extent to which an audience is aware of the seductive intentions of the speaker: where they lack such awareness there is the risk of manipulation. Van Dijk explains the difference between persuasion and manipulation and the consequences of the latter as follows:

> ... in persuasion the interlocutors are free to believe or act as they please, depending on whether or not they accept the arguments of the persuader, whereas in manipulation recipients are typically assigned a more passive role: they are *victims* of manipulation. This negative consequence of manipulative discourse typically occurs when the recipients are unable to understand the real intentions or to see the full consequences of the beliefs or actions advocated by the manipulator. This may be the case especially when the recipients lack the specific knowledge that might be used to resist manipulation. (Van Dijk 2006: 361)

Metaphor can be manipulative but is more commonly persuasive. What we may note from images such as the 'Iron Curtain', the 'moral compass' and the 'rivers of blood' is that they are sufficiently vague to permit multiple interpretations and such vagueness is highly attractive in political debate because the politician cannot be subsequently held to account. For example, American politicians cannot be held responsible for their failure to realise the American Dream since the notion itself is sufficiently vague that we would never know when it had been attained. It is an idea that, like paradise, is just around the corner at an indeterminate point in the future. Yet at the same time these images are striking and memorable: it is often the iconicity of metaphors that leads to them becoming historical myths. It is through such encoding processes that social cognition is influenced by highly symbolic forms of mental representation.

Metaphor is a figure of speech that is typically used in persuasive political myths and arguments; this is because it represents a certain mental representation that reflects a shared system of belief as to what the world is and culture-specific beliefs about mankind's place in it. It offers a way of looking at the world that may differ from the way we normally look at it and, as a result, offers some fresh insight. Because of this cognitive and culturally rooted role, metaphor is important in influencing emotional responses; as Martin (2000: 155) proposes: '... where affectual meaning is evoked, a distinction can be drawn between metaphorical language which in a sense provokes an affectual response... and non-metaphorical language which simply invites a response'. Metaphor *provokes* affective responses because it draws on value systems by exploiting the associative power of language; these systems may be embedded in a culture where certain types of entity are associated with positive or negative experiences, or they may be universal. As I have illustrated above, these associations may not always be ones of which we are conscious and successful leaders are those who can subliminally connect with our experiences of life and death.

When evaluating metaphor we should therefore always consider how far metaphors *conceal* a speaker's intentions; one of the purposes of this book is to develop a public awareness of rhetoric so that manipulation is more readily identified when it arises from metaphor. This is important because of the inherently persuasive power of metaphor. A greater understanding of how metaphor can be persuasive is a way of ensuring that audiences are not manipulated – even though they may be persuaded, as when they recognise that the implications of speakers' metaphors comply with their own best interests. When they do, the metaphors demonstrate that the speaker has the right intentions.

2.3 Critical metaphor analysis and cognitive semantics

Critical metaphor analysis is an approach to the analysis of metaphors that aims to identify the intentions and ideologies underlying language use (Charteris-Black 2004: 34). There are three stages to this approach: first metaphors are identified, then they are interpreted and then explained. Metaphors are identified using the criteria of whether a word or phrase is used with a sense that differs from another more common or more basic sense as demonstrated by identifying a source domain that differs from the target domain. This is a necessary stage for metaphor identification because without two separate domains there can be no transferred meaning. In each of the following chapters I illustrate some of the considerations that were used in identifying metaphors in the sections entitled 'Metaphor analysis'.

To assist in the interpretation of metaphors I employ the cognitive semantic approach towards metaphor. This was originated by Lakoff and Johnson's classic work *Metaphors We Live By*, and modified in later work (e.g. Lakoff and Johnson 1999, Lakoff 1987, 1993, 2002, Lakoff and Turner 1989, Johnson 1987). The basic claims of this approach are that the mind is inherently embodied, thought is mostly unconscious and abstract concepts are largely metaphorical (Lakoff and Johnson 1999: 3). The claim of conceptual metaphor theory is that because thought has evolved out of the sensory, motor and neural systems, metaphorical expressions originate in underlying (or conceptual) metaphors that originate in human bodily and neural experiences of space, movement, containment, etc. (Johnson 1987). There is a single idea (a proposition or a conceptual metaphor) linking a physical with a non-physical experience – that underlies a number of different metaphoric uses of language. I will illustrate the conceptual metaphor LIFE IS A JOURNEY by considering a few metaphors from Tony Blair's speech at the Labour Party Conference in 2003:

I remember when *our journey* to Government began … And what I learnt that day was not about the far left. It was about leadership. Get rid of the false choice: principles or no principles. Replace it with the true choice. *Forward or back. I can only go one way. I've not got a reverse gear.* The time to trust a politician most is not when they're taking the easy option. Any politician can do the popular things. I know, I used to do a few of them.

Blair creates a contrast between his supporters – 'modernising', New Labour whose critics accused it of lacking principles – and his opponents – traditional, 'Old' Labour and its claim to be based on principles. However, what was in reality a political choice between the left and right is represented as only a 'false choice' through metaphor (in italics) and is framed as 'going forward' or 'backward'. This frame is based on our embodied experience that we know what is in front of us (because we can see it) and that forward movement is inherently purposeful. These positive associations of forward motion show in expressions such as 'looking forward to' which is inevitably followed by something good (unless ironic). This positive self-representation is combined with the self-conviction that comes from the use of imperative forms ('get rid of', 'replace', 'trust'). It is reinforced by a proverb-like hyperbole – the image of a car without a reverse gear. Layer upon layer, the idea that he has the right intentions, is reinforced from all rhetorical angles, including pathos – as he then shifts to 'sounding right' by making a joke at his own expense.

As I indicated in Chapter 1, the essence of politics is about building trust, and Blair did this by establishing his moral credibility by appealing to ethos through metaphors from the source domain of journeys and then an appeal to pathos through humour. The appeal to ethos demonstrates what I describe as 'having the right intentions' and the appeal to humour as 'sounding right'. In logical terms the purpose of the metaphor is to simplify the complexity of leadership by defining in the straightforward terms of making up your mind, taking a decision and keeping to it. A very similar journey-based metaphor had been used by Margaret Thatcher in September 1980: 'To those waiting with bated breath for that favourite media catchphrase, the "U" turn, I have only one thing to say. "You turn if you want to. The lady's not for turning"'; here she was conveying her intention to continue with her policies in spite of a deepening recession and rising unemployment (cf. Jones 1996: 27). Blair's use of the metaphor was an allusion as he was emulating Thatcher's leadership style, but needed to avoid repeating the phrase 'not turning' by using a synonym 'only go one way'. The idea of 'turning' is a metaphor grounded in physical experience and refers to 'changing one's mind'; both leaders rejected this as incompatible with a style of leadership that was based on conviction, resolution and certitude.

I suggest a conceptual metaphor POLITICS IS A JOURNEY is a specific realisation of LIFE IS A JOURNEY that explains the choice of phrases such as 'forward or back' and 'U-turn'. This means that there are a range of metaphors where a complex abstract target (POLITICS) is systematically related to a source domain that is better known because it is grounded in bodily experience of movement (JOURNEYS). The conceptual metaphor takes the form A is B and represents the experiential basis that underlies a set of metaphors. It does not mean that metaphors can *only* take this form or *predict* all the forms that will occur, but it explains a pattern of language use by representing what is normal or expected in language use. The journey metaphor frame provides a mental representation that allows the various aspects of political experience to be understood and expressed through embodied experience of movement. The journey schema is rhetorically attractive to politicians and leaders because it can be turned into a whole scenario when they represent themselves as 'guides', their policies as 'maps' and their supporters as 'fellow travelling companions'. All of these entailments of the source domain contribute to the trust they seek to establish. Identification of conceptual metaphors assists in explaining the ideological motivation of language use. The use of journey metaphors and political myths enabled conflict to be represented as ethically motivated in the discourse of Tony Blair. Critical metaphor analysis therefore enables us to identify *which* metaphors were chosen and to explain *why* these metaphors were chosen by illustrating *how* they contribute to political myths.

Political myths can be identified by identifying conceptual metaphors that account for systematic preference by a politician for particular metaphors. I am not proposing that critical metaphor analysis is the *only* method for understanding and explaining a political myth. A number of other and related methods have been developed in critical discourse analysis by researchers such as Chilton (1996, 2004), Hodge and Kress (1993), Fairclough (1989, 1995, 2000, 2006), van Dijk[6] (1995, 1998, 2006, 2008, 2009) and Wodak and Meyer (2009). Van Dijk summarises critical discourse studies as 'typically interested in the way discourse (re)produces social *domination,* that is, the *power abuse* of one group over others, and how dominated groups may discursively *resist* such abuse' (van Dijk 2009: 63) and goes on to state that scholars working in this field 'aim to analyse, and thus to contribute to the understanding

---

[6] A full publication list for van Dijk is available at http://www.discourses.org/cv/Publications%20Teun%20A%20van%20Dijk.pdf

and the solution of, serious social problems, especially those that are caused or exacerbated by public text and talk, such as various forms of social power abuse (domination) and their resulting social inequality' (ibid.). Although the approach taken here is not directly oriented to power abuse of specific groups, it is motivated by providing insight into how power is maintained in democracies. This is because I am focusing on speeches by mainstream politicians addressed to the general public rather than to specific social groups.

Conceptual metaphor analysis is not the only way of identifying political myths; it is also possible to draw on other theories of metaphor such as blending theory. This theory proposes that metaphor is understood with reference to four distinct cognitive spaces. They arise when there is cross-domain mapping between two input spaces, a generic space that includes what is common to the two separate input spaces, and a blended space where the elements from the two input spaces are integrated; this blended space has an emergent structure where these fused elements can be elaborated. This theory challenges many assumptions in conceptual metaphor theory such as that the senses of words in 'source domains' are more basic or primary than the other senses in 'target domains'. By rejecting the distinction between source and target, it also rejects the idea of there being a direction of cognition from the literal senses to metaphoric ones. Instead, rather like gestalt theory, conceptual blending proposes that metaphor is holistic processing with only the blended integration taking place in the conscious mind. I will illustrate how the ideology behind some complex creative metaphors used by politicians can be analysed using blending theory. In this regard blending is simply a further theory that can be integrated into critical metaphor analysis.

Nor does critical metaphor analysis limit itself to the analysis of metaphors; it is equally concerned with metonyms. A metonym is when a word, or phrase, is used to refer to something within the same semantic field; for example, in politics a date such as 9/11 was used to refer to the attack on the World Trade Center; the date in some way stands for, or symbolises, the event. Similarly, the names of capital cities, and sometimes specific buildings or addresses are used as a form of shorthand meaning the governments of nation states. The essential feature of a metonym is that the two entities that are associated are closely related (or 'congruous') in experience; this is not the case with metaphor that may associate entities that are cognitively distant from each other. Metonyms tend to be more invisible than metaphors and therefore have even more ideological potential through creating hidden meanings and forming the very infrastructure of thought about political issues. However, they can be exploited creatively too; for example by blending: when Enoch Powell used the expression 'river of blood' in his anti-immigration speech in April 1968 he was blending two metonyms: BLOOD FOR CONFLICT and BLOOD FOR ETHNICITY – we know through our understanding of DNA that ethnicity and blood are closely related in experience and we also know that conflict is closely related, causally, with blood. It is the activation of metonymic thinking that made the image so powerful – especially when linked with a classical reference. Chilton (2004: 117) argues in his analysis of this speech:

> The speaker claims, explicitly or implicitly, to be not only 'right' in a cognitive sense, but 'right' in a moral sense. There is an important overlap in this domain with *feelings* as well as 'factual' representations. The speaker will seek to ground his or her position in moral *feelings* or intuitions that no one will challenge. The analysis suggests that certain intuitive, emotionally linked mental schemas are being evoked. Certain emotions that can be reasonably regarded as in some way basic are evidentially stimulated – most obviously fear, anger, sense of security, protectiveness, loyalty.

Figurative language – including metaphors and metonyms – is effective in combining this moral and emotional intuition. Similarly, in the lead-up to the Iraq War there was much discussion as to whether there was a 'smoking gun' that would prove that Iraq was in possession of weapons of mass destruction. Here 'smoking gun' was a particular type of metonym referring to all types of destructive weapon; in this case a single object stands for a whole script of events, the loading, aiming and shooting of a gun. The smoking gun activates a schema of intentional behaviour and therefore means 'evidence of culpability'. The metonym evokes emotions of fear and danger that arise from witnessing a gun crime. Metonyms therefore also contribute to sounding right.

In the second edition of this book I continue to suggest that persuasion in political speeches is realised through the effective choice of metaphors in combination with other rhetorical strategies. Critical metaphor analysis provides us with a methodology for the analysis and interpretation of ideology and illustrates how rhetoric is used for the purpose of legitimisation. Identification of conceptual metaphors is inevitably subjective, like all qualitative judgements, but the analytical method is clear and the reader is free to challenge metaphor classifications. As I have argued in my definition of metaphor, there is an element of subjectivity in *all* experience of metaphor – and this is inevitable because it is not possible to anticipate or fully predict an individual's experience of discourse and the extent to which he or she will experience words as having meanings that are transferred from other contexts of use. This does not mean that language-based enquiry should be restricted to what is predictable. Identification and discussion of possible ideological intentions underlying metaphor choices through conceptual metaphor analysis is a way of forming theories about persuasive language use.

When analysing political speeches using critical metaphor analysis the cognitive semantic approach needs to be complemented with a summary of the social context in which the speeches were made and of the overall verbal context of metaphor. Cognitive characteristics of metaphor cannot be treated in isolation from other persuasive rhetorical features in the discourse context. One attraction of the cognitive semantic approach is that it allows us to compare how metaphor is used by different politicians, both in terms of what metaphors are chosen and the concepts, ideologies and myths that underlie these. Although politicians sometimes use different metaphors, others are common to many, and for most politicians metaphor is a method that enables them to display their expertise in political rhetoric through knowledge and command of one of its major linguistic characteristics. In order to understand questions such as *why* one metaphor is preferred to another we need necessarily also consider rhetorical issues such as the leader's intentions within specific speech-making contexts: metaphors are not a requirement of the semantic system but are matters of speaker choice. Cognitive semantics and critical metaphor analysis are important linguistic contributions towards a theory of rhetoric and persuasion for political communication.

2.4 Summary

In these first two chapters I have argued that metaphor is vital to the language of leadership because it mediates between the conscious and rational basis of ideology and its unconscious mythical elements. Metaphor draws on the unconscious emotional associations of words, the values of which are rooted in cultural knowledge. For this reason it potentially has a highly persuasive force because of its activation of both conscious and unconscious resources to influence our rational, moral and emotional response, both directly – through describing and analysing political issues – and indirectly by influencing how we feel about things. It therefore plays a crucial social role in communicating ideology that I have argued is vital to the discourse of politics.

I have argued that metaphor does not work in isolation from other rhetorical strategies: to the contrary, I have outlined a range of strategies – such as metonymy – that occur independently or in conjunction with metaphor. Many of these strategies have continued in traditions of public speaking even after we have forgotten the classical rhetorical terms that were originally used to describe them. Metaphor becomes more persuasive when it is used in combination with other strategies. When a political leader employs a rhetorical strategy in isolation the audience is quick to identify that there is a conscious persuasive strategy at work. They become aware of the presence of a performer at work and their defences or 'cheat detectors' may be aroused against his or her linguistic exploits. However, when strategies occur in combination with each other, the audience is more likely to give itself over to the speaker because the focus of attention is on processing the message itself rather than on how it is communicated. Rhetoric therefore creates uncritical followers and political leaders may legitimise themselves most effectively through an interaction of rhetorical strategies because the total effect is greater than when each occurs separately. Persuasion is a multi-layered discourse function that is the outcome of a complex interaction between intention, linguistic choice and context.

The aim of this second edition is to raise further critical awareness of the rhetoric that is used by political leaders to persuade others of their thoughts, beliefs and values through establishing trust, convincing them that they are right thinking, that they sound right *and* can tell the right story. I propose that a better understanding of the conceptual basis for metaphor – and how this relates with other aspects of rhetoric and persuasion – will provide a clearer understanding of the nature of these thoughts, beliefs and values and the myths through which they are communicated. Critical awareness of how discourse is used to persuade and to create legitimacy is an important area of knowledge for those who wish to engage politically within a democracy. We can only ever have the possibility of trusting potential leaders once the language of leadership is better understood.

3
Winston Churchill: Metaphor and Heroic Myth

3.1 Background

Churchill was the past master of twentieth-century political oratory and has set the standards that subsequent politicians have often sought to emulate – especially in crisis situations for which his rhetorical style is the benchmark. Soon after his election George W. Bush declared that he had placed a bust of Churchill in the White House Oval Office. His post September 11 speeches adopted Churchill's rhetorical style and in early 2004 Bush claimed that Churchill was not just 'the rallying voice of the Second World War' but also 'a prophet of the Cold War'.[1] It is significant that a politician who attached great personal importance to oratory in the classical sense was also the one who had the greatest opportunity to employ it for that most vital of political objectives: national survival. Churchill has been able to set the benchmark for political speaking in the modern period precisely because he believed in the power of the spoken word to motivate by winning over hearts and minds and demonstrated this belief through command of wartime rhetoric; as he said in 1954 'To jaw-jaw is better than to war-war'.

Churchill had unknowingly spent much of his earlier life preparing for his role as a wartime orator. He published the first volume of his speeches before he was 30 and eventually went on to publish 18 volumes. In 1897 he published an essay 'The Scaffolding of Rhetoric' arguing for the importance of oratory, and yet it was not until 43 years later that his mastery of persuasion directly led to his appointment as Prime Minister. His command of delivery was such that he

---

[1] Speech opening Churchill exhibition at the Library of Congress.

memorised by heart the complete pre-prepared scripts for his speeches. Although his radio broadcasts provided leadership during a time of national crisis, his greatest political performances were in the House of Commons. For Churchill oratory was both the artist's brush and the bully's cudgel that could goad opponents into submission – he also knew when to use the brush and when the cudgel.

His most successful oratory was certainly during the Second World War when the impression of strength and inflexibility conveyed through his gravelly tone made him the symbol of a national resolve to withstand invasion. As Cassirer (1946: 278) argues:

> Even in primitive societies where myth pervades and governs the whole of man's social feeling and social life it is not always operative in the same way nor does it always appear with the same strength. It reaches its full force when man has to face an unusual and dangerous situation . . . In desperate situations man will always have recourse to desperate means – and our present-day political myths have been such desperate means.

In 1939 after the collapse of the Munich agreement and faced with the threat of an aggressive force expanding over Central Europe, Britain was in precisely such a position of danger. Churchill's appointment to the Admiralty on 3 September 1939 was against an unpromising background:

> He was politically déconsidéré, largely ignored even by those who agreed with his attitudes on foreign affairs. His career since 1915 had been, in the main, a story of failure. Now in his sixty-fifth year, after some forty years in active political life, he was given his opportunity. (James 1973: 108)

However, the loss of confidence in the government created a situation in which there were opportunities for myth creation. Indeed, his subsequent elevation to Prime Minister on 10 May 1940 can be attributed to the impact that his speeches were having in the early part of that year. The social function of his radio broadcasts was to raise morale by communicating the impression of specific actions being planned and implemented. The creation of a sense of strategy – even though often illusory – was essential if the public were to retain confidence in their leader's capacity to attain the stated objective of military victory. This use of the media was a completely novel, and effective, leadership strategy. As James argues – 'What will always be remembered as the "blood, sweat and tears" speech was a real turning point' (ibid.: 108). He goes on to claim:

> Here was the authentic voice of leadership and defiance. It was Churchill's outstanding quality as a war leader that he made the struggle seem not merely essential for national survival, but worthwhile and noble. (Ibid.: 109)

3.2 The rhetoric of Winston Churchill

In the following analysis I will argue that Churchill's primary rhetorical objective was telling a story in which the actions of Hitler and Germany are represented as forces of evil in contrast to those of Britain and its Allies that are represented as forces of good. I describe this narrative as a heroic myth and argue that metaphor was the prime rhetorical method for expressing this myth. This is evident in the metaphors – in particular personifications – as in the following excerpt:

> Side by side, unaided except by their kith and kin in the great Dominions and by the wide empires which rest beneath their shield – side by side, the British and French peoples have advanced to rescue not only Europe but mankind from the foulest and most soul-destroying tyranny which has ever darkened and stained the pages of history. Behind them – behind us – behind the Armies and Fleets of Britain and France – gather a group of shattered States and bludgeoned races: the Czechs, the Poles, the Norwegians, the Danes, the Dutch, the Belgians – upon all of whom the long night of barbarism will descend, unbroken even by a star of hope, unless we conquer, as conquer we must; as conquer we shall. (19 May 1940)

Central to Churchill's heroic myth is the claim that Britain was not fighting purely for national self-interest but was the embodiment of forces of good that would rescue all mankind from tyranny and barbarism.

A hallmark of Churchill's use of metaphor is that nation states are conceptualised as human heroes, villains or victims. In his rhetoric nations are attributed with mental and affective states that lead them to have thoughts, beliefs and feelings and this contributes to his sounding right. It was, of course, the people who inhabited these nations who may have undergone such experiences, but Churchill's heroic myth described international political and military affairs *as if they were* personal hopes and anxieties. Metaphor created the possibility for representation of Britain and its allies as motivated by altruism and as having the right intentions and for Germany and its allies as motivated by self-interest. This use of personification can be represented by an underlying metaphor – THE NATION IS A PERSON.[2]

For Churchill metaphor had a dual rhetorical role of sounding right and establishing himself as having the right intentions; this was crucial to creating confidence and confirming his identity as a successful leader. At other times, metaphor could be seen as a distraction from the primary goal of deliberating on political decisions. Metaphor was a resource for projecting a set of beliefs, and for creating social cohesion by telling the right story; this contrasts with the way that Hitler used metaphor for the conceptualisation and formation of actual political policy. It is for this reason that I describe Churchill's use of metaphor as heroic myth – a myth in which Churchill serves as a metonym for a righteous and heroic Britain.

Metaphor was only one amongst several rhetorical strategies. Quite large sections of Churchill's wartime speeches are characterised by a complete absence of metaphor; this is especially when he is describing the current military situation and summarising military strategy. There are very few occurrences of metaphor in a number of the most famous quotations for which Churchill is remembered. If we consider his first speech as Prime Minister – the 'blood, sweat and tears' speech – images of physical and mental suffering combine hyperbole with metonymy because the *effects* of blood, sweat and tears refer to the suffering and hard work that *cause* them, so the effects are used to refer to their cause. The speech also contains extensive use of repetition, matching clauses (parisons) and rhetorical questions. In the following excerpt from this speech repeated matched items are underlined and questions are shown in italics:

> We have before us an ordeal of the most grievous kind. <u>We have before us</u> many, many long months of struggle and of suffering. You ask, *what is our policy?* I can say: It is to wage war, by sea, land and air, with all our might and <u>with all</u> the strength that

---

[2] See Lakoff (1991) and Rohrer (1995) for a discussion of this metaphor in relation to the 1990 Gulf crisis.

God can give us; to wage war against a monstrous tyranny, never surpassed in the dark, lamentable catalogue of human crime. That is our policy. You ask, *what is our aim?* I can answer in one word: It is victory, victory at all costs, victory in spite of all terror, victory, however long and hard the road may be; for without victory, there is no survival. Let that be realised; no survival for the British Empire, no survival for all that the British Empire has stood for, no survival for the urge and impulse of the ages, that mankind will move forward towards its goal. (13 May 1940)

While the speech also contains metaphors, the essence of its rhetorical force is in repeated elements and rhetorical questions rather than metaphors. The effect of repetition and reiteration is to convey persistence and obduracy that sounds right because it is based on conviction. The structure of this part of the speech is organised around repetition in response to rhetorical questions; in answer to the first question about policy 'wage war' is repeated, in answer to the second regarding aims, 'victory' is repeated. Reiteration also assists in generalisation from *British* war 'policy' and 'aims' to the 'goals' of *mankind in general*. Here the underlying intention is to equate specific British objectives with general human aspirations and so to raise the status of military action from the personal to the heroic, from the prosaic to the sublime.

Often lexical repetition is combined with parallelism to produce an even more marked use of repetition at the levels of both vocabulary and grammar, as perhaps is most well known in:

We shall go on to the end, we shall fight in France, we shall fight on the seas and oceans, we shall fight with growing confidence and growing strength in the air, we shall defend our Island, whatever the cost may be, we shall fight on the beaches, we shall fight on the landing grounds, we shall fight in the fields and in the streets, we shall fight in the hills; we shall never surrender. (4 June 1940)

Repetition of 'we' implies unity of purpose and 'shall' clearly predicts the future; particular locations, landing grounds, etc. are then slotted into a syntactical frame:

WE + SHALL + 'MILITARY' VERB + LOCATION.

Repetition implies physical and mental obduracy since, like the staccato effect of a machine gun, opposition will continue – even when the bullets run out: it sounds right! Reiteration of the syntactical structure communicates strength and conviction and Churchill also sometimes uses it with poetic effect:

> The empires of the future are the empires of the mind. (6 September 1943)

Hyperbole is such a favoured rhetorical strategy that it becomes a mode of discourse for Churchill, as in his tribute and eulogy to the airmen who fought in the Battle of Britain:

> The gratitude of every home in our Island, in our Empire, and indeed throughout the world, except in the abodes of the guilty, goes out to the British airmen who, undaunted by odds, unwearied in their constant challenge and mortal danger, are turning the tide of the World War by their prowess and by their devotion. Never in the field of human conflict was so much owed by so many to so few. (20 August 1940)

Rhetorical force is achieved by the strategy of combining reiteration with contrast ('so much', 'so many': 'so few'). Metaphor also plays a marginal role for example in conceptualising the war as a sea with a changing tide. In other cases hyperbole is created by the use of superlative forms:

> Let us therefore brace ourselves to our duties, and so bear ourselves that, if the British Empire and its Commonwealth last for a thousand years, men will still say, 'This was their finest hour.' (18 June 1940)

In yet other cases contrast (or antithesis) is employed for an effect that can be both memorable and witty as in the following:

> There is nothing wrong with change, if it is in the right direction.

> The problems of victory are more agreeable than those of defeat, but they are no less difficult.

In some instances this is combined with chiasmus (clause inversion):

> An optimist sees an opportunity in every calamity; a pessimist sees a calamity in every opportunity.

Chiasmus could be used for morale raising in memorable fashion when describing the various stages of the war:

> Now this is not the end. It is not even the beginning of the end. But it is, perhaps, the end of the beginning. (10 November 1942)

This reminds us that in addition to strategies such as repetition, clause matching, inversion, antithesis and hyperbole, another hallmark of Churchill's oratory is his ability to replicate the structural patterns and discourse function of English phraseology. Consider, for example, his use of proverb-like utterances such as: 'We make a living by what we get, we make a life by what we give'; or 'If you mean to profit, learn to please' and 'It is better to do the wrong thing than to do nothing.' These clearly have a discourse function of warning similar to that of many English proverbs but they are also characterised by their formal linguistic pattern. They are comprised of two phrases in a relation of symmetry in which the second phrase reiterates structural elements from the first.

In other cases – again those that are often quoted because structural reiteration encourages memorisation – there are the characteristics of maxims or adages. Examples would include: 'The price of greatness is responsibility'; 'I never worry about action, but only inaction'; 'Censure is often useful, praise often deceitful' and 'Success is going from failure to failure without losing your enthusiasm'. All these phrases replicate ideas and linguistic patterns with which his audience would be familiar because they characterise the phraseology of the English language. This enhances the likelihood for subsequent quotation and these are therefore key linguistic techniques for myth creation. It is the ability to coin phrases that share the structural patterns of familiar maxims and express widely held cultural outlooks that enhanced Churchill's persuasiveness. It is no coincidence, then, that the phrase 'blood, sweat and tears' has entered into English phraseology and provides evidence of how sounding right contributes to linguistic innovation.

3.3 Metaphor analysis

For the analysis I selected a corpus of 25 of the major wartime speeches (see Appendix 1). There is a bias towards those speeches given in the earlier part of the war because this was a period when persuasive communication was most necessary to sustain public morale after the fall of France, the evacuation from Dunkirk and during the Battle of Britain. This was a crucial period in determining the outcome of the war. As A.J.P. Taylor (1969: 31) has put it:

His confidence that victory, though perhaps not easy, was certain, in time inspired others, and appeasement seemed to be unnecessary as well as dishonourable. Churchill's arguments mattered less than the tone in which he said them and his voice ultimately made him, in British eyes, the architect of victory.

The corpus contains approximately 50,000 words and at least 385 metaphors; therefore, one expression that is classifiable as a metaphor (using the definition given in Chapter 1) occurs on average every 130 words. For comparative purposes I also examined a 50,000-word corpus of Hitler's speeches; this revealed over double the frequency of metaphors found in the Churchill corpus.

Initially, I classified metaphors according to their source domains; this is because in establishing how metaphor can be used to create myth we need to identify the typical social values that are attached to the domains on which metaphor draws (see Appendix 2). These values arise from our bodily experience and knowledge of the value attached to these domains in particular cultural practices; for example, we know that light is a prerequisite for growth as well as sight while darkness is associated with inability to see and the resulting possibility of dangerous experiences. We know that families are normally associated with close human relationships and therefore associated with a positive evaluation. Our experience of journeys is that they are normally purposeful and goal orientated and that different types of experiences, difficulties, etc. may be encountered. Analysis of how metaphors are used to create the myths that underlie an ideology begins with identification of their source domains.

The approach summarised in Appendix 2 allows us to identify the preferred metaphor types of a particular politician; this facilitates comparison of different speakers and is valuable in identifying the metaphors that characterise their oratorical style. I should first comment briefly on the above figures: they are not necessarily comprehensive and I do not claim that other metaphor analysts would come up with slightly different numerical classifications. A particular difficulty, as we will see later, is when a number of different source domains occur in close proximity in what I will describe as 'nested metaphors' (see section 3.7); consider, for example, the following italicised metaphors:

Very few wars have been won by mere numbers alone. Quality, will power, geographical advantages, natural and financial resources, the command of the sea, and, above all, a cause which rouses the spontaneous *surgings* (1) of the human spirit in millions of hearts – these have proved to be the decisive factors in *the human story* (2). If it were otherwise, how would the race of men have risen above the apes; how otherwise would they have conquered and extirpated dragons and monsters; how would they have ever evolved the moral theme; how would they have *marched forward* (3) across the centuries to broad conceptions of compassion, of freedom, and of right? How would they ever have discerned those *beacon lights* (4) which summon and guide us across the *rough dark waters* (5) and presently will guide us across *the flaming lines of battle* (6) towards better days which lie beyond? (20 January 1940)

I suggest that the numbered metaphors draw on the following conceptualisations:

1. The spirit is an ocean
2. Evolution is a narrative
3. Human progress is a journey
4. Safety/hope is light
5. Danger/fear is darkness
6. War is fire

According to my analysis, there is a water metaphor (1), a narrative or 'story' metaphor (2), a journey metaphor (3), two light and darkness metaphors (4 and 5) and a fire metaphor (6). However, the journey metaphor is extended over several phrases (e.g. from 'marched forward' to a double repetition of 'guide'); similarly, the light metaphor occurs in 'beacon light' and 'dark waters' and the fire metaphor is in both 'beacon' and in 'flaming'. So in such cases is there one metaphor or two? ('Beacon' is particularly problematic since it is potentially both a light metaphor and a fire metaphor.)

Where metaphors from the same source domain occur in the same phrase my method was to count them as *single* metaphors. Where there is evidence of different source domains in the same phrase, I would identify which source domain was *primary* and only count this – especially where the secondary use was also part of *another* metaphor. For example, 'beacon' – though potentially part of a fire metaphor – is primarily a light metaphor (because the function of a beacon is to create light rather than heat) so I did not *also* count it as a fire metaphor. A similar practice was followed when the same source domain occurs in different phrases, so although 'guide' is potentially a journey metaphor, since 'march' had already led me to identify a journey metaphor and 'guide' is *also* part of a light metaphor it is not counted again. This procedure aims to avoid counting the same word or phrase as more than one metaphor and gives a rather conservative count of the number of metaphors used. The purpose of counting metaphors was to direct our interest towards underlying conceptualisations that were important in influencing core value judgements in Churchill's creation of political myth. Quantitative data are helpful in determining the relative importance to be attached to each of the different source domains for metaphor that he employed.

Appendix 2 shows that a relatively small number of domains provide the linguistic and cognitive basis for Churchill's metaphors. They include those for which the potential audience may be assumed to have had some experience – journeys, animals, buildings, family, etc. – and some that would be naturally resonant for British people because of their cultural and historical experience – such as the sea and the weather. Comparison with the Hitler corpus showed that Churchill draws on a much wider range of source domains. This may reflect a different discourse role for metaphor as Churchill is more concerned with sounding right and having the right intentions, while Hitler employs metaphor in actual policy formulation – that is thinking about what in his view was right. The stylistic preference for use of personification by Churchill reflects a preference for a grandiloquent and classical rhetorical style that is motivated by a desire to sound right as a national leader. This literary and aesthetic role for metaphor as a source of embellishment can be related to his earlier experience of historical writing. I used the findings shown in Appendix 2 to identify those domains worthy of a detailed analysis; these were personification, journeys, light and darkness and slavery.

3.4 Personification

Personification was easily the most common figure in Churchill's oratory, accounting for around 37 per cent of all his metaphors. It is a linguistic figure in which an abstract and inanimate entity is described or referred to using a word or phrase that in other contexts would be used to describe a person. We may therefore think of 'person' as the source domain. Personification is persuasive because it evokes our attitudes, feelings and beliefs about people and applies them to our attitudes, feelings and beliefs about abstract political entities and is therefore a way of heightening the emotional appeal. Typically, the ideological basis for using personification is either to arouse empathy for a social group, ideology or belief evaluated as heroic, or to arouse opposition towards a social group, ideology or belief that is evaluated as villainous. This is done by associating social groups, ideologies and beliefs that are positively evaluated with heroic human attributes – such as courage and determination – and by associating negatively evaluated social groups, ideas, etc. with villainous attributes – such as cowardice and treachery. A typical example of positive evaluation is when 'Britain' or 'us' is described as if it is a plucky hero who is prepared to fight to the death:

> And now it has come to us to stand alone in the breach, and face the worst that the tyrant's might and enmity can do... here, girt about by the seas and oceans where the Navy reigns; shielded from above by the prowess and devotion of our airmen – we await undismayed the impending assault. (14 July 1940)

> Britain, other nations thought, had drawn a sponge across her slate. But instead our country stood in the gap. There was no flinching and no thought of giving in, never give in, never, never, never. (29 October 1941)

> ... to look ahead to those days which will surely come when we shall have finally beaten down Satan under our feet and find ourselves with other great allies at once the masters and the servants of the future. (3 September 1943)

In these metaphors there is evidence of the concepts: BRITAIN IS A HERO and GERMANY IS A VILLAIN. In the corpus there are 11 occurrences where Churchill uses personifications to refer to 'we', 'us' or 'ourselves' – this forms a metonymic chain in which he stands for the people and the people stand for nation. The chain implies that the qualities that are attributed to the nation are also to be attributed to himself and the people. In this way, Churchill's rhetoric was successful in representing himself and his country as a champion prize fighter and identifying the people and himself with the acts of bravery and physical courage undertaken by servicemen. The effect of sounding right was to satisfy the political objective of harnessing the efforts of the civilian population to the military effort. This use of personification combined with first-person reference was a highly effective linguistic instrument for creating a myth in which he is a symbol of a heroic nation. The heroic myth of BRITAIN IS A HERO is quite evident in his speech to the VE day crowds:

> This is not victory of a party or of any class. It's a victory of the great British nation as a whole. We were the first, in this ancient

island, to draw the sword against tyranny. After a while we were left all alone against the most tremendous military power that has been seen. We were all alone for a whole year. (8 May 1945)

Hawkins (2001) describes an iconographic frame of reference comprised of three images: the hero, the villain and the victim; and he refers to this as the 'Warrior Iconography'. Though, of course, these roles are also implied by Edelman's Valiant Leader and Conspiratorial Enemy myths. Churchill's warrior iconography is one in which Churchill and Britain are the hero, Hitler and Germany are the villain and France and other conquered nations of Europe are the victims. The villain and victim roles are evident in the following:

> ... and against that other enemy who, without the slightest provocation, coldly and deliberately, for greed and gain, stabbed France in the back in the moment of her agony, and is now marching against us in Africa. (20 August 1940)

This activates a mental representation for treacherous and cowardly behaviour that is associated with the type of unprovoked assault one would expect of a villain – someone who has the wrong intentions. Everything that is associated with life is positively valued while everything that is associated with death carries an extreme negative value. It seems that what is important here in communicating value judgements is the creation of a polar contrast between forces of good and evil as well as those of life and death. In some instances personification creates an emotive link between Nazism and death as in the following:

> So we came back after long months from the jaws of death, out of the mouth of hell, while all the world wondered. (8 May 1945)

In other places the mythic role of 'monster' replaces that of 'villain':

> ... so many States and kingdoms torn to pieces in a few weeks or even days by the *monstrous force* of the Nazi war machine. (14 July 1940)

> It is to wage war, by sea, land and air, with all our might and with all the strength that God can give us; to wage war against a *monstrous tyranny*, never surpassed in the dark, lamentable catalogue of human crime. (13 May 1940)

...because, while France had been bled white and England was supine and bewildered, a *monstrous growth* of aggression sprang up in Germany, in Italy and Japan. (3 September 1943)

In this iconographic frame if Germany is the villain, then Nazism is the monster created by it; this provides evidence of an underlying concept NAZISM IS A MONSTER. I would like to suggest that motivating this concept is a combination of a conceptual metaphor and a conceptual metonym. The conceptual metaphor is A NATION IS A PERSON; it is this which permits the actions of nations to be represented as if they were either the actions of heroes or villains and other passive nations to be cast in the role of victim. The conceptual metonym is POLITICAL LEADER FOR NATION; the leader of the government of a nation is taken to represent that nation because he has an ultimate decision-making capacity. We see this in conventional expressions such as 'Mussolini has reeled back in Albania' or 'the smear of Hitler has been wiped from the human path'. The metonym and the metaphor work in conjunction with each other – since the metonym encourages us to think of the political actions of countries as if they were the actions of a particular person in those countries. The conventional use of metonym creates the conceptual basis for personifications motivated by the conceptual metaphor A NATION IS A PERSON.

Against this cognitive background, battles between nation states are conceived in heroic terms appropriate to a struggle between medieval warriors:

> *Shielded by* overwhelming sea power, possessed of invaluable strategic bases and of ample funds, France might have remained one of the *great combatants* in the struggle. By so doing, France would have preserved the continuity of her life, and the French Empire might have advanced with the British Empire to the rescue of the independence and integrity of the French Motherland... The Czechs, the Poles, the Norwegians, the Dutch, the Belgians are still *in the field, sword in hand*, recognized by Great Britain and the United States as the sole representative authorities and lawful Governments of their respective States. (20 August 1940)

Churchill's use of personifications based around the conceptual metaphor THE NATION IS A PERSON implies an evaluation based on a historical schema for medieval warfare in which allies are heroes and enemies are villains.

Table 3.1 Summary of metaphor targets in Churchill's personifications

	Positive evaluation	Total	Negative evaluation	Total	Total
Country/ political grouping	France (9) Nations (5) Countries (4) British nation (4)	41	Japan Germany	3	44
Abstract concept	Destiny (4) Freedom (4) Justice (2) Progress (2) History (2)	21	Death (4) War (3) Disaster (2) Woe (2)	17	38
Social grouping	We/us (11) Mankind (4) Motherland (2)	22	Foe (3) Enemy Evil doers	5	27
Military grouping	British army French army Navy	9	Gestapo German aircraft	2	11
Ideology	Western democracies	1	Nazi regime Communism Tyranny (5)	8	9
Other		11		4	15
Total		105		39	144

Because of the importance of personification in conveying value judgements and ideology through an emotional appeal I decided to quantify the types of metaphorical targets for which evaluation is given by a personification (see Table 3.1).

Not surprisingly, the most preferred target for a personification is a country/a political grouping or an abstract concept – these accounted for around two-thirds of the total uses of this figure. The metaphors in the following speech to the VE-day crowd refer to historical processes:

London can take it. So we came back after long months from *the jaws of death*, out of *the mouth of hell*, while all the world wondered. When shall the reputation and faith of this generation of English men and women fail? I say that in the long years to come not only will the people of this island but of the world, wherever *the bird of freedom chirps* in human hearts, look back to what we've done and they will say 'do not despair, *do not yield to violence and tyranny*, march straightforward and die – if need be – unconquered'. (8 May 1945)

Churchill shifts from personifications of abstract entities that have a negative evaluation (e.g. death and tyranny) and are linked to negatively evaluated targets (e.g. Germany and Japan) to those that have a positive evaluation (e.g. freedom) and are linked with positively evaluated targets (e.g. the British Empire and its Allies). This gives a mythical dimension to the struggle between good and evil and creates a polar relation between them: the use of personification is effective when combined with antithesis as it creates an evaluation based on a metaphysical domain. Personification was therefore a major rhetorical means for persuasion in Churchill's efforts to unify and to raise morale during a period of military conflict because it allowed him both to sound right and to express the right intentions.

3.5 Journey metaphors

Journey metaphors were originally introduced into cognitive linguistics by Lakoff and Johnson (1980) who proposed a metaphor LOVE IS A JOURNEY to account for expressions such as 'our relationship is at a crossroads', though this was later developed into the more general LIFE IS A JOURNEY (Lakoff and Turner 1989). They trace the literary and biblical origins of this metaphor in terms of how choices can be made between good and evil paths and how God can be conceived as 'a guide' and death as 'a departure' (ibid.: 10). This was later reformulated into PURPOSEFUL ACTIVITY IS TRAVELLING ALONG A PATH TOWARD A DESTINATION (Lakoff 1993). Charteris-Black (2004: 74) suggests that *social* purposes can be viewed as destinations just as much as individual ones. Evidence for this idea can be found in metaphoric uses of 'step', 'burden', 'forward', etc. I also propose that Conservative discourse typically employs journey metaphors to refer to movements forward in time while in Labour discourse movement is typically spatial rather than temporal. Chilton (2004) highlights the importance of spatial concepts in political discourse and argues that what is *close* to the speaker is evaluated as morally and legally *good*, while what is *distant* from the speaker is evaluated as morally and legally *bad*.

Journeys are a potent source domain for metaphor because of the availability of a clear schema that includes *required* elements – such as start and end points connected by a path and entities that move along the path; this is usually represented in cognitive linguistics as a SOURCE–PATH–GOAL. However, *optional* elements are equally important in political speeches; these include mode of travel, guides, companions, etc. It is the flexibility of these optional elements that serves as a richer basis for inferential reasoning and evaluation than the required elements that are so much part of our experience that we are barely conscious of them. For example, we know that on journeys there is the potential for both positive experiences – such as making friends and seeing new places – and for negative ones – such as meeting a dead end or getting lost. However, unlike personifications that create relations of contrast between the poles of good and evil, the rhetorical purpose of journey metaphors is to create solidarity in order that positively evaluated purposes may be successfully attained. In this respect journey metaphors encourage followers to accept short-term suffering for worthwhile long-term objectives.[3]

'Journeys' was the second most common source domain for metaphor in the corpus with a total of 48 linguistic forms. Typical linguistic forms were: *road, path, journey, toiling up a hill, milestone, feet, forward* and *march*. Over 75 per cent of the journey metaphors had one of four metaphor targets; these were: the British war effort ($n = 15$), human progress in general ($n = 10$), military victory ($n = 7$) and the American war effort ($n = 5$). All the metaphors convey a strong positive evaluation of these targets as we can see from the following examples which are chosen to illustrate the first three of these metaphor targets:

> ... And the whole preparation of our munitions industries under the spell of war has *rolled forward* with gathering momentum. (27 January 1940)

> The course of world history is the noblest prize of victory. *We are still toiling up the hill; we have not yet reached the crest-line of it*; we cannot survey the landscape or even imagine what its condition will be when that longed-for morning comes. (10 August 1940)

> Duty inescapable remains. So long as our *pathway to victory* is not impeded, we are ready to discharge such offices of good will toward the French Government as may be possible... (14 July 1940)

While all Churchill's journey metaphors carry a positive evaluation of the overriding war aim of defeating Germany, different aspects of the source domain are highlighted according to the rhetorical intention within the context of the speech. For example, when the metaphor target is some aspect of the British war effort – whether in terms of military

---

[3] Journey metaphors are also discussed in detail in sections 4.42 and 12.3.4.

or civilian activity – it is usually the knowledge that journeys involve expenditure of effort that is highlighted by the metaphor. So typically, movement towards a desirable social goal is difficult and involves some form of short-term suffering or struggle to overcome resistance. This was clearly effective in giving a sense of purpose to the suffering and difficulty that people encountered in their everyday lives during war. However, there are also other related ideas that realised Churchill's rhetorical intention of persuading by telling the right story. He sought to emphasise that journeys once started have to be completed (whatever the cost in human suffering) and that there was no 'going back' because of the desirability of the 'destination':

> ... the Prime Minister *led us forward* in one great body into a struggle against aggression and oppression, against a wrong-doing, faithlessness and cruelty, from which there can be *no going back*. (27 January 1940)[4]

Some optional elements from the journey source domain are explicitly rejected – for example, the knowledge that rests are sometimes taken during a journey:

> But from them also we may draw the force and inspiration to *carry us forward upon our journey* and *not to pause or rest* till liberation is achieved and justice done. (27 January 1940)

However, since the purpose of journey metaphors was to raise morale and create a feeling of optimism, they are also frequently goal-focused and refer explicitly to the end point, or destination, of the journey – and here the metaphor target is military victory:

> The *road to victory* may not be so long as we expect. But we have no right to count upon this. Be it long or short, rough or smooth, we mean *to reach our journey's end*. (10 August 1940)

Churchill frequently used the phrase 'the road to victory' as it emphasises the fact that there is always a predetermined destination – unlike say a path which could either meander around in circles or take us to an unknown destination. Churchill's use of journey metaphors shifts from

---

[4] Tony Blair used a similar journey metaphor to reject the idea of retreating from his chosen path when he claimed 'I can only go one way. I have not got a reverse gear' in his Labour Party conference speech of September 2003.

emphasising personal suffering to highlighting the irreversibility of the war effort according to the rhetorical objective of the stage in the speech.

The most important example of the power of language to influence political outcomes through the journey schema was when Churchill persuaded the USA to join the Allied cause – in this respect they contributed also to right thinking by providing a political argument. The choice of journey metaphors to describe both the British and the American war effort was a heuristic for forging a political link between the two countries – this was a vital objective in 1940 and journey metaphors encouraged the Anglo-American alliance. For example, the knowledge that journeys are generally social rather than solitary endeavours was exploited in the speech 'The Price of Greatness is Responsibility' which was designed to encourage American involvement in the war. Journey metaphors are shown in italics in the following excerpts:

> We may be quite sure that this process will be intensified with every *forward step the United States make* in wealth and power.
>
> Not only do we *march and strive shoulder to shoulder*[5] at this moment under the fire of the enemy on the fields of war or in the air, but also in those realms of thought which are consecrated to the rights and the dignity of man.
>
> I like to think of British and Americans *moving about freely* over each other's wide estates with hardly a sense of being foreigners to one another. (3 September 1943)

These metaphors show evidence of an underlying concept BRITAIN AND THE USA ARE TRAVELLING COMPANIONS. Here each use of the metaphor profiles a different aspect of the journey domain. First is the idea of journeys being purposeful, next is the idea of going on a journey together with someone else, and finally, the idea of travelling with someone implies unrestricted rights of access to each other's territory. This heuristic probably encouraged the government of the USA to enter the war and to commit itself to the rescue of its 'travelling companion'. Churchill's use of metaphor is systematically linked with underlying rhetorical and political intentions. These are achieved by highlighting different component elements of the schema that people have for journeys in the construction of an ideological perspective. Systematic

---

[5] The same metaphor was subsequently used by Tony Blair in a speech intended to demonstrate British support for the USA following the September 11 attacks on the World Trade Center and the Pentagon.

extension and elaboration of a particular metaphor schema are a very effective way of using metaphor both to develop a political argument and to give stylistic coherence to a speech.

Another good example of how metaphor forms coherent mental representations or frames occurs in the speech 'The First Five Months' of 27 January 1940. There are a total of five metaphors from the source domain of journeys that are distributed at near equal distances throughout the speech as follows:

1. ... the Prime Minister *led us forward* in one great body into a struggle against aggression and oppression, against a wrong-doing, faithlessness and cruelty, from *which there can be no going back*.
2. ... the whole preparation of our munitions industries under the spell of war *has rolled forward* with gathering momentum...
3. The men at the top may be very fierce and powerful, but their ears are deaf, their fingers are numb; they cannot feel their feet as *they move forward in the fog and darkness of the immeasurable and the unknown*.
4. ... wickedness has cast its shadow upon mankind and seeks *to bar its forward march*...
5. But from them also we may draw the force and inspiration *to carry us forward upon our journey* and not to pause or rest till liberation is achieved and justice done.

The first two metaphors highlight the directionality and force of the war effort. In the first Churchill is a heroic leader inspired by a sense of moral self-righteousness. In the second we know that – like a journey – the war effort cannot be reversed; the third one then describes the Nazi command as being lost on a journey because they are ignorant of the route (perhaps because they have no guide or no adequate maps). The last two then describe the general notion of inevitability of human progress in terms of a successful and purposeful journey – but one which may encounter impediments that need to be overcome. This illustrates the flexibility of the journey metaphor in developing arguments. It is used to examine different aspects of the military and political conflict in such a way as to imply that the British efforts are successful because they have direction while those of their enemy are not because they are without direction.

Analysis of metaphors can add to our understanding of how specific rhetorical goals are achieved through the use of metaphors that match the speaker's intentions with the audience's mental schemata and scripts for journeys. Evidently the creation of such metaphorical coherence is an important skill in speech making and is likely to add to the attainment of its persuasive objectives. These were primarily the creation of social and political unity by telling the right story and reflects in the use of 'space' metaphors of the left rather than the 'time' journey metaphors of traditional Conservatives (cf. Charteris-Black 2004: 74–6).

3.6 Metaphors of light and darkness

Originally, Lakoff and Johnson (1980: 48) cited evidence for UNDERSTANDING IS SEEING in conventional expressions such as 'I see what you are saying' and 'can you elucidate your remarks'. In these expressions there is the implication that light is an experiential prerequisite for sight which is, in turn, a necessary precondition for knowledge. Lakoff and Turner (1989: 190) reformulated the metaphor as KNOWING IS SEEING and on Lakoff's home page there are other metaphors such as HOPE IS LIGHT, IDEAS ARE LIGHT SOURCES and INTELLIGENCE IS A LIGHT SOURCE. Since knowledge is equated with light in this schema, darkness is by implication equated with ignorance. Cognitive linguistic treatment of light metaphors has been traced to the association between light and life (plants rely on a light source) and between darkness and death (it is dark underground where we are buried). However, their origin in universal knowledge overlooks the importance of cultural and social knowledge in influencing the mythical quality of metaphors.

I would suggest that *cultural* knowledge is more important in determining the type of evaluation conveyed by light in Churchill's use of light metaphors. Light and dark metaphors are very common in Christian religious discourse and link light, faith, goodness and Jesus; for example, these notions are central to the creation of coherence in John's Gospel. Light metaphors contrast with dark metaphors in which there is an equivalence between darkness, spiritual ignorance, evil and Satan, leading to such familiar expressions in the domain of the supernatural as 'the forces of darkness' and 'the dark powers' (cf. Charteris-Black 2004: 185ff.). In this respect, within Christian discourse, 'light' carries a positive evaluation as being prototypically good while 'dark' carries the negative one of being prototypically bad. This is not necessarily mediated by any knowledge that we may have of the conditions necessary for plant survival – indeed some plants prefer dark and shady locations to light ones. This cultural knowledge contributes to Churchill's narrative of Britain as a force of light – and therefore heroic – and Germany as a force of darkness and therefore villainous.

In political speeches metaphors drawing on the source domain of light and darkness are frequently used as a way of offering evaluation through exploiting their potential for antithesis. This is typically how Churchill employs light and dark metaphors; in fact he uses more dark metaphors than light metaphors and the majority of his dark metaphors use a morphological variant of 'dark' such as 'darkness' – his most common metaphor is the phrase 'The Dark Ages'. By contrast, there is a wider diversity of light metaphors and these include 'beacon', 'shining', 'flickering' and 'gleam'. Table 3.2 shows how light and dark metaphors invariably convey a strong evaluation.

Typically, Churchill's light metaphors are based on the conceptual metaphor HOPE IS LIGHT which complies with the rhetorical purpose of raising morale. The only exceptions to this are when he uses light in relation to science as in 'the light of perverted science' ('The Few') which is motivated by the concept KNOWING IS SEEING. For added persuasive effect, Churchill frequently heightens the contrast between the forces of good and the forces of evil by juxtaposing light and dark metaphors, as in the following passage referring to Finland's struggle to prevent a Nazi invasion:

> ... *If the light of freedom which still burns so brightly* in the frozen North should be finally *quenched*, it might well herald a return *to the Dark Ages*, when every vestige of human progress during two thousand years would be *engulfed*. (20 January 1940)

In addition to a contrast between light and dark, there is evidence of fire metaphors nesting within a metaphor frame for light – hence the selection of 'burns', 'quenched' and 'engulfed' (since we know from

Table 3.2 Evaluation in light and dark metaphors

Light: positive evaluation	Dark: negative evaluation
Not so easily shall the *lights of freedom* die	Many hundreds of naval homes in our dockyard cities *have been darkened* by irreparable loss
The veritable *beacon of salvation*	Wickedness has *cast its shadow* upon mankind
The qualities of Allied troops *have shone*	*Long dark months* of trial and tribulation lie before us
British qualities *shine the brightest*	*The dark curse* of Hitler will be lifted from our age

experience that fires can be extinguished if they are absorbed by a liquid).[6] Fire and light when combined as metaphor source domains have the rhetorical effect of hyperbole.

As a stylistic feature, this type of intensification of meaning is important at particular stages in a speech and Churchill frequently uses light metaphors at the end position of speeches; for example, these are the final lines of the speech 'The Air Raids on London':

> Our qualities and deeds must burn and glow through the gloom of Europe until they become the veritable beacon of its salvation. (8 October 1940)

And the speech 'War of the Unknown Warriors' ends:

> ... but let all strive without failing in faith or in duty, and the dark curse of Hitler will be lifted from our age. (14 July 1940)

As well as the creation of contrast and the use of light and dark metaphors in speech endings he also uses them to create relations of cohesion between paragraphs. One important instance of this is the important post-war speech 'The Sinews of Peace' in which he outlines his vision for Anglo-American relations after the occupation of part of Germany by the Russian forces. Early on in the speech he describes 'opportunity' as '*clear and shining* for both our countries'; subsequently he warns 'The *dark* ages may return, the Stone Age may return on the *gleaming* wings of science.' In the next paragraph he claims that: 'A *shadow* has fallen upon the scenes so lately *lighted* by the Allied victory ...'. Then the following paragraph commences: 'In front of the *iron curtain* which lies across Europe are other causes for anxiety.' Later in the speech he refers again to: 'In front of the *iron curtain* that lies across Europe ...' and in the next paragraph but one:

> I have felt bound to portray the *shadow* which, alike in the west or the east, falls upon the world. (5 March 1946)

Here it seems that the genesis of the politically potent image of the iron curtain can be analysed as an extension of the light–dark source domain. Our knowledge of the function of a curtain is that it is designed both to exclude light and to prevent someone outside from looking in; one

---

[6] The idea of one metaphor nesting within another is developed in section 3.7.

made of iron would be all the more impenetrable to light and all the more secretive. This iconic metaphor implies that Russia was allied with forces of darkness and also did not wish to be seen – since it had drawn the curtain. This negative evaluation is reinforced by our knowledge that iron is visually unattractive and has the properties of being hard and inflexible (a heavy curtain would be much more difficult to draw). These attributes were later taken up and exploited by the Russians in the phrase 'the Iron Lady' to refer to Margaret Thatcher (a metaphor for which skilfully reversed the rhetorical effect by re-representing inflexibility as strength). So the iron curtain metaphor fits with the view of Russia as secretive, potentially dangerous and an obstacle to open communication.[7] Here we can see how influential and persuasive Churchill's choice of metaphor became since the metaphor in the original image weakened over time as 'the iron curtain' came to refer to a literal geopolitical reality. However, it is not clear that it ever lost the important connotative and evaluative meaning that underlay its original choice.

3.7 Nested metaphors

'Nested metaphor' is the term that I have used to describe the rhetorical practice of placing a metaphor from one source domain within a metaphor from another source domain (cf. Charteris-Black 2004). In the last section I showed how fire and light metaphors could be nested within one another. There is no limit to the number of metaphors that can be connected in this way – and knowledge of both source domains as well of the relations between them is necessary to fully interpret the metaphor. 'Nested metaphor' is not to be confused with the term 'mixed metaphor'; this implies that there is a degree of inappropriateness or over-elaboration in metaphor choice.[8] We are not always aware of nested metaphors in the same way that we may be of 'mixed metaphors' because of the congruence of source domains and they can be highly persuasive ways of creating a subtle and sophisticated use of language.

Churchill often nests journey metaphors within other source domains in order to heighten their persuasive effect by creating interactions

---

[7] The 'Iron Curtain' metaphor is also discussed in relation to conventional metaphor in section 2.1.3.

[8] For example, Brewer's defines a mixed metaphor as 'a figure of speech in which two or more inconsistent metaphors are combined' (Kirkpatrick 1992).

between a range of source domains. This use of metaphor is not conventional and can be described as poetic because of the novelty of the images that are created. Churchill's passion for English literature reflects in his desire to employ such poetic uses of metaphor. In the following a personification ('History is a person'), light and fire metaphors (in bold) and combat metaphors (underlined) are nested within a journey metaphor frame (in italics):

History with its **flickering lamp** *stumbles along the trail* of the past, trying to reconstruct its scenes, to revive its echoes, and **kindle** with **pale gleams** the passion of former days. What is the worth of all this? The only *guide* to a man is his conscience; the only shield to his memory is the rectitude and sincerity of his actions. It is very imprudent *to walk through life* without this shield, because we are so often mocked by the failure of our hopes and the upsetting of our calculations; but with this shield, however the fates may play, *we march always* in the ranks of honour. (12 November 1940)

The past is represented as if it were the life of a man; a light metaphor based on UNDERSTANDING IS SEEING is blended with a fire metaphor based on INTENSE FEELING IS HEAT (ANGER IS HEAT; cf. Lakoff and Kövecses 1987). These domains are connected by the underlying metaphor LIFE IS A JOURNEY that is implied by 'stumbles', 'guide', 'walk' and 'march'. Then a combat metaphor is introduced; this we can represent as RIGHT ACTION IS A SHIELD. So – given that the 'destination' is death – and all that remains is our memory of a person, the combination of light, combat and journey metaphors provides a poetic account of the metaphor target of the whole text: 'the right way to live'. The genre of a eulogy permits an elaborate use of metaphor in which a range of different source domains interact with each other creating a diversity of images in order to evoke sentiments appropriate for this occasion. This would not of course always be an option in other speech-making contexts.

Nested metaphors are also in evidence when Churchill was at the height of his speech-making powers in terms of sounding right and telling the right story. Consider, for example, the last section of his crucial morale-raising speech paying tribute to the airmen who defended the country in the Battle of Britain:

What General Weygand called the Battle of France is over. I expect that the Battle of Britain is about to begin. Upon this battle depends the survival of Christian civilization. Upon it depends our own British life, and the long continuity of our institutions and our Empire. The whole fury and might of the enemy must very soon be turned on us. Hitler knows that he will have to break us in this Island or lose the war. If we can stand up to him, all Europe may be free and the life of the world may *move forward into broad, sunlit uplands*. But if we fail, then the whole world, including the United States, including all that we have known and cared for, will sink into the abyss of *a new Dark Age* made more sinister, and perhaps more protracted, by *the lights of perverted science*. Let us therefore brace ourselves to our duties, and so bear ourselves that, if the British Empire and its Commonwealth last for a thousand years, men will still say, 'This was their finest hour'. (18 June 1940)

Here I have underlined three personifications and italicised the other metaphors; by using the *same* figure – personification – for three *different* metaphor targets ('Christian civilization', 'the British way of life' and 'the world') Churchill creates a relationship of equivalence between them. This is rhetorically persuasive as it implies that the interests of Britain are identical with – and representative of – those of Christian civilisation and the world in general. Britain has the right intentions because it is fighting for these global altruistic objectives. It also tells a story that contradicts the reality that Britain was at this time militarily isolated by implying that morally it is Germany that is alone. A journey metaphor is then conflated with a light metaphor in the image of 'the world' moving 'forward into broad, sunlit uplands' – here HOPE IS LIGHT. This is contrasted with 'Dark Age' where darkness implies absence of hope and – because it is 'sinister' – absence of morality too. This creates an antithesis to the underlying metaphor UNDERSTANDING IS SEEING by implying that knowledge can become 'perverted'. In this way Churchill employs metaphor effectively to construct ethos: a tone of morally inspired authority. This prepares the way for the famous use of hyperbole in the coda position of the speech in which his own evaluation of a social group (airmen) is attributed to mankind in general.

By identifying himself with all mankind and by appointing himself as an arbiter of morality, Churchill communicates the central idea that the British were a heroic people fighting for the cause of Christian civilisation; metaphor is therefore essential for expressing the legitimacy of their cause.

3.8 Summary

In this chapter I have argued that metaphor was vital in Churchill's speeches for the creation of a narrative I have described as a heroic myth in which Britain and her Allies are constructed as forces of goodness while Germany was constructed as a force of evil. These are summarised in Figure 3.1.

Although used along with other linguistic characteristics that contributed to sounding right such as repetition, reiteration, hyperbole and the coining of patterns based on English phraseology, metaphor was crucial to the formation of this heroic myth. Personification based on the conceptual metaphor THE NATION IS A PERSON was used to create a narrative in which Britain was a warrior, Germany a villain or a monster and France an innocent victim.

As I have illustrated, Churchill's systematic use of journey metaphors aimed to raise morale by giving a sense of purpose to the war effort but also had the political argument of engaging the Americans as fellow travelling companions. Light and dark metaphors were employed to offer evaluations of the combatants and sounded right by invoking cultural knowledge such as the metaphoric associations of light and dark in the Bible. I have also described his most contrived use of metaphor as nested metaphors where a number of different source domains interact to create myth. As Cassirer (1946: 280) summarises:

> In all critical moments of man's social life, the rational forces that resist the rise of old mythical conceptions are no longer sure of themselves. In these moments the time for myth has come again. For myth has not been really vanquished and subjugated. It is always there, lurking in the dark and waiting for its hour and opportunity. This hour comes as soon as the other binding forces of man's social life, for one reason or another, lose their strength and are no longer able to combat the demonic mythical powers.

Churchill's mythic use of metaphor was precisely devised to combat the mythical powers that Hitler's oratory had revived in Germany and came at a time when the social forces binding the political structures of Europe were disintegrating. While Hitler's metaphors were directed to specific political arguments, as well as sounding right, Churchill's were chosen on the basis primarily of sounding right and on having the right intentions – he represented his struggle as being on behalf of civilisation

Personification	Light metaphors
THE NATION IS A PERSON	HOPE IS LIGHT
BRITAIN IS A HERO	BRITAIN IS LIGHT
GERMANY IS A VILLAIN	GERMANY IS DARKNESS

Journey metaphors	Social metaphors
PURPOSEFUL ACTIVITY IS TRAVELLING ALONG A PATH TOWARD A DESTINATION	THE NATION IS A PERSON
	NAZISM IS A MONSTER
BRITAIN AND THE USA ARE TRAVELLING COMPANIONS	ETHICAL BEHAVIOUR IS A SHIELD

Figure 3.1   Summary of conceptual metaphors for Churchill's heroic myth

and mankind in general rather than part of it. The ideological struggle was therefore fundamentally also one of political communication in which metaphor was a weapon in the drawing of battle-lines, as competing narratives drew on competing metaphor systems for unifying and motivating participants. Churchill's creative use of metaphor extended the rhetorical methods developed in classical times, and which he knew about as a historian, to the purpose of persuasive wartime leadership.

4
Martin Luther King: Messianic Myth

4.1 Background

Martin Luther King was the greatest twentieth-century American political speaker and, arguably, is the greatest North American orator whose voice is still known to us though now closely rivalled by Barack Obama. This is because he was able to draw on the rich traditions of slave preachers whose discourse had sustained black people during their time of suffering. His father had been a minister in the Baptist Church and within this tradition the ability to preach was (and still is) held as a sign of a divine calling. As Ling (2002: 12) explains:

> Ultimately, King would also come to see the advantages of a liturgy, which, through communal singing and an emotive, interactive style of preaching, prepared ordinary people to do extraordinary things. The charismatic leader, the revered minister of his flock, could inspire his followers to overcome their fears, to confront wrongdoers, and to demand justice.

From an early age King became sensitised to the potential of the spoken word to arouse pathos through the musical qualities of cadence and rhythm and to understand the persuasive influence of the spoken language. He also showed early promise of having an excellent memory – as Ling (2002: 14) continues:

> As a toddler, he loved to listen to his grandmother's 'Momma Williams' – tell vivid Bible stories. An amazing memory enabled him to recite Biblical passages verbatim and sing entire hymns by the age

of 5. This remarkable aural memory meant that ideas because fixed in the cadence of particular phrases so that in his later career as a scholar and a preacher, he would commonly quote extensively words he had read or heard.

Repetition is a prime means of cultural transmission within oral cultures and, as Miller (1992) argues, the issue of plagiarism does not arise because nobody owns oral culture. Borrowing adds authority by merging speakers' voices with earlier sanctified bearers of the Word and also enables audiences to participate because they can predict what the speaker is going to say next. We will see later that King's memory – as well as his practice of keeping a catalogue of his previous speeches – enabled him to recycle phrases and metaphors in speeches and sermons that were delivered many years apart: what sounded right once would sound right again.

The details of Martin Luther King's life are quite well known from a number of excellent biographies[1] (see Ling 2002 for a summary). From early adulthood King advocated non-violent means to oppose all aspects of racial segregation in the USA (e.g. segregated seating on buses, segregation of schools, housing). In 1957 he was elected as president of the Southern Christian Leadership Conference that sought to improve the condition of African Americans through what came to be known as the Civil Rights movement. These included political goals, such as voting rights, social goals, such as an end to segregation, and economic goals such as a more equal distribution of wealth. He aimed to achieve these objectives through a number of extended campaigns including those in Montgomery, Birmingham, Chicago and Memphis; a range of modes of protest were employed including rallies, marches, voter registration and bus boycotts. This was in spite of a great deal of harassment, brutality, imprisonment and worse that was inflicted on many of the participants in these campaigns (King included). He was awarded the Nobel Peace Prize in Oslo in 1964. In the latter part of his life he became an active opponent of the war in Vietnam – although he insisted on keeping the Civil Rights campaign separate from the anti-war movement.

Throughout his life King had an intuition of his own death. In 1957 during the Montgomery campaign, soon after a bombing wave, he prayed 'Lord, I hope no one will have to die as a result of our struggle for freedom in Montgomery. Certainly, I don't want to die. But if

---

[1] For example Oates (1994) and Garrow (1978, 1988).

anyone had to die, let it be me!' Later, after 12 sticks of dynamite failed to explode outside his home, he told his Dexter congregation: 'If I have to die tomorrow morning I would die happy, because I've seen the promised land and it's going to be here in Montgomery' (Garrow 1988: 89). His own death then became a recurrent theme in his discourse, culminating in his final speech given the day before his assassination in Memphis on 4 April 1968.

4.2 Messianic myth

While reflecting on the stabbing wounds he had received after an attack at a Harlem book signing in 1958, King said: 'So like the Apostle Paul I can now humbly yet proudly say, I bear in my body the marks of the Lord Jesus' (Miller 1992: 172). This is one of a number of instances that give support to the idea that King was encouraged by those around him to adopt a messianic narrative in which the telling of a story was essential to persuasion. Miller continues:

> In 1961, after hearing King calm an unruly crowd, the president of the Atlanta Chamber of Commerce remarked, 'I had heard him called "Little Jesus" in the black community. Now I understand why...during the Selma crusade Stokely Carmichael commented that rural blacks regarded King 'Like a God'. Coretta King observed that, during his sojourn to Chicago the following year, ghetto dwellers regarded her husband 'almost like a Messiah'. (Miller 1992: 173)

The reason why King came to be perceived in this way is because he spoke the charismatic language of a messianic prophet rather than of a conventional political leader. His conviction that he had the right intentions in seeking human equality irrespective of race, creed or colour formed the core ethos of his rhetoric. It was his ability to draw on the language of the past to create a narrative of an imagined community of humanity that warranted his status as a prophetic leader. As Lischer (1995: 176) explains:

> In his sermons and civic addresses King executed a ritualized series of prophetic functions. In the middle years of his career King produced an imaginative picture of a better America.... King's prophetic imagination enabled Americans to envision a society in which skin colour was incidental to friendship, goodness, and achievement. Many

white Americans could not 'imagine' eating with Negroes, sending their children to the same schools, living in the same neighbourhood, or working as equals with another race.

King's linguistic ability to communicate an image of a future in which such things were feasible created a highly persuasive myth that gave meaning to the lives of many Americans. His creation of a moral vision encompassing *all* Americans offered a version of the American Dream that had popular appeal because at its basis was the elimination of ethnicity in the formation of American national identity – this was a vision that Barack Obama would develop later (see Chapter 11).

The rhetorical strategy for communicating this moral vision was to merge biblical time with present time so as to create a narrative in which the present is viewed as a continuation of a sacred past. At the heart of this story is the belief that the experiences of the Hebrews recur throughout history. Initially, Old Testament characters and events serve as prototypes for New Testament ones, and these in turn serve as prototypes for heroic leaders in *all* historical periods including the present. The rhetorical intention of King's 'messianic discourse' is to explain how contemporary circumstances correspond with biblical ones. King's use of metaphor projects listeners into biblical settings so that the sacred biblical past becomes perpetually present. I suggest that underlying a narrative that views present events as modelled on a sacred past is a conceptual metaphor: THE SECULAR PRESENT IS THE SACRED PAST.

King was nicknamed 'De Lawd' by colleagues such as Ralph Abernathy and they often used messianic terms when they introduced him at rallies (Ling 2002: 172). This seems to have originated in an incident in the Albany campaign when William Anderson, looking at King in his cell, declared 'You are Jesus and we are the saints. The hosts that no man can number' (Ling 2002: 91). I will argue that metaphor is central to the creation of this messianic narrative and that analysis of King's rhetorical choices provides insight into how he legitimised himself as a charismatic leader. Perhaps the clearest illustration of these rhetorical choices occurs in King's prophetic last speech made on 3 April 1968 – the day prior to his assassination:

> Because I've been to the mountaintop. And I don't mind. Like anybody, I would like to live a long life. Longevity has its place. But I'm not concerned about that now. I just want to do God's will. And He's allowed me to go up to the mountain. And I've looked over. And I've

seen the promised land. I may not get there with you. But I want you to know tonight, that we, as a people will get to the promised land. And I'm happy, tonight. I'm not worried about anything. I'm not fearing any man. Mine eyes have seen the glory of the coming of the Lord. (3 April 1968)

Here, at the final stage of the journey, King satisfies the messianic goal of leading his followers to their ultimate place of redemption. Metaphor choices communicate the assumption that the speaker knows right from wrong – good from evil – and that by knowing this he becomes their arbiter. Choices of verb modality communicate the conviction that his actions are divinely inspired. The spiritual powers that are implied by messianic myth include the ability to make predictions in the form of visionary dreams. The creation of unity through conviction was crucial to the self-fulfilling impact of King's discourse: once his discourse had united the Civil Rights movement behind him, it became inevitable that it would attain its goals. Messianic myth was, then, the basis for an ideological strength that would have a real and lasting impact on the American political system and formed the rhetorical basis for King's, and later Obama's, charismatic leadership.

4.3   The rhetoric of Martin Luther King

For the analysis of Martin Luther King's discourse 14 speeches were selected, including addresses given at major rallies, speeches and sermons (see Appendix 3). King sometimes employed ghostwriters for essays and books, and occasionally for speeches, but never did so for sermons (Miller (1992: 118). One letter is included because it is written in the style of a speech and subsequently became the most widely read of King's writings. The speeches cover the main topics of the Civil Rights movement: human rights, racial and social equality of African Americans within a Christian ideology. I have not included his speeches on the Vietnam War because that was a secondary area of interest. The corpus size is approximately 50,000 words.

Readers are invited to consider the passages I select for discussion with reference to the full versions of the speeches; these are available on the following websites:

http://www.mlkonline.com/
http://www.stanford.edu/group/King/
http://www.nps.gov/malu/documents/king_speeches.htm

It is perhaps only possible to understand fully King's persuasive force by listening to recordings of these speeches – many of which are available on these sites and others. His personalised oral style, resonant voice quality and southern accent all contribute to the rhetorical effect of sounding right. As Jamieson (1985: 80) argues:

> Generally speaking, it is the rhetoric not the content, which provides the most immediate effect. The rise and fall in speech tone and the dramatic gesture punctuate and compel, and in so doing they provide an indication of the speaker's emotive involvement with the contents of the communication, not only the speaker's involvement, but also the desire which he possesses for his audience to be similarly involved.

The major linguistic characteristics of his speeches are repetition, matching clauses, contrast, analogy, rhetorical questions and other rhetorical characteristics of religious discourse. For example, many sermons and speeches are organised around biblical quotations, religious references and other stylistic characteristics particular to African American preachers. These include the punctuation of the speech by phrases of encouragement or by outbreaks of applause from the audience/congregation; interactive verbal responses also sometimes lead to outbreaks of communal singing. The interaction between speaker and audience gives the speech momentum and a feeling of shared purpose and unity. The speaker's confidence grows and the audience's involvement engages them as participants in the creation of discourse: messianic myth is not a solitary activity but a social process in which language plays the primary, though not an exclusive, role.

A good example of all these rhetorical characteristics occurs at the climax of the speech given on 25 March 1965 in Montgomery; the speech coda commences with repeated rhetorical questions evoking verbal responses from the audience:

> I know you are asking today, 'How long will it take?' (Speak, sir) Somebody's asking, 'How long will prejudice blind the visions of men, darken their understanding, and drive bright-eyed wisdom from her sacred throne?' Somebody's asking, 'When will wounded justice, lying prostrate on the streets of Selma and Birmingham and communities all over the South, be lifted from this dust of shame to reign supreme among the children of men?' Somebody's asking, 'When will the radiant star of hope be plunged against the nocturnal bosom of

this lonely night, (Speak, speak, speak) plucked from weary souls with chains of fear and the manacles of death? How long will justice be crucified, (Speak) and truth bear it?' (Yes, sir)

There is an increase in the frequency and loudness of audience responses in reaction to the hyperbole of King's personifications and images; King himself reacts by reducing the time between questions and by providing syntactically parallel responses to them:

I come to say to you this afternoon, however difficult the moment, (Yes, sir) however frustrating the hour, it will not be long, (No sir) because 'truth crushed to earth will rise again.' (Yes, sir)
How long? Not long, (Yes, sir) because 'no lie can live forever.' (Yes, sir)
How long? Not long, (All right. How long) because 'you shall reap what you sow.' (Yes, sir)
How long? (How long?) Not long: (Not long) ...
How long? Not long, because the arc of the moral universe is long, but it bends toward justice. (Yes, sir)

Here we can see two hallmarks of the black folk pulpit: the call-and-response exchange and the calm-to-storm delivery. The calm-to-storm pattern involves a slow, placid beginning; a middle that gradually becomes more rhythmical; and a tumultuous and rapturous climax (Miller 1992: 35). Once the audience is fully engaged through these interactive processes, King offers an explanation of his answer by breaking into a familiar hymn:

How long? Not long, (Not long) because:
Mine eyes have seen the glory of the coming of the Lord; (Yes, sir)
He is trampling out the vintage where the grapes of wrath are stored; (Yes)
He has loosed the fateful lightning of his terrible swift sword; (Yes, sir)
His truth is marching on. (Yes, sir) etc. (25 March 1965)

This is typical of what I describe as 'messianic discourse' in which King identifies the audience with the chosen people and himself with Jesus. When the situation required and the mood was right King was a persuasive speaker because of the skill with which he integrates a diverse range of rhetorical features into an effective and harmonious whole. It is this ability to combine the rhetorical figures of hyperbole, repetition, parallelism, question and answer with the pace, rhythm and musical quality of his delivery that draws on the black Baptist tradition. And, as Miller (1992) notes, his sermons reduplicate themes using a technique that combines deductive and inductive modes of argument. He deduces from a general set of moral laws found in biblical sources such as Exodus, Amos, Isaiah, etc. and then illustrates these inductively from American political culture with references to Lincoln and Jefferson. His speeches are ritualistic because they assume that truth is fixed by the founding text of Christianity and is then revealed as a narrative unfurling through history. Underlying the structure of this narrative are metaphors based on the concept THE SECULAR PRESENT IS THE SACRED PAST: this forms the basis for the creation of his own particular version of political myth that I describe as messianic myth.

Another dimension of King's rhetorical ability to sound right was his harnessing the new media of television to communicate the prophetic vision of a better future and the struggle that was necessary to achieve it. The dramatisation of issues through 'messianic discourse' attracted media attention and, once the cameras were there, the brutality of his opponents could be revealed. For King, the television cameras provided an invisible shield of protection, as he put it in relation to the Selma–Montgomery march on 17 March 1965: 'We will no longer let (white men) use their clubs on us in the dark corners. We are going to make them do it in the glaring light of television' (Garrow 1978: 111). Therefore, the more appealing King's myth the more people would come to the marches and the greater the media attention would be. Evidently, metaphor was crucial in creating a high level of drama – the marchers could be conceptualised in terms of the biblical escape of the Hebrews from Egypt, and he could be conceptualised as what he came to be – a martyr for the holy cause of equal rights for African Americans. The narrative of King's life and his death was constructed through language. Moreover, the techniques of the medium of television also facilitated the development of particular tensions between King's spoken language and the type of physical response it evoked from pro-segregation racist groups. As Ling (2002: 313) summarises:

> His powerful oratory and persuasive presentation of the African American case both sustained local struggles from Birmingham to Memphis and gave key concerns a vital public prominence. In this respect, he was also a transitional figure who took presentational skills nurtured in the older public sphere of direct oratory and showed

how they could be powerfully transferred to the new medium of television... Combining the cinematic power of photomontage and the domestic intimacy of radio, television placed King's emotive voice in a special context. His calm voice of reason in countless press conferences was juxtaposed in newscasts to scenes of brutal disorder and viewed by people as they sat in what was supposed to be the moral sanctuary of their own homes.

Juxtaposition of images of the brutality inflicted on Civil Rights supporters interspersed with audio clips of King's calm voice provided an ethical social context for the moral vision of his speeches. Inevitably, a link was made with other symbols of innocence destroyed; the use of metaphor within such a context made King a symbol of *all* victims of social, economic or political injustice; for this reason metaphor was fundamental to what I describe as 'messianic discourse'. The combination of the dramatic tension created by the new media and the semantic tension created by King's oratory was highly effective in creating a coherent and persuasive political narrative.

4.4   Metaphor analysis: source domains

4.4.1   Introduction to findings

After a close reading of the speeches a total of 354 metaphors were identified in the corpus – or one every 147 words – which is a little less frequent than in the Churchill corpus. Initially, I classified them according to the source domains shown in Appendix 4.

First I will explain the counting procedure: the numbers shown in Appendix 4 are the actual instances (or tokens) of metaphor. Since King frequently reused evocative metaphors, the number of metaphor types would be less than this. A good example of this is the phrase 'let freedom ring'; this is repeated 11 times with a cumulative effect in his speech of 10 April 1957 and I have counted these as 11 separate instances of metaphor. It seemed difficult to determine whether the words 'chained' and 'manacled' were from the domain of slavery or imprisonment and so it seemed preferable to merge these source domains. King shows a definite preference for five source domains that occurred more than 20 times in the corpus; these were journeys, landscape, slavery/imprisonment, light and bells.

I have used the most frequent domains as the basis for discussion in the following sections. However, one danger from treating source domains separately is that it may overlook other ways of classifying them. Subsequently, I analysed clusters of metaphor for the two most common *target* domains for metaphor (i.e. what the metaphors refer to): racial segregation and non-violence. I then examined the interaction of metaphors with other characteristic rhetorical features, for example where two metaphors occur in close proximity but are taken from either similar or contrasting source domains. This permitted consideration of how metaphors interact with each other in order to create coherence – at a local level, as regards complete speeches and throughout King's discourse. The rhetorical effect arising from interactions between metaphors supports the claims for a discourse role for metaphor (cf. Charteris-Black 2004: Ch. 11).

4.4.2   Journey metaphors

Journeys are the most common metaphor source domain in the corpus, accounting for around 39 per cent of all the metaphors, and they are a defining feature of King's political discourse. In some respects King's use of journey metaphors is similar to that of Churchill's in that they create feelings of solidarity and encourage toleration of short-term suffering for the purpose of achieving long-term political objectives. They contribute both to sounding right and to having the right arguments. Journey metaphors imply purposeful activity and are end-focused because a purposeful journey implies arrival at a predetermined destination. King uses our familiarity with *arriving* as a way of predicting the *success* of the Civil Rights movement; it follows from this that whenever he evaluates an action *positively* he uses a metaphor implying *forward movement* and whenever he evaluates an action *negatively* he uses a *stopping* metaphor.

The persuasive potential of journey metaphors can be explained when we recall that marching was the most effective protest method employed by the Civil Rights movement. Major events such as the marches on Birmingham, Montgomery, Memphis, etc., were all based on actual journeys – sometimes very long journeys – since marching attracted media attention to their cause. In this respect journey metaphors were likely to be highly salient for activists because they provided a frame to understand abstract political objectives in terms of actual physical events. They were familiar with the sufferings entailed by these journeys (both because of the journeys themselves as well as the physical opposition to them), but they were also aware that Civil Rights marches arrived at their destinations and so the metaphors implied that objectives could be attained.

Journey metaphors are part of what is referred to in the literature as the location event-structure metaphor:

The source domain is the domain of motion-in-space. The target domain is the domain of events. This mapping provides our most common and extensive understanding of the internal structure of events and it uses our everyday knowledge of motion in space to do so... some movements are movements to desired locations (called destinations). Some movements begin in one bounded space and end in another. Some movements are forced, others are not... There are various kinds of impediments that can keep someone from moving to a desired location, for example, blockages or features of the terrain. (Lakoff and Johnson 1999: 179)

While Lakoff and Johnson's account provides a very general way of thinking and talking about journeys, there is the distinct ideological resonance of a socially placed historical perspective in King's use of journey metaphors. They provide evidence of a mental representation or conceptual metaphor: THE CIVIL RIGHTS MOVEMENT IS A SPIRITUAL JOURNEY. In this respect the freedom to vote, to sit where one wants when travelling on a bus are conceived by this metaphor as spiritual (rather than civil) objectives and as *stages* on a journey because not all civil rights will be granted at the same time. King's self-representation is as a spiritual rather than as a political leader: one who has divine knowledge of his own mortality. It is the interaction between the secular and the spiritual that is conveyed by his use of journey metaphors and provides support for the view that this was a prime linguistic method for the creation of a messianic myth that served to communicate his ideology.

A very important ideological motivation originates in King's social role as a religious leader and preacher. The basic storyline in King's use of journey metaphors is that African Americans are a chosen people who are escaping from a place of oppression towards the Promised Land. Frequently his metaphors draw an analogy between the situation of the blacks in American post-war society and that of the Hebrews prior to their exodus from Egypt. It is precisely this analogy that provides the basis for messianic myth. As Miller argues:

The main source for King's theme of deliverance from oppression – which he propounded in virtually every sermon, speech, essay, interview, column, and book of his entire career – was the folk religion of American slaves. His equation of black American and the Hebrew people revived and updated the slaves' powerful identification with the Israelites suffering under the yoke of the Pharaoh. And his interpretation of the Exodus as an archetypal event expressed the distinctive worldview of those who longed for a new Moses to emancipate them from an American Egypt. (Miller 1992: 17)

Consider, for example, the opening of his sermon delivered at the Dexter Avenue Baptist Church in 1957:

I want to preach this morning from the subject: 'The Birth of a New Nation'. And I would like to use as a basis for our thinking together a story that has long since been stenciled on the mental sheets of succeeding generations. It is the story of the Exodus, the story of *the flight of the Hebrew people from the bondage of Egypt, through the wilderness, and finally to the Promised Land.* It's a beautiful story...the struggle of Moses, the struggle of his devoted followers as they sought to get out of Egypt. *And they finally moved on to the wilderness and toward the Promised Land.* This is something of the story of every people struggling for freedom. It is the first story of man's explicit quest for freedom. And it demonstrates the stages that seem to inevitably follow the quest for freedom. (7 April 1957)

Here, King draws on knowledge of the stages in the narrative sequence of the biblical Exodus to create a general model or ideology for *any* oppressed people, and this evokes the historical experience of slavery of his African American audience. The secular present is brought into contact with the sacred past *through* the experience of slavery. Then, towards the end of the speech, he returns to the same underlying analogy:

The road to freedom is a difficult, hard road. It always makes for temporary setbacks. And those people who tell you today that there is more tension in Montgomery than there has ever been are telling you right. Whenever you *get out of Egypt*, you always confront a little tension, you always confront a little temporary setback... *The road to freedom is difficult.* (7 April 1957)

Interestingly, the narrative stages of the Exodus can be related to the five stages of an argument developed in classical rhetoric that were described in Chapter 1; see Figure 4.1.

Table 4.1 shows how the narrative stages fit with the rhetorical stages for building an argument.

Journey metaphors represent deliverance as arising from an extended period of struggle so that it becomes part of a mythic narrative. This is an

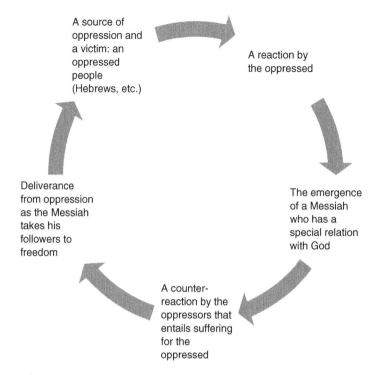

Figure 4.1   Stages of the messianic myth

Table 4.1   Rhetorical and narrative stages in messianic myth

Narrative stages	Rhetorical stages
A source of oppression (Pharaoh/supporters of racial segregation) and a victim: an oppressed people (Hebrews/African Americans)	Introduction
A reaction by the oppressed (flight from Egypt/ political campaigns such as boycotting public buses and marching)	Outline of argument
The emergence of a leader who has a special relation with God (Moses/King)	Support of argument
A counter-reaction by the oppressors that entails an extended period of suffering for the oppressed	Counter-argument
Deliverance from oppression (physical and spiritual) as the Messiah takes his followers to freedom	Appealing conclusion

effective rhetorical strategy because it raises expectations of confrontation and does not promise short-term attainment of political, social and economic goals. It is a struggle that takes as its moral justification the fact that the oppressed people are divinely chosen and that freedom from oppression is part of their spiritual birthright – this creates an appropriate ethos. But since it is in the nature of messianic myth to overcome obstacles that are in the path of the chosen people, the struggle will be successful.

The persuasive outcome of the myth is to make suffering seem a natural and inevitable part of the struggle:

> Sometimes it gets hard, but it is always difficult *to get out of Egypt*, for the Red Sea always stands before you with discouraging dimensions. (*Yes*) And even after you've crossed the Red Sea, *you have to move through a wilderness* with prodigious hilltops of evil (*Yes*) and gigantic mountains of opposition. (*Yes*) But I say to you this afternoon: *Keep moving.* (*Go on ahead*) *Let nothing slow you up.* (*Go on ahead*) *Move on* with dignity and honor and respectability. (*Yes*) I realize that it will cause restless nights sometimes. It might cause losing a job; it will cause suffering and sacrifice. (*That's right*) It might even cause physical death for some. But if physical death is the price that some must pay (*Yes sir*) to free their children from a permanent life of psychological death (*Yes, sir*), then nothing can be more Christian. (*Yes sir*) Keep going today. (*Yes sir*) Keep moving amid every obstacle. (*Yes sir*) *Keep moving amid every mountain of opposition.* (17 May 1957)

As I have argued elsewhere, there is a higher-level concept LIFE IS A STRUGGLE FOR SURVIVAL that motivates many language choices in politics and is closely related to a conceptual metaphor POLITICS IS CONFLICT (Charteris-Black 2004: 91–2). In spite of the hardships, part of the ideology of messianic myth is the assurance that struggle by a chosen people (led by a messiah who is in direct communication with God) will *inevitably* succeed:

> *Don't go back* into your homes and around Montgomery thinking that the Montgomery City Commission and that all of the forces in the leadership of the South will eventually work out this thing for Negroes, it's going to work out; *it's going to roll in on the wheels of inevitability.* (7 April 1957)

In this mythical framework King was also keen to convey the length of the journey; this is conveyed rhetorically through repetition of particular journey metaphors highlighting forward movement towards a desired goal. Just as the slaves were delivered from slavery – African Americans will be delivered from segregation. Rhythmic repetition becomes an incantation that is a very distinctive hallmark of his political discourse. Consider his address at the Freedom Rally:

> You see, all I'm trying to say to you is that we've come a long, long way since 1619. (Yes) But not only has the Negro come a long, long way in reevaluating his own intrinsic worth, but he's come a long, long way in achieving civil rights. We must admit that. Fifty years ago or twenty-five years ago, a year hardly passed that numerous Negroes were not brutally lynched by some vicious mob. But now the day of lynching has just about passed. We've come a long, long way. Twenty-five or fifty years ago, most of the Southern states had the poll tax, which was designed to keep the Negro from becoming a registered voter. And now the poll tax has been eliminated in all but five states. We've come a long, long way. (Amen) We have even come a long, long way in achieving the ballot etc. (10 April 1957)

Here we can see that the achievements of the Civil Rights movement over a period of time are conceptualised as the stages on a journey. The repetition of 'We've come along way' provides a rhythmic beat – like the feet of those who walked for miles because they had boycotted the segregated buses. The conflation of time and space domains provides further evidence of the conceptual metaphor: THE CIVIL RIGHTS MOVEMENT IS A JOURNEY – though here it is a political rather than a spiritual journey.

Later in the speech King introduces an antithetic element into the repetition of journey metaphors where he contrasts *movement forwards* with *stopping*:

> And so *we've come a long, long way since 1896.* And my friends I've been talking now for about fifteen or twenty minutes and I *wish I could stop here. It would be beautiful to stop here.* But I've tried to tell you *about how far we've come,* and it would be fine if every speaker in America *could stop right there.* (*Yeah, That's right*) But *if we stopped here* we would be the victims of a dangerous optimism. (*Yeah*) [*applause*] *If we stopped here* we would be the victims of an illusion wrapped in superficiality etc. (10 April 1957)

The value here of antithesis is that it activates our knowledge of journeys to evaluate political choices. African Americans have the opportunity of deciding between continuing on the journey or of stopping; King's rhetoric argues in favour of 'moving forwards' because, in messianic myth, 'stopping' is always evaluated negatively. Here we find three quite distinct rhetorical techniques in combination: metaphor, repetition and contrast. It is the interaction of these different techniques that adds momentum to his arguments in a way that is particularly effective in the spoken word: the contrastive relation implied by moving forward and stopping provides a rhetorical framework for the metaphors and repetition adds a rhythmic effect that is part of sounding right for an African American audience. Metaphor repetition of this type is a highly distinctive feature that occurs throughout King's speeches and one that I comment on at various points in this chapter.

Another advantage of journey metaphors that King exploits with a persuasive intention is that there are different modes of transport and the speed of a journey is determined by the choice of transport mode. Typically horse transport conveys slow progression towards the desired goal, car transport conveys steady and unstoppable progress while jet transport communicates very rapid progress. On several occasions contrast between a prototypically slow mode of transport and a prototypically fast one is employed to highlight the choice between slow and rapid progress towards desired social, political and economic goals:

> The nations of Asia and Africa are *moving with jetlike speed* toward gaining political independence, but we *stiff creep at horse-and-buggy pace* toward gaining a cup of coffee at a lunch. (17 May 1957)

Here the slow pace of social and political progress in the USA is contrasted with much more rapid progress of independence movements in Asia and Africa. It is likely that the horse and buggy image activates associative meanings that are based on the way that people travelled in the southern states of the USA during the period prior to emancipation from slavery. King uses the same metaphor in the speech he gave at the Great March on Detroit, 23 June 1963. The recurrence of the same horse and buggy and jet metaphor in speeches delivered six years apart reminds us that King used his records when planning speeches. Use of the same metaphor shows that King intended to convey the same unchanging messages. It is such intertextual reference that adds coherence to his political communication and supports the view of political discourse as stylistically unique.

In a similar way metaphors based on modes of transport communicate the argument that progress towards the destination of equality is an *unstoppable* force once momentum has been gained; compare the metaphor in the first row of Appendix 4 with this one from 1963:

> 'Well,' they're saying, '*you need to put on brakes.*' The only answer that we can give to that is that the *motor's now cranked up* and we're *moving up the highway of freedom* toward the city of equality, [*Applause*] and *we can't afford to stop now* because our nation has a date with destiny. *We must keep moving.* (23 June 1963)

Since the automobile has always been the most widespread mode of transport in the USA, the idea of vehicles following predetermined routes – rather than the meandering journeys associated with walking – argues for the inevitability of reaching destinations. Although there may be obstructions along the way, it is certain that destinations will be reached because a road always leads somewhere – rhetorically, this allows delays to be conceived as only temporary setbacks. It is interesting to note that motor vehicle metaphors are *not* contrasted with other modes of transport when it is inevitability of arrival rather than speed that is highlighted by the metaphor.

4.4.2.1 Summary of journey metaphors

The final, and in some ways most important, aspect of journey metaphors is that they offer a mental representation in which individual spiritual progress is equated with the social progress towards freedom. The Civil Rights movement is mentally represented as a personal struggle for salvation:

> *Death is not a blind alley* that leads the human race into a state of nothingness, but an *open door which leads man into life eternal.* (18 September 1963)

From the perspective of messianic myth, a journey in this life is only the start of the journey into another life: so in this respect while LIFE IS A JOURNEY so death is also a journey towards a desired spiritual destination. Forward movement is therefore always positively evaluated for political ends. This metaphor is perhaps most evident in King's last speech where the whole of human history is likened to a journey in which human intellectual, aesthetic and social progress can be represented by a conceptual metaphor THE HISTORIC STRUGGLE FOR FREEDOM IS A JOURNEY:

> As you know, if I were standing at the beginning of time, with the possibility of general and panoramic view of the whole human history up to now, and the Almighty said to me, 'Martin Luther King, which age would you like to live in?' – I would take my mental flight by Egypt through, or rather across the Red Sea, through the *wilderness on toward the promised land*. And in spite of its magnificence, *I wouldn't stop* there. I *would move on* by Greece, and take my mind to Mount Olympus. And I would see Plato, Aristotle, Socrates, Euripides and Aristophanes assembled around the Parthenon as they discussed the great and eternal issues of reality etc. (3 April 1968)

King again uses the antithesis between positive evaluation of forward movement and negative evaluation of stopping. The reason that the speech is so extraordinary is that in this – the last speech prior to assassination – he takes on the perspective of a supernatural agent moving through the epochs of human history. These are conceptualised as the stages on a journey – as seen, perhaps, by an astronaut examining human events from afar. From the perspective of messianic myth, merging time and space metaphors draws on the rhetorical potential of both domains to create an effect of sublime reassurance. The traveller takes control over his decisions as to how far to advance within the space of a single human lifespan towards the goal of spiritual and social freedom. It is likely that King travelled considerably *further* in terms of spiritual self-discovery than any of his political successors were able to do. Ultimately, just as Moses led the Hebrews out of Egypt, so King's use of journey metaphors construes the myth of himself as a messiah: they are therefore fundamental to the creation of the messianic myth that was essential to his charismatic leadership.

4.4.3   Landscape metaphors

Landscape metaphors contribute to the creation of messianic myth because the landscape that occurs in Martin Luther King's metaphors is the landscape of the biblical Holy Land. King was greatly influenced by the following passage from Isaiah:

Then I can hear Isaiah again, because it has profound meaning to me, that somehow, 'Every valley shall be exalted, and every hill shall be made low; the crooked places shall be made straight, and the rough places plain; and the glory of the Lord shall be revealed, and all flesh shall see it together'. (Isaiah 40: 3–4)

I have argued that biblical metaphors serve to conceptualise the struggle against racial injustice as a divinely motivated messianic myth in which King is the messiah who will lead the African Americans out of the mythical Egypt. Therefore, landscape metaphors communicate the same ideology as journey metaphors. They also have a polarity according to whether they evaluate negatively the forces of opposition or positively evaluate the Civil Rights movement. When the evaluation is negative the metaphor refers to harsh physical landscapes using metaphorical senses of words such as 'wilderness' and 'mountains'; these metaphors can be conceptually represented as: POLITICAL STRUGGLE IS A HARSH LANDSCAPE. The following are a few examples of metaphors in which landscape metaphors contrast the suffering of the present with an anticipated end to suffering in the future:

They discover the difficulties of the wilderness moving into the promised land, and they would rather go back to the despots of Egypt because it's difficult to get in the promised land. (17 November 1957)

They have broken loose from the Egypt of colonialism, and now they are moving through the wilderness of adjustment toward the Promised Land of cultural integration. (7 April 1957)

From these we can see that landscape metaphors that evaluate a target positively can be represented conceptually as RACIAL EQUALITY IS THE PROMISED LAND. Within the framework of messianic myth, journeys across barren landscapes imply the need for a guide:

In every community there is a dire need for leaders (*Yes*) who will lead the people, who stand today amid the wilderness toward the promised land of freedom and justice. (10 April 1957)

King represents himself as a leader of a people who are escaping from oppression; the hardships of the political struggle are a wilderness, but this is contrasted with a Promised Land of racial equality. Within the framework of messianic myth, the struggle is for the survival of an oppressed group sharing a common ideology and needing a leader who is a source of divine inspiration because he is in touch with God. Indeed in his prophetic last speech (see above, 3 April 1968), King makes clear his view of himself as no more than a divine mouthpiece. Nowhere else in his political discourse is the notion of messianic myth more clearly articulated by metaphor. Indeed the notion of arriving at a 'mountain top' implies an end to a political struggle:

Keep moving amid every mountain of opposition. (17 May 1957)

There will still be gigantic mountains of opposition ahead and prodigious hilltops of injustice. Let us remember (*Yes*) that there is a creative force in this universe working to pull down the gigantic mountains of evil. (17 May 1957)

Because the struggle is like climbing a mountain, at times the mountain itself represents the feelings of despair that can arise from the lack of quick attainment of goals:

And with this faith I will go out and carve a tunnel of hope through the mountain of despair. (23 June 1963)

But in other places the struggle itself is referred to positively as a mountainside; the most commonly repeated metaphor from this source domain is 'from every mountainside, let freedom ring'. This becomes one of King's rhythmic choruses and is interesting because it implies that being on the mountainside – in which the mountain represents the opposition – implies that one is already beginning to conquer the opposition. Once the mountain has been ascended political and social goals have been attained:

Moses might not get to see Canaan, but his children will see it. He even got to the mountaintop enough to see it and that assured him that it was coming. (7 April 1957)

This is why political aims are conceptualised as a levelling of the mountain – once the mountain is no longer there, there is no longer any opposition to the attainment of racial equality:

I have a dream that one day every valley shall be exalted, every hill and mountain shall be made low. (28 August 1963)

What is interesting is that King repeatedly returns to the same metaphors in communicating his political objectives and is able to integrate journey metaphors with landscape metaphors and to fit these conceptually with evaluation metaphors such as FORWARD MOVEMENT IS GOOD/STOPPING IS BAD; GOOD IS UP/BAD IS DOWN. A particular realisation of these top-level conceptual keys[2] is the conceptual metaphor DESPAIR IS A VALLEY. There are a number of instances of this in the corpus such as:

> Now is the time to rise from the dark and desolate valley of segregation to the sunlit path of racial justice. (28 August 1963)
>
> Let us not wallow in the valley of despair. (28 August 1963)
>
> We have walked through desolate valleys and across the trying hills. We have walked on meandering highways and rested our bodies on rocky byways. (25 March 1965)

Because valleys are places metaphorically associated with low feelings, they are also places that can become inverted in moments of transcendence when political success is attained because a spiritual world is conceived as the inversion of a corrupt one. This explains King's reiteration of the passage from Isaiah: 'Every valley shall be exalted, and every hill shall be made low'.

So far I have analysed Martin Luther King's metaphors in terms of two source domains that were shown be the most common in the corpus – journeys and the landscape. In practice, I have shown them to be related conceptually through the concept of messianic narrative. They have also worked in similar ways as regards their potential for persuasive argument according to contrasting negative and positive evaluations that originate in familiar physical experiences. We know that journeys are usually purposeful and that climbing a mountain is physically hard, but that the view from the top can make it spiritually rewarding. I will now consider two salient target domains that were used more in developing political arguments: metaphors that describe King's views on racial segregation and the means by which he sought to end it: non-violence.

---

[2] See Charteris-Black (2004: 15–16) for a discussion and explanation of the term 'conceptual key'.

4.5   Metaphor analysis: target domains

4.5.1   Segregation metaphors

Ending racial segregation was a primary political objective of the Civil Rights movement; in the early days bus segregation was a major source of racial conflict, and it may be worth illustrating why this was the case. The first ten seats of all public buses were reserved for white passengers and the last ten seats for black passengers; after purchasing their tickets black passengers had to disembark to re-enter through the back door of the bus to avoid passing through the white section. The middle 16 seats could be for either race; however, in the event of the white section being full, a white passenger could request up to four black passengers in the middle section to give their seats up so as to remain segregated (Fairclough 1995: 17–18). Increasingly, blacks became aware that such a request was only permitted if there was a seat available in the black section, and would refuse to give up their seats (Ling 2002: 35). At this point the driver was authorised to intervene – often leading to conflict.

Of course, segregation affected many other walks of life such as allocation of houses and schooling, but it seems that it was in relation to public transport that the issue came to a head: the system was overcrowded and the majority of passengers were black. Campaigns such as the Birmingham bus boycott led to blacks walking long distances to get to and from their places of employment; it is possible that this was the origin of the marching campaigns that I have suggested motivated the use of journey metaphors. For King, then, segregation was wrong on moral grounds because it conflicted with biblical injunctions that all men are created equal and because it dehumanised people.

The word 'segregation' occurs 68 times in the corpus; in 26 of these segregation is described using a metaphor. Not surprisingly, these metaphors invariably offer a negative evaluation through the associations created by our experience of the semantic domains on which they draw. These are, in order of frequency, illness, prisons and slavery. I suggest that the first group implies a conceptual metaphor SEGREGATION IS AN ILLNESS that contains the implied argument that whatever actions are undertaken to end it are legitimate ones; in some cases there is a neutral term for illness:

> Frankly, I have yet to engage in a direct-action campaign that was 'well timed' in the view of those who have not suffered unduly from the disease of segregation. (16 April 1963)

Segregation is something of a, a tragic sore that debilitates the white as well as the Negro community. (10 April 1957)

But more commonly metaphor source domains refer either to a very serious medical condition or to death itself:

Segregation is a tragic cancer which must be removed before our democratic health can be realized. (10 April 1957)

...with the conviction that segregation is on its deathbed in Alabama, and the only thing uncertain about it is how costly the segregationists and Wallace will make the funeral. (25 March 1965)

Of course, drawing on knowledge of illness implies the possibility of being restored to health through a cure:

Segregation is a cancer in the body politic, which must be removed before our democratic health can be realized. [*Applause*] (*Yeah*) (23 June 1963)

Now it's true as I just said, speaking figuratively, that old man segregation is on his deathbed. But history has proven that social systems have a great last-minute breathing power and the guardians of the *status quo* are always on hand with their oxygen tents to keep the old order alive. [*Applause*] (10 April 1957)

Health metaphors generally have a strong persuasive role in discourse because they can be employed systematically in the creation of evaluation frameworks.[3] If a negative evaluation arises from the association between segregation and illness, then there is a political argument that favours the activities of those who are struggling to end segregation because, metaphorically, they are restoring the body politic to health. In this respect King's use of health and illness to conceptualise the struggle between opponents and proponents of racial segregation contributes to right thinking.

The next most frequent domain for metaphors that describe segregation refers to buildings:[4]

---

[3] See Sontag (1989) for an early treatment of health metaphors and Boers (1999) for their use in socio-economic reporting.

[4] See Charteris-Black (2004: 70 ff. and 95 ff.) for a discussion on building metaphors in politics.

... racial segregation was still a structured part of the architecture of southern society. During this era the entire edifice of segregation was profoundly shaken. (16 August 1967)

However, more specifically they refer to buildings whose function is to imprison:

Dungeons of segregation and discrimination for another hundred years... (7 April 1957)

Easily the most common expression in this domain is 'the walls of segregation'; these are always described as 'falling down':

... and walk the streets of Montgomery until the sagging walls of segregation were finally crushed by the battering rams of surging justice.

In assault after assault, we caused the sagging walls of segregation to come tumbling down. (10 April 1957)

The destruction of a prison is a metaphor for ending racial segregation. In this respect building metaphors are used rather differently than is common in general political discourse where they usually refer to political actions that are positively evaluated (as in 'laying the foundations' of a policy, 'a window of opportunity'; Charteris-Black 2004: 70–4). Since King was involved with a protest movement, building metaphors are adapted in a way that implies a positive evaluation of the *destruction* of a type of building that is negatively evaluated – in this case, I suggest, a prison. There is, then, evidence of an underlying conceptual representation SEGREGATION IS A PRISON. This also contains the argument that it should be escaped from since the imprisonment is unjust.

The third metaphor source domain for segregation is slavery. In some cases the similarity between the two forms of oppressive social practice is made explicitly:

Segregation is wrong because it is nothing but a new form of slavery covered up with certain niceties of complexity. (10 April 1957)

In other cases it is implicit and refers to the symbols and practices of slavery:

One hundred years later, the life of the Negro is still sadly crippled by the manacles of segregation and the chains of discrimination. (28 August 1963)

There were clear historical links between slavery and segregation since segregation was closely associated with the Republican Southern states. However, since segregation was practised extensively, and probably not thought of as slavery by those who practised it, there is a clear enough semantic tension arising from transferred meaning to classify this as metaphor. Certainly the semantic tension was much less for those who were the victims of both forms of social practice and felt them to be quite literal. However, since King's rhetoric reminded his opponents of the very close parallels between slavery and segregation, I suggest a third conceptual metaphor SEGREGATION IS SLAVERY. This also contains the argument that it should be ended.

Illness, imprisonment and slavery were not the only types of metaphor for describing segregation; at times it was conceived as immoral sexual behaviour:

Segregation is wrong because it is a system of adultery perpetuated by an illicit intercourse between injustice and immorality. (23 June 1963)

And at times using reification:[5]

But not until the colossus of segregation was challenged in Birmingham did the conscience of America begin to bleed. (25 March 1965)

What is interesting, though, is that while metaphors recur in sufficient frequency and with sufficient rhetorical force to describe them as integral to King's ideology, there is also important scope for variation. The rhetorical characteristic that all three domains share is that, through a relation of contrast, they could readily shift from describing segregation to describing desegregation: illness metaphors could be inverted to health metaphors; prison and slavery metaphors to metaphors of liberty and freedom. Indeed we will find that such relations of contrast and inversion are fundamental to the flexibility of Martin Luther King's

---

[5] Reification is referring to something that is intangible or abstract using a word that in other contexts refers to something that is tangible or concrete.

political arguments. Nowhere is this more the case than in his use of metaphor to describe his views on non-violence.

4.5.2   Metaphors for non-violence

In political, social and moral terms it is non-violence that makes King stand out from amongst other political leaders of the time. We should recall that other African American political leaders such as Malcolm X exhorted their followers to use violent means to attain civil rights and the separation of 'blacks' and 'whites'. However, King's religious beliefs would not permit him to advocate violence and he was strongly influenced by the philosophy of Gandhi. Non-violence is fundamental to demonstrating the right intentions, since those who respond to violence by non-violence must take their inspiration from spiritual intentions. The most characteristic type of metaphor for describing non-violence is by reification; generally, this is done when nouns from the domain of conflict are used to describe abstract notions such as non-violence. For example, on 10 July 1966, King defended his non-violent philosophy with the argument that: 'Our power does not reside in Molotov cocktails, rifles, knives and bricks' but in 'the powerful and just weapon' of non-violence, 'a sword that heals' (Ralph 1993: 106–7). Abstract words from the domain of spiritual belief are contrasted with concrete words from the domain of conflict. We may describe this use of reification as polar metaphor: this is where the source and target domains of metaphor are antonyms.

One of his final speeches, 'The Drum Major Instinct', is constructed entirely around a metaphor contrast of the spiritual and the physical:

> Yes, if you want to say that I was a drum major, say that I was a drum major for justice. (*Amen*) Say that I was a drum major for peace. (*Yes*) I was a drum major for righteousness. (4 February 1968)

So King inverts the expected collocation of lexis from the domain of conflict to describe its antonyms: peace, harmony and spiritual fulfilment. The use of polar metaphor expresses the spiritual basis for his philosophy of non-violence.

4.6   Metaphor interaction

We have seen at various points in the above analysis that metaphor is not a discrete rhetorical strategy and that metaphors from different domains do not occur in isolation from each other. Typically, metaphors combine with another rhetorical techniques – parison, antithesis, etc. – and interact with other metaphors. Antithesis requires two contrasting elements and leads to the symmetrical patterns of parallelism. In the following examples I have italicised the parallelisms:

> The strong person is the person who can cut off *the chain of hate, the chain of evil.* (17 November 1957)

> They have something to say to every politician (*Audience: Yeah*) who has fed his constituents with *the stale bread of hatred* and *the spoiled meat of racism.*

> Let us all hope that *the dark clouds of racial prejudice will soon pass away* and *the deep fog of misunderstanding will be lifted* from our fear-drenched communities. (16 April 1963)

Usually it is two phrases that are reiterated within a single sentence, but in some cases the metaphor extends over two sentences:

> Hate at any point is a cancer that gnaws away at the very vital center of your life and your existence. It is like eroding acid that eats away the best and the objective center of your life. (17 November 1957)

The use of metaphor with parallelism creates a well-balanced and rhythmic syntactical symmetry that contributes to sounding right. The effect of reiteration is to enhance the rhetorical force of the metaphor because repetition of meanings overlaps with repetition of sounds and rhythm. Such use of metaphor involves repetition of the same proposition and the same evaluation – this allows more time for the semantic content to be understood and for the evaluative component to be recognised. Syntactic parallelism enhances the force of the metaphor because it is a form of hyperbole. Metaphoric parallelism also facilitates the learning and recall of metaphor – as we have seen in a number of places from King's tendency to reuse metaphors over long periods of time.

For example, the metaphor 'until justice runs down like water, and righteousness like a mighty stream' was first used in a speech given on 5 December 1955. It was then reused in a slightly modified form in the letter from Birmingham jail (16 April 1963): 'Let justice roll down like waters and righteousness like an ever-flowing stream'. Then, on 16 August 1967, he uses a combination of these two earlier versions: 'Let justice roll down like waters and righteousness like a mighty stream';

this version is then repeated in his last speech of 3 April 1968. Evidently, the image is a powerful one and evokes images of baptism that would be highly salient for his audience. I suggest that such symmetry and intertextual reference are a rhetorical hallmark of King's messianic discourse. They are a characteristic that unifies different speeches on different occasions over long periods of time – they support King's messianic discourse by making it sound right because it is inherently biblical.

Another interaction of rhetorical strategies is where metaphor is integrated with antithesis; this is also a highly characteristic feature of King's messianic discourse. The following are some representative illustrations of the 20 instances of metaphors containing contrasting propositions in the corpus:

> And somehow the Negro came to see that every man from *a bass black to a treble white* he is significant on God's keyboard. (10 April 1957)

> Now is the time to rise *from the dark and desolate valley of segregation to the sunlit path of racial justice.* (28 August 1963)

> There is a recalcitrant *South of our soul revolting against the North of our soul.* ... There is something within all of us that causes us to cry out with Plato that the human personality is like a charioteer with two headstrong horses, each wanting to go in different directions. (17 November 1957)

> Death is not *a period* that *ends* the great sentence of life, but *a comma* that *punctuates* it to more lofty significance. Death is not *a blind alley* that leads the human race into a state of nothingness, but *an open door* which leads man into life eternal. (18 September 1963)

The use of contrasting metaphors enhances their persuasive effect – because the relation of semantic contrast in the source domain argues for the same relation in the target domain – and provides an evaluation that is rhetorically based on two opposing poles. For example, if CIRCUMSTANCES ARE WEATHER, then a contrast between good and bad weather will form the basis of the evaluation. Similarly, if THE CIVIL RIGHTS MOVEMENT IS A JOURNEY, then we know that journeys can be fast or slow, involve moving on, or stopping, and that these form the basis of positive and negative evaluations. Contrasting metaphors are therefore always used to provide both an evaluation based on the right intentions and right thinking.

4.7 Summary

We have seen in this chapter that there is extensive evidence that King combines metaphor with other rhetorical strategies – in particular parison and antithesis – to produce a type of symmetry that creates rhythmic utterances, and has the persuasive effect of strengthening an evaluation. This is done by reinforcing propositions or by making contrasting evaluations that contribute to sounding right and to right thinking. Contrasting metaphors also draw out the systematic or isomorphic relations that hold between our knowledge of what occurs in the source domain and the meaning in the metaphor target domain to frame a particular mental representation. King's conceptual metaphors are summarised in Table 4.2.

There is evidence of the effect of King's messianic narrative in the following eulogy given by his mentor Benjamin Mays:

> If Amos and Micah were prophets in the eighth century B.C., Martin Luther King, Jr. was a prophet in the twentieth century. If Isaiah was called of God to prophesy in his day, Martin Luther was called of God to prophesy in his time. If Hosea was sent to preach love and forgiveness centuries ago, Martin Luther was sent to expound the doctrine of non-violence and forgiveness in this third quarter of the twentieth century. If Jesus was called to preach the gospel to the poor, Martin Luther was called to give dignity to the common man. If a prophet is one who interprets in clear and intelligible language the will of God, Martin Luther King, Jr. fits that designation. If a prophet is one who does not seek popular causes to espouse, but rather the causes he thinks are right Martin Luther qualifies on that score. (Lischer 1995: 173)

Table 4.2 The conceptual metaphors of Martin Luther King

THE SECULAR PRESENT IS THE SACRED PAST
THE CIVIL RIGHTS MOVEMENT IS A SPIRITUAL JOURNEY
THE HISTORIC STRUGGLE FOR FREEDOM IS A JOURNEY
POLITICAL STRUGGLE IS A HARSH LANDSCAPE
RACIAL EQUALITY IS THE PROMISED LAND
SEGREGATION IS ILLNESS
SEGREGATION IS A PRISON
SEGREGATION IS SLAVERY

From the perspective of messianic myth, suffering is a necessary experience for a chosen people because it demonstrates that this is indeed a mythical struggle. The long struggle of the Civil Rights movement was constructed by Martin Luther King as a spiritual struggle for the forces of good. The primary goal in King's political discourse was the creation of a messianic myth that by telling this story legitimised Civil Rights objectives by framing them as spiritual. The benefit of alluding to, and drawing on, images from the Bible is that it overcame tension between social and personal aspects of struggle: it created social cognition by integrating King's personal spiritual beliefs with the social aspirations of African Americans and extended these further into a narrative of the spiritual self-realisation of humanity. This was a narrative that Barack Obama later continued to tell.

5
Enoch Powell: the Myth of the Oracle

5.1 Background

In this chapter I will consider the British politician Enoch Powell, the author of a speech that has become known as the 'Rivers of Blood' speech that expressed vehemently fears that Britain would not be able to absorb the number of immigrants who had been given the right to citizenship following the break-up of the British Empire. Although he is most remembered for his stance on immigration, there were four major positions that defined his career: opposing changes to the British constitution, opposing immigration, opposing British entry into the Common Market and support for Ulster Unionism in opposition to a united Ireland. It is worth noting that all of these positions reflected a traditional conservative opposition to change and looked back to the days when Britain was 'Great'. Along with a commitment to free market principles, control of the money supply and opposition to intrusive government, these stances – when combined with a powerful sense of nationhood – were raised to the status of an ideology with the coinage of 'Powellism'.

While the undeniable charisma of this great individualist and eccentric polymath developed an iconic, mythological status, he remained a distant and aloof figure on the edge of real political power because of the difficulty he had in building political alliances. After a brief biographical introduction, I will describe Powell's mythic thinking that expressed itself in speculative prophecy before analysing his rhetorical strategies. I will then undertake a detailed analysis of his use of metaphor and how this relates to an overarching myth that I will refer to as 'The Oracle'.

Enoch Powell brought intellectual brilliance, commitment and passion to whatever causes he adopted; he was the youngest ever Professor of Classics to be appointed at the University of Sydney (aged 25 while only Nietzche had become a professor at the age of 24), then became the youngest man ever appointed to the rank of brigadier in the Second World War. He was frustrated at not seeing combat – especially after the death of former associates – and the adversarial style of his speeches may have arisen because of his experience of war and the subsequent loss of the British Empire. He was a driven individual with great intellectual ability but flaws of character that inhibited political success – making it ultimately fleeting and his position peripheral. He encountered difficulty in forming close personal relations and pushed away those who sought to ally themselves with him. His individualism and his view of Britain as unique contributed to a staunch anti-Americanism that was based on a conviction that the primary American war aim was the destruction of the British Empire. His biographers emphasise his nationalism:

> Powell was never ashamed of his nationalism, to him 'the nation is the ultimate political reality. There is no political reality beyond it.' The parliament was the focus of the nation; he would fight for its sovereignty. As his anti-imperialism developed, and as his reluctance to have Britain interfere in the affairs of other nations became more marked, these ideas too led on from his concept of nation. (Heffer 1999: 153)

A similar view of his principal ideology is given by his other major biographer:

> Having entered politics as one of the last of the ardent imperialists, he soon sloughed off the skin of Empire and spent the rest of his career berating his fellow countrymen for their failure to renounce completely the myth of Empire. But he also had an exceptional talent for articulating and expressing his assumptions and attitudes, and making them seem part of a convincing whole in what became known as 'Powellism'. This was possibly because he appeared to take the beliefs and perceptions of a particular nation and epoch as fundamental truths. (Shepherd 1997: 505)

There is always something of a riddle about Powell; what is certain is that he was a highly complex individual whom few could really fathom;

however, he was someone who people listened to because he was persuasive and he was persuasive because he articulated their underlying beliefs with great conviction and emotional intensity. It was this ability to access the 'voice within' that is perhaps the most significant quality of his rhetoric. As Heffer puts it:

> A politician crystallises what most people mean, even if they don't know it. Politicians are word-givers, when they have spoken, individuals recognise their own thoughts. Politicians don't mould societies or determine destinies. They are prophets in the Greek sense of the word – one who speaks for another and gives words to what is instinctive and formless. (Heffer 1999: 474)

Powell gave form to feelings of loss associated with imperial decline and sought to overcome these with feelings of national pride that originated in victory in the Second World War; like many from the political right, his rhetoric was based on heightening the emotional appeal of resistance to invasion. Powell was able to crystallise fears that originated in the response to the social and political changes arising from the experience of loss of Empire. Fears that the geographical boundaries of an island state were permeable as a result of the demographic processes of decolonisation can be traced to the idea of communities as 'containers' that are threatened by outside forces. The impact of his speeches on the policies of his time is less than his legacy as a symbolic figure for the political right, since he has gained a place in historical memory as a prototypical national hero who sought to preserve a sense of national identity at a time when the international processes of the break-up of Empire and European convergence were working in opposite directions.

5.2 The rhetoric of Enoch Powell

I assembled a corpus of 48,194 words from 24 speeches (Appendix 5) spanning the period 1953 until 1988; the majority of the speeches are selected from the period 1968–71 as this was the height of his political influence. When Enoch Powell spoke, people listened. The reason they listened was because of the unique combination of classical erudition with popular phraseology that characterised his rhetorical style and the extremely high level of commitment with which he expressed points of view. Powell's primary claim to legitimacy was based on the authority with which he spoke on issues ranging from national sovereignty, government bureaucracy and economic policy to the two topics for which he is most remembered: opposition to immigration and opposition to entry to the Common Market (the predecessor of the European Union). The epistemic, or knowledge, basis of his claims appealed to having the right arguments – as well as the right intentions.

In addition, the conviction with which he expressed predictions had a distinct way of sounding right that I will describe as the voice of 'The Oracle' and relied on a narrative strategy I will refer to as 'speculative prophecy', a term that originated from Powell himself. Speculative prophecy was his distinct style of myth creation. He became persuasive through a range of rhetorical strategies that contributed to mental representations. These include the use of popular phraseology and personalisation through apparently authentic anecdotes, in which he reports conversations with particular constituents, or from their letters. There is also extensive evidence of what Wodak refers to as 'topoi' – arguments based on particular warrants such as the use of numbers, appeals to justice or the displacement of the native population.

On the basis of this curious blend of objective data and subjective experience, classical rhetoric and popular phraseology, he developed a rhetorical strategy based on sounding like the Delphic oracle. He provided answers to questions that he framed as being posed by the 'inner voice' of the British public, or rather that part of it that identified with the symbolic nationhood of 'England's green and pleasant land'. Such hypothetical questions were claimed by Powell to be ones that people were too embarrassed, too afraid or too ashamed to ask overtly because of the taboos surrounding open discussion of issues of race: this, he implied, rightly, like sex and religion, was a potentially threatening topic and therefore not very 'British'. The answers that he gave to these imagined questions took the form of speculative prophecy; the most well-known example of this is the most cited (and misnamed[1]) of all his speeches, the so-called 'Rivers of Blood' speech:

> As I look ahead, I am filled with foreboding. Like the Roman, I seem to see 'the River Tiber foaming with much blood'. That tragic and intractable phenomenon which we watch with horror on the other side of the Atlantic but which there is interwoven with the history and existence of the States itself, is coming upon us here by our own volition and our own neglect. Indeed, it has all but come. In numerical terms, it will be of American proportions long before the end of

---

[1] Enoch Powell never used the expression 'rivers of blood' in this speech; the actual words (shown in the quotation) is an allusion to Virgil's *Aeneid*.

the century. Only resolute and urgent action will avert it even now. Whether there will be the public will to demand and obtain that action, I do not know. All I know is that to see, and not to speak, would be the great betrayal. (20 April 1968)

The mythic thinking and speculative prophecy that underlay much of Powell's rhetoric occur in this extract. As I explained in Chapter 2, there is evidence of the blending of a conceptual metaphor CONFLICT IS BLOOD with a conceptual metonym BLOOD FOR ETHNICITY. The use of water metaphors to convey strong emotion ('filled', 'foaming'), the evocation of classical heritage through reference to 'the Roman' and 'tragic'; a rather spurious historical analogy between the race situation in Britain and in the USA and claims based on numbers: all are rhetorical methods that contribute to speculative prophecy. This rhetoric is one of high modality, and part of demonstrating that the speaker has the right intentions is to argue that he is *forced* to speak since 'not to speak, would be the great betrayal'. Voicing semi-conscious anxieties was a highly persuasive way of sounding right and contributed further to the arousal of such anxieties. Speculative prophecy contributes to modality because by speaking what were represented as the thoughts of the majority he was able to construct a mental representation of himself as the inner voice of the nation; as a result few doubted the strength of his commitment to the propositions that he expressed. Like the oracle, there is no mid-ground in the modality of Enoch Powell: it is at a high level – epistemically and deontically[2] – and there is an outright obligation for him to speak because, for Powell, speech and myth creation were action. The expression 'speculative prophecy' was used by Powell in the following:

The first and most important thing to say about British entry into the European Economic Community is that it is not going to happen. I cannot undertake to tell you precisely how or, at what stage or date that will become self-evident, nor when the statement I have just made will pass across the boundary between the realm of bold and speculative prophecy and the region of what everybody knew all along. Of the fact however, I have no doubt. Without the 'full-hearted consent of her Parliament and people' Britain cannot be made to undertake the permanent and binding merger of herself into a new

---

[2] 'Epistemic' refers to being right in the sense of what is true (rather than false), while 'deontic' refers to being right in terms of the right intentions (i.e. morally right rather than wrong).

political amalgam.... That condition manifestly is not, and will not be, fulfilled; and from that the consequence follows as the day the night. (13 September 1971)

Here we see the mythical claim to be speaking what others are only thinking 'what everybody knew all along', and here Powell defines 'speculative prophecy' as voicing the unspoken fears, hopes and anxieties of the people – those almost subliminal concerns that only the oracle could articulate. It was true that there would need to be consent before Britain joined the Common Market; however, there is no actual evidence presented that the majority of people were opposed to European entry – other than a presupposition of the speaker that they would be opposed, based on a claim that he predicts will become 'self-evident'. A presupposition that something is 'self-evident' rests on the status of the speaker as a source of knowledge and contributes to myth formation.

In mythical terms and in terms of sounding right Powell's use of persuasive strategies bears close resemblance to Churchill's in that he conceived of Britain as a bastion of freedom and heroism for which any sacrifice would be worth making; as he put it: 'Never indeed since Rome had there been a national will so strong, steady and persistent as Britain's' (Papers of the late Enoch Powell, 1943). While for Churchill the outer threat to an island nation was an expansionist European foreign power, for Powell it was the prospect first of 'invasion' by inhabitants of the former British Empire who had citizenship rights in the UK and then of loss of sovereignty and decision-making powers through absorption into a larger Europe. Underlying the world view was an inherently mythical view of a homogeneous nation that traces a shared ancestry through historical time:

> We have a meaning in this place only in so far as in our time and generation we represent great principles, great elements in the national life, great strands in our society and national being. Sometimes, elements which are essential to the life, growth and existence of Britain seem for a time to be *cast into shadow, obscured, and even destroyed*. Yet in the past *they have remained alive; they have survived; they have come to the surface again, and they have been the means of a new flowering*, which no one had suspected. (3 March 1953)

Here we have a myth-based narrative of the nation as a living entity that has sustained itself over time and whose identity overrides that of individuals; the use of metaphors (in italics) conveys concepts of destruction followed by rebirth in a mythical view of time as cyclical rather than linear. Early in life Powell had been exposed to myth:

> His encounter with the Golden Bough was the most powerful intellectual experience of his boyhood. More than any other influences, it set him adrift from the Church of England. By demonstrating, 'beyond all doubt', that the Christian belief in the killing, eating and resurrection of Christ was merely one variant of similar belief-systems throughout human history. (Shepherd 1997: 9)

A mythical world view in which Christian notions of 'evil' could be reapplied in the language of myth is reflected in the ease with which Powell saw 'evil' around him and as threatening to this living nation:

> Some problems are unavoidable. *Some evils* can be coped with to a certain extent, but not prevented. But that a nation should have saddled itself, without necessity and without countervailing benefit, with a wholly avoidable problem of immense dimensions is enough to make one weep. That the same nation should stubbornly persist in allowing the problem, great as it already is, to be magnified further, is enough to drive one to despair. (9 February 1968)

Here we have a view of the nation as having an agency to make decisions as if it were a conscious entity; for Powell anything that threatened the British constitution or the position of the monarch within it was 'evil':

> When we come to the proposed new style for the United Kingdom, I find in it three major changes, all of which seem to me *to be evil*. One is that in this title, for the first time, will be recognized a principle hitherto never admitted in this country, namely the divisibility of the Crown...

> However, *the underlying evil* of this is that we are doing it for the sake not of our friends but of those who are not our friends. We are doing this for the sake of those to whom the very names 'Britain' and 'British' are repugnant. (3 March 1953)

Britain was conceived as a living entity that, in a highly emotive way, was under attack from without and, through immigration, from within; anything that sought to preserve its national life was inherently 'good' while anything that challenged it through change was self-evidently 'evil'. His world view was clearly defined and the nature of sources of good and evil could be identified by those, like him, who were able to access the barely voiced and unconscious wishes of ordinary British people who were only partially aware of the dangers that faced them and to articulate such wishes.

5.3   Rhetorical strategies

Powell developed a wide range of rhetorical strategies through which he could represent the claimed repressed or unconscious wishes of the British people; these included first the use of popular phrases and expressions that contrasted with his own erudite classical voice; second, the use of reported dialogues with an interlocutor who speaks in a plain voice – in contrast to his own grandiloquent, classical style – and third, the use of narrative techniques that simplified complex processes by representing them as part of a national folk tradition. The first appealed by sounding right, the second appealed to right thinking, while the third was a broader appeal to be telling the right story. I will illustrate each of these three strategies in turn before going on to consider his use of metaphor.

5.3.1   Popular phrases: sounding right

In the following he condemns current British immigration policy by using a popular phrase that he explicitly refers to as originating in the language of children in the playground:

> They must think that, to use a famous phrase, we are 'stark, staring bonkers' to offer all illegal entrants a prize for breaking the law, by promising that if they slip through they can stay here for keeps. It sounds like a children's playground game, not the policy of a nation which through its own past sins of omission is menaced with a problem which at the present rate will by the end of the century be similar in magnitude to that in the United States now. (9 February 1968)

Negative evaluation is made through the alliterative and rather puerile hyperbole 'stark, staring, bonkers' and this contrasts with his own prophetic voice that we hear in 'sins of omission'. The choice of these phrases sounds right because it contrasts two styles: that of the ordinary man and of the politician. The link between the ordinary and an evaluation of government policy is made through the phrase 'children's playground game'; this phrase activates a frame for the playground that provides a warrant for an evaluation based on an argument of useless-ness. The accusation of governmental incompetence is combined with a scare tactic through using words such as 'sins', 'menaced' and 'mag-nitude' that imply the argument that immigration is dangerous. In a speech on the Commonwealth Powell argued that member countries should be allowed to leave without resistance by Britain and should even be encouraged to do so since the Commonwealth was, in essence, a fic-tion based on charitable sentiment. Powell was opposed to charity as it undermined self-sufficiency – and had the negative effect of enabling immigration into Britain. In the coda to the speech he summarises his argument using a popular phrase:

> All the greater burden rests upon Her Majesty's Opposition, whose lack of immediate administrative responsibility confers on them a rel-atively wider freedom of thought, speech and expression, not to leave unvoiced and unrepresented a major and relevant aspect of public opinion in this country. There comes always a time 'when the kissing has to stop'. In my belief it has come. (14 January 1966)

The use of 'kissing' implies that relations between nations are analo-gous to those between people. This succinct popular phrase reformulates what he has already said with the greater complexity by a double negative 'not to leave unvoiced and unrepresented'. He also refers to 'unvoiced' but 'major' public belief which allows him to sound as a voice of revelation. Accessing popular appeal through the use of phraseology is a common strategy for sounding right by being in touch with public opinion. He drew on this strategy right through his career:

> 'Unity' and 'union' are words which trip lightly off tongues when something called 'Europe' is discussed. The old jingle says that 'one is one, and all alone, and evermore shall be so'; but there is already and soon will be still more, a tremendous quantity of double talk about political unity and the Common Market. (19 June 1971)

Here Powell is aware of how 'jingles' that 'trip lightly off tongues' can become naturalised ways of thinking – and therefore of the need to be critical of these.

5.3.2 Reported dialogue with interlocutors: thinking right

The integration of popular perspectives into his discourse is more explic-itly signalled in the reporting of supposedly authentic dialogues, but these are also used to develop political arguments. The dialogues are with individuals who are referred to in terms of broad social categories with whom many could identify. A salient example occurs in the so-called 'Rivers of Blood' speech:

> A week or two ago I fell into conversation with a constituent, a middle-aged, quite ordinary working man employed in one of our nationalized industries. After a sentence or two about the weather, he suddenly said: 'If I had the money to go, I wouldn't stay in this country.' I made some deprecatory reply, to the effect that even this government wouldn't last for ever; but he took no notice, and continued: 'I have three children, all of them been through grammar school and two of them married now, with family. I shan't be satisfied till I have seen them all settled overseas. In this country in fifteen or twenty years time the black man will have the whip hand over the white man.' (20 January 1968)

We know that many of Powell's supporters were ordinary, middle-aged working men. Here the strategy of sounding natural through direct reported speech is used to develop the argument that the native population will be displaced: the idea that the white native British will be forced out of their homeland is a highly emotive and highly persuasive one. The choice of the popular phrase 'to have the whip hand' evokes a scenario for slavery in which there has been a reversal of roles with the white man now in the role of slave and the black man in the role of brutal slave owner. Notice how Powell distances himself from such points of view through indirect reported speech: 'the government won't last for ever'. He continues with an evaluation of his personal response to what he has reported his constituent as saying:

> Here is a decent, ordinary fellow-Englishman, who in broad daylight in my own town says to me, his Member of Parliament, that this country will not be worth living in for his children. I simply do not have the right to shrug my shoulders and think about something else. What he is saying, thousands and hundreds of thousands are saying and thinking – not throughout Great Britain, perhaps, but in the areas that are already undergoing the total transformation to which there is no parallel in a thousand years of English history. (20 April 1968)

There is generalisation from an individual's anecdote, via the medium of the political representative, the speculative prophet, to a multitude since the interlocutor is now generalised into an 'ordinary fellow-Englishman' – that is one who is no longer defined by class or age. Others, even though they may not be 'saying' what this particular interlocutor has said, are nevertheless claimed to be 'thinking' it; we are moving here from individual to representations that contribute to social cognition. The authority of the prophet comes from reading people's minds as well as the future. The use of phrases such as 'broad daylight' and 'shrug one's shoulders' sounds right because they evoke popular conversational expressions. The extent of the change in the balance of population is then communicated through a hyperbole that alludes to Churchill's famous Second World War speeches. The articulation of barely articulated points of view is represented as morally necessary and emphasises the right intentions because a politician's role in a democracy is to express the beliefs of the people. The voice of the oracle cannot be challenged since myths establish their own legitimacy as forms for interpreting reality. The overarching myth for Powell is the myth of the nation – this was a type of mental representation that was unchallenged and taken for granted.

Powell claimed that, even among immigrants themselves, there are supporters of repatriation programmes. Rather than using direct speech, as he does when reporting the voices of his native white constituents, the views of immigrants are reported using indirect speech: 'I can only say that, even at present, immigrants in my own constituency from time to time come to me, asking if I can find them assistance to return home' (20 April 1968); the immigrant voice is present but more distanced from the audience because we do not hear his actual words – only an *indirect* version of them. Contrast this with the following from a speech rejecting the responsibility of the trade unions for causing inflation, where *direct* speech is used to report the views of an archetypal British working man:

> Who shall complain, then, if even the sturdy common sense of the British working man gives way at last under the onslaught? 'I suppose,' he murmurs, 'it must be my fault, since everybody says so. I don't understand how it possibly can be but apparently I ought to try to be ashamed of myself and to mend my ways in some unexplained manner.' (11 May 1968)

The words sound authentic because we hear the actual words and how they are spoken – murmured. Although an expression such as 'unexplained manner' sounds more like the register of an academic than a working man, the use of the first-person pronoun and of direct speech allies the hearer with the point of view expressed. Powell continues:

> Yet all the time the common sense of the people tells them that it is not so. Everyone has heard the story of how Galileo, as he rose from his knees after recanting the heresy that the earth moves round the sun, was heard to remark softly to himself: 'But all the same it does.' A dangerous situation builds up when an accusation which they feel in their bones to be false is fastened upon whole classes of men and women, indeed upon a whole people. They become resentful, and not without reason, feeling that everyone is leagued in a conspiracy against them to pretend that black is white and innocent is guilty. (11 May 1968)

Here further strategies are employed – the historical allusion to Galileo is an appeal to right thinking, followed by the argument of danger that heightens the emotional appeal followed by an appeal to having the right intentions. The imaginary interlocutor also asks questions that are then answered by Powell as the oracle: 'For a long time now the British have been asking one another: "When and how are we going to get back our pride and our confidence in ourselves?"' The importance given to multiple voices in creating an understanding of the truth was first proposed by Bakhtin (1981) who argued that individual voices were shaped by those of others; it certainly seems to be the case that the legitimacy of Powell's arguments arises from the claim that they are based on the articulated opinions, or as Bakhtin called it 'the polyphony' of *many* others – 'whole classes of men and women' – rather than on himself alone. Speaking with the voices of many is the way that Powell sounds convincing and is closely related to myth creation by narrative.

5.3.3 Narrative: telling the right story

As I argued in Chapter 1, narrative is a means for forming persuasive mental representations; it can either be through narrating events that are represented as being authentic by incorporating the voices of others or in the use of the moral or cautionary tale. When analysed using a text pattern approach, we see that Powell's mini-narratives focus on communicating the setting and outlining the nature of the problem – rather than on providing a solution to it; it is essentially a fear-arousing discourse rather than a fear-assuaging one. A good example of this is when

Powell claims evidence of multiplicity of voices in the amount of correspondence he has received, and uses this to introduce a narrative told from the perspective of a victim of immigration:

> In the hundreds upon hundreds of letters I received when I last spoke on this subject two or three months ago, there was one striking feature which was largely new and which I find ominous. All Members of Parliament are used to the typical anonymous correspondent; but what surprised and alarmed me was the high proportion of ordinary, decent, sensible people, writing a rational and often well-educated letter, who believed that they had to omit their address because it was dangerous to have committed themselves to paper to a Member of Parliament agreeing with the views I had expressed, and that they would risk either penalties or reprisals if they were known to have done so. The sense of being a persecuted minority which is growing among ordinary English people in the areas of the country affected is something that those without direct experience can hardly imagine. I am going to allow just one of those hundreds of people to speak for me. She did give her name and address, which I have detached from the letter which I am about to read. She was writing from Northumberland about something which is happening at this moment in my own constituency.
>
> Eight years ago in a respectable street in Wolverhampton a house was sold to a negro. Now only one white (a woman old-age pensioner) lives there. This is her story. She lost her husband and both her sons in the war. So she turned her seven-roomed house, her only asset, into a boarding house. She worked hard and did well, paid off her mortgage and began to put something by for her old age. Then the immigrants moved in. With growing fear, she saw one house after another taken over. The quiet street became a place of noise and confusion. Regretfully, her white tenants moved out. (20 April 1968)

The voice of a particular individual is represented as typical of 'ordinary English people' and the claimed anonymity of the particular letter from which he is 'about to read', arises from fear of breaking the taboo on voicing criticism of immigrants and immigration. The act of reading a letter personalises the narrative as well as attributing it to a legitimate source since we know that constituents write letters to their MPs: it validates the authenticity of the narrative. But the claim that it is typical of many he has received is a way of making a personal anecdote into a social myth with persuasive force. The discourse is that the native English have been displaced and become a victimised minority in their own locality; it follows the theme of role reversal in which 'black' becomes 'white' thereby usurping what is taken to be the natural order of things. The multiplicity of voices is emphasised as evidence of how this claim can be generalised and the letter continues with an account of isolation, displacement and abuse by immigrants:

> The telephone is her lifeline. Her family pay the bill, and help her out as best they can. Immigrants have offered to buy her house – at a price which the prospective landlord would be able to recover from his tenants in weeks, or at most a few months. She is becoming afraid to go out. Windows are broken. She finds excreta pushed through her letterbox. When she goes to the shops, she is followed by children, charming, wide-grinning piccaninnies. They cannot speak English, but one word they know. 'Racialist', they chant. When the new Race Relations Bill is passed, this woman is convinced she will go to prison. And is she so wrong? I begin to wonder. (20 April 1968)

Here we notice the positive evaluation of the family solidarity of the in-group as contrasted with the financially and morally exploitative practices, as well as verbal and physical abuse, perpetrated by an out-group. This leads to the use of a naming strategy with the racist labelling 'piccaninnies'; this lexical choice is derived from *pequenino*, a term of endearment for a young child in Portuguese. It contrasts with the label 'racialist' (rather than the more current 'racist') that Powell attributes to the limited lexicon of the 'piccaninnies' and implies a rejection of the legitimacy of the Race Relations Act that would uphold the rights of the out-group at the expense of those of the in-group. Throughout this section of the 'Rivers of Blood' speech Powell is engaging in persuasive storytelling.

Another narrative strategy that communicates ideology is through the use of proverbial or fable-like utterances referring to the animal world:

> One can hardly retch at the Guyanese gnat after having swallowed, if not digested, all those enormous Asiatic and African camels. (14 January 1966)

> To draw attention to those problems and face them in the light of day is wiser than to apply the method of the ostrich which rarely yields a satisfactory result – even to ostriches. (9 February 1968)

While space constrains explaining the full context of these extracts they demonstrate how the use of exotic animals gives Powell's rhetoric both a humorous as well as a popular style – evoking the image of a father reading a bedtime story.

5.4 Metaphor analysis

Powell followed Aristotle in believing that mastery of metaphor constituted the height of political expression – aesthetically, emotionally and in terms of its persuasive force – and also, like Aristotle, he is the only politician analysed in this book who explicitly discusses in his speeches what metaphor is, and how it can be used persuasively. Powell was aware of the cognitive framing role of metaphor in creating a perspective on a political issue, its role in developing arguments and counter-arguments, as well as its emotional role in arousing popular opinion. Martin (2000) develops a model of appraisal that distinguishes between emotive 'affect', moral 'judgement' and aesthetic 'appreciation'; however, for Powell there was no division between the moral, the emotional and the aesthetic. Metaphor inherently has an aesthetic appeal, and he combines judgement with affect so that his moral views on the world are essentially emotional ones concerned with the protection and defence of a homeland – which is generally 'England' rather than 'Britain' – against an invasion from within. Effectively, for Powell, the presence of people from different cultural and religious backgrounds constituted a 'fifth column' whose loyalty to the nation could never be fully relied upon and the right intention was therefore resistance to them. The concept of 'an invasion' implied a potentially heroic role for a leader who would resist such an 'invasion'.

A full overview of the quantitative findings for the types of metaphor employed by Powell, based on a close analysis of the corpus, is given in Appendix 6. In comparison with other politicians, Powell employs a high number of metaphors from the source domain of water, using words such as 'flow' and 'tide' to conceptualise movements of people; he also draws on metaphors from the natural world such as 'animals', 'plants' and 'landscape' to invoke natural processes and nature in general to argue in support of his political policies. He is less reliant on conventional journey metaphors than other politicians – perhaps because this would profile the movement of immigrants, and also because as I have mentioned, spatial metaphors are more closely linked to the rhetoric of the political left, while the political right is oriented to time-based metaphors. His use of metaphor is rather more calculated and stylistically unique – less dependent on conventional imagery and he shows a greater awareness of the strategic use of metaphor for emotive effect – this is especially the case in the use of the source domain most salient in his discourse – water metaphors.

As Charteris-Black (2006) points out, the metaphors used by the political right in relation to immigration typically refer to large movements of water (van Dijk 1998, van Teeflen 1994, El Refaie 2001, O'Brien 2003, Chilton 2004, Semino 2008). However, it was perhaps Enoch Powell who established the prevalence of such metaphors in modern right-wing discourse on immigration. For example, the use of 'swamp' by Margaret Thatcher and Norman Tebbit (see section 1.4.3) is motivated in part by the same frame of water and the depersonalisation that is implied. The effectiveness of water metaphors can be traced back to the idea that metaphoric meaning originates in bodily experience, because when strong emotions are experienced they are associated with the rapid movement of blood from one part of the body to another; hence a number of emotion terms in English have conventional uses of metaphors such as 'fill', 'pour', 'outpour', 'drain', etc. and their related conceptual metaphors (Goatly 1997, Kövecses 2003).

Powell contributed to this use of metaphor when he uttered – misquoting the *Aeneid*: 'Like the Roman, I seem to see the river Tiber foaming with much blood'. The classical reference evoked his status as a scholar; there are three words related to water that create a scenario for social violence, in which the image of a river stained by the colour of 'blood' implies a series of violent actions leading to assaults on victims whose blood drained into the river. It is more effective because it relies on inferencing: the audience would not know the details of the classical source, the violence is not explicit nor are the victims identified. Rivers could also be stained with blood if, for example, an *abbatoir* was in the proximity of a river; like many figures of speech in political rhetoric its persuasiveness comes from its imprecision and the mental images evoked. As I have argued above, the persuasive force of this figure also originates in its power of prediction – Powell speculated with the authority of the oracle of Ancient Greece and foretold the future of his own worst imaginings. His power as a myth maker is that through the use of 'tide' and 'flow' he established the rhetorical tradition of thinking about immigration as a movement of water, and this has led others to extend this to notions of 'tidal wave' and 'flood' – neither of which occurred in the speeches analysed here.

Underlying Powell's rhetoric, and his use of metaphor, is an orientation either to cognition, by developing an argument or counter-argument, or to emotion through the argument of danger; for example, the expression 'River Tiber foaming with much blood' coerces his audience emotionally by employing metaphors that are likely to arouse fears. Apart from danger, the most common of these fear-arousing political arguments is that of displacement combined with arguments based on numbers – this is the view that an out-group (New Commonwealth citizens) will displace the in-group (native white English people) by outnumbering them and taking over their social and economic resources as in the following:

> There is no comparable official figure for the year 2000; but it must be in the region of five to seven million, approximately one-tenth of the whole population, and approaching that of Greater London. Of course, it will not be evenly distributed from Margate to Aberystwyth and from Penzance to Aberdeen. Whole areas, towns and parts of towns across England will be *occupied* by different sections of the immigrant and immigrant-descended population. (16 November 1968)

Both arguments based on ideas of displacement and of danger are influenced by metaphors motivated by the conceptual metaphor IMMIGRATION IS INVASION – consider the lexical choice of 'occupied' in the extract above or that of 'invasion' in the following:

> We can perhaps not reduce the eventual total of the immigrant and immigrant-descended population, much, if at all, below its present size: with that, and with all that implies, we and our children and our children's children will have to cope until the slow mercy of the years absorbs even that *unparalleled invasion of our body politic.* (16 November 1968)

Powell's use of 'invasion' creates the space for him to 'occupy' by offering himself as the solution to such a peril. However, Powell was also linguistically aware of criticisms of his use of language and such explicitly racist metaphors are generally avoided; his awareness shows in the following:

> From these whole areas the indigenous population, the people of England, who fondly imagine that this is their country and these are their home towns, would have been *dislodged* – I have deliberately chosen the most neutral word I could find. (16 November 1968)

Here, following the somewhat ironic tone in 'fondly imagine that this is their country', the use of 'dislodged' still argues that the indigenous population is being displaced, but the choice of a metaphor that is not related to invasion is less emotionally coercive, and this more 'neutral' choice is something that Powell comments on explicitly. However, militaristic and conflict-oriented metaphors re-emerged in this opposition to British entry into Europe but only to specific audiences; for example, when addressing the right-wing Monday Club he employs an extended metaphor of defence against attack from abroad:

> It is not my intention today *to fire even a musket-shot in the new Battle of Britain* which is just commencing and which I have pleasure in announcing *will in due course be won by Britain, as the Battles of Britain always have been in the past.* However, at this early stage, *before even the battalions have been deployed, let alone the first salvoes of artillery discharged*, there may be use for all of us in analysing calmly the ideas of dependence, independence and interdependence in British economic policy. (13 July 1971)

There is evidently explicit reference to the Second World War and Powell was desperate to engage in military combat when he first entered the war and subsequently frustrated by being given logistical roles that denied him an opportunity for a heroic death. By treating both immigration and entry to the European Union as potential 'invasions' of British sovereignty he was able to satisfy the mythical need of the hero to sacrifice himself, and there is no doubt that Powell was emotionally willing to offer himself as such a sacrifice for his country.

Another type of metaphor for immigration that might be described as emotionally coercive – and is highly characteristic of the political right because of its tendency to naturalise political actions – is the use of disease metaphors for negative judgements on the basis of the inherent legitimacy of preventing and eliminating disease; Powell uses a metaphor that originates in the source domain of plant diseases in the following:

> To claim special communal rights (or should one say rites?) leads to a dangerous fragmentation within society. *This communalism is a canker*; whether practised by one colour or another it is to be strongly condemned. (20 April 1968)

The use of 'canker' implies that the process of migration is something from the non-human world of plants; we find a similar use of depersonification in the following:

> ... an important part of my argument at Birmingham was the fact of reverse discrimination – that it is not the immigrant but the Briton who feels himself the *'toad beneath the harrow'* in the areas where the immigrant population *is spreading and taking root.* (16 November 1968)

The first metaphor could be analysed as a conceptual blend as shown in Figure 5.1.

In this figure the circles show the mental spaces, the solid horizontal line represents the mapping between the input space, and the dotted lines represent the inter-space mapping between the input spaces, the generic space and the blended space. While a 'toad' is hardly a flattering metaphor, it is blended with 'the Briton'; they are in object position and are threatened because of their location in relation to an inanimate 'harrow' that is blended with immigrants who are in subject position. In the second metaphor there is a blend between 'immigrants' in the first input

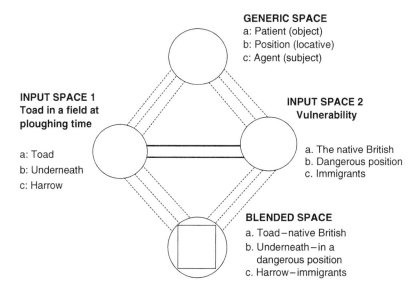

Figure 5.1 Analysis of 'toad beneath the harrow' using blending theory

space, and 'weeds' in the second input space, based on the concepts of 'expansion' and 'danger to other entities' in the generic space. The two metaphors together represent the native Briton as a victim (a toad, or a flower) who warrants sympathy and the immigrant population as dangerous because of its apparently inevitable or natural growth; 'taking root' implies that the source of the danger is invisible because it is underground – but the political argument of the metaphors is that once the gardener is aware of the danger he can drag out the weed by the roots and prevent it from spreading further.

As discussed at the start of this section, the inanimate source domain of water is commonly used to refer to the process of immigration. However, while 'water' metaphors usually refer in some way to motion so as to conceptualise the movement of people, Powell also uses the source domain of stationary water:

> ... there is sufficient for a further 25,000 dependants per annum ad infinitum, without taking into account *the huge reservoir of existing relations* in this country. (20 April 1968)

The notion of a 'reservoir' implies size – almost of an unlimited type – since reservoirs rarely run dry and the metaphor emphasises the scale of past immigration and heightens fear of future immigration. What is interesting is that Powell employs metaphor to describe both the process of immigration (rather than immigrants) and the experience of the native indigenous population who are represented as being on the defence; in the following they are in an essentially passive role:

> There is a sense of hopelessness and helplessness which comes over persons *who are trapped or imprisoned,* when all their efforts to attract attention and assistance bring no response. This is the kind of feeling which you in Walsall and we in Wolverhampton are experiencing in the face of the continued *flow of immigration* into our towns. (9 February 1968)

Here, using two parallel word combinations, he employs a metaphor of containment to argue that the natives of the named cities have lost their power of agency against an irrevocable and overwhelming force; 'flow' implies the movement of people in contrast to the unmoving 'reservoir' discussed above. The argument that immigration is something inanimate, yet both moving and increasing, is conveyed most aesthetically using a metaphor from the source domain of the weather:

The cloud no bigger than a man's hand, that can so *rapidly overcast the sky*, has been visible recently in Wolverhampton and *has shown signs of spreading quickly*. (20 April 1968)

This curious image of a cloud that is measured with reference to a human body part and can spread so quickly that it can obscure the sun implies an inevitability about a social process; the argument is not entirely clear since there is little that can be done to control the weather, and so complaining about immigration becomes rather like grumbling about the weather. However, the metaphor takes the perspective of the native English who experience the weather – which is usually perceived badly – and by taking this perspective establishes solidarity with the sort of people who grumble about overcast skies even though they may be inevitable. The meaning is opaque and relies on inferencing from clues such as 'Wolverhampton' – known to have a high immigrant population – and the indirectness guards against accusations of 'racialism'. To analyse the way that the metaphor combines both right thinking with sounding right we could employ blending theory as shown in Figure 5.2. This is because it is not entirely clear as to whether the source or target domain of the metaphor is the weather and so the directionality of the metaphor is not entirely clear.

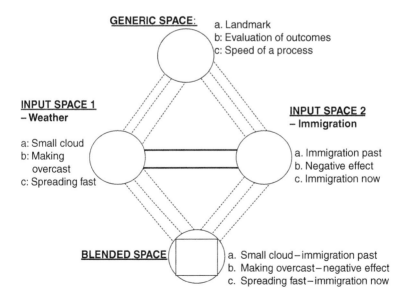

Figure 5.2 Analysis of 'immigration' metaphor using blending theory

In Figure 5.2 the circles show the mental spaces, the solid horizontal line represents the mapping between the input space, and the dotted lines represent the inter-space mapping between the input spaces, the generic space and the blended space. The blended space shows that the 'cloud no bigger than a man's hand' is referring to immigration that has already taken place, that the cloud is increasing in size implies immigration is increasing with the negative effect of obscuring the sun. This is an emotionally coercive argument. Powell's fear was that if whole areas of British cities became inhabited by immigrants ('alien wedges' as he once provocatively called them) they would inevitably come into conflict with the native population leading to civil strife. Use of the same metaphor in an earlier speech gives a clue as to a very interesting origin of his views on the dangers of immigration:

> We have just been seeing in Wolverhampton *the cloud no bigger than a man's hand in the shape of communalism*. Communalism has been the curse of India and we need to be able to recognize it when it *rears its head here*. (9 February 1968)

Use of the word 'communalism' may have originated in his experience in India, and refers to when groups of different religions – Muslim and Hindu – engaged in cycles of extreme revenge attacks. There is something in the choice of a metaphor implying a snake ('rears its head') that is reminiscent of Gandhi's metaphor for the British Empire as a snake (see Charteris-Black 2007: 75); it is emotionally coercive because it introduces the notion of danger. Ironically, while Powell was very emotionally attached to India and felt an affinity with Indian people, he also saw the potential conflicts that could arise when people of different religions lived in close proximity and then extrapolated from this specific historical situation to speculate about what would happen generally in British society – predictions that have largely proven to be unfounded – just as his prediction that Britain would remain outside of Europe has also proved to be inaccurate. However, further evidence of the influence of his experience in India occurs in another metaphor that represents immigration from the perspective of the inhabitants of the country that is migrated to:

> Those whom the gods wish to destroy, they first make mad. We must be mad, literally mad, as a nation to be permitting the annual inflow of some 50,000 dependants, who are for the most part the material

of the future growth of the immigrant-descended population. *It is like watching a nation busily engaged in heaping up its own funeral pyre.* (20 April 1968)

Here there is a curious shift from a quotation from Shakespeare's *King Lear* to the notion of a nation (rather than a person) 'building its own funeral pyre'; the use of pyres, something that is not normally practised in British funerals, is characteristic of Indian culture. At the time of writing a British person of Indian origin has established for the first time a legal right to be cremated in the open air in accordance with his Hindu beliefs. We should notice that the perspective is that of someone 'watching' inactively, which highlights the essential passivity of the English in the face of immigration and implies that they should do something about it. There seems to be an underlying mental representation that PERMITTING IMMIGRATION IS NATIONAL SUICIDE for which there is also evidence in Powell's account of legislation to prevent racial discrimination:

This is why to enact legislation of the kind before Parliament at this moment is *to risk throwing a match on to gunpowder.* (20 April 1968)

It is curious that legislation intended to reduce social tensions between immigrant and native should be represented as 'inflammatory' but fits with Powell's general world view of the inherent evil of mixing people of different races. It is a prelude to the final metaphor for the displacement of the natives:

For reasons which they could not comprehend, and in pursuance of a decision by default, on which they were never consulted, they found themselves *made strangers in their own country.* (20 April 1968)

This extreme image of isolation and displacement was present in the narrative about the elderly lady who was represented as the only white left in her street. These myths of isolation and separateness embody Powell's own feelings of apartness – in a political sense and in terms of developing rich personal relationships. Powell's metaphors therefore both make an argument as well as arousing feelings that are represented as both natural and right. The convergence of rational and emotional influences in a coercive rhetoric of legitimacy occurs in relation to political issues other than immigration alone. For example, in his opposition to overseas aid:

> If the Western nations were to confer on the rest of mankind not, as at present, just a tiny fraction of their goods and capital, but were, literally, in the words of the epistle, to 'bestow all their goods to feed the poor' their wealth would only disappear, *like a snowflake on boiling water, into the maw of these vast and astronomically increasing populations*, and the outcome would be a common level of poverty and incompetence. (10 December 1965)

Here the metaphor – which I classified under 'reification' rather than under 'weather' – emphasises both the speed and inherent danger arising from giving aid. The recipients of charity are represented as potentially dangerous by the use of the metaphors 'boiling water' and 'maw' – both images that imply the potential to injure either the donor or what is donated.

In terms of domestic policy Powell was an advocate of absence of government intervention and therefore employed metaphor for highly negative representations of it:

> And so the merry game goes on, of *choking and drowning Britain* in a mass of paper planning. One is hard put to it to know whether to laugh or cry... All the myriad, diverse, unforeseeable activities of the whole economy have to be surveyed and predicted, until the simple act of putting a tablecloth on a table or making a portion of Bechamel sauce becomes a government statistic, and no one can move or act or breathe without the agency of government. It is lunacy, yes: but *it is a lunacy towards which we are heading by general connivance and with the speed of an express train.* (17 February 1968)

Here there is incorporation of metaphor with humorous irony of 'merry game' and 'Bechamel sauce' and hyperbole in images that threaten survival – 'drowning' and being in the path of 'an express train'. Similarly, he creates an association between socialist-oriented central planning and danger or death (as later characterised Margaret Thatcher's metaphors for the Labour Party):

> The National Economic Plan of the DEA – we are threatened with another, you know – and the Diet and Health Survey of the General

Register Office, *they are all branches, some tiny, some large, of this same pervasive, poisonous upas tree of contempt* for the independence, dignity and competence of the individual. (20 April 1968)

The naming of the plans and documents is ironic and the metaphor visualises what are otherwise abstract ideas. The danger of illness was also associated with joining Europe:

... economically as part of the Community has as little basis as the contrary assumption that it would 'grow' slower or fare worse. Belief in the so-called 'dynamic effect' of membership and the theory of *growth-by-infection* are pure superstitions... (19 June 1971)

Powell's metaphors exhibit a convergence of all types of appeal – those based on having the right intentions, right thinking and heightening the pathos through fear of danger and death; they also contain specific arguments that assume that the primary role of the politician is to protect his followers from danger by making them aware of dangers that are invisible – and metaphor fulfils this purpose effectively.

Unusually in political rhetoric, drawing on his background as a classicist, Powell demonstrates a metalinguistic awareness of metaphor that underlay his use of it as a rhetorical resource. In the following extract he explicitly draws attention to metaphor by using a metaphor for metaphor; he then goes on to develop a counter-argument that those who supported British entry into Europe on economic grounds are thinking metaphorically because of the essentially political nature of what is supposedly an economic Union:

In short, there is a danger that we may fall prey to one of the most dangerous of political epidemics – that of metaphor. I am using the word in its proper sense of transfer – the importation or transfer of words and ideas from the sphere where they belong to one where they do not. It is my thesis that much of the language of our current debate is unconscious metaphor of the most dangerous kind: the confusion of the economic and the political. (13 July 1971)

The idea that metaphor spreads like an 'epidemic' is, of course, itself a metaphor and as a true linguist he goes on to define metaphor before providing an illustration of it in relation to the discourse on the Common Market.

He also draws attention to metaphoric thinking to develop counter-arguments to charity by arguing that any extension of the meaning of morality to a collective entity was a transfer of meaning since charity was essentially a personal or individual decision rather than a social one:

> Charity is essentially the act of a person. The commandment of perfection, 'Thou shalt love thy neighbour as thyself', turns upon the verb 'love', which is meaningful only when applied to an individual human (or divine) being. It is a personal emotion; and self-sacrifice in which it results is something peculiar to individual persons: '...Morality, religious or ethical, is about persons. *Wherever the terms of morality are applied to collective or inanimate entities, they are either being used metaphorically, or they apply in fact to the individuals underlying the collective or inanimate entity.* (6 May 1965)

Of course this view was not consistent with the highly social nature of his mystical belief in the British nation, and the social cognition that he sought to arouse by opposing immigration. However, when it suited his arguments he drew attention to the metaphoric nature of the thinking that underlay the arguments of his opponents. For example, a major argument in support of unification of Europe was that it would prevent future wars by creating 'family' relationships between nations; Powell picks up on this metaphor ironically and elaborates it as not being compliant with the historical experience of conflict in Europe:

> 'If we are to avoid a third conflict,' he wrote, '*we must turn Europe into a family.'* In the past Europe has been a group of independent warring states at the cost of thousands of lives. Had there been a genuine *fraternity of nations*, these terrible tragedies might have been avoided...(13 September 1971)

He goes on to undermine the conceptual metaphor EUROPE IS A FAMILY:

> By now we are a long way from banishing war by '*turning Europe into a family'*. We are back in the old familiar world of force; but even in that world the answer carries little conviction, because for twenty-five years we have been protesting that the only defence against Russian attack is the American nuclear armoury. So our European '*family of nations'* would have to be furnished with its nuclear arsenal on an

American scale; and I wonder whether anyone thinks that would enable them or their children or their children's children to sleep more soundly in their beds. (13 September 1971)

Powell had a linguist's awareness of the power of language that had originated in his mastery of languages, being a fluent speaker of German, Italian, French, Greek and Urdu; he canvassed in these languages and was aware of the importance of language in defining national and personal identity (these were very similar in Powell's world view). This comes over in the use of metaphors to contribute to an argument in the following speech that he delivered competently in French:

Perhaps the fact that I address you this evening in French is the beginning of my explanation, why the British have this preponderant sense that their national destiny cannot be merged in that of the Community. I mean that observation in the most serious manner possible. With equal delight and effort, *like those who have climbed a frontier range of mountains, one surmounts the linguistic watershed and looks out, like Winckelman looking from the Alps into Italy, over another land – a different past, and a different future.* There is no more ignorant vulgarity than to treat language as an impediment to intercourse, which education, habit, travel, trade abolish and remove. The function of language in *the life of nations*, as a means both of differentiation and of self-identification, *is rooted* in the very origin of humanity, and increase of knowledge tends to enhance its significance rather than diminish it. Everything that nationality means is represented and, as it were, symbolised by language, which becomes less and less like *a common currency* the more one penetrates its inner meaning. (12 February 1971)

The metaphor here is that languages, like geography, define boundaries between national groups and are central to the 'life of nations'; he uses metaphors to express his idealised view of language – as being alive and as 'rooted' in myth and history; though he rejects the idea of language as a 'common currency' precisely because of its role in providing a national identity that is inherently separate and distinct. It is ultimately this world view that expresses the tension between social forces towards integration – through travel, trade, etc. – and the need for the individual to retain an identity in this world of flux. His use of metaphor to

articulate such needs as if they were a natural process is highly powerful and persuasive, and when we hear metaphor in Powell's speeches we
know that this is his own erudite voice, rather than that of the other
interlocutors.

5.5 Summary

Through mythical thinking Powell was able to remain apart from other
people and his main political philosophy was to keep people of different
racial backgrounds apart as well as keeping his nation apart from other
nations; ultimately it was this heroic individualism that is most characteristic of his rhetoric. His mythic perspective on Britain may have
originated in his conviction that he would die fighting for his country;
as one of his biographers summarises: 'He had decided he would die in
the war, and decided with such certainty that he would never come to
terms with being wrong about it, least of all when he saw others meet
the fate he had settled for himself' (Heffer 1999: 54). This death wish
may explain the fearlessness with which he voiced what were potentially dangerous views and, at times, his apparent attempts to commit
political suicide by being unnecessarily provocative through his use of
extreme rhetoric. The sense of himself as a historical agent, one who
could see further into the future because he knew more about the past,
underlies the sense of conviction with which his speculative prophecies
are expressed. The prophet is obliged through moral necessity to protect
what he, and only he, foresees as threatened through creating awareness
of what he, and only he, foresees as the source of danger:

> The English as a nation have their own peculiar faults. One of them
> is that strange passivity in the face of danger or absurdity or provo-
> cation, which has more than once in our history lured observers
> into false conclusions – conclusions sometimes fatal to the observers
> themselves – about the underlying intentions and the true determi-
> nation of our people ... but we must be told the truth and shown the
> danger, if we are to meet it. Rightly or wrongly, I for my part believe
> that the time for that has come. (16 November 1968)

In this passage he identifies a 'strange passivity' and implies that it
is only he who really knows the 'underlying intentions ... of our people' and is the politician who can reveal 'the truth' and – through his
command of popular rhetoric – 'show' the 'danger'.

Throughout Powell's political career there was a sense of separateness and isolation that ultimately made him relatively unsuccessful in an activity that is mainly concerned with forming alliances and sustaining loyalties. He saw himself as a solitary hero leading by example and gives an appropriate image of this that originated in his military experience: 'I wanted to end the war, so to speak, or perhaps not so to speak, riding into Berlin on a white horse' (Heffer 1999: 58). This sense of isolation also added to his undoubted charismatic appeal and the distance that he maintained through rather remote language served to contribute to the myth of the oracle. Who would expect the oracle to speak in a prosaic style? Who would expect the oracle to speak like other men? Hence Powell alternates between the highly poetic voice of the speculative prophet, where metaphor predominates, and rhetorical strategies such as popular phraseology and narrative, where we hear the voices of ordinary mortals. This rhythmic alternation between two voices, those of the speaker and the audience, creates a dialogue for sustaining the myth of a nation threatened from without and from within, and it was ultimately a popularist rather than a racist rhetoric.

6
Ronald Reagan and Romantic Myth: 'From the Swamp to the Stars'

6.1 Background – romantic myth

Ronald Reagan became an icon for many Americans because his presidency preceded the collapse of the Soviet Union and initiated a period in which the USA became, prior to the rise of China, the world's only superpower; he therefore became associated with political success, and national well-being. During a moderately successful career as an actor in which he appeared in 52 films, he developed an interest in politics as President of the Screen Actors Guild. After serving two terms as Governor of California, he enjoyed two successful presidencies, surviving an assassination attempt during the first of these; he fought a long battle against Alzheimer's after becoming President at the age of 74.[1] His policies of reducing government spending at home, while supporting anti-Communist movements abroad, contributed to the destruction of the Berlin Wall in 1989, an event that is taken to symbolise the fundamental realignment of international power relations that gave the USA – at least for a period – an exclusive claim to being *the* global superpower.

His domestic policies became known as 'Reaganomics' and have been summarised as follows:

> Governor Ronald Reagan campaigned in 1980 on an economic policy platform that proclaimed the federal government was responsible for the economic problems of the United States. He proposed to solve these problems by diminishing the role of the federal government in

---

[1] There is some dispute over the timing of the onset of Alzheimer's; he was not formally diagnosed until 1994, but one of his sons claims that there was evidence of the illness as early as 1984 (Reagan 2011).

the economy to foster a recovery led by the private sector. To do so, Reagan proposed to cut taxes, to cut public spending, to curtail public interference and thus promote economic growth, which he claimed would eventually lead to a balanced budget. (Hogan 1990: 157)

While his domestic policy emphasised a reduction in the role of government, his foreign policy encouraged its expansion; his description of the Soviet Union as 'The Evil Empire' symbolised a dramatic, mythical struggle in which the USA was cast as hero and the USSR as villain. The policy was based on reviving the Cold War through opposing the 'demonic' Soviet Union and entailed support for anti-Communist right-wing groups in Africa, Asia and Latin America. Military expenditure was increased and Reagan was associated with the development of a system of defence against nuclear attack through ground- and space-based systems that became popularly known as 'Star Wars'. One commentator has summarised the appeal of Reagan as follows:

By 1980 he had a well-established track record as a campaigner. He was physically attractive and highly photogenic; on the television screen he came across as a man of warmth and charm. It should be added that Reagan was not all style and no substance. He was not an intellectual; he made constant use of anecdotal evidence and some of his views bordered on the banal. But one of his great strengths has always been his resolute attachment to a few simple conservative themes. This gave his candidacy a clear sense of direction that others have lacked. Voters may not have agreed with Reagan, but they had no doubt where he stood. (Mervin 1990: 83)

In contrast to policies that were often confrontational, his communication was marked by a largely positive lexical content and a relaxed and easy-going style, often humorous, that incorporated enough one-line quips and anecdotes for him to gain the nickname 'the Great Communicator'. Above all, unlike his predecessor, he did not take himself too seriously: prior to having an operation to remove a bullet following an assassination attempt in March 1981, he is reported to have said jokingly to one of the surgeons 'I hope you are all Republicans'. There was certainly a striking contrast between the potential seriousness of the political issues of the time – such as the arms race, conflict in Central America and the Soviet invasion of Afghanistan – and a leader who responded to crises with messages of hope, optimism and confidence.

Reagan's keywords[2] were 'growth', 'recovery', 'freedom', 'peace', 'faith', 'dreams' and 'spirit'. Following his acceptance of the Republican nomination in 1984, Reagan enthused that it was 'morning again in America' and invited opponents to 'go on and make my day'. However, for others, such as Patricia Schroeder, his style gave the impression of superficiality and led to a less complimentary nickname: 'The Teflon President' – implying that style came at the expense of substance. There is no doubt that his acting experience enabled him to present a confident and relaxed front in situations where others, such as Jimmy Carter, had displayed stress and anxiety.[3] Reagan had also developed skills related to acting such as the ability to memorise 'lines', to improvise and to play diverse 'roles'. As one early analyst notes:

> By the time he got to the White House he had spent more than fifty years using every communications medium save Morse code and smoke signals. He had been a successful actor in high school and college. A pioneer in the young radio business, a journeyman screen performer, a television personality, a speechmaker to audiences of all description, author of a syndicated newspaper column. (Barrett 1984: 33)

Above all, Reagan learnt how the persuasive force of myth that underlies so many successful film scripts could readily be transferred to accounts of political situations and events. Mental representations and schemata that had already been formed through Hollywood could be used to frame political narratives. A mythic approach to politics seems to characterise the decade of the 1980s when the American superhero came to the fore in comic books. There is evidence in Reagan's rhetoric of all of Edelman's main types of myth. The Conspiratorial Enemy myth underlay the epithet 'The Evil Empire' which revived the Cold War rhetoric of McCarthyism; the United We Stand myth underlay a patriotic appeal to idealism such as:

> It is the American sound. It is hopeful, big-hearted, idealistic, daring, decent, and fair. That's our heritage; that is our song. We sing it still. They are the entrepreneurs, the builders, the pioneers, and a lot

---

[2] Keywords are those which statistically he used more frequently than all the other politicians in this book when they are combined.

[3] This was particularly during the Iran hostage crisis in 1979 which seriously damaged his reputation.

of regular folks the true heroes of our land who make up the most uncommon nation of doers in history. You know they're Americans because their spirit is as big as the universe and their hearts are bigger than their spirits. (27 January 1987)

However, it was perhaps the Valiant Leader myth that was most readily transferable from his career as an actor to the domain of politics. Reagan was able to draw on the heroic roles that he had taken on as a B movie actor in films such as *Knute Rockne, All American* and *Kings Row* to create an image of a leader who could bring peace to a world filled with fear – as one of his biographers notes:

> From his earliest teenage years as a lifeguard, when he pulled ashore drowning swimmers, to his last presidential days in office, when he sought to obtain the release of hostages in Lebanon, Reagan saw himself as a rescuer, the romantic hero who saved life from the treacherous currents of nature and politics. He saw himself doing as an individual – a head of state who, in the spirit of Emerson, headed history in the right direction. (Diggins 2007: 40)

When he fought his first election campaign American confidence had been shattered by the sight of blindfolded hostages taken from the American Embassy in Tehran, and Reagan offered a vision of the valiant individual that demonstrated how a nation filled with such individuals, could, through a combination of persuasion and the threat of force, restore its position as a global leader. This image of the valiant leader was reinforced by his personal physical bravery and mental strength when he was the victim of an assassination attempt in March 1981; he is reputed, humorously, to have said to his wife: 'Honey, I forgot to duck'– rescripting an assassination attempt as a shootout in a cowboy movie.

Given the primacy of myth in his political communication, in this chapter I account for the persuasiveness of Reagan's mental representations through the notion of 'Romantic Myth'. 'Romantic Myth' brings individual human relationships into the spotlight and gives them a role in the affairs of the world. Though a romance is, by definition, a relationship between individuals, it is also one in which individuality is heroically sacrificed for the sake of the relationship. Describing myth as 'romantic' does not undermine its potential to change the world: the possibility of a romantic future was highly significant in melting the hard socialist realism of the Soviet Union, in which party relationships overrode individual ones, especially after the economic collapse of the 1980s. The prospect of a better world combined with other Soviet failures, such as the military defeat in Afghanistan, ultimately led to the collapse of the Berlin Wall, the break-up of the Soviet Union and the resulting American hegemony. The romantic myths of the Valiant Leader, and myths based on extraterrestrial exploration, eventually replaced the myth of the Conspiratorial Enemy because as the enemy became less of a threat it also became less necessary to represent it as conspiratorial.

6.2 The rhetoric of Ronald Reagan – the actor politician

To investigate Reagan's rhetoric 13 speeches were selected over the period 1981–87 forming a corpus of approximately 51,000 words. Reagan's rhetorical intention during this period was to respond to the major issues of the time with a sense of optimism and hope; this was important to his supporters because Carter's inability to resolve the Iranian hostage crisis symbolised a period of uncertainty and lack of national self-esteem. Reagan restored a sense of national confidence through the use of light-hearted narratives that evoked positive emotions, such as 'Recession is when your neighbour loses his job, Depression is when you lose your job and Recovery is when Jimmy Carter loses his'. His wit and the impression of being at ease with himself raised the confidence and self-esteem of many Americans and gave them the hope that they could come through bad times; the effect of his rhetoric on the general morale inspired a sense of well-being that is more significant than the details of the policies that he espoused. When Reagan explained policy he often did so by listing numbers and statistics that he had researched but which did not come across convincingly as a coherent argument. His rhetoric became persuasive when it created an empathetic climate based on the impression that he was a fundamentally good man acting heroically upon a bad world. He established an ethical image as saviour of the free world from the totalitarian oppression of the Communist bloc, and his status as a stereotypical American – humorous, romantic, heroic – gave empathetic proof of his appeal. Reagan can therefore best be interpreted as an actor who became a motivator: a spinner of romantic fantasies who could inspire; and it is not therefore surprising that he relied on the transformational potential of metaphor.

Of all the politicians analysed in this study, Reagan and Obama used metaphor the most frequently; in the 13 speeches analysed in detail,

479 metaphors were identified (as compared with 447 for Obama), this works out at 9.4 metaphors per 1000 words as compared with Thatcher (3.76 per 1000 words) or Clinton (7.18 per 1000 words). Along with Obama, he also used nearly all the source domains for which evidence has been found among the other politicians analysed; some were unique to him such as metaphors from the world of cinema and entertainment: 'Family and community are the co-stars of this great American come-back' which alludes to his movie acting career. This was something that he used to humorous effect: 'Thank you all very much, and may I just say that every bit of show business instinct that is within me says that perhaps it would be better if the entertainment followed the speaker. You are a tough act to follow.' For Reagan what was important was to create empathy with his audience – whether immediate or remote; as one of his more favourable biographers comments:

> ... he was a liberal romantic who opened up the mind to the full blaze of Emersonian optimism. Like the poet, the president left the American mind innocent, without knowledge of power and evil and the sins of human nature. The Reaganite ethos of morning in America, of the country as always in a state of becoming, as the land of tomorrow, is old New England Transcendentalism somehow find-ing a home in Illinois, Hollywood, Sacramento, and then the White House. (Diggins 2007: 51–2)

The untarnished idealism of his romantic myths fitted well with the cul-ture of American popular comic superheroes. This easy idealism rejected cynicism and negativity:

> The critics were wrong on inflation, wrong on interest rates, wrong on the recovery, and I believe they'll be wrong on the deficit, too, if the Congress will get spending under control. If optimism were a national disease, they'd be immune for life. Isn't it time that we said no to those who keep saying no to America? (2 March 1984)

Here his claim that his critics were wrong is supported by a medical metaphor that draws an inference from the hypothesis that optimism is 'a disease'; this works rather like an oxymoron by harnessing together something that is by definition positive, optimism, with an entity that is inherently negative, disease – and therefore represents opponents negatively. He concludes his second inaugural speech with the following script for a romantic, positive-thinking optimism:

> It is the American sound. It is hopeful, big-hearted, idealistic, daring, decent, and fair. That's our heritage; that is our song. We sing it still. For all our problems, our differences, we are together as of old, as we raise our voices to the God who is the Author of this most tender music. And may He continue to hold us close as we fill the world with our sound – sound in unity, affection, and love – one people under God, dedicated to the dream of freedom that He has placed in the human heart, called upon now to pass that dream on to a waiting and hopeful world. God bless you and may God bless America. (21 January 1985)

It is significant that he draws on metaphors from music and sound – listening to his speeches is like watching *Gone with the Wind*, a narrative in which good always wins in the service of a divinely appointed national purpose. This readily contrasts with the negative pessimism of less romantically minded opponents. We should also notice that it is 'the world' that is both filled with an American sound and provides an expectant audience for the American song – and I will consider a little later how this construal of 'the world' contributed towards a rhetoric of America as the global superpower. In the following speech he associates America, and by implication his own policies, with romantic dreams of hope, glory and adventure:

> The difference between the path toward greater freedom or bigger government is the difference between success and failure; between opportunity and coercion; between faith in a glorious future and fear of mediocrity and despair; between respecting people as adults, each with a spark of greatness, and treating them as helpless children to be forever dependent; between a drab, materialistic world where Big Brother rules by promises to special interest groups, and a world of adventure where everyday people set their sights on impossible dreams, distant stars, and the Kingdom of God. We have the true message of hope for America. (2 March 1984)

'Opportunity', 'glory', 'greatness' 'and 'dreams' are contrasted with 'coercion', 'mediocrity', 'drabness' and 'materials'; but more significantly, political endeavour itself is conceptualised as a world of adventure, where there are, as in the cinema, or the superhero comic book, no hard and fast boundaries between fantasy and reality; after all fictive worlds often bring us closer to whatever 'truth' may be out there than the factual ones of materialism. In this respect Reagan was aware of the need to instil an emotional climate that encouraged acceptance of his metaphors and he demonstrated his rhetorical 'spark' by the actor's ability to improvise and find the right 'line' for a specific situation:

> His rhetoric was light on substance but quick on slogans (for example, 'Are you better off today than you were four years ago?', 'It's morning in America' and 'Go ahead, and make my day'. Reagan knew that the public neither understands the intricacies of issues nor focuses much attention on their resolution. What matters is the short, memorable response that electrifies the viewing audience. Reagan was able to give that response when it was necessary. (Woodward 1990: 117)

Reagan's ability to provide the 'short memorable response' became legendary and demonstrated a quick-wittedness that demonstrated emotional intelligence. His ability to stay calm under pressure was a considerable quality given the political tensions during a reactivation of the Cold War as well as conflicts with other nations such as Libya and Nicaragua:

> What the actor as politician needs to display, wrote Miller, is 'relaxed sincerity.' This was a 'certain underlying cool, a self-assurance that suggests the heroic.' Ronald Reagan had it ... He 'disarmed opponents by never showing the slightest sign of inner conflict about the truth of what he was saying.' His critics may have found him simplistic, but what counted was the sincerity he summoned, which 'implies honesty, an absence of moral conflict in the mind of its possessor.' Reagan has the actor's ability to incorporate reality into the fantasy of his role. (Diggins 2007: 116)

Reagan's rhetoric combined the impression of having the right intentions with 'sounding right' and framed these within telling the right romantic myth. His political success implies that whatever was lacking in terms of thinking was readily compensated by his expertise in the other components of persuasive communication.

6.3   Sports metaphors and the broadcaster politician

Reagan's skill in telling a story may have originated in his early experience as a sports broadcaster in Des Moines of which he wrote in his autobiography:

> I did possibly forty-five football games from virtually every major press box in the Midwest. I covered by telegraph more than 600 big league baseball games, plus swimming meets (and) track meets. Those were wonderful days. I was one of a profession just becoming popular and common – the visualiser for the armchair quarterback. (Reagan (with Hubler) 1981: 40)

Sports were attractive to Reagan both because they satisfied his desire for heroism, within a competitive context, and the inherent opportunities for drama and narrative that the sports field, like the cinema, offers; sometimes sporting events provided scripts that could be adapted to either cinema or politics. His use of 'visualiser' reflects an ability that is essential to successful sports broadcasting: the ability to create images in the mind of his audience so that political scenarios can readily be interpreted in terms of a sporting event, as he does in the following:

> In fact, the liberal conduct of foreign policy reminds me of a little football game that was played at Notre Dame back in 1946, when Notre Dame player Bob Livingstone missed a tackle. And his teammate, all-American Johnny Lujack, screamed, 'Livingstone, you so-and-so you,' and he went on and on. And then, Coach Frank Leahy said, 'Another sacrilege like that, Jonathan Lujack, and you'll be disassociated from our fine Catholic university'. Well, in the very next play, Livingstone missed another tackle, and Coach Leahy turned to the bench and said, 'Lads, Jonathan Lujack was right about Robert Livingstone'. And that's why it's important to go to the record. (30 January 1986)

Here we see some of the traits of Reagan's rhetoric: his use of analogy drawing on popular American culture, his use of anecdote for rather scurrilous effect, his recall of word-for-word dialogue so that it sounds authentic. Reagan's interest in sports was something that – like his interest in cinema, his mild hedonism, and his humorous style – contributed to an impression of empathy with many millions of ordinary Americans: he was not aloof or morally superior, in contrast to his predecessor

Carter, or later, John Kerry. For Reagan the political arena was not fundamentally different from the sports arena: both were equally characterised by struggle, spectacle, and the idea that victory or defeat arose from self-reliance. The concept that POLITICS IS SPORT was present both in relation to domestic and foreign policy; domestic policy was conceived as a race against inefficiency:

> But we cannot win the race to the future shackled to a system that can't even pass a federal budget. We cannot win that race held back by horse-and-buggy programs that waste tax dollars and squander human potential. We cannot win that race if we're swamped in a sea of red ink. (4 February 1986)

Here we can see evidence of the concept SPEED IS SUCCESS for which we see further evidence in his foreign policy when it became framed as an 'arms race':

> We've been striving to give the world the facts about the international arms race. Ever since our nearly total demobilization after World War II, we in the West have been playing catch-up. Yes, there's been an international arm's race, as some of the declared Democratic candidates for the presidency tell us. But let them also tell us, there's only been one side doing the racing... (18 February 1983)

An arms 'race' implies that the side that obtains either more or better arms will succeed by becoming more powerful, but Reagan claims that it is only the Soviet Union that has been 'racing'. Above all, sport, like Reagan's representation of politics, was based on a romantic heroism in which success on the sports field was a manifestation of divine approval, as in the following where efforts in sport are likened to spiritual struggle:

> Let us be sure that those who come after will say of us in our time, that in our time, we did everything that could be done. We finished the race; we kept them free; we kept the faith. (25 January 1984)

> And in those moments when we grow tired, when our struggle seems hard, remember what Eric Liddell, Scotland's Olympic champion runner, said in *Chariots of Fire*: 'So where does the power come from to see the race to its end? From within. God made me for a purpose, and I will run for His pleasure.'

If we trust in Him, keep His word, and live our lives for His pleasure, He'll give us the power we need—power to fight the good fight, to finish the race and to keep the faith. (2 March 1984)

Sporting success was related to divine experience since sports provided an opportunity to display motivation and determination based on God-given abilities. This outlook reflected a secular interpretation of Christianity which is a hallmark of Reagan's beliefs, in contrast to more fundamentalist Christian outlooks that have predominated in the rhetoric of other American politicians such as George Bush and Sarah Palin. The sports stadium provides a secular cathedral and athletes are worshippers at the temple of the body. Sports success symbolised a range of values that Reagan identified with: effort, independence and self-reliance. Reagan had noticed when working as a lifeguard how apparently unthankful, and even angry, swimmers were when they were saved from drowning – and interpreted this as being because it undermined such feelings of independence and self-reliance. We should recall the importance of sports in everyday American lifestyle – in activities such as junior American football known as 'little league', and his version of government was based on the sort of local initiatives that participation in local sports events typified:

> You see, we knew then what we know now: that the real big leaguers aren't here in Washington at all; they're out there in the heartland, out in the real America, where folks go to work every day and church every week, where they raise their families and help their neighbors, where they build America and increase her bounty and pass on to each succeeding generation her goodness and splendour... And it's here we find the explanation for the success of the last five years, the reason why on issue after issue the liberals in this town have lost and are still losing: they've forgotten who's in charge, who the big leaguers really are. (30 January 1986)

Reagan's experience as a sports broadcaster gave him the skills of creating drama by heightening emotional tension and appealing to the incontrovertible legitimacy implied by framing human affairs in terms of 'winning' and 'losing' – after all no supporter wants his team to lose. Competitive sports were something in the blood of many Americans and were so unquestionably a source of pleasure that metaphors based on sports readily satisfied the purpose of establishing empathy with an audience – as well as representing complex issues using a readily intelligible frame. In the contemporary period we have seen how politicians such as Berlusconi have employed a similar naturalised rhetoric of sports to establish legitimacy (Semino and Masci 1996).

6.4 Reaching for the stars: intergalactic myth

Reagan had a fascination with space – not only because it symbolised a new 'frontier' for scientific and technological advance – but also because it became, as it did for many scriptwriters, an arena for the projection of his greatest hopes and worst fears. In some respects it was the contrast between the possibilities of space exploration and the reality of human destruction that formed a rhetoric based on a set of narratives that I will term 'intergalactic myth'. Intergalactic myth appealed to Reagan's imagination because 'space' was the next 'frontier' and seemed to provide an arena for scientific and technological innovation that would impact on the practical aim of economic growth; as he put it:

> Nowhere is this more important than our next frontier: space. Nowhere do we so effectively demonstrate our technological leadership and ability to make life better on Earth. The Space Age is barely a quarter of a century old. But already we've pushed civilization forward with our advances in science and technology. Opportunities and jobs will multiply as we cross new thresholds of knowledge and reach deeper into the unknown. (25 January 1984)

The space programme was held by Reagan to provide technological spin-offs that would enhance American productivity and technological supremacy:

> In the zero gravity of space, we could manufacture in 30 days lifesaving medicines it would take 30 years to make on Earth. We can make crystals of exceptional purity to produce super computers, creating jobs, technologies, and medical breakthroughs beyond anything we ever dreamed possible. (6 February 1985)

'Space' is viewed as presenting opportunities over and beyond those that are available on earth and therefore as providing a fresh arena for the application of American know-how. Intergalactic myth fitted well with Reagan's optimism about the outcomes of space exploration – economic expansion based on science and technology. This myth was not in conflict with religious faith, but would reinforce it:

> Well, today physicists peering into the infinitely small realms of subatomic particles find reaffirmations of religious faith. Astronomers build a space telescope that can see to the edge of the universe and possibly back to the moment of creation. So, yes, this nation remains fully committed to America's space program. We're going forward with our shuttle flights. We're going forward to build our space station. (4 February 1986)

However, the motivation behind intergalactic exploration was not something detached from America's past – the search of the Pilgrim Fathers for a new world and the pioneering spirit behind the opening of the west:

> In conquering the frontier we cannot write off our traditional industries, but we must develop the skills and industries that will make us a pioneer of tomorrow. This administration is committed to keeping America the technological leader of the world now and into the 21st century. (25 January 1983)

The notion of a 'pioneer of tomorrow' contrasts the ideal of a pure 'New World' with a corrupt old world – and has a central appeal in American political rhetoric; the space exploration programme was a key element in the rebirth of this search for a 'new world':

> Just as the oceans opened up a new world for clipper ships and Yankee traders, space holds enormous potential for commerce today. Sunrise industries, such as computers, micro-electronics, robotics, and fiber optics – all are creating a new world of opportunities. (25 January 1984)

The mythic belief that space itself will generate fresh opportunities could be seen as a very modernist faith in the future – one which more recent periods of pessimistic postmodern doubt have seriously eroded.

There was something fantastical and essentially cinematic about Reagan's enthusiasm for space exploration and how he framed political issues as intergalactic myth. For example, he frequently refers to 'earth' – especially in a narrative representing America as heroic:

> Now America must meet another: to make our strategic defense real for all the citizens of planet Earth.

> Surely no people on Earth hate war or love peace more than we Americans.

> Almost 25 years ago, when John Kennedy occupied this office during the Cuban missile crisis, he commanded the greatest military power on Earth.

This way of framing policy followed the script of a popular science fiction series *Star Trek*, and allusions to film scripts were sometimes quite explicit, as when he referred to the science fiction film series *Star Wars*: 'The Strategic Defense Initiative has been labelled Star Wars. But it isn't about war. It's about peace... If you will pardon my stealing a film line – the force is with us.' His willingness to exploit lines from film scripts shows how policies could emerge from mythic thinking in which fantasy and reality were blended – so that intergalactic myth became a heuristic for policy conception. Telling the right story formed the basis of an appeal to be thinking right. He talks frequently about the 'Earth' and about the 'world' – especially during the unfurling crisis in Eastern Europe from 1987. His use of both 'earth' and 'world' are usually incorporated into an argument that America's actions are legitimate because they are not based on narrow self-interest but on the hopes and aspirations of all people everywhere towards democracy and American values. This romantic view of America concealed the interests of the military–industrial complex that gained considerable influence during his presidencies and must have seemed hypocritical to those who were struggling for genuine democracy against oppressive governments in Central and South America. It also contributed to a discourse in which Reagan represented the USA as *the* global superpower – something that occurred rhetorically before the collapse of the former Soviet Union made it into a reality.

The shift from more local and national concerns to international notions of 'world' leadership can be measured linguistically in a very simple way: the word 'world' occurs nearly twice as frequently in Reagan's second inaugural speech in 1987 as compared with his first inaugural speech in 1982 – 17 times as compared with 9 times – although the speeches are very similar in their overall length. When we consider the collocations of 'world' they are typically very positive words such as 'free' and 'peaceful', since the rhetorical purpose is to give a highly attractive representation of American world hegemony. Consider, for example, the following:

> And as we renew ourselves here in our own land, we will be seen as having greater strength *throughout the world*. We will again be the exemplar of *freedom and a beacon of hope* for those who do not now have *freedom*. (20 January 1981)

Here there are metaphors of rebirth, power and light, embodied by a positive image of the USA. Another feature we can notice from the mythic representation of American global leadership is the collocation of prepositions such as 'throughout' and 'around' with 'world' – since notions of spatial dominance seem central to the representation of American influence and power.

> Yes, the American people want an administration that pursues every path to peace, but they also want an administration that is realistic about Soviet expansionism, committed to resisting it, and determined to advance the cause of freedom *around the world*. (30 January 1986)

It is worth noting, however, the relative infrequency of the word 'global' in this period prior to what has been referred to as 'globalisation' – even though the increased use of 'earth' and 'world' indicates awareness of processes that would eventually influence all countries to varying degrees. When Reagan uses 'earth' rather than 'world' the perspective is rather different, since 'earth' exists in semantic contrast to 'space' in a way that 'world' does not, implying a dualistic rather than a unitary concept. Therefore 'earth' is used both in arguments for developments of the space programme and sometimes to give what might be described as an intergalactic perspective on 'world' affairs that contributes to the objectivity of Reagan's knowledge claims. Both of these were important since it was the Strategic Defense Initiative (based on the idea that nuclear weapons could be prevented from hitting their target) that ended the philosophy of 'mutually assured destruction', and is thought to have had a significant influence on Gorbachev's policy in Eastern Europe.

When Reagan contrasts 'earth' with 'space' he is also arguing for an expansion of national power and influence: 'Our second American revolution will push on to new possibilities not only on Earth but in the next frontier of space.' Here 'earth' is conceptualised in terms of an earth–space dualism – in which 'earth' is represented as bounded by having a 'frontier' – and evoking the historical myth of the nineteenth-century opening of the 'wild' west. However, the notion of space as a 'frontier' is metaphoric since it is not only spatial but also a frontier of knowledge – so that knowledge is framed as occupying physical space. In this intergalactic myth, the USA, since it is leading space exploration, is seen as the most likely contributor to the chances of human survival and this is encapsulated in a particular phrase 'the last best hope of man on Earth' that he used in a number of speeches over a period of time:

> Let us so conduct ourselves that two centuries from now, another Congress and another President, meeting in this chamber as we're meeting, will speak of us with pride, saying that we met the test and preserved for them in their day the sacred flame of liberty, this *last, best hope of man on Earth*. (26 January 1982)

> How can we not believe in the greatness of America? How can we not do what is right and needed to preserve *this last best hope of man on Earth?* (25 January 1984)

> Again, let us remember that though our heritage is one of blood lines from every corner of the Earth, we are all Americans pledged to carry on *this last, best hope of man on Earth*. (21 January 1985)

The phrase is an allusion to Thomas Jefferson's first inaugural address, given on 4 March 1801, in which the President referred to the government of the United States as 'the world's best hope', and it was used by Abraham Lincoln to refer to the Union in its struggle for emancipation; however, it is the addition of 'on earth' that adds the particular colour of Reagan's intergalactic, romantic myth of global domination – that the USA is equivalent to 'America', and that America is equivalent to the planetary interest of the whole 'earth'. So the dualism of 'earth' and 'space' contributes to a discourse of world domination.

For Reagan, space, and later the nuclear defence programme that became known as 'Star Wars', symbolised a romantic aspiration towards a peaceful world based on science and technology. However, like knowledge itself, the other side of science and technology was that it also offered the potential for self-destruction. Reagan was terrified by the prospect of the arms race leading to the devastation of nuclear holocaust – especially after he realised the possibility of a nuclear war being embarked on by accident:

> Lately I've been wondering about some older prophecies – those having to do with Armageddon. Things that are new today sound an awful lot like what was predicted would take place just prior to 'A' day. Don't quote me.

As one of his biographers observes: 'It may be that what he feared was not a struggle between good against evil but one of evil against the evil that America would become were it to use nuclear weapons to pre-emptively destroy an enemy or even retaliate after a first strike' (Diggins 2007: 195). Space also incorporated fantasy and reality in such a way that he found it increasingly difficult to separate the two. The appeal of the space programme and its technological spin-offs eventually became the lynchpin of his international policy when it was transformed into the Strategic Defense Initiative popularly known as Star Wars. While many saw Reagan as a warmonger other more recent accounts have revised this earlier view:

> Deep down he never saw himself as a nuclear warmonger but as one who, like a religious savior and classical hero, was the bringer of peace. Reagan also sensed something else: the connection between confronting the 'evil empire' and being tempted by it, the trial of facing a sinful enemy and still claiming innocence of sinlessness. Star Wars was Reagan's way of having America preclude facing a situation where a second strike would have to be resorted to after the United States had taken a first hit. It would protect America not only from Russia but from itself. To renounce the doctrine of retaliation also meant that America avoided the guilt of using nuclear weapons. (Diggins 2007: 292)

It does seem that Reagan was genuinely concerned about the possibility of nuclear holocaust leading to the destruction of modern civilisation; he was profoundly moved by the dystopian film *The Day After* that portrays life after a nuclear holocaust, and the experience had an influence on his subsequent policy. He refers explicitly to such a possibility: 'What, then, is our course? Must civilization perish in a hail of fiery atoms? Must freedom wither in a quiet, deadening accommodation with totalitarian evil?' (London, June 1982). There is evidence that through the 'Star Wars' programme he saw a real possibility of avoiding the 'hail of fiery atoms':

> It is a Strategic Defense Initiative aimed ultimately at finding a nonnuclear defense against ballistic missiles. It's the most hopeful possibility of the nuclear age. But it's not very well understood. Some say it will bring war to the heavens, but its purpose is to deter war in the heavens and on Earth. (6 February 1985)

We should recall that the film industry where Reagan first pursued his career is one that depends on the projection of light through images and has its own highly conventional metaphor of 'stars' that I will explore in the next section. Reagan's intergalactic myth represented himself as a star lighting the way to a future that would not be characterised by horrendous levels of radiation but by joy, prosperity and romance. He had a mythic belief in the power of optimism to restrict nightmare scenarios to their proper realm – that of the cinematic dystopia. It was the dramatic contrast between the horrors of nuclear Armageddon and the possibilities of life in the future – an essentially secular interpretation of the contrast between good and evil – that connected intergalactic myth via other aesthetic appeals with myths of technology:

> America believes, America is ready, America can win the race to the future – and we shall. The American dream is a song of hope that rings through night winter air; vivid, tender music that warms our hearts when the least among us aspire to the greatest things: to venture a daring enterprise; to unearth new beauty in music, literature, and art; to discover a new universe inside a tiny silicon chip or a single human cell. (4 February 1986)

6.5   Intergalactic metaphors and light metaphors

I argue throughout this work that metaphors are systematically employed in the creation of political myths and in the case of Ronald Reagan I have illustrated in the previous section how his blending of fantasy and reality in his exploitation of cinematic narratives developed into what I have called 'intergalactic myth'; in this section I will demonstrate how 'intergalactic metaphors' further contributed to this rhetorical objective. An 'intergalactic metaphor' is one in which words from the semantic field of intergalactic entities such as 'stars', 'planets' or 'space' can serve either as the source or as the target domain of metaphor. For example in the following, space exploration is the target domain when it is represented metaphorically as a 'frontier': 'Our second American revolution will push on to new possibilities not only on Earth but in the next frontier of space.' By talking about space as a 'frontier' Reagan hoped to arouse the same enthusiasm for space exploration that had motivated the pioneers in the 'opening up' of the American West – with the implied associations of the source domain such as new territory, new wealth, etc. The space programme was literally 'spatial' and therefore naturally attracted metaphors relating to physical motion towards a predetermined objective that are motivated by the SOURCE–PATH–GOAL frame that underlies journey metaphors.

By contrast, in the following metaphor Reagan uses 'space' as a source rather than as a target domain for metaphor:

> American private enterprise will be blasting off toward new horizons of hope, adventure, and progress – a future that will dazzle our imaginations and lift our spirits. (2 March 1984)

Here the potential of success for private enterprise, the metaphor target, is conceptualised as a rocket 'blasting off' – the intergalactic source domain – and the metaphor elaborates various aspects of the source domain such as excess of light ('dazzle') and upwards motion ('lift'). Hopes are conceptualised spatially in terms of 'horizons' and as 'lifting' in line with the metaphor HAPPY IS UP. We could analyse this metaphor using blending theory as shown in Figure 6.1.

In Figure 6.1 the circles show the mental spaces, the solid horizontal line represents the mapping between the input spaces, and the dotted lines represent the inter-space mapping between the input spaces, the generic space and the blended space. In input space 1 there is 'private enterprise' and in input space 2 there is 'rocket launch'; in the blended space the expansion of business is blended with the force and speed of a rocket taking off and the notion of success in business is blended with the destination of a rocket. At the generic level, motion, speed/force and purpose comprise part of the SOURCE–PATH–GOAL schema. In a sense the point of the metaphor is that we could potentially describe a rocket launch as private enterprise (as in 'launching a new company') just as much as we can describe private enterprise in terms of a rocket launch. Blending theory is therefore helpful in understanding how intergalactic metaphors work at the level of conceptualisation.

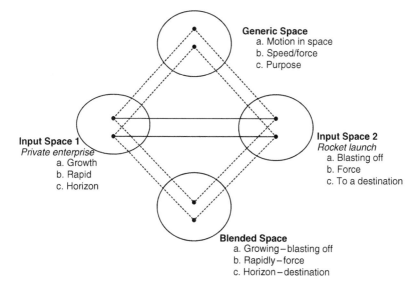

Figure 6.1 Analysis of 'intergalactic metaphor' using blending theory

Intergalactic metaphor was rhetorically appropriate, because – like the space programme – it permitted exploration of possibilities without commitment to specific or predetermined goals since metaphors allow imaginative reflection through the heuristic 'how would it be if we thought of "a" in terms of "b"?'. One characteristic of the way Reagan integrated fantasy into persuasive rhetoric was by an orientation towards future temporal states with the spatial metaphor of 'reaching' as in the following:

> America has always been greatest when we dared to be great. We *can reach for greatness again*. We can *follow our dreams to distant stars*, living and working in space for peaceful, economic, and scientific gain. (25 January 1984)

Even when faced by disaster, with the loss of the *Challenger* spacecraft, Reagan once again drew on the romantic myths based on light and stars to provide hope at a time of despair:

> Other brave Americans must go now where they so valiantly tried to lead – a fitting place, I've always thought, for Americans – *'the stars and beyond.'* (30 January 1986)

The tragedy of the Shuttle Seven will only serve to strengthen the resolve of America to pursue their dream of *'the stars and beyond.'* (30 January 1986)

And I hope that we are now ready to do what they would want us to do: Go forward, America, and *reach for the stars*. We will never forget those brave seven, but we shall go forward. (4 February 1986)

The 'stars', then, proved to be a source domain of metaphor that fitted well with the romantic association with Reagan's film star roles but also with his faith in technology that was evident in both space missions and the Star Wars policy. We can gain further insight into intergalactic metaphors by once again analysing a particular case – 'reach for the stars' – drawing on blending theory as shown in Figure 6.2.

The metaphor of 'reaching for the stars' is a type of spatial–temporal metaphor in which the physical action of moving towards the stars refers metaphorically to intentional actions in the future that have a generally positive purpose. Input space 1 is concerned with physical movement: 'reaching' is a physical action and the 'stars' also refer to a physical entity. Input space 2 is a mental space for hoping, this

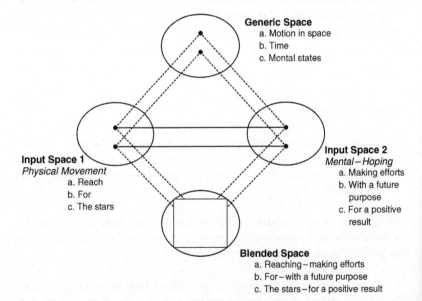

Figure 6.2   Analysis of 'reach for the stars' using blending theory

is oriented to a positive expectation for the future. The physical and mental domains are blended in the blended space, drawing on generic knowledge concerning space, time and mental states. The stars can refer to a positive mental state, perhaps because they are pretty, sparkle and are mysterious; they combine a rich blend of cultural, mythological narratives with scientific, astronomical interests. It is this metaphorical blending of space, time and mental states that underlies Reagan's use of the metaphor to enthuse his followers; it also contributed to actual policy formation in relation to the space programme as it became a metonym for human aspiration in general.

It was effective because it also activated associations of Reagan's career as a B-movie film star and therefore was rhetorically coherent. It is worth at this point also considering what underlies the dead metaphor of a 'movie star'; of course a star is observed from below and is looked up to, similarly film stars are admired and the growth of celebrity culture is testimony to the apparent need for icons to admire. Stars emit light in the same way that a movie star radiates idealised human emotions, spiritual qualities or simply personality and good looks; stars are also remote and in the same way movie stars are detached from everyday life and inaccessible, living behind a screen of security measures. In developing myths for space exploration Reagan's intergalactic metaphors emphasise the remoteness and distance of the 'stars':

And as long as it's real, work of noble note will yet be done, work that could reduce the harmful effects of x rays on patients and enable astronomers to view *the golden gateways of the farthest stars*. (4 February 1986)

We can follow our *dreams to distant stars*, living and working in space for peaceful, economic, and scientific gain. (25 January 1984)

While stars are far removed physically they are emotionally very near, and intergalactic metaphor draws on two sets of heroic associations arising from the polysemy of 'stars'– those of space exploration and those of successful actors – and therefore served well Reagan's self-construal as a myth-making actor-politician.

'Light' metaphors also contribute towards the romantic myth by integrating a secular perspective into religious discourse. The source domain of light is related to intergalactic metaphor since stars emit light; light metaphors are often based on the concept KNOWLEDGE IS LIGHT which in turn arises from a metaphor source domain drawing on religious beliefs motivated by the concept – GOD IS LIGHT (Charteris-Black 2004). Reagan's mythic exploitation of light metaphors shows in the common collocation of 'light' with 'world':

> We have *lighted the world* with our inventions, gone to the aid of mankind wherever in the world there was a cry for help, journeyed to the moon and safely returned.

> My friends, we *live in a world that is lit by lightning*. So much is changing and will change, but so much endures, and transcends time. (21 January 1985)

Light, music, hope, humour, all these contribute to the essentially optimistic perspective of Reagan's romantic myths, and his use of 'stars' as a metaphor demonstrates how the axes of up and down and of light and dark could be harnessed to whatever he selected as a source of inspiration. When Reagan refers to the stars, he appeals to an altruistic sense of national purpose and it sounds right because the imagery is consistent: 'We believe *faith and freedom must be our guiding stars*, for they show us truth, they make us brave, give us hope, and leave us wiser than we were' (February 1985).

Intergalactic rhetoric was something novel that Reagan brought to political communication through speeches and incorporated coded references to both the popular culture of cinema and the significant technological developments of the time. The essential corollary of the national dimension of an intergalactic myth in which America symbolised all positive entities was a demonisation of the Soviet Union. As predicted by this metaphor frame, the former Soviet Union is represented through metaphors of darkness – in fact more often than it is given the attribute 'evil' – as in the following:

> ...when strategically vital parts of the world fall under *the shadow of Soviet power*, our response can make the difference between peaceful change or disorder and violence. (26 January 1982)

> ...when Americans courageously supported the struggle for liberty, self-government, and free enterprise throughout the world, and turned the tide of history away from *totalitarian darkness* and into the warm sunlight of human freedom. (21 January 1985)

Telling the right story usually involves heroes *and* villains. However, while Reagan was oriented to the future, his hopes and ideals were also firmly rooted in the past; and here also he draws on the metaphor of the 'shining city' to communicate a sense of the USA as an ideal location, bounded in space but existing as a conceptual entity as much as a physical reality. The metaphor draws on the source domain of light and in one of his speeches he explains both its origin and its meaning:

> And that's about all I have to say tonight, except for one thing. The past few days when I've been at that window upstairs, I've thought a bit of the 'shining city upon a hill'. The phrase comes from John Winthrop, who wrote it to describe the America he imagined. What he imagined was important because he was an early Pilgrim, an early freedom man. He journeyed here on what today we'd call a little wooden boat; and like the other Pilgrims, he was looking for a home that would be free. (11 January 1989)

The image of the shining city originates in Jesus' Sermon on the Mount that refers to 'A city that is set on an hill cannot be hid', and became a significant myth-creating image in early American political rhetoric. It communicated the idealistic motives of those who sought a 'New World', rather than just survival; the image of a shining city on a hill implies a point of view from below, one that is looking upwards and therefore, following the concept GOOD IS UP, and KNOWLEDGE IS LIGHT, towards a superior or 'higher' moral and intellectual life. It had previously been used by John F. Kennedy amongst others. Reagan goes on to give his own interpretation of this most American of myths:

> I've spoken of the shining city all my political life, but I don't know if I ever quite communicated what I saw when I said it. But in my mind it was a tall, proud city built on rocks stronger than oceans, windswept, God-blessed, and teeming with people of all kinds living in harmony and peace; a city with free ports that hummed with commerce and creativity. And if there had to be city walls, the walls had doors and the doors were open to anyone with the will and the heart to get here. That's how I saw it, and see it still. (11 January 1989)

This image of the USA as an Ancient Greek city state implies a liberal philosophy of freedom of movement and trade through the notion of a walled city with 'open doors' – a container that has apertures. It is a highly idealised version of the American Dream of a nation that, symbolised by the raised beacon of its Statue of Liberty, welcomes the oppressed, as in the 1983 poem by Emma Lazarus:

> Give me your tired, your poor,
> Your huddled masses yearning to breathe free,
> The wretched refuse of your teeming shore.
> Send these, the homeless, tempest-tossed to me,
> I lift my lamp beside the golden door!

Here there are 'light' and 'container' metaphors – the 'lamp' and a 'golden door' that can be opened or shut. This romantic myth is the one that Reagan identified with and fits with his idealised view of America as the idealised 'shining city' that other nations would seek to emulate. Reagan did contribute to a 'golden door' point of view when he signed the Immigration Reform and Control Act in 1986 that gave amnesty to approximately 3 million illegal immigrants who entered prior to 1982 and had lived continuously in the US – so at times myths framed policy. He employed 'light' metaphors to argue that this would draw illegal immigrants out of the shadows:

> The legalization provisions in this act will go far to improve the lives of a class of individuals who now must *hide in the shadows*, without access to many of the benefits of a free and open society. Very soon many of these men and women will be able *to step into the sunlight* and, ultimately, if they choose, they may become Americans. (6 November 1986)

The USA as a shining city is coherent with intergalactic myth and is sustained by the use of metaphors drawing on the source domain of light and its associations with spirituality and knowledge; it is entirely consistent with Reagan as an illusionist who could cast his spell on audiences – whether on the silver screen or the rainbow screen of politics. His use of light metaphors also reflects a 'light' touch on language – his humour and his ability to self parody: it drew on his experience of the light show. Intergalactic and light metaphors proved effective for Reagan as they did not require logical evidence but instead relied on the artistic proof of pathos – the hallmark of the romantic myths that his cinema career had also sought to create. In the following he combines self-parody with further exploitation of the ambiguous 'star' metaphors:

So, friends and neighbors, salute Halley's Comet. Salute that space shot 'U-ra-nus' – I'm too old-fashioned to call it 'U-ra-nus.' I just remember politics in 1985 was also a celestial phenomenon, Steven Spielberg all the way. (30 January 1986)

Reagan was not an intellectual like Theodore Roosevelt nor was he a great classical orator like Barack Obama, however he has some claim through his command of persuasion to at least being a 'celestial phenomenon'.

6.6 Conclusion

In this chapter I have identified Reagan's extensive and systematic use of metaphors from many different source domains to perpetrate a set of romantic myths that gave hope, confidence and optimism to the USA at a time when these states of mind were much needed. While not naturally endowed intellectually, he made the most of the resources at his disposal; these included looks and the ability to memorise short scripts; he then employed these effectively to produce a discourse characterised by humour, lightness of touch and a rosy perspective on the world. His use of sports metaphors facilitated popular identification, and his ability to tell events as if they were a sports commentary made him easy to listen to.

His mythic belief in space and technology – although at times making him sound like an American comic-book hero – contributed to what I have called the intergalactic myths that initiated the period of globalisation. Metaphors referring to the stars and also metaphors that use 'stars' to refer to other positively evaluated entities fitted well with his rhetorical representation of earth in a dualistic relation with space. Telling the story in this way also provided the argument that the space programme would generate new knowledge and therefore contribute to economic growth. His use of metaphors of darkness for his ideological opponents, combined also with an ability to negotiate with them, prevented any major confrontation between the superpowers. However, there are many in Central and South America who would have good reason to doubt the authenticity of Reagan's appeals to freedom and democracy because of the assistance he gave to groups who only paid lip-service to these ideals. Indeed for them the Reagan era was a journey from the stars to the swamp.

It seems that one of the ironies of democracies is that they empower individuals who have the ability to appeal using the same skill sets as actors, or celebrities; these skills may not be those most likely to contribute to most ethical types of government. There is a difference between having the right intentions and acting as if one does. In reality it may be that the best leaders in meritocracies are *not* those who appeal most to public opinion during election campaigns through their looks, their familiarity or their command of a popular rhetoric. However, when these deficiencies become evident there is at least the option of casting out these actor-politicians – if we can bear to sacrifice the dreams they offered. In the meantime actor-politicians are likely to be the most entertaining, with the most enchanting of narratives, who persuade us through metaphor and mythic thinking.

7
Margaret Thatcher and the Myth of Boudicca

7.1 Background – the Iron Lady

Born in Grantham in Leicestershire in 1925, Margaret Thatcher was destined to become the most influential female politician in British twentieth-century history. She was elected as leader of the Conservative Party in 1975 and became Prime Minister in 1979, and remained so until her resignation in November 1990. Her guiding beliefs were similar to those of Reagan and have been summarised by her biographer Hugo Young as follows:

> She saw a smaller state, a more market-orientated economy, a citizenry required to make more choices of its own. She wanted weaker unions, stronger businessmen, an enfeeblement of collective provision and greater opportunities for individual self-help. All of these she succeeded in filling with a sense of moral purpose, which proved that she was, in some sense, right, and socialists were with equal certainty wrong. (Young 1993: 604)

It was a sense of moral conviction combined with effective image management that was at the basis of Margaret Thatcher's dominance of British politics throughout the 1980s and explains why she became the political icon of her time – both nationally and internationally. She succeeded in winning elections in 1979, 1983 and 1987 and, joining forces with Reagan, became the symbol of Western resistance to the Soviet Union. It is perhaps worth considering the significance of the nickname originally coined in 1976 by the Soviet magazine the *Red Star* – 'The Iron Lady'. Whatever the original intentions of its author, this metaphorical phrase came to be reinterpreted as a mark of respect rather than of criticism.

It established her importance: for nobody unimportant would be worth the Russians' while to attack. It gave her an identity as an international, and not merely a domestic, politician. It also neutralised the danger still seen to lurk in the fact that she was a woman, completely unversed in the male world of high diplomacy. Nobody could be too disturbingly feminine who was not presented as being made of iron. (Young 1993: 170–1)

Why did her Soviet detractors choose 'iron' as a metaphor – with obviously pejorative intentions? Presumably because of its qualities of hardness and inflexibility – attributes traditionally associated with males rather than females. Iron is inanimate and unlikely to be touched by the milk of human (let alone feminine) kindness. Margaret Thatcher took pride in giving the 'Iron Lady' epithet an ironic sense: 'Ladies and gentlemen, I stand before you tonight in my green chiffon evening gown, my face softly made up, my fair hair gently waved ... the Iron Lady of the Western World' (31 January 1976). This ironic use of a metaphor became a powerful weapon in establishing her identity as a woman in a man's political world. Because her party did not traditionally have female members in its higher echelons Margaret Thatcher deliberately set out to sound right rhetorically through the characteristics that are conventionally attached to men: authority, courage, firmness, determination and the will to succeed.

Margaret Thatcher was the first British politician to appreciate the need for the manufacture and projection of a political image and this played an important part in the creation of an effective political myth. Under the guidance of her public relations adviser Gordon Reece she improved her voice by accentuating its huskiness and eliminating its shrillness – so as to literally 'sound right'. The self-reference to her clothes and hair in her response to the Iron Lady epithet is not incidental, since hairstyle and clothes contributed to the overall impression of signifying power, authority and other desirable political attributes. As Bruce (1992: 55) notes, 'Clothes convey messages, because they involve choice, and those choices express personality.' Awareness of the effect of these choices was enhanced through the use of the marketing consultants Saatchi and Saatchi. Their influence was noticeable in the 1983 when 'Their surveys revealed a powerful nostalgia for imperialism, thrift, duty and hard work which chimed in the Prime Minister's own beliefs' (Johnson and Elebash 1988: 278).

Subliminal messages about firmness and strength conveyed through non-verbal means were reinforced in the spoken language as we can see from the following well-known quotations that contributed to the effect of sounding right:

I don't mind if my ministers talk, as long as they do what I say!

This country belongs to the courageous, not the timid.

I'm NOT handing over, I'm not handing over the islands now. (To Ronald Reagan on the Falklands crisis, 1982)

You turn if you want. The Lady's not for turning. (October 1980)

On occasions she reversed conventional stereotypes:

If you want something said, ask a man. If you want something done, ask a woman.

Thatcher played upon a relation of contrast between the values that were socially expected of a woman and her own singularly aggressive masculine stance. This gender contrast coupled with her belief in the inherent rightness of her point of view was the dynamo that drove her discourse and created her political image. Her self-conviction shows clearly in the following:

Deep in their instincts people find what I am saying and doing right. And I know it is, because that is the way I was brought up in a small town. We knew everyone, we knew what people thought. I sort of regard myself as a very normal, ordinary person, with all the right instinctive antennae. (*Sunday Times*, 3 August 1980)

In this chapter I will argue that Margaret Thatcher communicated a moral conviction that was her defining ethos, by combining the rhetorical strategy of contrast with metaphor and that an interaction between metaphor and antithesis was at the basis of a rhetorical appeal to having the right intentions. I will propose that antithesis underlay her metaphors because this was the most effective means for communicating a perception of political reality based on conflict that emphasised the polar opposition between her own positions and those of her political opponents. Contrastive metaphors create what I describe as a gender-based political myth – the Iron Lady was a mythic recreation of the legendary Boudicca.

7.2   The rhetoric of Margaret Thatcher

I analysed the rhetoric of Margaret Thatcher initially with a corpus comprised of 11 of the party conference speeches that she delivered as leader of the Conservative Party during the period 1977–87. This produced a corpus of approximately 50,000 words. Party conference speeches were chosen because appeals to the party faithful are likely to draw on the full rhetorical resources of the leader to unite the party through clear ideological statements. Margaret Thatcher was a leader who led from the front and did not seek to conceal her objectives behind a veil of obscurity. This is why her ideology attained the status of a political philosophy in its own right: not since Karl Marx and Lenin has the suffix -ism been added to the name of a politician with such regularity. The rationale for the choice of the period is that this was when her rhetoric was at its most persuasive in terms of political success. It covers the years just prior to her election in 1979 and includes the last party conference speech made during a year that she won an election (1987). She certainly seemed to lose her rhetorical edge in the latter part of her period as Prime Minister. However, for the purpose of illustration reference will also be made to speeches made outside this period.

I will argue that the reason Thatcher's name came to be associated with an ideology was because of her systematic use of metaphor to provide a frame through a political myth based on conflict. It was this that provided the coherence between the cognitive and the emotive dimensions of her political speaking and accounts for the persuasive force of her discourse. Edelman argues convincingly for the importance of notions of conflict in political discourse:

> Because politics involves conflict about material advantages, status, and moral issues, some people are always pitted against others and see them as adversaries or as enemies. Political enemies may be foreign countries, believers in distasteful ideologies, groups that are different in any respect, or figments of the imagination; in any case they are an inherent part of the political scene. They help give the political spectacle its power to arouse passions, fears, and hopes, the more so because an enemy to some people is an ally or innocent victim to others. (Edelman 1988: 66)

This view is also supported by Sego (2001) who argues for a notion of 'political otherness', suggesting that there is polarity between the political identity of the politician and his or her immediate followers on the one hand and the political policies that are *not* their own on the other. Sego does not argue that there is anything inherently wrong with the notion of 'otherness' – since a normal part of the political process in creating an identity is to distinguish one's own policies from that of the other party or parties. We have already seen how Thatcher used her femininity to communicate a unique political identity through exploiting the 'The Iron Lady' epithet. However, problems arise from extreme developments of the concept of political otherness: 'Finally, comes the instrumentation, or acting on the awareness of the "otherness" previously constructed, in such a way that the other is perceived to be the opposition, even at times the enemy' (Sego 2001: 111).

An impression of underlying bellicosity arises from Margaret Thatcher's telling of narratives that are based on conflict rather than on reconciliation. In Thatcher's discourse we find that what began as simple differences of ideology readily progressed from conceiving political opponents as 'the other', through transitional stages, to conceiving of them as 'the enemy'. In a visit to Australia in 1981 shortly before the Conservative Party conference she said that consensus was achieved by 'abandoning all beliefs, principles and values'; she went on to ask, 'Whoever won a battle under the banner "I stand for Consensus?"' (Young 1993: 224). She defined herself by a complete rejection of the consensus politics that had been pursued by her predecessor Edward Heath. This was most evident when Argentina's invasion of the Falkland Islands in April 1982 provided the opportunity for a post-colonial military expedition. As McNair (2003: 205) notes: 'In a sense the conflict became in itself an act of political communication, loaded with symbolic resonance and echoes of Britain's imperial past.' An example of this was when 'At the 1983 conference, the first following the Thatcher government's victory in the Falklands, the stage resembled nothing more than a great, grey battleship, on which the Tory leadership sat like conquering admirals' (ibid.: 141).

I propose that the most frequent conceptual metaphor underlying Margaret Thatcher's speeches is POLITICS IS CONFLICT, and that, typically, conflict metaphors are used to frame government policies as a military campaign. Conflict metaphors imply a type of evaluation because the agent of conflict is positively represented as a heroine – a Boudicca – while that which is struggled against is negatively represented as an alien invading ideology. Margaret Thatcher – who became a metonym for the Conservative Party – constructs herself as the heroine who struggles against an imagined enemy. These enemies can be classified into groups based on the targets of her metaphors: the political opposition of the Labour Party; the social and economic problems of inflation, unemployment and crime and specific groups in society such as trade unions and the police. Finally, come a range of abstractions including private enterprise, Western civilisation, socialism, freedom, terrorism, markets, heritage, etc. I will classify each of these metaphor targets as domain-specific metaphors of the ideologically based conceptual metaphor POLITICS IS CONFLICT.

7.2.1   SOCIAL AND ECONOMIC PROBLEMS ARE ENEMIES

The two main social and economic problems that are the targets of conflict metaphors are inflation and unemployment. Frequently they occur in combination with other rhetorical strategies, for example contrastive pairs:

> That is why it is not a question of choosing between the conquest of inflation and the conquest of unemployment. Indeed, as one of our speakers reminded us yesterday, we are fighting unemployment by fighting inflation. (16 October 1981)

Here a contrast is set up between two options – battling inflation and battling unemployment; however, this is effectively a straw man argument since the second sentence resolves the tension between the contrasting premises by explaining that there is a causal relation between the two policies.

In other cases the underlying metaphor is a personification INFLATION IS AN ENEMY:

> Inflation is the parent of unemployment, it is the unseen robber of those who have saved. (10 October 1980)

> Inflation threatens democracy itself. We've always put its victory at the top of our agenda. For it's a battle which never ends. It means keeping your budget on a sound financial footing. (10 October 1980)

Here an abstract economic phenomenon is conceptualised as if it were a combatant; this is an effective way of providing a warrant for economic policies (such as controls on consumption) aiming to 'attack' inflation. Similarly, personification is used to represent unemployment as an 'enemy'. There is no attempt to explain how the types of economic policy that are usually introduced to control inflation (e.g.

restricting consumer spending by interest rates) are going to assist in reducing unemployment. However, the use of metaphor removes the necessity of explaining logical cause–effect relations for describing economic processes and relies on a readily accessible mental modal for conflict.

In the later speeches there is also evidence of the representation of other types of social problem as enemies; these include terrorism and drugs:

> Britain has taken the lead in tackling practical issues in Europe which are of real benefit to people – reform of the Common Agricultural Policy, completion of the Single Market, the fight against terrorism and drugs. (14 October 1988)

There are also some instances of an inversion of the metaphor so that what is positively evaluated – such as freedom – is also something that we have to fight *for*:

> We pledge in this Party to uphold these principles of freedom and to fight for them. We pledge it to our allies overseas. And we pledge it to this country which we are proud to serve. (12 October 1990)

In an analysis of party political manifestos I have claimed that the Conservative Party typically employs conflict metaphors to represent itself as the defender of values that are represented as being under attack by Labour (Charteris-Black 2004: 70). I will now consider how the availability of a mental model for conflict became a powerful force in the representation of political issues in the later 1970s and early 1980s.

7.2.2 INDUSTRIAL RELATIONS IS A BATTLE

The latter part of the political climate of the 1970s was characterised by uneasy relations between the Labour government and the trade union movement; there were a number of lengthy strikes, though the situation was not significantly worse than it had been at other times in the 1970s. What changed was the way that industrial relations were constructed as a public spectacle by party political rhetoric and by the media. The Conservative Party under Margaret Thatcher identified the disharmonious relation between the Labour Party and its traditional ally as an opportunity to exploit the conceptual metaphor POLITICS IS CONFLICT to activate another metaphor: INDUSTRIAL RELATIONS IS A BATTLE as in the following:

> For years the British disease has been the 'us' and 'them' philosophy. Many in industry are still infected with this virus. They still treat the factory not as a workplace but as a battlefield. (12 October 1978)

Thatcher used a mode of representation in which the trade unions were the cause of all Britain's sufferings; as Edelman (1988: 89) proposes:

> To blame vulnerable groups for the sufferings and guilt people experience in their daily lives is emotionally gratifying and politically popular, and so the construction of enemies underlies not only domination, oppression, and war, but the policy formation, the elections, and the other seemingly rational and even liberal activities of the contemporary state as well.

There was clearly an emotional gratification from having identified the cause of all the nation's ills; if the factory was a 'battlefield' we may ask ourselves who exactly were the armies? We can see that they were not only workers and management but also the workers themselves:

> Our success was not based on Government hand-outs, on protecting yesterday's jobs and fighting off tomorrow's. It was not based on envy or truculence or on endless battles between management and men, or between worker and fellow worker. (12 October 1979)

The Conservative Party was always aware of its need to retain the loyalty of its working-class supporters and therefore was keen not to represent the conflict between management and worker as a simple class war as this would permit Marxist interpretations. So the strategy here was to represent it as a battle between workers. It was also a battle in which one side could invoke the use of government to pass legislation (for example to end secondary picketing[1]). There was also an aim to represent the government (with its full legislative powers) as acting on behalf of the weak (i.e. non-unionised workers) as well as the strong (shareholders) and on behalf of the majority. There was an awareness of the

---

[1] Secondary picketing is when one group of striking workers form a picket line outside the place of work of another group who are not on strike to encourage them to join the strike.

political importance of shareholders as contrasted with trade unionists; since it was only because of trade union members who went on strike that the trade unions could be conceptualised as the 'enemy'. However, politicians frequently like to mix messages of anxiety with promises of hope for the future and Thatcher looked forward to a time when share ownership would alter the numerical balance between the two social groups:

> Soon there will be more shareholders than trade unionists in this country. Of course, not all trade unionists are shareholders – yet. But I hope that before long they will be. (9 October 1987)

Attributing the origins of Britain's problems to trade unions was an effective way of rallying opinion behind her since it created an identifiable enemy, as Edelman (1988: 20) argues:

> Language about origins is therefore not likely to convert people from an ideology to a contrary one very often ... Its effect ... is to sharpen the issue, sometimes to polarize opinion, and in any case to clarify the pattern of opinion oppositions available for acceptance. The construction of problems and of the reasons for them accordingly reinforces conventional social cleavages: those long standing divisions of interest in which relative power sanctions the limits of rivalry are well established and widely recognised.

Representing groups in society as the causes for problems inevitably led to the representation of political opponents associated with these social groups as combatants.

7.2.3 POLITICAL OPPONENTS ARE ENEMIES

Having drawn on the POLITICS IS CONFLICT conceptual metaphor to represent both social and economic problems and social groups as 'enemies' it is not surprising that Thatcher also uses it as a way of thinking about opposition political parties:

> Home ownership too has soared. And to extend the right to council tenants, we had to fight the battle as you know, the battle in Parliament every inch of the way. Against Labour opposition. And against Liberal opposition. (9 October 1987)

Through what Lakoff and Johnson (1999: 59) describe as inferential structures the cognitive framework of this primary metaphor carries with it the full range of implications from the domain of war; for example, the view that holding political power is equivalent to control of territory in a ground war. A favoured phrase of Margaret Thatcher was: 'Rolling back the frontiers of socialism'. Here socialism is not represented as an ideology but as an enemy state that has undertaken an invasion and occupation; therefore, any measures to oppose it are conceived of as heroic efforts to resist an alien ideology. We can therefore extend the metaphor POLITICAL OPPONENTS ARE ENEMIES to POLITICAL IDEOLOGIES ARE ENEMIES.

Once the conflict framework is accepted it brings with it a whole set of experiences that are emotive because they are based on collective historical memory:

> I have reminded you where the great political adventure began and where it has led. But is this where we pitch our tents? Is this where we dig in? (9 October 1987)

Emblems of territorial possession symbolising historical identity, such as flags and banners, occur frequently through the party conference speeches of Margaret Thatcher. I suggest that words such as 'flags' and 'banners' establish a powerful emotional link between what they refer to and a particular value judgement because they evoke iconic images that resonate with historical myths. These support the argument that she based much of her use of metaphor on the myth of Boudicca – with images of Ancient Britons rallying around a strong female leader to oppose an alien invasion:

> Would 'consolidate' be the word that we stitch on our banners? Whose blood would run faster at the prospect of five years of consolidation? (9 October 1987)

Here the use of the expression 'stitch on our banners' is a very clear example of the merging of verbal with image-based modes of communication. It is for this reason that we may consider the use of the term 'flag' to activate the POLITICS IS CONFLICT conceptual metaphor. It occurs extensively in the party conference speeches to refer metonymically to the political parties and their associated ideologies:

A new battle for Britain is under way in our schools. Labour's tattered flag is there for all to see. Limp in the stale breeze of sixties ideology. (12 October 1990)

We Conservatives have run up our flag. Choice, high standards, better teachers – a wider horizon for every child from every background. (12 October 1990)

Since the role of the flag was to identify opposing generals in the thick of combat on a battlefield, clearly it is intended to evoke emotions associated with protection of territory, family, tribe, etc. Reference is made to the Union Jack – closely associated with the Conservative Party:

The Conservative Party now and always flies the flag of one nation – and that flag is the Union Jack.

While this is contrasted with other iconic symbols of the alien invader – typically this was the 'Red' flag associated with Communism:

Our people will never keep the Red Flag flying here. There is only one banner that Britain flies, the one that has kept flying for centuries – the red, white and blue. (14 October 1983)

I am extremely disinclined to be deceived by the mask of moderation that Labour adopts whenever an Election is in the offing, a mask now being worn, as we saw last week, by all who would 'keep the red flag flying here'. (14 October 1977)

By setting up a contrast at the iconic level between the Union Jack and the Red Flag, Thatcher creates symbolic associations between the native, indigenous patriotism of the Conservative Party and between the invading ideology of Communism and the Labour Party. Clearly, such metaphors are intended to tell a story that evokes ancient and emotive historical identities. In this mental model there is an ideological struggle for the victory of a native ideology and the defeat of ideas that are conceptualised as the outsider and as the 'enemy'.

The flag is not the only symbol of patriotism that she refers to; there is also the rose:

The rose I am wearing is the rose of England. (10 October 1986)

Ironically, it was the red rose that was later taken up as the symbol of New Labour. The advantage of a metaphor model based on notions of national identity is that it can readily be invoked to identify the Conservative Party with national 'insider' interests that are opposed to foreign 'outsider' interests such as the European Union:

> We were elected with a clear commitment to the European Community and to fight tenaciously for British interests within it. We have honoured that commitment. We have both fought for our interests and extended our influence. But we are not half-hearted members of the Community. We are in, and we are in to stay. And I look forward to another famous victory in the European elections next June. (14 October 1983)

Or against the internal enemy that threatens national survival which, from Thatcher's perspective, included supporters of unilateral disarmament:

> It was Labour's Hugh Gaitskell who promised the country to fight, fight and fight again against the unilateral disarmers in his own party. That fight was continued by his successors. Today the fight is over. (10 October 1986)

However, perhaps the clearest manifestation of the POLITICS IS CONFLICT conceptual metaphor in relation to ideological struggle is her extensive and pervasive use of figurative language in relation to socialism. There are in fact two stages to this representation; the first is to create a metonym in which the Labour Party stands for socialism. In the second stage she draws on a rich conceptual framework to employ metaphor to demonise socialism. The evaluative and persuasive force of conflict metaphors originates in an association between socialism, immorality and evil that I will explore further in the next section.

7.2.4   Summary of Margaret Thatcher's rhetoric

From the point of view of the hearer – in this case the political audience – there is a cumulative effect of figures of speech in which different metaphor targets are all explained with reference to the domain of conflict. By using the conceptual frame of conflict to describe *all* types of opponent – whether they are social and economic problems, trade unions, political opponents or actual ideologies such as socialism – the negative associations evoked by metaphors evaluating any one of these apply to *all* the others. The metaphor frame therefore sets up relations of equivalence through which she is able to create a subliminal association between social problems, economic problems, political opponents and ideologies and one that implies causal relations between them. We saw this in Chapter 1, where an association with the social outcome of crime, partially attributable to unemployment, was linked with Labour housing policies; inflation is equated with Labour economic policies and the implication is that it is *caused* by them. The conflict metaphor frame therefore encourages a transfer of evaluations between *everything* that is labelled as an opponent: this erodes the ability to identify rational explanations of social and economic problems – because emotionally they have already been explained.

Thatcher's use of conflict metaphors to describe her views on social and economic problems, industrial relations and political and ideological opponents is indicative of some of the inherent characteristics of her leadership style. Her reliance on conflict as a basic way of conceptualising *all* human relations may explain what her biographer describes as a 'salient and potentially destructive feature in her political personality'. He continues:

> This was her persistent inability to make common cause with the relatively few colleagues she ever found around whose strength of purpose matched her own. It had been a habitual problem, measurable by the succession of ministers, strong as well as weak, allies as well as enemies, whom she had despatched from office. The absence of fraternity became a hallmark of the Thatcher style from the beginning. (Young 1993: 543)

Essentially construing both her ideological and personal relations as a rejection of consensus inevitably led her to rely on a discourse of conflict that reflects in antithetic metaphors. It seems that conflict was the animus that inspired Thatcher's political actions and her political discourse. Young (1993: 242) reports Douglas Hurd's view was that:

> ... she was at her happiest when she was up against the wall. When she wasn't embattled, she needed to imagine or invent the condition: embattled against the cabinet, against Whitehall, against the country, against the world, 'I am a rebel head of an establishment government,' she once startlingly announced to a private party in Downing Street, kicking off her shoes and standing on a chair to give an impromptu speech.

It is because of the centrality to this self-perception as a heroic warrior embattled against large and dangerous forces from the outside, and her dependence on conflict as an animus that I have proposed that we may represent Thatcher's political discourse as originating in the myth of Boudicca.

7.3 Metaphor analysis

A close reading of the corpus revealed a total of 186 metaphors or one metaphor every 269 words; this was a less frequent use of metaphor than in the other politicians analysed so far. Metaphor types are summarised in Appendix 10 and show that over 25 per cent of all the metaphors drew on the domain of conflict. Although some politicians demonstrate an even higher reliance on a single source domain (for example, 39 per cent of Martin Luther King's metaphors were journey metaphors), this is a much higher use of this domain than any other politician analysed in this book. This is the reason why I have identified conflict as the psychological basis for her rhetoric.

7.3.1 Journey metaphors

Journey metaphors are typically used to reinforce the relation of contrast that I have argued underlay the myth of Boudicca. In metaphors from this source domain the relation of antithesis is highlighted by contrasting unimpeded movement along a path with inability to move – as in the following:

> But there are others with special gifts who should also have their chance because if the adventurers who strike out in new directions in science, technology, medicine, commerce, industry and the arts are hobbled there can be no advance. (10 October 1975)

The curious use of 'hobbled' also activates the idea of physical injury preventing forward movement. Conservative ideology is represented as the cause of rapid, unobstructed forward movement, while the ideology of Labour is conceptualised as a source of obstruction that causes failure to progress along the path or very slow movement. There is also a contrast between unimpeded and impeded movement in the following:

> We must get private enterprise back on the road to recovery. (10 October 1975)

> No wonder investment in industry has slowed to a crawl. (4 October 1976)

That is the programme that will lead to expansion – picking up speed over the years. (4 October 1976)

But without any genuine common ground parties that cannot advance on their own feet tend to be trodden on by their partners. (8 October 1982)

In this metaphor-based model the enemy is constructed as a negative force – like gravity – that constrains the vital and vigorous force of Conservative ideology. In some cases the contrast is evoked in a metaphor extending over several phrases:

I look to the day when we throw off the Socialist yoke and together turn to the task of setting our country on the road to a real and lasting recovery. (14 October 1977)

Mr President there are just as many evaders and short-cutters around today in the Labour Party . . . In real life such short cuts turn out to be dead ends. (11 October 1985)

Here the phrase 'short cuts make dead ends' alludes to a saying 'short cuts make long returns'. I suggest that these contrasting concepts based on movement and knowledge of journeys provide evidence of two underlying conceptualisations: CONSERVATIVE POLICIES ARE UNIMPEDED MOVEMENTS and LABOUR POLICIES ARE IMPEDED MOVEMENTS. These metaphor choices assist in creating a myth in which the party policies actually *cause* either fast or slow progress towards political objectives. There is slippage from a metaphoric relation of association to a logical relation of causation. In some cases metaphors for constraint are combined with literary allusion as in the following:

You are pinning down the swift and the sure and the strong, as Gulliver was pinned down by the little people of Lilliput. A society like that cannot advance. (12 October 1978)

In other cases two different metaphorical schemas are blended in a nested metaphor:

But is this where we pitch our tents? Is this where we dig in? Absolutely not. Our third election victory was only a staging post on a much longer journey. (9 October 1987)

Here the inherently contrastive domain of war – based on the notion of two opposing forces – is blended with the contrast from the journey domain between movement forwards and stopping. In other cases the desire for conflict is attributed to the opposition:

> Mr. Kinnock told Mr. Scargill publicly that there was no – and I quote – 'no alternative but to fight – all other roads are shut off'. (11 October 1985)

Margaret Thatcher continued using journey metaphors right to the end of her time as leader of the Conservative Party; as she said on the appointment of John Major as Prime Minister: 'I shan't be pulling the levers there but I shall be a very good back-seat driver' (*The Independent*, 27 November 1990). The iconic image of the mythical Queen of the Ancient British is of a warrior travelling in a chariot and evidently the myth of Boudicca was effectively developed by her journey metaphors. Images of Boudicca are inseparable from driving her chariot and so it is no surprise that Thatcher draws on journey metaphors in her discourse of leadership.

7.3.2   Health metaphors

Metaphors from the domain of health and disease can be used for evaluating groups in society, ideologies and other metaphor targets. It seems that the power of health metaphors derives from a basic paired set of fundamental human experiences: life and death. Between these extremes, there are degrees of health so that metaphors can be graded anywhere on a scale of good and bad health according to the strength of the intended evaluation. For example, mild forms of evaluation are expressed by metaphoric uses of *bout* or *recovery*; stronger evaluations are conveyed with *wounds* or *healthy* and very strong evaluations are conveyed by metaphoric uses of *paralysis* or *robust*. It is the underlying bodily experience of health and illness – rooted in the deeper biological facts of life and death – that provide the potential for health metaphors to be persuasive because they automatically imply that anyone who is seeking to restore health has the right intentions and is thinking right.

Margaret Thatcher's use of these metaphors is equally distributed between those conveying positive and negative evaluations. However, they tend towards the extreme ends of either scale, reflecting a preference for hyperbole that corresponds with her tendency to simplify issues by emphasising the contrast between two positions. There is also clear evidence of health metaphors combining with other rhetorical strategies such as parallelism:

> Without a healthy economy we cannot have a healthy society. Without a healthy society the economy will not stay healthy for long. (10 October 1980)

In the following there is a quadruple reiteration of a health metaphor (in italics) that is combined with a dual contrast (shown by letters):

> A Britain that was known as *the sick man of Europe* – And which spoke the language of compassion (A) but which suffered the winter of discontent (B).
>
> Governments had failed to tackle the real problems *which afflicted us*.
>
> They dodged difficult problems rather than face up to them. The question they asked was not '*Will the medicine work*?' (A) but '*Will it taste all right?*' (B) (11 October 1985)

In fact the use of sickness and remedy metaphors is the start of a chain of contrasting pairs in which there is a problem followed by a solution:

> We were told you can't reform trade union leaders, you can't reform the trade unions – their leaders won't let you. But we did. (11 October 1985)

The use of the initial health metaphor is effective in activating a structure that permeates a set of contrasting pairs. In health metaphors there is a clear contrast between Conservative policies that are described by using metaphors based on restoring good health and Labour policies that are described by metaphors based on causing illness. This can be conceptually represented as CONSERVATIVE POLICIES ARE A MEDICINE and LABOUR (= SOCIALIST) POLICIES ARE A DISEASE. If Britain is the sick man of Europe, then these metaphors reinforce an underlying problem–solution discourse pattern in which the Conservative Party is the doctor offering its policies as a remedy to the afflictions caused by Labour policies:

> The waste of a country's most precious assets – the talent and energy of its people – makes it the bounden duty of Government to seek a real and lasting cure. (10 October 1980)

On a number of occasions Thatcher refers to the 'British sickness' or to Britain as 'The sick man of Europe'. Drawing on the problem–solution pattern, the notion of an illness implies the necessity for treatment and she offers herself as an embodiment of a Conservative Party that will administer the cure. In this metaphor model the Labour Party is a quack doctor whose solutions are relabelled as problems:

> Labour's real prescription for Britain is the disease half the world is struggling to cure. (13 October 1989)

The analysis of Thatcher's health metaphors reveals that they are systematically organised by a relation of contrast. Everything that is good and healthy is associated with Conservative policies and everything that is bad and diseased is associated with the condition of Britain arising from Labour policies. These associative relations may readily be interpreted as causal ones. The rhetorical effect of this contrast is to reinforce and heighten the differences between the two parties. This basic polarity contributes to the creation of a political myth in which British society is in conflict – like a body struggling against a virulent form of illness. This frame arouses emotions associated with the fear of illness and the struggle for health. In this respect we can say that her use of metaphor communicates a political myth that is part of an extremist ideology: that Britain was a fundamentally divided society threatened by the alien disease of socialism. In fact, it was her rhetoric – and her use of metaphor in particular – that told the story of a country that was at war with itself.

7.3.3 Metaphors for religion and morality

Margaret Thatcher did not attempt to conceal the fact she was motivated by a personal spiritual and moral conviction; she is reported as having said: 'I am in politics because of the conflict between good and evil, and I believe that in the end good will triumph' (*Daily Telegraph*, 18 Sept. 1984). And: 'Economics are the method; the object is to change the soul' (*Sunday Times*, 3 May 1981). She uses metaphors from the domain of religion and morality to present Conservative policies as *the cause* of inherently good moral values such as trust, honour and faith and Labour policies as *the cause* of immoral values such as duplicity and dishonesty. The underlying notions of goodness and evil provide a very clear scale for the evaluation of political parties and their ideologies. This fits with the general pattern of conflictive metaphor in which linguistic choices are made from the extreme ends of this scale. Rhetoric becomes persuasive when linguistic choices communicate an underlying value system or ethos of the speaker.

The use of metaphors of religion and morality also implies a transfer from the phenomena that are being described to the actual ethos and behaviour of the politician. An important objective for political leadership is to create a perception that the speaker is to be trusted because they have a plan for a future that is inherently good; in this respect a very common choice of metaphor is that of 'vision'. Although partly motivated by the conceptual metaphor UNDERSTANDING IS SEEING (Lakoff and Johnson 1980: 48), this metaphor also activates the religious idea of a visionary – or one who has supernatural powers to see into the future. The ability to see into the future also implies that the speaker is inherently good and Thatcher commonly tries to make this association in the coda position in her speeches:

> And I have tried to tell you something of my personal vision, my belief in the standards on which this nation was greatly built, on which it greatly thrived, and from which in recent years it has greatly fallen away. (10 October 1975)

> Three years ago I said that we must heal the wounds of a divided nation. We must learn again to be one nation or one day we shall be no nation. That is our Conservative faith. It is my personal faith and vision. (12 October 1978)

Here we can see an appeal to two myths: that of the contrast between how bad things are with how good they were, and the myth of herself as an active participant uniting a divided people. This, of course, is ironic since I have already identified how Thatcher's discourse systematically *divided* the British people through the creation of contrasts. The amplification of a minor problem is a political strategy for offering the policies of one's own party as a solution to it. It is interesting that what she describes as 'her personal vision' in the codas of the early speeches, becomes 'our vision' once the Conservative Party was elected:

> Of course, our vision and our aims go far beyond the complex arguments of economics ... (10 October 1980)

> That is our vision. It is a vision worth defending and we shall defend it. Indeed, this government will never put the defence of our country at risk. (12 October 1984)

The shift in the personal pronoun is intended to signify that what was a personal aspiration towards social improvement has broadened into a social movement. However, as Fairclough (2000: 164) points out in relation to New Labour, with the first-person plural pronoun it is never clear exactly who is included and who is excluded. The 'our' could refer to those present at the conference, to all party members or to all those who may potentially support the party. It is also possible that this anticipates her use of the royal 'We' that was most famously recorded in relation to her remark: 'We have become a grandmother' (4 March 1989). Often such vagueness is beneficial in political discourse because as it can lead to a wider group of hearers identifying with the speaker.

Interestingly, while 'vision' is used to conceptualise future political aspirations and objectives – those of the past are referred to by 'faith':

Through the long years of Opposition you kept faith; and you will, I know, keep faith through the far longer years of Conservative government that are to come. (12 October 1979)

Faith, then, is conceptualised as a state of belief that can sustain the party in times of hardship and rejection, whereas vision comes more to the fore once it has gained a position of power and is able to realise its hopes for the future.

As with the other domains analysed, metaphor is systematically integrated with antithesis – especially that between the past and the present – when Conservatism values are contrasted with those of Labour; typically Labour is associated with an absence of morality and religion while the Conservative Party is a source of moral strength:

Let Labour's Orwellian nightmare of the Left be the spur for us to dedicate with a new urgency our every ounce of energy and moral strength to rebuild the fortunes of this free nation. (10 October 1980)

As Young (1993: 420) explains: 'Religion was put to the most useful service it could perform for a crusading politician of the later twentieth century. It reduced to simple issues of personal morality highly complex questions of social and economic behaviour.' Metaphor targets from the domain of morality are not restricted to the Labour Party but attack the whole ideology on which Thatcher claims these policies are based – i.e. socialism. There is a consistent theme throughout her speeches on the immorality of socialism. Edelman (1988) argues that construction of the reason for social problems is one way that politicians are able to assign praise and blame. As he puts it:

A particular explanation of a persisting problem is likely to strike a large part of the public as correct for a fairly long period if it reflects and reinforces the dominant ideology of that era... In a crucial sense problems are created so that particular reasons can be offered for public acceptance, and... so that particular remedies can be offered. (Edelman: 1988: 18)

A very good example of this is the way that social and economic problems such as the low productivity and poor industrial relations that characterised the late 1970s were constructed as being the result of socialism. One way that Thatcher is able to develop this narrative framework is by presenting a conceptual framework that relies on a scale so that there are degrees of socialism that are described in relation to liquids:

The best reply to full-blooded Socialism is not milk and water Socialism, it is genuine Conservatism. (14 October 1977)

Here 'blood' is contrasted with 'milk and water' – this implies there is a good and bad type of socialism within the Labour Party. This is because blood is associated with danger – and perhaps the notion of full-blooded also evokes an image of raw sexuality, while milk and water are associated with safety and security. She then goes on to argue that the current party leadership is of the more extreme type – that is likely to be potentially dangerous:

And make no mistake, the leadership of the Labour Party wants what it has always wanted, the full-blooded Socialism that has been the driving force and purpose of its political life and leadership. (16 October 1981)

The use of an image such as 'full-blooded' is valuable in her rhetoric because it is a type of personification since we associate blood with something that is alive. Having given socialism the attribute + animate, it is then an easy step to associate the policies of the Labour Party with the behaviour of an immoral person following a conceptual metaphor: SOCIALISM IS AN IMMORAL PERSON. We find a number of instances in which the behaviour of socialism is described as immoral in terms of motive and destructive in terms of effect:

I am extremely aware of the dangerous duplicity of Socialism, and extremely determined to turn back the tide before it destroys everything we hold dear. (14 October 1977)

Today we know Socialism by its broken promises — above all by the broken promise of a fairer and more prosperous Society. (14 October 1977)

Mr President, this was the year when time ran out on Socialism. Marxist Socialism is not yet buried but its epitaph can now be written. It impoverished and murdered nations. (12 October 1990)

From these examples it is clear that there is a gradation by which socialism shifts from being simply dishonest to being a murderer – and at the end point of this scale it is identified with nothing less than original sin. Thatcher used personification systematically to reach this climax of hyperbole:

Mr President, Labour's language may alter, their presentation may be slicker, but underneath, it's still the same old Socialism. Far be it from me to deride the sinner that repenteth. The trouble with Labour is they want the benefit of repentance without renouncing the original sin. No way! (9 October 1987)

If Labour is equated with original sin, then it is not only *associated with* immorality but it is actually the *cause* of immorality – just as it was the cause of ill health.[2] Simplistic explanations of social ills had a strong appeal for those lacking critical skills to analyse such metaphors and often activate basic sources of fear such as illness (cf. 7.3.2) and animals (cf. 7.3.5).

Thatcher's use of metaphors conveying a strong negative evaluation of socialism was intended to polarise opinion and to activate deep underlying fears of the Labour Party. This is done by representing the Labour Party as the *cause* of unspecified dangers that are associated with socialism. It was certainly not clear that the Labour Party was a socialist party at this time, but the implication that it was readily lent support to the view that it was the cause of social dangers. By activating fear through her use of metaphor she was able to represent the Conservative Party as

---

[2] However, an advertising campaign prior to the 1997 election in which posters depicted Tony Blair with demon eyes had no discernible impact on public opinion.

a bastion of moral security and herself as a Boudicca who would rescue the nation from the dangers of invasion by alien value systems.

At times her use of metaphors of morality also bring in a humorous touch; her most original metaphor for socialism after the collapse of the Berlin Wall was to represent it as a second-hand car:

> At that election, Socialism offered yesterday's policies for today's problems. Socialism was routed. The other day at Brighton they were given a respray, polished and offered once again to the people. But they are still yesterday's policies, and even yesterday they did not work. (14 October 1983)

Although the negative evaluation is a constant, the emphasis has shifted from something that is dangerous to something that is simply unattractive because it is unreliable. Here again there is an underlying moral scale since second-hand car salesmen are typically thought to be untrustworthy. Once again the construction of problems paves the way for advocating certain types of solution: we will see later how the 'solution' offered by Thatcherism to the 'problem' of socialism is free enterprise.

7.3.4 Metaphors of life and death

As we saw in section 7.3.2, life and death provide a very basic scale for evaluation – along with other paired dualities such as day and night, good and evil, sickness and health; they are mythic archetypes that evaluate human experience as either positive or negative. As I showed in Chapter 2, Thatcher employs metaphor to exploit this underlying duality for the purpose of creating a political myth in which the policies of the Conservative Party – such as the encouragement of free enterprise – are associated with a life force:

> It is the spirit of enterprise that creates new jobs and it is Government's task to create the right framework, the right financial framework, in which that can flourish and to cut the obstacles which sometimes handicap the birth of enterprise, and also to manage our own resources carefully and well. (12 October 1984)

Conversely, the policies of the Labour Party and of socialism are represented as a force that actively *causes* metaphoric death:

> Marxist Socialism is not yet buried but its epitaph can now be written. It impoverished and murdered nations. (12 October 1990)

This way of thinking about ideologies may be conceptually represented as: CONSERVATIVISM IS A LIFE FORCE and LABOUR SOCIALISM IS A DEATH FORCE. Thatcher frequently makes the polar contrast between archetypal forces of life and death, good and evil in a single contrastive metaphor:

> The incentive that was once the dynamo of this county but which today our youth are denied. Incentive that has been snuffed out by the Socialist State. (4 October 1976)

> So it's ironic that as enterprise and liberty rise from the dead ashes of State Control, the Labour Party here is still trying to blow life into those old embers. (13 October 1989)

There is something about the simplicity of this rhetoric that enhanced its impact; there are no shades of grey in the portrayal of Conservative enterprise as a force of life and Labour socialism as a force of death. Such polarisation is a very typical hallmark of Thatcher's use of metaphor to form persuasive mental representations. The construction of politics as a battle between health and illness and between life and death also activates a basic schema for survival so that Conservative policies are associated with survival:

> The very survival of our laws, our institutions, our national character – that is what is at stake today. (4 October 1976)

While Labour policies would actively bring about the destruction of policies claimed to be valued by many:

> They have voted to stop the existing right to buy council houses, a policy which would kill the hopes and dreams of so many families. (10 October 1986)

By using the transitive verb 'kill' Thatcher articulates a causal and intentional relationship between Labour policies and death: killing does not occur by accident and implies an active participant. She also draws on the same mental model for survival to represent small businesses as an endangered species:

> We have turned small business from an endangered species to a vital and rapidly growing part of our economy. The habits of hard work, enterprise, and inventiveness that made us great are with us again. (14 October 1988)

Through political myth she was able to create a spectacle in which competing ideologies are conceived as forces of life and death in a constant struggle with each other. She was able to construct herself as a heroic female warrior who would battle for the survival of capitalist institutions that were represented as being weak and under attack, and to depict her opponents as an immoral force that would destroy without feeling. In this way she was able to ally herself with what in reality were the most powerful interests in society while representing herself as the champion of the weak. Such are the myths on which leadership is often based.

7.3.5   Animal metaphors

Animal metaphors can involve either nominal forms such as leopard, lion, insect, or verb forms such as to claw, burrow or gnaw. Typically animals are either insects that cause damage insidiously or animals that are prone to making violent attacks. They are almost invariably used to create a negative evaluation as in the following:

> Mr. Wilson has at last discovered that his own Party is infiltrated by extreme left-wingers – or to use his own words it is infested with them. (10 October 1975)

> And never let it be forgotten that Labour fought it tooth and nail in their local councils, in Parliament and through the courts. (8 October 1982)

Some instances that I have classified as animal metaphors draw on the domain of hunting through the notion of a trap. In these metaphors Labour is conceptualised as a wily hunter who is setting a trap for an innocent party:

> People who ask the question are already halfway into Labour's trap. They've swallowed the bait and are ripe for the catch. (14 October 1977)

In this respect there is a link with the metaphors for morality in that the setting of a trap profiles the duplicity and cunning of the trapper. On occasions she successfully combines irony with animal metaphors:

> Today, instead the voice of compassion, the croak of the Quango is heard in the land. (12 October 1978)

So it's back to square one for the Socialists. The Labour Leopard can't change its spots – even if it sometimes thinks wistfully of a blue rinse. (14 October 1988)

We can conclude that animal metaphors are employed to add colour and a touch of lightness and humour to political discourse. They fit in with her overall tone of humour and provide an alternative voice from the more typical political myth of Boudicca that I have outlined in the previous sections. Such style switching is an important contribution to successful rhetoric.

7.3.6   Master–servant metaphors

Margaret Thatcher frequently employs personification in metaphors that she uses to describe the state. Another polar contrast that is characteristic of her political discourse is that between servant and master. It is, of course, no coincidence that she employs social categories that are associated with the social structures that predominated in Britain prior to the First World War where domestic service was still a main form of employment. The upstairs–downstairs distinction between social classes fits well with her overall view of Britain as a socially divided society and evokes nostalgia for an imperial period when Britain was the dominant world power.[3] She exploits this metaphor to represent the contrasting views of the state held by the two major parties. Under Labour, she claims the state is the 'the master' and the people are the 'servant', whereas under the Conservatives these relations are to be reversed:

A man's right to work as he will to spend what he earns to own property to have the State as servant and not as master these are the British inheritance. (10 October 1975)

That Government is the servant of the people, not its master. (14 October 1988)

The dates of these examples indicate that the metaphor THE STATE IS A SERVANT is a constant theme of her party conference addresses; she contrasts this with what she depicts as the Labour view that THE STATE IS THE MASTER. If the state is the servant, this of course raises the

---

[3] In December 2010 there was a revival of the popular TV series *Upstairs Downstairs* that is set in a country house, indicating the ongoing nostalgic appeal of the class system to some British audiences.

question of who is the master? Curiously, though, this is not a question that she chooses to answer directly – although we can only assume that it is free enterprise and its associated social entities: business owners and shareholders.

7.3.7 Other metaphors

Thatcher used a wide range of other domains for metaphor – some of which I have analysed in relation to other politicians – however, I will only consider here those that support the claim that her rhetorical purpose was to create a myth of herself as a reincarnation of Boudicca. The most important of these metaphors are those that support the notion of Britain as a family – this may be represented conceptually as THE NATION IS A FAMILY.[4] However, Conservative policies have traditionally sought to ally themselves literally with the family and hold the family to be the source of the moral codes that are necessary for social life; this shows in Thatcher's discourse:

> And we must draw on the moral energy of society. And we must draw on the values of family life.

> For the family is in the first place where we learn those habits of mutual love, tolerance and service on which every healthy nation depends for its survival. (9 October 1987)

We should also remember that as the first female Prime Minister of Britain Margaret Thatcher was particularly keen to exploit any opportunity to activate mental scripts in which women could play a more central role. Evidently, fundamental to what I have described as the Boudicca myth is the notion of a strong and decisive female leader on whom the fate and destiny of her people depend.

From a traditional perspective one of the main domains of power was women's control of family finance – this was the norm at the onset of the Industrial Revolution. We should recall that the etymological origin of the word 'economics' is from the Greek *oikos* 'house' and *nomos* 'managing'. Indeed social and literary sources indicate that the practice continued in many traditional working-class communities of men giving their pay packet to their wife before being given their own allowance. This notion that money was safer in female hands is something that Thatcher exploits a number of times in metaphoric

---

[4] I discussed this conceptual metaphor in relation to Gordon Brown in Chapter 2.

descriptions of the national budget as analogous with the family budget as I analysed in Chapter 2. The reactivation of the historical sense of economics as 'household management' recreated a personification by which abstract financial decisions of government are described as if they were the more familiar financial decisions made by families. Perhaps the most memorable quotation relating to the family was: 'There is no such thing as Society. There are individual men and women, and there are families' (*Woman's Own*, 31 October 1987).

7.4 Summary

This analysis of Margaret Thatcher's party conference speeches has shown that she uses metaphor systematically for the purposes of evaluation and to heighten contrasts between her ideology and those of her opponents. Irrespective of the domain that is selected – conflict, journeys, health, morality, domestic service, life and death, etc. there is the exploitation of the semantic contrasts and antonyms that occur in words and phrases taken from these domains. Opposition between allies and enemies, between movement forwards and impeded movement, between health and illness, between honesty and duplicity, between master and servant, and between life and death form the very bedrock of a conflictive political myth that I have summarised as POLITICS IS CONFLICT. This is a way of telling the right story that creates a mental representation that underlies her persuasive effect. The role of metaphor is to represent *associations* between Labour and negative social phenomena and between the Conservative Party and positive social phenomena as straightforward *causal* relationships.

In the story told by Thatcher Britain is a sick and divided nation (as a result of Labour policies) that awaits the unifying force of a strong leader with policies that are linked to the positive ends of all these scales of metaphor. She represents herself as a militant, female, moral life force that will restore regenerative powers to overcome the insidious, immoral, death force of socialism and will bring an end to negative social phenomena. Metaphor is a prime rhetorical means by which the myth of Boudicca communicates a political ideology of right-wing Conservatism that is proposed as evidence of right thinking. Through the systematic creation of contrasts and bogus causal relationships she is able to activate a mental model of the British way of life as under attack by invasive, alien forces. Metaphor is, therefore, the prime means for the creation of an alien 'Other' whose threat provides the warrant for her policies. The recurrent use of contrast and false reasoning in her political myths may be explained by her sense of self-righteousness:

Her political style, as it developed while she was Prime Minister, always depended to an unusual degree on this search for 'rightness'. She was a woman with a low quotient of cynicism, about herself if not about her opponents. She believed that, being so absolutely and incontestably right, she could communicate her own convictions in the matter to a wide audience and eventually persuade them that any discomforts and disappointments were but minor pitfalls on the road to recovery. (Young 1993: 217)

This sense of rightness – although ultimately leading to conflict even with her closest allies – motivates a primary, or conceptual, metaphor for Margaret Thatcher's political discourse: POLITICS IS CONFLICT. I have argued that this has a number of entailments such as: POLITICAL OPPONENTS/IDEOLOGIES ARE ENEMIES, SOCIAL AND ECONOMIC PROBLEMS ARE ENEMIES and INDUSTRIAL RELATIONS IS A BAT-TLE. This metaphor frame establishes the rhetorical dynamic of thesis and antithesis arguments. This dynamic is reiterated through polar metaphors creating the political myths that offer themselves as both systematic explanations of the causes of social problems and solutions to them. These political myths are summarised in Table 7.1.

It was essential to the overarching political myth of a self-righteous and victorious female fighter that metaphor creates a contrasting set of conceptual dynamics for conflict. The establishment of a framework of conflict created a problematic situation to which she could present herself as the heroic solution. Unfortunately, so effective was her con-struction of political myth through metaphor that she probably created a misunderstanding of the realities of social and economic power in British society. Indeed it appears that her own personality and leadership

Table 7.1 Margaret Thatcher's political myths

Positive	Negative
CONSERVATIVISM IS A LIFE FORCE	LABOUR/SOCIALISM IS A DEATH FORCE
CONSERVATIVE POLICIES ARE A MEDICINE	LABOUR/SOCIALIST POLICIES ARE A DISEASE
CONSERVATIVE POLICIES ARE UNIMPEDED MOVEMENTS	LABOUR POLICIES ARE IMPEDED MOVEMENTS
CONSERVATIVISM IS MORAL/ HONEST	LABOUR/SOCIALISM IS SINFUL/ DUPLICITOUS
THE STATE IS A SERVANT	THE STATE IS THE MASTER

style relied so extensively on conflict that it contained within it the seeds of its own destruction. A conflict-based schema could only last until an alternative political myth could be offered – that of a consensual Third Way. Rather than identifying with one side of the debate, the success of New Labour was to reinvent itself as the party of the middle way, the party that could overcome conflict and restore social harmony to a nation divided by 19 years of Conservative rule. This was a nation in need of a new leader who could bring a fresh political myth that would rescue it from a discourse of conflict that had dominated British politics.

8
Clinton and the Rhetoric of Image Restoration

8.1 Background

Bill Clinton's presidency is perhaps best characterised by the contrast between the high-minded ideals and personal charm of the President and a series of increasingly severe scandals that culminated in his impeachment. These reflected on various dimensions of his ethical behaviour, ranging from his financial integrity (the Whitewater affair), personal habits (e.g. marijuana smoking), sexual integrity (the Paula Jones and Monica Lewinsky affairs) and his personal courage (the issue of draft dodging). Earlier presidents had been destroyed by political scandal but none had been threatened with impeachment for lying while under oath. Given the impact of these scandals on the American political scene of the 1990s, it was vital that Clinton was able to rely on techniques of image creation to maintain his stature as President. Accusations went far beyond policy criticisms and focused on his personal morality and therefore attacked the ethos at the bedrock of his rhetorical powers.

This chapter addresses the question: what communication skills did Clinton employ to restore his image as President? In answering this question I will argue that Clinton communicated that he was a leader who had the right intentions and that this was essential because the scandals had jeopardised this perception. I will also argue that his personality and appearance 'looked right' and that his use of metaphor contributed to his ability to 'sound right' as well as to 'tell the right story'.

8.2   The rhetoric of Bill Clinton: metaphor and image presentation

A very important strategy of persuasion employed by Clinton is to present himself as a potent symbol of regenerative nature – as he puts it in his first Inaugural address:

> My fellow citizens, today we celebrate the mystery of American renewal. (20 January 1993)

The idea of 'renewal' was essential to the development of Clinton's leadership image because it implied a recreation of the vitality associated with earlier periods of American history. Clinton's appeal to images of renewal and rebirth activates creation myths in which a God recurrently returns to bring about a cyclical regeneration; in Clinton's case he appealed to the restorative myth of J.F. Kennedy. The success of this myth accounts for his ability to survive the extensive investigations and eventual impeachment for lying under oath. Although the American public and media claimed to be scandalised by the revelations about his sexual relations with Monica Lewinsky, these were tolerated because they did not contradict this myth of renewal and regeneration. Sexual peccadilloes would have been much less acceptable from a politician who was less dependent on his virility as a symbol of national vitality – a politician such as his main rival in the 1992 election – George Bush. Images of renewal and rebirth are also associated with both the democratic process and the Democratic Party:

> This year, we must also do more to support democratic renewal and human rights and sustainable development all around the world. (25 January 1994)

> So let's set our own deadline. Let's work together to write bipartisan campaign finance reform into law and pass McCain–Feingold by the day we celebrate the birth of our democracy, July the 4th. (27 January 1997)

Here the rhetorical purpose is to create a subliminal association between the Democratic Party, patriotism and the positive connotations of birth and renewal. Clinton's rhetoric aimed to satisfy an American cultural yearning for a returning hero and the lost hope that had died with JFK. John Hellmann calls this search for the new hero a 'dream of resurrection', which was evident in the ceaseless attempts to place Kennedy once again in the White House (in Brown 1988). The myth here is that the Democrats, with Clinton at their helm, are going to heal America from the 'breaches' caused by Republican policies – and they will do so with divine approval:

> Just a few days before my second inauguration, one of our country's best-known pastors, Reverend Robert Schuller, suggested that I read Isaiah 58: 12. Here's what it says: 'Thou shalt raise up the foundations of many generations, and thou shalt be called *the repairer of the breach, the restorer of paths to dwell in.'*
>
> I placed my hand on that verse when I took the oath of office, on behalf of all Americans, for no matter what our differences in our faiths, our backgrounds, our politics, we must all be *repairers of the breach.* (27 January 1997)

Democratic policies are evaluated as constituting a form of 'repair', with the implication that those of the previous administration had in some way caused a 'breach' with the American tradition. This choice of metaphor fits well with the general claim that Clinton is introducing a new and vital narrative to restore values that were under attack. It was also important in reversing an association made by previous Republican presidents between spiritual states and right-wing values:

> As it was articulated during the Eisenhower–Dulles administration, prophetic dualism involved religious faith, the faith of our fathers, the ideals of freedom, individuality, a militant God, and the existence of evil in the world. The God officially invoked was the God who presided over the founding of America, the God who abhorred atheists and loathed communist savagery. (Wander 1990: 159–60)

Lakoff (2002) describes such political contrasts in terms of the 'Strict Father' morality of conservatives and the 'Nurturant Parent' morality of liberals. The story that Clinton told was that he would restore dynamism and vitality to American politics; this is especially evident from the choice of the italicised verbs:

> It is time to break the bad habit of expecting something for nothing: from our government, or from each other. Let us all take more responsibility, not only for ourselves and our families, but for our communities and our country. To renew America we must *revitalize* our democracy. (20 January 1993)

Tonight I announce that this year I will designate 10 American Heritage Rivers to help communities alongside them *revitalize* their waterfronts and clean up pollution in the rivers, proving once again that we can grow the economy as we protect the environment. (27 January 1997)

Persuasiveness arises from the cumulative effect of a rhetoric that creates a restorative myth in which Clinton himself symbolises the regeneration of America. Consider the italicised words in this passage from near the end of the first Inaugural speech:

I ask the congress to join with me; but no president, no congress, no government can undertake THIS *mission* alone.

My fellow Americans, you, too, must play your part in our *renewal*. I challenge a new generation of young Americans to a season of service, to act on your idealism, by helping troubled children, keeping company with those in need, reconnecting our *torn communities*. There is so much to be done. Enough, indeed, for millions of others who are still young in spirit, to give of themselves in service, too. In serving we recognize a simple, but powerful, truth: we need each other, and we must care for one another. Today we do more than celebrate America, we rededicate ourselves to the very idea of America, an idea *born in revolution*, and *renewed* through two centuries of challenge, an idea tempered by the knowledge that but for fate, we, the fortunate and the unfortunate, might have been each other; an idea ennobled by the *faith* that our nation can summon from its myriad diversity, the deepest measure of unity; an idea infused with the conviction that America's long, heroic *journey* must go forever upward. (20 January 1993)

'Mission' and 'faith' activate associations of high principle with a moral leader – these then interact with metaphors of birth and renewal to depict vitality as a morally purifying force. These metaphors were reinforced by Clinton's youthful appearance, charming manner and inviting personal demeanour. Positive creative images are contrasted with negative destructive ones in the phrase 'torn communities'. The speech is completed with a journey metaphor; this activates notions of heroism associated with the Pilgrim Fathers and of the journeys taken during the opening up of the West and possibly the idea of leading the way in space travel. Subliminally there is also a suggestion of a spiritual journey to heaven.[1] The cumulative rhetorical effect is to associate the President with a myth of American rebirth.

Blaney and Benoit (2001) identify a range of discourse strategies that were employed by Clinton to restore his image after the various political scandals in which he was involved. These include denial; evading responsibility; reducing offensiveness of the event; corrective action and mortification. From a pragmatic perspective these are speech acts based on the underlying speaker intention of saving face. One of the substrategies of their category of reducing offensiveness is 'transcendence'; this they define as putting the alleged misdeed in a broader context by highlighting important values. It seems that metaphor coincides most with transcendence, as a way of shifting from the immediate local context to broader issues. Consider Clinton's metaphors (in italics) from the ABC television programme *Nightline* on 12 February 1992:[2]

> Look for a person *with a vision*, with a plan, with a record, and with a capacity to change their lives for the better. I'm going to try to *give this election back* to the people, to *lift the cloud off this election*. For three weeks, of course, I've had problems in the polls. All I've been asked about by the press are a woman I didn't sleep with and a draft I didn't dodge. Now I'm going to *give them this election back*, and if I can *give it back to them* and *fight for them* and their future, I think we've got a chance to do well here and I know we can go beyond here and *continue this fight* to the American people.

There is a religious metaphor, a weather metaphor, two metaphors from the domain of conflict and several instances of what I describe as 'creative reifications'. In these the election is referred to as an object to be 'returned' to someone from whom it has been metaphorically 'stolen'. Clinton presents himself as a hero who protects the weak and skilfully reverses the roles of accuser and accused by depicting his critics as bullies who have 'taken something away' from the electorate. He transcends the allegation of unfaithfulness by substituting a heroic narrative.

Then in relation to the Lewinsky affair Clinton said:

> And so tonight, I ask you to turn away from *the spectacle of the past seven months*, to *repair the fabric of our national discourse*, and to *return*

---

[1] See Charteris-Black (2004: 94–5) for analysis of a similar use of journey metaphors by Lyndon Johnson.

[2] This was prior to his candidacy for the New Hampshire primary.

our attention to all the challenges and all the promise of the next American century. (17 August 1998)

In the phrase 'repair the fabric of our national discourse' he uses a creative reification to transcend the accusation of misconduct; language is presented as a garment that has been torn by the proponents of harmful allegations and so needs creative attention. In such a way Clinton becomes a great fabricator of American political discourse.

Blaney and Benoit (2001: 135) emphasise the importance of transcendence as a rhetorical strategy:

> The most important findings about individual strategies in this study address transcendence. Clinton's discourse addressing the various accusations presented in the preceding chapters was largely, if not uniformly, successful. One should note that a common strategic thread ran through all the discourse: transcendence. This ability to describe charges against him as unimportant in the larger context of the America's challenges was the key to his rhetorical success.

I would suggest that the use of a metaphor 'common strategic thread' to describe Clinton's discourse strategy indicates the importance of metaphors – in particular creative reifications – in his successful rhetoric of leadership. The use of metaphor activates two domains and it is the joint activation of these domains, and the interactions and tensions between them, that deflects the audience's focus from the charges made against him by his opponents. Metaphor had a crucial charismatic effect in the discourse of image restoration as it provided the rhetorical resources by which Clinton could transcend scandal by creating a myth of creation and rebirth.

8.3   Metaphor analysis

Initially I constructed a corpus of approximately 50,000 words comprising State of the Union speeches and Inaugural addresses (see Appendix 11 for details). These speeches cover the full span of Clinton's period as President, and are a valid sample of the speeches that he prepared for most thoroughly because of their electoral importance. I selected only part of the 1994 State of the Union address to ensure that the corpus did not exceed 50,000 words.

A close analysis revealed a total of 359 metaphors or one every 160 words – a marginally lower frequency than for Martin Luther King. The analysis revealed that nearly three-quarters of these could be classified as only three types of metaphor. The largest group can broadly be classified as reifications – that is, figures of speech that refer to an abstraction as if it were something tangible and concrete. This group was subdivided into two sections according to whether the event or entity referred to in the source domain is creative or destructive. The other two types were metaphors from the source domains of life/renewal and journeys.

Although Clinton relies *primarily* on a few types of metaphor, he also accesses a wide range of source domains. In total 23 source domains were identified and the number would exceed this if we were to subdivide reifications for creation/construction into discrete source domains. For example, a wide range of verbs including 'build', 'shape', 'weave' and 'forge' were classified together as 'creation' metaphors; each of these could have been classified by separate source domains such as building, sculpture, cloth-making, iron-making, etc. However, it seems to provide a more explanatory account if we treat all reifications from the lexical fields of creativity, manufacture and craft as semantically related because their intention is always to give a positive evaluation. A very popular metaphor for Clinton is 'tool', referring to an abstract entity such as a competence or skill as in the following:

> We must set tough, world-class academic and occupational standards for all our children and give our teachers and students *the tools they need to meet them*. (25 January 1994)

> We reinvented government, transforming it into a catalyst for new ideas that stress both opportunity and responsibility, and give our people *the tools they need to solve their own problems*. (27 January 1998)

These were classified as instances of reification drawing on the domain of creation. The range, diversity and content of metaphors suggest that creative use of language is an important persuasive means for Clinton to display presidential rhetoric. I will begin by considering creation; I will then analyse metaphors from the domains of life and rebirth, journeys and religion; finally I will give some attention to the diversity of metaphors employed and consider how they are integrated with a myth of everyday heroes.

8.3.1   Creation metaphors

Typically, reifications from the domain of creation describe mental processes as if they were material ones by phrases related to building and manufacture as indicated by italics in the following:

> From our Revolution to the Civil War, to the Great Depression, to the Civil Rights movement, our people have always mustered the determination to *construct from these crises the pillars* of our history. Thomas Jefferson believed that to *preserve the very foundations* of our nation we would need dramatic change from time to time. Well, my fellow Americans, this is our time. Let us embrace it. Our democracy must be not only the envy of the world *but the engine of our own renewal.* (20 January 1993)

Creation metaphors argue that government creates the circumstances in which people become more creative and productive in their own lives. Therefore the positive evaluation that we place on acts of creation transfers to the agent that is responsible for this – the administration with the President at its helm. This is evident in the linguistic pattern: a first-person plural pronoun is the subject of a modal form (obligation) of a transitive verb from the domain of creativity; these include 'shape', 'forge', 'create' or 'craft' followed by an abstract noun. The pattern can be summarised:

We + modal + verb (lexical field for creativity) + abstract noun

This pattern represents government as a collaborative process involving people and as active rather than passive. The following lines taken from the corpus illustrate this pattern and provide an indication of the way that choice of metaphor is governed by the immediate semantic context:

> We shaped a new kind of government for the information age.
> We will work together to shape change, lest it engulf us.
> There, too, we are helping to shape an Asia Pacific community of cooperation, not conflict.

'Shape' communicates an idea of controlling the future and usually refers to an action leading to an unknown future outcome. For this reason the outcomes that are 'shaped' are vague and abstract ideas such as 'change', 'an Asian-Pacific community', etc. Here Clinton invites a degree of trust since change by definition is unpredictable – especially when the objects of change are intangible ideas and abstract entities.

In particular 'shape' is used with reference to the technological revolution entailed by the spread of computers and the Internet:

> To realize the full possibilities of this economy, we must reach beyond our own borders, *to shape the revolution that is tearing down barriers and building* new networks among nations and individuals, and economies and cultures: globalization. It's the central reality of our time. (27 January 2000)

> At the dawn of the 21st century a free people must now choose *to shape the forces of the Information Age and the global society,* to unleash the limitless potential of all our people, and, yes, to form a more perfect union. (20 January 1997)

This conceptualisation of change is largely optimistic because it conveys the idea that the forces of technology are controllable. In reality whether they are perceived as controllable probably depends on how one is affected by them. Those who can purchase new technology probably believe that it enables them to have more control over their lives; however, those who lose their jobs as a result of technological change may believe themselves to be at the mercy of uncontrollable forces. The emphasis on technological expertise complies with an earlier tradition of Democratic presidents that Wander (1990) associates with Kennedy and Johnson and describes as 'technocratic realism'.

Clinton's use of creation reifications contributes to the persuasive style of his rhetoric by communicating an important characteristic of leadership: an optimistic and socially purposeful outlook. Where the emphasis is on some type of general social objective – rather than technological innovation – 'forge' is preferred to 'shape' as in the following:

> So tonight *we must forge a new social compact* to meet the challenges of this time.

> *We Americans have forged our identity,* our very union…

> So this year *we will forge new partnerships* with Latin America, Asia and Europe…

The choice of 'forge' emphasises collaborative effort because the associations of iron production arouse the idea of a number of people productively engaged towards a single common purpose. It may also imply an initial resistance from the object that is to be forged – one that is broken down by heat. However, if it were used in the context of technological change it might be inappropriate because of the lack of precise domain boundaries between industry and technology (for example, microchips are 'manufactured' rather than 'forged').

Other choices of creation metaphors are governed by particular collocations. For example, although the verb 'create' is used with a wide range of nouns in object position – including 'parks', 'schools', 'empowerment zones', 'technology centres' and 'training schemes' – easily the most common collocation was with 'jobs' (13 instances in the corpus) as in the following:

> We will put people to work right now and *create half a million jobs*...

> *we can create a million summer jobs* in cities and poor rural areas for our young people.

> At the same time, we need an aggressive attempt *to create the hi-tech jobs of the future*...

In such uses the political leader is thought of as a creative artist. However, where the object of 'creation' is a term relating to legal policy, the verb chosen is always 'craft':

> ...have reached across party lines here *to craft tough and fair reform*.

> I will convene the leaders of Congress *to craft historic bipartisan legislation*.

> You know, when the framers finished *crafting our Constitution in Philadelphia*, Benjamin Franklin...

Since we associate craftsmanship with attention to detail, the 'crafting' of legislation implies that there will be a degree of thoroughness. At times genuinely creative metaphors are used – for example those from the domain of fabric:

> Let us *weave these sturdy threads* into a new American community that once more stand strong against the forces of despair and evil because everybody has a chance to walk into a better tomorrow.

> *Our rich texture* of racial, religious and political diversity will be a Godsend in the 21st century.

Evidently the use of a wide range of creation metaphors plays a crucial part both in creating a presidential style of discourse and in making positive evaluations of the actions and purposes of government; this can be summarised by a conceptual metaphor: GOOD GOVERNING IS CREATING. The typical linguistic forms employed in such positive reifications are active verbs with first-person plural subjects; these invite the electorate to identify with government as a creative force.

In a study that compares the use of metaphor by candidates for the Democratic nomination in the 1996 election, Hodgkinson and Leland (1999) identify Clinton's use of metaphors of creation and contrast this with Dole's metaphors of tradition. They explain how Clinton's metaphors look forward to the future with the goal of bridging between centuries, while Dole's metaphors are retrospective and less likely to appeal to those looking to the future:

> Whereas Clinton's metaphors of construction enabled the audience to envision a future with Clinton as their engineer, Dole's metaphors of tradition turned the audience to the past. (Hodgkinson and Leland 1999: 160)

However, sometimes in order to create it is necessary first to destroy and just as we will find later, Clinton's use of life metaphors are contrasted with death metaphors, so reifications of creation are contrasted with reifications of destruction.

8.3.2 Destruction metaphors

Destruction metaphors employ verbs that entail some degree of sudden movement or force and will cause material damage over time. The purpose of such metaphors is invariably to convey a negative evaluation of a particular type of abstract social phenomenon or entity, such as crime, conflict, or an unnamed source of aggression. Underlying the use of reifications for destruction is a metaphor schema in which negatively evaluated social phenomena are associated with damage and destruction; this can be summarised in the form: BAD GOVERNING IS DESTROYING. These metaphors imply a mental schema in which various social processes that erode social cohesion are negatively evaluated because they entail serious material damage. These metaphors are often verbs – either in active or passive mood:

> Our purpose must be to bring together the world around freedom and democracy and peace, and to oppose *those who would tear it apart*. (27 January 2000)

All over the world people are *being torn asunder by racial, ethnic and religious conflicts* that fuel fanaticism and terror. (4 February 1997)

Sometimes targets of negative metaphors collocate with a particular verb choice; for example, economic phenomena are negatively evaluated by 'explode' – a verb that is also associated with force and sudden movement – to refer to an undesirable increase in quantity:

For years, debt has exploded.

Health premiums that don't just explode when you get sick or you get older,

Any one of us can call for a tax cut, but I won't accept one that explodes the deficit or puts our recovery at risk.

'Explode' implies a rapid change that results from the building up of pressure over a period and can also have a non-economic target:[3]

We must all work together to stop the *violence that explodes* our emergency rooms.

In other cases there is the use of adjectival or nominal forms, or verbs in the infinitive, to refer to the results of negatively evaluated processes occurring over a period of time:

... how we can repair the *damaged bonds* in our society ...

... to understand *the damage* that comes from the incessant, repetitive, mindless violence ...

... from giving terrorists and potentially hostile nations the means *to undermine our defenses.*

Nothing is done more *to undermine our sense* of common responsibility than our failed welfare system.

Here the focus is on the outcome of some form of bad government rather than on the behaviour itself – as was the case with more dynamic

---

[3] See Charteris-Black (2004: 158–67) for an analysis of verb choices in financial reporting.

verbs such as 'tear' and 'explode'. The damage is shown as the cumulative effect of harmful actions over a period of time and implies the existence of an insidious but dangerous source of fear.

Interestingly, the same metaphor source domain can be used for both reifications of creation and of destruction. For example, we saw in the previous section that words from the domain of fabrics such as 'weave' or 'texture' convey a positive evaluation; conversely, where the metaphor describes the negative effects of time (or inappropriate washing) on fabrics the evaluation is negative:

> ... when the century's bitterest cold swept from North Dakota to Newport News it seemed as though the world itself was *coming apart at the seams*. (25 January 1994)

> The common bonds of community which have been the great strength of our country from its very beginning *are badly frayed*. (25 January 1994)

> We must expand that middle class and *shrink the underclass*. (24 January 1995)

In other cases creation and destruction reifications are contrasted with each other as in the following:

> And as I have said for three years, we should work to open the air waves so that they can *be an instrument of democracy* (creation) not *a weapon of destruction* (destruction) by giving free TV time to candidates for public office. (24 January 1995)

> We cannot accept a world in which part of humanity lives on *the cutting edge of a new economy* (creation), and the rest *live on the bare edge of survival* (destruction). (27 January 2000)

The rhetorical figure contrasts a positively with a negatively evaluated material entity to communicate an opposition between a positively and a negatively evaluated social or economic phenomenon. In some cases an expression that refers to destruction can also have a positive evaluation because the thing that is eliminated is negatively evaluated:

> Once we reduced the deficit and put the steel back into our competitive edge (creation), the world echoed with the sound of falling trade barriers (destruction). (25 January 1994)

As we have seen in the discourse of other politicians such as Margaret Thatcher, the integration of contrast and antithesis with metaphors from specific domains such as health and disease, morality and immorality are an important strategy for heightening rhetorical effect by going to the extreme ends of a scale. The combination of hyperbolic contrast with creation and destruction metaphors for the purpose of evaluation is a salient and very persuasive characteristic of Clinton's rhetoric.

8.3.3 Metaphors for life, rebirth and death

Metaphors for life and rebirth account for a further 23 per cent of the metaphors in the corpus and also contrast positive with negative evaluations. Metaphors for life greatly outnumber metaphors for death – although these also occur in the corpus. A similar preference for life over death metaphors shows in a simple analysis of lexical frequency in the corpus; 'life' and 'live' occur a total of 153 times (once every 353 words) while 'death' and 'dead' occur a total of only 17 times (once every 3182 words). This finding is corroborated by other lexis such as 'new' and 'renew'; together these words occur 388 times (once every 139 words). As I have suggested in section 8.1, these frequencies imply that Clinton relies strongly on a discourse in which life and renewal are very central ideas. However, these metaphors are not unique to Clinton, as I have also described how Margaret Thatcher used a life and death contrast to describe the Conservative and Labour parties respectively. For Clinton, it is typically 'America' that is represented as being in need of 'renewal':

> And so tonight, let us resolve to continue the journey of renewal, to create more and better jobs, to guarantee health security for all, to reward welfare – work over welfare, to promote democracy abroad and to begin to reclaim our streets from violent crime and drugs and gangs *to renew our own American community.* (17 February 1993)

This example and the others cited in section 8.1 come from the early period of Clinton's presidency when there were clear rhetorical advantages in highlighting the novelty of a Democratic President.

Clinton also uses verbs such as 'seize' because they are in keeping with his image as a dynamic force acting swiftly to bring about improvements in the nation's fortunes. Although such uses could also be classified as creation metaphors, I chose to include them as 'life' metaphors. Examples include the following:

While America rebuilds at home, we will not shrink from the challenges nor fail to *seize the opportunities* of this new world. (20 January 1993)

After so many years of gridlock and indecision, after so many hopeful beginnings and so few promising results, Americans will be harsh in their judgements of us if we fail to *seize this moment*. (17 February 1993)

But if we're honest, we'll all admit that this strategy still cannot work unless we also give our people the education, training and skills they need *to seize the opportunities of tomorrow*. (27 January 1994)

This verb is often used to evaluate positively a government response to technological change and globalisation:

The new promise of the global economy, the Information Age, unimagined new work, life-enhancing technology – all these are ours *to seize*. (4 February 1997)

Other verb choices emphasise the life-generating effect that his policies will have on the economy:

Ports and airports, farms and factories will *thrive with trade and innovation and ideas*. (4 February 1997)

Together, we must make our economy *thrive* once again. (17 February 1993)

Given Hawkins's (2001: 34) claim that life and death constitute a fundamental scale for evaluation – with life symbolising everything positive and death symbolising everything that is negative – it is not surprising that Clinton also uses metaphors that refer in some way to the experience of death. These are generally adjectival compounds as italicised in the following:

We'll ask fathers and mothers to take more responsibility for their children. And we'll crack down on *deadbeat parents* who won't pay their child support. (17 February 1993)

Deadwood programs like mohair subsidies are gone. (24 January 1995)

If you know somebody who's caught in a *dead-end job* and afraid he can't afford the classes necessary to get better jobs for the rest of his life, tell him not to give up, he can go on to college. (27 January 1998)

If his policies are represented as a life force for the regeneration of American society, it follows that those negative social phenomena that they aim to change are depicted as a death force. At times the contrast between death and life – between the policies of the past and present administration – is made quite explicit:

Well, we did. We replaced *drift and deadlock with renewal and reform.* (17 February 1993)

And so today we pledge an end to the era of *deadlock and drift,* and a new season of *American renewal* has begun. (20 January 1993)

Here alliteration is combined with other features, such as metaphor blending, since a death metaphor is blended with a journey or path metaphor. It is interesting also to see how 'life' metaphors are used to sustain the myth of rebirth particularly in the period leading up to the new millennium in the year 2000:

We should challenge all Americans in the arts and humanities to join with their fellow citizens to make the year 2000 a national celebration of the American spirit in every community, a celebration of our common culture in the century that is past and in *the new one* to come in a *new* millennium so that we can remain the world's *beacon* not only of liberty but of *creativity* long after the *fireworks have faded.* (19 January 1999)

America is to be reborn and is heralded with images of religion, fire and creativity. What is interesting, though, is how skilfully Clinton represents himself and Hillary Clinton as the hero and heroine of this myth:

In that spirit, let us lift our eyes to the new millennium. How will we mark that passage? It just happens once every thousand years. This year, Hillary and I launched the White House Millennium Program to promote America's *creativity and innovation* and to preserve our heritage and culture into the 21st century. Our culture *lives* in every community, and every community has places of historic value that tell our stories as Americans. We should protect them. (19 January 1999)

Here there is a clear merging of the identity of 'Hillary and I' with American creativity and innovation. Given the tarnishing of his image by the Monica Lewinsky affair, it was important that Clinton was able to utilise the millennium celebrations to manage the impression of marital fidelity. Metaphors of rebirth, regeneration and creation are central rather than peripheral in the creation of a rhetoric of image restoration designed to overcome the sense of public outrage caused by his behaviour.

Clinton's choice of life metaphors is intended to invoke both a better past and divine approval as the basis for the regeneration of American society. His policies are contrasted with a social situation that is associated with death and with blockage. It is not surprising therefore that another important domain for metaphor is that of journeys.

8.3.4 Journey metaphors

Given that journey metaphors also occurred in the discourse of the other politicians analysed in earlier chapters, I became interested in how far they are used generically by politicians to communicate purposeful activity in the achievement of objectives and how far they are used in ways that are stylistically unique.

In the 1996 presidential campaign the Democrats were faced with the problem of ensuring that the TV networks covered both the Democratic convention and their presidential candidate. Their solution to this problem was for Clinton to travel across America by train; the associations of train were largely positive because they evoked America's past. This provided a powerful emotional link between past and present. Journeys in space evoked journeys in time and Clinton employs the journey frame to emphasise shared emotions of solidarity and collaboration across the divides of time and space. This shows in the collocation of journey metaphors with a reference to the nation or with a first-person plural pronoun:

> It has been too long – at least three decades – since a President has challenged Americans to join him on *our great national journey*, not merely to consume the bounty of today but to invest for a much greater one tomorrow. (20 January 1993)

> ... an idea infused with the conviction that *America's long, heroic journey* must go forever upward. (20 January 1993)

For all of us are on that same *journey of our lives*, and our journey, too, will come to an end. But the *journey of our America* must go on. (20 January 1997)

Clinton employs journey metaphors to create the idea of travelling in time in order to relate the present to an idealised version of America's past history – this is a more general spiritual aspiration than the specifically biblical one of Martin Luther King. Nostalgia is an effective rhetorical strategy because of its emotional resonance for Americans and because of the identification it creates between political leaders and their audiences. Clinton's campaign film-makers employed nostalgia to create an association with the progressive era of Theodore Roosevelt and also constantly replayed images of a handshake between J.F. Kennedy and the young Bill Clinton.

Journey metaphors are generally employed by politicians to conceptualise long-term purposes; in the case of Martin Luther King the link was with the journeys of the biblical past, while for Bill Clinton journeys were either nostalgic in tone or looking into the future. This is why, although Clinton's metaphors share a rhetorical resonance that emphasises the spiritual nature of the journey, these metaphors also combine with other metaphors for life, rebirth and renewal that imply forward movement in time:

And so tonight, let us resolve to continue the *journey of renewal*, to create more and better jobs, to guarantee health security for all, to reward welfare. (24 January 1994)

To all of you, I say, it is a *journey* we can only make together, *living* as one community. (27 January 1998)

This is the *heart* of our task. With a new vision of government, a *new* sense of responsibility, a *new* spirit of community, we will sustain *America's journey*.

The promise we sought in a *new* land we will find again in a land of *new* promise. (20 January 1997)

So what is distinctive about Clinton's journeys is that they represent the journey itself as a powerful regenerative experience: an experience of life and rebirth. This serves to create a strong positive evaluation. However, equally effectively, and again quite distinctively, he is able to contrast these purposeful regenerative journeys with other types of journeys that lack purpose and therefore are not regenerative. This is typically done through the use of images of slow and purposeless movement implied by the verb 'drift':

> We know we have to face hard truths and take strong steps, but we have not done so. Instead we *have drifted, and that drifting* has eroded our resources, fractured our economy, and shaken our confidence. (20 January 1993)

> For too long *we drifted without a strong sense of purpose*, responsibility or community, ... (20 January 1993)

> But for too long and in too many ways, that heritage was abandoned, and *our country drifted*. (24 January 1994)

In some instances this sense of purposeless movement is *contrasted* with the journey of renewal:

> And so today we pledge an end to the era of deadlock and *drift*, and a new season of American *renewal* has begun. (20 January 1993)

In other instances of negative evaluation, the metaphor highlights not simply movement that is slow and directionless but movement that ceases altogether; this is typically done through the use of the nominal form 'gridlock':

> After so many years of *gridlock and indecision*, after so many hopeful beginnings and so few promising results, ... (24 January 1994)

> And I want to thank every one of you here who heard the American people, who *broke gridlock*, who gave them the most successful teamwork between a president and a Congress in 30 years. (24 January 1994)

> Then our nation was gripped by economic distress, social decline, *political gridlock*. The title of a best-selling book asked: 'America: What Went Wrong?' (27 January 2000)

Lakoff and Johnson (1999: 188) would classify such metaphors using the submapping: the Suspension of Action is the Stopping of Movement. However, my analysis of metaphor in political discourse shows that there is a strong pragmatic and rhetorical motivation in Clinton's use of journey metaphors. This is to convey evaluations that comply systematically with the underlying myth of rebirth. It is this coherence and systematicity in metaphor use that characterise his rhetorical use of language to create the image of a purposeful and successful leader.

Journey metaphors describe a wide range of metaphor targets. For example, when the emphasis is on steady progress towards political objectives – perhaps based on a mapping 'Making Progress is Forward Movement' (ibid.: 191) – the most common choices of metaphor are words from the domain of walking such as 'step', particularly in the phrase 'step by step':

> But this is just the start of our journey. We must also *take the right steps* toward reaching our great goals. So I'm asking you that we work together. Let's *do it step by step*. (24 January 1995)

> Now, again I say to you, these are *steps, but step by step,* we can go a long way toward our goal of bringing opportunity to every community. (27 January 2000)

However, when the metaphor target is 'distance' from the attainment of political objectives the selection is of metaphors from the domain of car travel:

> But there is a *long, hard road ahead.* And *on that road* I am determined that I and our administration will do all we can to achieve a comprehensive and lasting peace for all the peoples of the region. (24 January 1994)

> We pursued a strategy of more police, tougher punishment, smarter prevention with crime-fighting partnerships, with local law enforcement and citizen groups, where *the rubber hits the road.* (27 January 1998)

Given that automobile travel is the most common in the USA, it is not surprising that Clinton uses this domain quite effectively to transfer knowledge of various aspects of road travel to the political domain. For example, we know that successful arrival at an unknown destination frequently requires use of a map:

> Within a decade, gene chips will offer *a road map* for prevention of illnesses throughout a lifetime. (27 January 1998)

> In 1992, we just *had a road map*; today, we have results. (27 January 2000)

The notion of a road map is a helpful reification for politicians because they can represent their policies as a guide for forward movement. Tony Blair has described his policy for progress in the Israeli–Palestinian conflict as a 'Road Map' for peace.[4] This choice of metaphor also fits with the more general use of journey metaphors to contrast remaining on a predetermined route and diverting from that route:

> Because we refused to *stray from that path*, we are doing something that would have seemed unimaginable seven years ago. We are actually paying down the national debt. (Applause.)

> Now, if *we stay on this path*, we can pay down the debt entirely in 13 years and make America debt-free for the first time since Andrew Jackson was President in 1835. (Applause.) (27 January 2000)

The idea of getting lost does not seem to be covered in Lakoff and Johnson's (1999) model in which Difficulties are conceptualized either as Impediments to Movement, Blockages, Features of the terrain, Burdens or as Counterforces (ibid.: 188–9). Evidently, the notion of maps and avoiding getting lost fits well with a political target in which a leader provides a set of policies that are then implemented. The leader takes society *towards* the realisation of predetermined objectives and is conceptualised as a guide. Metaphors of getting lost create the fear and uncertainty that help to create the social preconditions for leaders to emerge. As well as sounding right, journey metaphors are exploited in storytelling because the audience have rich schemata for journeys; this is one reason why they are generally appealing to politicians rather than stylistically unique.

There are other uses of journey metaphors in the discourse of Bill Clinton that are also fairly typical of political discourse. Aspects of political policy that are in reality the result of conscious political choices are represented as inevitable. An example of this is the role of technology in society. Invariably scientific and technological innovation is positively evaluated using journey metaphors; for example:

> Tonight, as part of our gift to the millennium, I propose a 21st Century research fund for *pathbreaking* scientific inquiry, the largest funding increase in history for the National Institutes of Health,

---

[4] See Semino (2008: 110ff.) for a detailed analysis of the road map metaphor.

the National Science Foundation, and the National Cancer Institute. (27 January 1998)

Technology is represented through the metaphorical use of the noun 'march' as something that is *given* rather than as something that is *chosen*:

> A third challenge we have is to keep this inexorable *march of technology* from giving terrorists and potentially hostile nations the means to undermine our defences. (27 January 2000)

> We should also offer help and hope to those Americans temporarily left behind with the global marketplace or by *the march of technology*, which may have nothing to do with trade. (27 January 1998)

> To accelerate the *march of discovery* across all these disciplines *in science and technology*, I ask you to support my recommendation of an unprecedented $3 billion in the 21st Century Research Fund, ... (27 January 2000)

'March' implies that the progress forwards is highly purposeful, orderly, swift and will inevitably lead to arrival at a predetermined destination. Imagine, for example, the difference had words such as 'stroll' or 'plod' been chosen in these contexts. This is of course a different way of conceptualising change from that implied by using 'shaped', since the noun 'march' implies that one either joins an army or is eliminated by it. What is interesting is how Clinton constructs technological change as something that is both inevitable and requires a positive evaluation. In this respect a significant metaphor, originating in the pre-industrial mode of travel by horse, is the verb 'harness':

> ... action to strengthen education and *harness the forces of technology* and science; ... (4 February 1997)

> To prepare America for the 21st century, *we must harness the powerful forces* of science and technology to benefit all Americans. (4 February 1997)

> We began the 20th century with a choice, *to harness the Industrial Revolution* to our values of free enterprise, conservation, and human decency. (20 January 1997)

The verb 'harness' evokes both nostalgic images and images of a powerful rider and I will discuss it further in the following chapter on Tony
Blair.[5]

8.3.5   Religious metaphors

Uses of words such as 'sacred', 'crusade' and 'faithful' in politics were
classified as metaphors from the domain of religion. I also included
'spirit' and 'mission' where they have a religious rather than a secular
sense. For example, in the following there are two uses of 'mission':

> In Bosnia and around the world, our men and women in uniform
> always do their *mission* well. Our *mission* must be to keep them well-
> trained and ready, to improve their quality of life, and to provide the
> 21st century weapons they need to defeat any enemy. (27 January
> 1998)

Neither use is classified as metaphor because there is no clear activation
of the religious sense as they refer to military and political tasks. Here
'mission' is treated as a synonym for a secular activity or 'task'. The
religious source implies the purity of intention since these metaphors
imply that political motives are religious ones:

> Though we march to the music of our time, our *mission is timeless.*
> (20 January 1993)

> The *preeminent mission* of our new government is to give all
> Americans an opportunity – not a guarantee, but a real opportunity –
> to build better lives. (20 January 1997)

The rhetorical objective of choosing words from the domain of religion is to enhance the ethos of the speaker because they imply that
political decisions are made on the basis of high principle rather than
crude self-interest. Religious belief has always been an acceptable pre-
text for political action in American politics. This can be traced back
historically to the early settlers and its presence in the wording of the
American constitution. As Wander (1990: 158) argues, morality has reg-
ularly been employed in political rhetoric designed to appeal to the
Protestant Establishment. We have already seen how effectively biblical

---

[5] See also Charteris-Black (2004: 53) for a discussion of 'harness' in relation to
'technology' and 'working people'.

218 Politicians and Rhetoric

knowledge was employed by Martin Luther King to construct a timeless present. The pragmatic effect of religious metaphors is to create a myth of political leadership as equivalent to spiritual guidance – in terms of the equivalence of principle on which both are presupposed. This entails a rejection of any clear-cut division of human motivation and behaviour into the secular and the sacred.

For Clinton, the principles he claims for political action are inherited from a historical lineage of politicians who share the same ideals. The inheritance of idealism from the past is most evident in the use of the word 'sacred':

> Posterity is the world to come, the world for whom we hold our ideals, from whom we have borrowed our planet, and to whom we bear *sacred responsibilities*. We must do what America does best, offer more opportunity to all and demand more responsibility from all. (20 January 1993)

> For we are the keepers of the *sacred trust* and we must be faithful to it in this new and very demanding era.

> More than stale chapters in some remote civic book they're still the virtue by which we can fulfil ourselves and reach our God-given potential and be like them. And also to fulfil the eternal promise of this country, the enduring dream from that first and *most-sacred covenant*. (24 January 1995)

Whereas Martin Luther King looked back to biblical history and the history of slavery, Clinton evokes a sense of historical destiny in which America's early political figures – the Pilgrim Fathers – were entrusted to sustain the religious principles that had led them to flee from religious persecution in Europe. It is this sense of historical awareness, originating as it did in religious belief, to which (along with many other presidents) he claims ownership. We can see how this reactivation of earlier ideals fits in closely with the notion of the myth of rebirth and renewal. Appeals to the religious motivation for altruistic behaviour support Clinton's claim to be renewing American idealism through activating resonant historical myths. By reducing the distance between politics and religion Clinton is claiming a spiritual authority for his actions – this is important as it creates himself as a leader with the potency to generate American spiritual revival.

Religious metaphors, therefore, fit well with other metaphor choices based on creation and rebirth; while for the purposes of analysis I have separated these metaphors into discrete categories, in practice they have a combined rhetorical effect on the audience. Choosing metaphors that send the same message, but from different directions, is an important skill of leadership because the effect is subtler and more difficult to detect and yet has a subliminal rhetorical impact of creating positive evaluations.

8.4 Metaphor diversity and everyday heroes

We can see from Appendix 12 that Clinton draws on a very wide range of source domains in his use of metaphor; a similar point could be made about the range of rhetorical objectives that are attained by metaphor. Metaphors from the domains of life, rebirth and creativity cast his policies in a positive light, those from the domain of journeys often evoke nostalgia, while those of religion focus on the ethos of trustworthiness and his credentials as a spiritual leader and evoke historical myths. In other cases the use of metaphor is persuasive in a different way, it is to establish himself as a normal American who shares the same interests, passions and outlook as any other 'normal' American male. This use of metaphor to create a familiar or 'laddish' contemporary image is perhaps most evident in his use of sports metaphors such as the following:

> Now those who commit crimes should be punished, and those who commit repeated violent crimes should be told when you commit a third violent crime, you will be put away and put away for good, *three strikes and you are out*. (24 January 1994)

> The people of this nation elected us all. They want us to be partners, not partisans. They put us all right here in the same boat. *They gave us all oars, and they told us to row*. Now, here is the direction I believe we should take. (4 February 1997)

> I think Senator Dole actually said it best. He said: '*This is like being ahead in the fourth quarter of a football game*; now is not the time to walk off the field and forfeit the victory.' (27 January 1998)

Here political issues are conceived in terms of baseball, running, rowing and American football – perhaps the key male national pastimes. Sports metaphors often have the effect of evoking associations with harmless, ordinary, though competitive, and generally male, behaviour. These instances are spread at different time intervals throughout the corpus and reflect a politician who is always keen to be identified with the ordinary American. It is a common ploy of American politicians; George W. Bush did not attempt to conceal the fact he was watching American football when he passed out after choking on a pretzel and Barack Obama incurred an injury playing basketball while serving as President. We can see this as a way of bridging the credibility gap between the heroic politician and the ordinary citizen by evoking contemporary areas of interest. In terms of rhetorical effect it is very similar to the common practice of completing State of the Union addresses by personalising heroism through the nomination of individuals who are present in the audience. This is a technique used extensively (though not exclusively) by Clinton:

> I'd like to give you one example. His name is Richard Dean. He is a 49-year-old Vietnam veteran who's worked for the Social Security Administration for 22 years now. Last year he was hard at work in the Federal Building in Oklahoma City when the blast killed 169 people and brought the rubble down all around him. He reentered that building four times. He saved the lives of three women. He's here with us this evening, and I want to recognize Richard and applaud both his public service and his extraordinary personal heroism. (23 January 1996)

Indeed, the heroes themselves can be sports heroes:

> You know sports records are made and sooner or later, they're broken. But making other people's lives better and showing our children the true meaning of brotherhood, that lasts forever. So for far more than baseball, Sammy Sosa, you're a hero in two countries tonight. Thank you. (19 January 1999)

Sometimes the same method of personal nomination and adulation refers to fallen heroes:

> And this October, a true American hero, a veteran pilot of 149 combat missions and one five-hour space flight that changed the world, will return to the heavens. Godspeed, John Glenn! (27 January 1998)

The notion of *everyday* heroes shows that part of the myth-making power of metaphor is to transform everyday individuals into heroic icons who can have the right stories told about them. By contrast, Clinton's use of sports metaphors transforms his image from the heroic to the status of an ordinary American. Therefore the rhetorical effect of metaphor contributes both to a myth making, but also to myth debunking.

8.5 Summary

In this chapter I have argued that rhetoric was a crucial means by which Clinton was able to create and restore an image of himself as a President and that metaphor contributed significantly to overcoming the scandals that characterised his presidency and therefore convincing the electorate that – in spite of appearances – he had the right intentions. I have suggested that metaphor – given its reliance on creating semantic tension – was the most powerful means by which Clinton communicated the tensions that characterised his political image. Parry-Giles and Parry-Giles (2002) identifies tensions between past and present, masculine and feminine, war and peace, black and white and between private and public. For example, in their analysis of the 1992 campaign film entitled *The Man from Hope*, they identify how – through personal reminiscences from a childhood that involved an alcoholic and abusive father – Clinton was able to manipulate his private life for public consumption. The intention here was to create a persona that was *accessible* to the electorate precisely *because of* its vulnerability. The authors make the important point that 'as they exhibit their intimate selves via television, they sacrifice the interpersonal distance that is necessary to perform the heroic dimensions of the presidency' (ibid.: 25). I propose that Clinton's uses of metaphor – in particular his use of metaphors of creation and metaphors of life and renewal – enabled him to restore his heroic image as President by telling a story about himself that convinced his hearers even if he had at times strayed from the path, underneath he always had the right intentions. I have represented this narrative conceptually as: GOOD GOVERNING IS CREATING. This metaphor frame enabled him to transcend the, at times, sordid details of his personal sexual behaviour and create an image of himself as an ethical leader who had the right intentions.

Clinton was also highly skilled in heightening emotional appeals by sounding right, through a narrative that would pull the heartstrings:

A compassionate empathetic leader who had risen from humble middle-class roots to the pinnacles of power and success because of hard work and intelligence. He overcame the hardships of a broken

home, domestic abuse, and alcoholism, and he brought to his political leadership an ability to 'feel the pain' of the average American.
(Parry-Giles and Parry-Giles 2002: 125)

Ultimately, Clinton's rhetorical skills made him highly persuasive: he
integrated having the right intentions, with sounding right. He told
the right story because the rhetorical contrasts of his metaphors corresponded with his personal psychological tensions and the electorate was
able to identify and empathise with these. In addition, he also looked
right. By combining the effects of his rhetorical resources with those of
his appearance and personal charm, he was able to turn situations that
would have destroyed other politicians to his own advantage, to become
eventually a charismatic statesman.

9
Tony Blair and Conviction Rhetoric

9.1 Background

In terms of legacy, Tony Blair will be remembered for his position on the international stage – one that was established through an interventionist foreign policy in the fashion of the late-Victorian Liberal Gladstone. Wherever there was wrong in the world – the Balkans, Sierra Leone or Iraq, like the superhero of an American comic story, Blair saw it as his destiny to get involved on the side of 'good'. Commitment to an ethical position was fundamental to Blair's self-representation and has continued to characterise his rhetorical style since the apparent failure of the war in Iraq – as measured in terms of lives lost and bodies maimed. In his 2010 autobiography he resisted any temptation to apologise for his decision to support George W. Bush in attacking Iraq by an appeal to ethos that follows a chain of journey-related metaphors (in italics):

> The difference between the TB (Tony Blair) of 1997 and the TB of 2007 was this: faced with this opposition across such a broad spectrum in 1997, I would have *tacked to get the wind back behind me.* Now I was not doing it. I was prepared to go full into it if I thought it was the only way *to get to my destination.* 'Being in touch' with opinion was *no longer the lodestar.* 'Doing what was right' had replaced it. (Blair 2010: 659)

This ethically self-righteous position was not one on which Blair was prepared to compromise. Rhetorically, he rejects the 'journey' metaphors that we will see characterised his time as leader of New Labour. His legacy is the claim that it was both right and necessary to topple Saddam Hussein: to engage in 'regime' change. It is unlikely that his critics would have thought any better of him had he done otherwise by apologising in his autobiography – persuading and apologising being two different speech acts.

What is the origin of the moral certainty that underlay this self-righteousness? I would suggest that the answer is in the psychology of a man whose response to a shift in family fortunes from a position of security to insecurity was to adopt a firmly Christian morality. When he was only 11 years old his father had suffered a devastating stroke. His sister was struck by Still's disease – a severe form of infantile rheumatoid arthritis – and his grandmother lived with the family after she developed Alzheimer's disease. As a result his mother was largely occupied with family matters and unable to give a great deal of time to the son whom she adored. In spite of these difficulties, he obtained a second-class degree at Oxford, passed the Bar exams and used the combination of a youthful appearance, personal charm and self-effacing manner to forge a successful career in the Labour Party. But during these times he also acquired very strong religious beliefs that continued to motivate him throughout his political career. Although these beliefs had always been covert when in power, once he had retired from a leadership role he swiftly converted to Roman Catholicism – something his political judgement would have prevented him from doing while serving as Prime Minister.

Tony Blair viewed the biggest Tory mistake of recent times as the deposing of Margaret Thatcher (interview in the *Fettesian*, December 1991). This is because he realised how successfully she had developed a personality cult based on certainty and aggression and this is something that ultimately – in spite of appearances of consensus – his rhetoric sought to emulate. According to his biographer Rentoul, Blair also 'marked well how she (Thatcher) used language to identify her "common sense" with popular values' (2001: 276). As he aged, Blair dropped the meek and diffident manner of his youth to become a preacher-politician employing what I will describe as Conviction Rhetoric. His period as the pre-eminent political figure in British history will be remembered for this ambivalence of consensus and conflict, of the lamb and the wolf.

In this chapter I first look at some general characteristics of his rhetorical style – his ability to sound right – at times through hesitancy and informality while at others through a Conviction Rhetoric that communicated opinions defining what was right and wrong in no uncertain terms. I will then examine how metaphor systematically contributed to his ability to tell a story that was right because it was grounded in beliefs about 'good' and 'evil' and formed powerful myths of creation and destruction.

9.2 Blair, communication and leadership

A vital component of Blair's success as a political leader was his style of communication; this was based on a fundamental understanding of the importance of constructing messages that are persuasive in modern communication media. As McNair (2003: 149) argues:

> ...Tony Blair was elected largely because of his perceived ability to look and sound good for the cameras, and to communicate, with this image, to the electorally crucial voters of southern England. Nick Jones argues that Blair was indeed the first UK party leader to have been chosen for his ability to say 'only what he wanted to say and what he believed to be true'.

His understanding of the contemporary media communication principles such as brevity, clarity and simplicity shows in an article for *The Times* newspaper in 1988:

> Our news today is instant, hostile to subtlety or qualification. If you can't sum it up in a sentence, or even a phrase, forget it. Combine two ideas or sentiments together and mass communication will not repeat them, it will choose between them. To avoid misinterpretation, strip down a policy or opinion to one key clear line before the media does it for you. Think in headlines. (In Rentoul 2001: 146)

Message content and style, policy and presentation, are so subtly blended in Blair's discourse that one is never quite sure which one is responding to. He was always an exponent of the 'sound bite'; as Jones (1996: 27) argues:

> Effective political communication has always relied on easily understood slogans and phrases aimed at promoting and justifying the policy decisions of governments and their opponents. Radio, and subsequently television, provided politicians with an opportunity to explain their objectives to a mass audience in a personal and

friendly way … Therefore the most important point in any speech, broadcast or interview has to be delivered briskly and summarised as concisely as possible. Politicians want the public to remember their punch line.

However, Blair's rhetoric relies on more than just sound bites alone, the essence of his ability to persuade lies in the ability to integrate ethos – having the right intentions – with pathos – sounding right – and even if he did not always look right, he looked better than Gordon Brown and was able to tell the right story. Together these create the image of a sentient moral being who is touch with the morality of ordinary people.

This new style of communication was in direct contrast to that of the Labour Opposition during the period of Margaret Thatcher's domination. In 'Old' Labour discourse there was a divergence between the discourse of party politics and the discourse of ordinary people. New Labour responded to developments in American political discourse:

> Blair noticed the parallels with the lessons the Democrats learnt in the United States, where David Kusnet, later a speechwriter for president Clinton, wrote a book called *Speaking American*, about how the Democrats needed to use language which helped persuade ordinary voters that the party shared their basic values. Blair knew, through bitter personal experience, the Labour Party has been just as bad at 'Speaking English'. (Rentoul 2001: 276)

The content of his policy and the persuasive discourse in which it has been communicated are based on reason and simplicity. For example, his view that party members (rather than MPs alone) should also be involved in the election of the party leader was based on the reasonable claim that all Labour Party members are equal. This was communicated by simple repetition in the phrase: 'one member one vote' and this became the sound bite for those seeking reform in leadership selection. Another very successful sound bite was 'Tough on crime, tough on the causes of crime'. The emphasis on simplicity and slogans has influenced Conservative rhetoric, with his Tory successor coining the slogan 'The Big Society' to refer to civic engagement.

While avoiding the deficiencies of earlier Labour Party rhetoric, Blair was also quick to learn from the Conservatives. *Marxism Today* suggested that Blair's communication style reflected Margaret Thatcher's influence. One way he did this was by expressing points of view that reflected popular opinion and he developed an informal style by using familiar colloquial phrases such as:

> We didn't revolutionise British economic policy – Bank of England independence, tough spending rules – for some managerial reason or as *a clever wheeze to steal Tory clothes*. (2 October 2001)

> Do not fall for the right wing nonsense that the extra money so far *has been poured down the drain*. (22 February 2002)

The use of these colloquial phrases in a political speech indicated a register downshift. 'Stealing someone's clothes' seems to originate in the world of clever wheezes of the English public schools – that of the then fashionable Harry Potter. 'Down the drain' draws on the everyday experience of disposing of waste materials while also linking into the negative connotation associated in cognitive linguistics with downwards orientation (e.g. 'feeling down', 'down in the dumps', 'a downer'). What is interesting is that the use of everyday expressions – those that might be used between colleagues or friends in informal settings – occurred in the traditionally formal register of a political speech. Fairclough (2000: 7) has commented on this in relation to Blair's statement on Princess Diana's death:

> But threaded into this conventional public language is a more personal language (Blair begins speaking for himself, in the first person singular, and about his own feelings) and a more vernacular language. It is as if Blair (with his advisers – the speech has been attributed to Alistair Campbell) had started with the official form of words, then personalised and informalised it … and part of the power of his style is his ability to combine formality and informality, ceremony and feeling, publicness and privateness.

We should recall that television often involves close-up shots of the speaker and seems to open the way for a more intimate style of discourse. I would like to suggest that this shift towards informal discourse in the use of everyday phraseology is a characteristic of the personalised discourse style that has been developed by Tony Blair – specifically for television broadcasting. It implies a covert positive evaluation by placing the speaker as a member of the same group as the audience. By speaking the same language as the electorate Blair reduces the rhetorical distance between himself and the mass audience he aims to reach. What is significant in his register choice is that, even when speaking to a party conference audience, he does so in a language that mirrors popular conversational norms rather than those of the political class. I suggest that the use of register-shifting to legitimise his policies is his unique innovation in political speaking.

9.3   Blair and the rhetoric of legitimisation: the epic battle between good and evil

A number of commentators have noted Blair's predilection for what I have described as ethical discourse (Charteris-Black 2004: Ch. 3). For example *The Times'* Parliamentary observer Matthew Parris commented:

> Scan his abstract nouns and you will sniff a curious blend of the pulpit and school assembly. The vocabulary is of trust and honour; of compassion, conviction, vocation; of humanity, integrity, community, morality, honesty and probity; of values, standards; faiths; and beliefs. (*The Times*, 2 June 1995)

Analysis of Tony Blair's speeches indicates how contrasting ethical terms such as right and wrong, good and evil are used in conjunction with metaphors, and this is a general characteristic of New Labour discourse (Fairclough 2000: 37ff.). In response to public concern over the influence of special advisers in 2003, Tony Blair announced the appointment of an 'ethics adviser' to investigate ministerial sleaze.

As a young man Blair had kept his strong Christian beliefs largely to himself; while living the life of would-be pop star and music promoter, this aspect of his personality was largely covert. It was not until he joined the Christian Socialist Movement in June 1992 that he effectively 'came out' as a Christian and only much later that he came out as a Catholic. Blair's underlying moral perspective is evident in his 1995 Labour Party conference address:

> It is a moral purpose to life, as to values, a belief in society, in co-operation. It is how I try to live my life; the simple truths. I am worth no more that any other man, I am my brother's keeper, I will not walk by on the other side. We aren't simply people set in isolation from each other, face to face with eternity, but members of the same family, community, the same human race. This is my socialism.

This was a clear rejection of the values implied by Margaret Thatcher when she claimed that 'There is no such thing as society'. There is certainly extensive evidence in the corpus I collected on Blair of the importance of morality and ethics; words associated with these occur with the following frequency:

right – 95
value – 74
justice – 61
good – 40
equal – 39
commitment – 19
fair – 19
wrong – 15
bad – 13
evil – 13
mission – 12
honest – 9
TOTAL 390

Blair employs a word from the domain of ethics and morality at least once every 128 words in his speeches.[1] If we compare the frequency of the same words in the Thatcher corpus we find that the total occurrence is 271 times – or once every 183 words. The only words in the above list that occur more frequently in the Thatcher sample are 'good' and 'fair'; however, 'value' occurs four times more frequently in the Blair corpus, and 'justice' and 'evil' occur six times more frequently. This seems to confirm the impression that ethical discourse is a particular characteristic of Tony Blair. As Rose argues, the use of ethical language is very much in keeping with prevalent social values at the end of the twentieth century:

> Ethico-politics ... concerns itself with the self-techniques necessary for responsible self-government and the relations between one's obligation to oneself and one's obligations to others ... Ethico-politics has a particular salience at the close of the 20th century. For it appears that somehow 'we' – the subjects of advanced liberal democracies – in the absence of any objective guarantees for politics or our values, have become obliged to think ethically. Hence it is likely to be on the

---

[1] In a similar analysis of the 2001 Labour Party conference speech I found an ethical word once every 50 words (cf. Charteris-Black 2004: 59).

terrain of ethics that our most important political disputes will have to be fought for the forseeable future. (Rose 1999: 188)

As Rose goes on to comment in relation to 'practices for ethical self-formation':

... these practices and techniques that take up and disseminate the idea that the consumer is an ethical citizen; consumers can and should consciously seek to manage themselves and their conduct in an ethical fashion according to principles that they have chosen for themselves. (Rose 1999: 191)

Therefore Blair's rhetoric is based on the underlying idea that POLITICS IS ETHICS. In order to create value in a marketplace of ethics there is a need to make bold rhetorical contrasts between right and wrong, between good and evil. Blair positions himself as an active agent in this market by communicating ethical ideas using conflict metaphors as if conflict is a necessary precondition for the pursuit of high ethical standards. Moral contrasts pave the way for a Conviction Rhetoric that draws its rhetorical force from conflict with those who have different moral and ethical interpretations. For example, the war against Iraq was morally and ethically justified for Blair (and many Iraqi exiles) because of the inherent evil of Saddam Hussein and his policies. Yet for many others it was wrong because it entailed the maiming and death of thousands of Iraqis who had had little personal choice in whether or not they were combatants. The debate is over whether the ends justifies the means; for Blair they evidently did, but for much of the rest of the international community, as well as for the majority of the British public, they did not, and at the time of writing – nearly eight years after the Iraq War had supposedly ended – yet another tribunal is questioning the legality of the decision to embark on war.

The communication of moral and ethical ideas employing conflict metaphors implies a conceptual metaphor MORALITY IS CONFLICT; for Blair values are something that need to be fought for:

So this is a battle of values. Let's have that battle but not amongst ourselves. The real fight is between those who believe in strong public services and those who don't. That's the fight worth having. (2 October 2001)

These are values that every Labour leader from Keir Hardie onwards would recognise. Scottish values. British values. Labour values. Values that are worth fighting for. (22 February 2002)

One danger in using language originally from the domain of conflict to describe Labour Party policies was that metaphors became literal descriptions of policy in relation to the Balkans, Afghanistan and Iraq. In these scenarios the language of conflict in relation to moral values provided the basis for actual military conflict. Therefore, the two conceptual metaphors POLITICS IS ETHICS and MORALITY IS CONFLICT reflect a crusading mentality in which there is a religious basis for military engagement:

> What began as *a moral crusade* is now also the path to prosperity. (26 September 2000)

In logical terms, if political decisions are conceptualised as moral decisions and moral decisions entail conflict, then it follows that political decisions also entail conflict. This produces exactly the same concept framework that I have described in relation to Margaret Thatcher's political discourse. This was communicated using the same integration of conflict metaphors with ethical antitheses. In ideological terms Tony Blair has developed a Conviction Rhetoric that Margaret Thatcher initiated in the creation of a marketplace of ethics. Significantly, Blair claims to actually take a personal satisfaction in political conflict:

> We are in a fight and it's a fight I relish. For it is a fight for the future, the heart and the soul of our country. A fight for fairness. A fight for jobs. A fight for our schools. A fight for our hospitals. A fight for a new vision in which the old conflict between prosperity and social justice is finally banished to the history books in which it belongs. (26 September 2000)

The danger of using metaphors of conflict to describe moral and political beliefs is that it blurs the boundaries between target and source domains of metaphor. When Blair uses words from the lexicon of morality and conflict together it is not clear whether he is talking about *morality in terms of conflict* or about *conflict in terms of morality*. The danger of this lack of precision is that it blurs the hypothetical world of metaphor with the reality-orientated world of literal language – although it may sound as if he has the right intentions, it does not necessarily imply that he was thinking right. This is because it can lead to a lack of a clear grasp of how moral beliefs can in any way be *separate from* politics and can lead to a position in which ethical struggles between good and bad entail that it is right to engage in actual physical conflict. Blair's blurring of the boundary between issues of Church and issues of state – between religious ideals and secular realities – is revealed by analysis of his language and the underlying myths and metaphors that are found there.

The myth that supported Blair's Conviction Rhetoric was the most basic of all myths – that of the struggle between good and evil. In this myth, Blair, and those who are 'on-message', are represented as agents of good involved in a struggle against the forces of evil. We can analyse this by identifying shifts in what Blair refers to as 'evil'; prior to 11 September 2001, various forms of social injustice and its causes were 'evil':

> Crime, anti-social behaviour, racial intolerance, drug abuse, destroy families and communities. They destroy the very respect for others on which society is founded. They blight the life chances of thousands of young people and the quality of life of millions more. Fail to *confront this evil* and we will never build a Britain where everyone can succeed. (26 September 2000)

However, subsequently, it was terrorism in general that came to embody 'evil':

> This mass terrorism is the new evil in our world today. It is perpetrated by fanatics who are utterly indifferent to the sanctity of life and we, the democracies of this world, are going to have to come together and fight it together and *eradicate this evil* completely from our world. (11 September 2001)

Subsequently, the 'regime' (not 'government') of Saddam Hussein was cast as 'evil':

> Looking back over 12 years, we have been victims of our own desire to placate the implacable, to persuade towards reason the utterly unreasonable, to hope that there was some genuine intent to do good in a regime *whose mind is in fact evil*. (18 March 2003)

The personification of evil had shifted from Osama Bin Laden (once he had evaded his would-be captors) to Saddam Hussein. The link was made by historical association with earlier embodiments of evil:

There's a lot of it about but remember when and where this alliance was forged: here in Europe, in World War II when Britain and America and every decent citizen in Europe joined forces to liberate Europe from *the Nazi evil*. (1 October 2002)

We may notice that Blair gives an epic dimension to his own political action since the ability to classify certain political entities as 'evil' implies moral authority on the part of the speaker. The identity of the evil enemy may transmute over time – indeed from his theological perspective he may believe that evil is elusive and shifting by its very nature; however, Blair creates a role for himself in this epic narrative as a prophetic agent of the forces of good. There are dangers in employing epic myths to produce a discourse of ethics:

> It is all too easy for all this talk about ethics to become merely a recoding of strategies of social discipline and morality. That is to say, political strategies which prioritize the ethical reconstruction of the citizen seem almost inescapably to try to propagate a code which once again justifies itself by reference to something that is natural, given, obvious, uncontestable: the virtues of work, the importance of family, the need for individual responsibility to be shown by respect for the basic contours of the existing state of affairs. Apart from its other difficulties, such a moralizing ethico-politics tends to incite a 'will to govern' which imposes no limits upon itself. (Rose 1999: 192)

Blair did not conceal his 'will to govern' and to lead New Labour to a third election victory; however, there have been a number of negative consequences of his desire to impose his own moral view on the rest of mankind. Fairclough (2000: 40–1) notes an association between moral and authoritarian discourses particularly in relation to youth crime. We may recall the intended on-the-spot fines for young offenders (soon after his own son was discovered drunk on the streets by police). Then there was the requirement for parents to sign a reading pledge and most recently a proposal to fine parents £100 for taking their children on family holidays during school time. These policies confused minor issues and took their motivation from the American concept of 'zero tolerance'. Tony Blair competed with official state sources for ethics and morality such as the High Court and the Archbishop of Canterbury; the ethical legitimisation implied by Conviction Rhetoric concealed a will to govern.

9.4   Metaphor analysis

The corpus on Tony Blair totalled approximately 50,000 words and comprised the 14 speeches as shown in Appendix 13. A close analysis revealed a total of 295 metaphors or one every 169 words – a little less frequent than in the Clinton corpus – and four major metaphor types: journeys, conflict, personification and reification. Reification was further subdivided according to whether the process was creative, destructive or neutral. Neutral evaluation in fixed phrases was an important category because such patterning is a strategy of rhetorical positioning by register-shift. While Tony Blair had a preference for journey metaphors he was not over-reliant on any single source domain for metaphor and his discourse was characterised by variety in depth. The findings of the analysis of source domains of metaphor are summarised in Appendix 14, and as conflict metaphors have already been discussed the following discussion focuses on journey metaphors and reifications.

9.4.1   Journey metaphors

Since the attempt to restart the Middle East peace process that followed September 11th was labelled by Blair as 'The Road Map', it is not surprising that journeys are the most productive source domain in the corpus, accounting for 25 per cent of all metaphors. The path schema has been a highly productive source domain of metaphor for the politicians examined so far. As with other politicians such as Martin Luther King, Bill Clinton or Margaret Thatcher, these metaphors are evidence of the conceptual metaphor LONG-TERM PURPOSEFUL ACTIVITIES ARE JOURNEYS. Underlying my analysis of this type of metaphor was the question of how far Blair's use of journey metaphors is similar to, or differs from, that of the other politicians. In some cases he employs familiar journey metaphors such as *path, route, step, destination*, etc. One characteristic that he shares with Bill Clinton is his use of nominal phrases in which 'journey' is qualified by a post-modifier:

> That will not complete the *journey of renewal* for the NHS, but it will take us a long way towards our destination. (22 March 2000)

> We are on a *journey of renewal*. Before us lies a path strewn with the challenges of change. (26 September 2000)

> This party's strength today comes from the *journey of change* and learning we have made. (2 October 2001)

In Opposition, Labour was trying to escape policies we didn't believe in. It was a *journey of conviction*. (1 October 2002)

This is not the time to abandon our *journey of modernisation* but to see it through. (1 October 2002)

In these cases Blair's 'journeys' refer primarily to the processes of change associated with the modernising programme of New Labour; after the initial objective of improving party democracy, this focused on two major areas of policy: education and health. Phrases such as 'journey of change' and 'journey of renewal' highlight the worthiness of the motive for the journey. In the phrase 'journey's end' (four occurrences in the corpus), there is also a focus on the worthiness of the journey's outcome – rather than on the journey itself. This signifies Blair's concern with the measurement of results within the fixed time span of a government and, perhaps, with his own place in history. Blair never seems quite to believe that his luck will last and the journey's end is probably the next appeal to the electorate on which the will to govern relies in democracies.

We have seen in the previous chapter how the metaphor of 'harnessing' was popular for Bill Clinton and drew on the nostalgic domain of travel by horse. My analysis of the 1997 election manifesto shows how it is typically working people and technology that are 'harnessed' in New Labour discourse (Charteris-Black 2004: 53–4). Because they are both conceptualised as being in need of control, this is a rhetorical strategy by which Blair communicates his will to govern:

A plan to *harness new technology* to spread prosperity to all. (26 September 2000)

... a world in which a civil war in one country can lead to mass migration in an entire continent; a world in which a bunch of terrorists can *harness the good of aviation*, modern architecture, mass communication, and turn it into an evil that terrorises not just the US but the entirety of civilisation. (22 February 2002)

'Harness' implies a compromise between something that will 'progress' anyway and something that can be controlled by a human agent. Lakoff and Johnson (1999: 193) discuss such as follows:

... historical images that are preserved through cultural mechanisms (movies showing runaway horses, often pulling buckboards and stagecoaches) can be preserved in the live conceptual system. In this case the issue is the control of external events conceptualized as large moving entities that can exert force on you. Here those entities are horses, which can be controlled with strength, skill, and attention, but which otherwise, get out of control. This special case thus focuses on external events that are subject to control, but require strength, skill, and attention if that control is to be exerted.

I propose that use of the verb 'harness' is motivated by a will to govern in which the political leader is construed as strong and skilful, and in control of making decisions about external forces of technological change. This is a very effective component of political myth because it encourages the public to rely on valiant leaders who are able to make the decisions necessary to ensure their well-being. What is interesting is that Blair shows a flexible adaptation of the journey metaphor to provide an evaluation of whatever policy he is describing – generally this is a positive evaluation that invites acceptance of change, modernisation and reform. However, he also exploits the metaphor to provide a negative evaluation of counter-policies as in:

Theirs is a *journey of convenience* and it fools no-one least of all themselves. (1 October 2002)

Evidently, then, Blair's use of journey metaphors – while showing many similarities with that of other politicians – is typically phraseological. This preference for coining phrases that appear to have the ring of truth – 'journey of change', 'journey's end', 'harnessing new technology', etc. – creates the illusion that he is drawing on a common stock of popular knowledge. The use of familiar metaphors rooted in the language of popular imagery is in fact an important rhetorical component of the Conviction Rhetoric.

9.4.2 Blair and reification

The most characteristic type of metaphor employed by Blair was reification; as we have seen in the previous chapter, this is a type of metaphor in which mental states and processes are represented as if they were material ones. It was Blair's way of explaining abstract political, economic and social policies using words that refer to tangible things; one effect is to make these abstract processes more intelligible. It is persuasive because it is a covert linguistic process, as the substitution of nouns for verbs conceals the fact that a metaphor is being used in the first place. A rejection of these policies could only be countered by a rejection of the metaphor on which they are based. This is all the more difficult since the metaphor is not overt and therefore its rejection could only come through in-depth analysis of linguistic uses. Blair used reification as a way of presenting political arguments as grounded in right thinking.

I agree with Rentoul that the presence of metaphors of creation and destruction in Tony Blair's discourse may be partially attributed to the influence of Bill Clinton and the Democratic Party:

> It was not until his visit to the United States in January 1993 that anything resembling a 'great movement' became evident, as Blair suddenly gained a sense of perspective, and acquired a language in which to express his latent 'social moralism', a set of beliefs which were to provide him with a distinctive platform for the leadership of the Labour Party. (Rentoul 2001: 195)

However, this point of view suggests that the primary influence has been in relation to a communication strategy rather than to an actual policy:

> Blair did not simply transplant an ideology from America. He used the similarities between the ideas of the modernisers on both sides of the Atlantic in order to apply some of the Democrats' vivid language to a body of ideas which he had already largely developed. (ibid.: 197)

Blair drew on the American Democrats to develop a discourse in which political arguments are based on a claim that the intentions were right.

Reifications can be subdivided into those that refer to creative and destructive acts. However, unique to Blair is an additional category that I have termed neutral reification; this is where the evaluation itself is highly covert and embedded in a style of phraseology. I will consider the first two types now and the third later in the chapter.

9.4.2.1   *Creation and life metaphors*
Reifications from the source domain of creation and life highlight creative processes, or swift and decisive action. There was an implication of creativity in the renaming of the party as 'New Labour' and this is reflected in the frequent occurrence of 'new' and 'renew' in the Blair corpus. These words are also reminiscent of Clinton's discourse. For example, 'new' and 'renew' occur 207 times in the Blair corpus – this compares with a total of 388 occurrences in the Clinton corpus; 'create'

occurs 22 times in the Blair corpus as compared with 50 times in the Clinton corpus. Following the GOOD GOVERNING IS CREATING conceptual metaphor, the typical use of 'create' is as a positive evaluation of a policy initiated by New Labour:

> Not every Labour government has *created jobs* in record numbers. But this week we announced the strongest job growth for three years. (28 February 2003)

> It is this Government that *created the minimum wage* and equal pay, new rights to work, new rights for part time as well as full time workers, new rights for women workers. (28 February 2003)

We will recall the high frequency of the collocation 'create new jobs' in the discourse of Bill Clinton. The New Labour government and its youthful leader are not the only forces that are referred to as agents of creation – even globalisation itself can be:

> It is true we currently face a difficult economic environment; *globalisation creates constant challenges*. (15 February 2003)

This is an interesting example of how the positive evaluations of a word can be used to communicate a covert message – here a strong positive evaluation of globalisation. We may inquire what *human* agents are concealed under the abstract notion of 'globalisation' and recall that the effect of the decisions of these human agents may be to make people's skills redundant. Evaluation of globalisation as a creative force implies complicity with the motives, aims and ideology of the covert agents of economic change.

In other cases we are reminded closely of Clinton's use of verbs that refer to creative processes; these include *build* (33 occurrences) and *shape* (4). When 'build' is used in the Blair corpus, the noun in object position invariably refers to an aspect of New Labour policy that is positively evaluated – typically, this is some type of alliance based on identification of a common outlook:

> But reaching out to the Muslim world also means engaging with how those countries move towards greater democratic stability, liberty and human rights. It means *building pathways of understanding* between Islam and other religious faiths. (7 January 2003)

From the same domain of building there are other creative reifications of this type in the use of words such as 'foundations' or 'framework':

> So I do not claim Britain is transformed. I do say the *foundations of a New Britain are being laid.* (28 September 1999)

> Sixth, we need to *construct a better framework* within which the international institutions, like the IMF and World Bank, help countries deal with their difficulties and make progress... Britain has the political and intellectual capacity to help create this framework. (7 January 2003)

What is interesting about the use of creation terms is that they are always rather vague and imprecise in terms of actual reference: it seems at times as if 'building a framework' or 'laying the foundations' simply refers to positively evaluated *intentions* rather than *actual* political achievements. A similar rather loose positive evaluation is found in other words that also characterised Bill Clinton's discourse; for example, consider the use of 'shape' and 'craft' in the following:

> Of the institutions and alliances that will *shape our world* for years to come. (18 March 2003)

> The point is that unless there is real energy put into *crafting a process* that can lead to lasting peace, neither the carnage of innocent Israelis nor the appalling suffering of the Palestinians will cease. (7 January 2003)

They evaluate various policy initiatives as creative but they are not verbs that specify the nature of political action; this reflects in the absence of any apparent agent for these verbs: it is not clear precisely *who* will do the shaping or the crafting (cf. Fairclough 2000: 35). This lack of specificity reflects in the use of 'process' – it is not 'peace' that will be crafted but *a process that can lead to peace.* This seems to place the end result a stage further removed from the action of a political agent. In other cases the associations of verbs from the domain of life positively evaluate the subject of the verb as in the following:

> And if we wanted to, we could breathe new life into the Middle East Peace Process and we must. (2 October 2001)

Here the Middle East is represented as an ailing patient or victim who passively awaits resuscitation by an active and dynamic life force. Blair's choice of verbs, then, either conceals or enhances the status of the political leader. There is further evidence of this type of metaphor in words that were classified in the analysis of Clinton as metaphors relating to the domain of life and rebirth; these include the dynamic verbs *grasp* and *seize*:

So we should *grasp the moment* and move, not let our world slip back into rigidity. We need boldness, grip and follow through. (13 November 2001)

The starving, the wretched, the dispossessed, the ignorant, those living in want and squalor from the deserts of Northern Africa to the slums of Gaza, to the mountain ranges of Afghanistan: they too are our cause. This is a *moment to seize*. (2 October 2001)

So let us *seize the chance* in this time, to make a difference. Future generations will thank us if we do; and not forgive us if we fail. (13 November 2001)

It is no coincidence that Clinton and Blair both considered themselves as young and dynamic leaders of their parties and this reflects in the choice of verbs that are associated with quick reflexes. It is also an interesting reversal of polarity since in other contexts *seize* can have a negative connotation; for example:

And let the oil revenues – which *people falsely claim we want to seize* – be put in a Trust fund for the Iraqi people administered through the UN. (15 February 2003)

Iraq is a wealthy country that in 1978, the year before *Saddam seized power*, was richer than Portugal or Malaysia.Today it is impoverished, 60% of its population dependent on Food Aid. (15 February 2003)

This reversal of polarity is an indication of how New Labour can create new uses of language by activating an alternative area of a word's semantic field so as to develop fresh associations. The rhetorical goal of the legitimisation of policy that is inherent in the will to govern leads to linguistic innovation. However, there is also a danger in the use of metaphors of creation and rebirth that is noted by Blair's most critical biographer, Leo Abse:

The myth of renewal and rebirth is a dangerous ploy to introduce into politics. It is the myth which some historians, notably Roger Griffen, have described as the palingenetic myth. Etymologically, the term palingenesis, derived from *palin* (again, anew) and *genesis* (creation and birth), refers to the sense of a new start or regeneration after a phase or a crisis of decline. It is precisely that myth, when it has invaded politics of 20th century Europe, notably in Nazi Germany, that has wreaked havoc. (Abse 2001: 146)

We will recall from section 2.2.2 how Margaret Thatcher used life metaphors to support her policies for urban renewal through free enterprise and the Falklands War; therefore creation and life metaphors may be readily adapted for purposes of legitimisation in right- or centre-left-wing political rhetoric.

9.4.2.2 Metaphors of destruction and death

Many negative reifications in the corpus are verbs whose literal senses refer to a degree of force that will cause material damage. Blair – like Clinton – uses a number of verbs such as *root out, stamp out, scourge, strip* and *shatter* – as in the following:

Today world events can lift or shatter that confidence. (13 November 2001)

At times, verbs that imply a degree of physical force or even violence can take on a positive evaluation when their object is something that is negatively evaluated – and therefore which it is beneficial to 'break':

We must strip away barriers to enterprise, encourage venture capital, promote technology and above all invest in education and skills. (22 February 2002)

We know, also, that there are groups or people, occasionally states, who trade the technology and capability for such weapons. It is time this trade was exposed, disrupted, and stamped out. (14 September 2001)

Conceptually this shows a reversal of the metaphor GOOD GOVERNING IS CREATING to produce GOOD GOVERNING IS DESTROYING; this is the case when the entity that is destroyed is something negative such as 'barriers' or the illegal weapons trade. This reversal indicates a switch from positive self-representation to negative representation of opponents. This semantic switch is a powerful weapon of metaphor in the hands of the skilled rhetorician, because aggressive words activate an emotional response and allow positive evaluation of the expression of powerful feelings. Words expressing Conviction Rhetoric can be combined with other powerful images in which there are strong contrasts of connotation between the positive and negative poles:

> The war against terrorism is not just a police action to *root out* the networks and those who protect them, although it is certainly that. It needs to be a series of political actions designed to remove the conditions under which *such acts of evil can flourish* and be tolerated. (13 November 2001)

This reversal of polarity of words from the domain of physical force, and even violence, constitutes the will to govern of the 'Third Way' – unlike the pacifist or neutralist orientation of 'Old' Labour, New Labour is prepared to take the angel's cause in a dynamic and interventionist fashion. The Conviction Rhetoric of New Labour is reflected semantically by the adoption of words that may be associated with fascism because they imply the use of force; for example: *seize, strip away, expose,* etc. The regeneration of New Labour is therefore characterised by the adoption and appropriation of lexis typically associated with right-wing leaders for what are apparently left-wing objectives such as social equality. As Abse goes on to comment:

> Repeatedly we have witnessed, during the Second World War, and in pre- and post-war Europe the Fascist vision of a new vigorous nation growing out of the destruction of an old system... All these fascisms offered, and continue to proffer, regeneration; they promise to replace gerontocracy, mediocrity and national weakness with youth, heroism and national greatness, to bring into existence a New Man in an exciting new world in place of the senescent, played-out one that existed before. (Abse 2001: 149)

As with fascist discourse, Blair's contrasts metaphors of violence, destruction and death with metaphors of creation and rebirth to maximise rhetorical tension. Consider the following metaphor combinations:

> ... so that people everywhere can see the chance of a better future through the hard work and *creative power* of the free citizen, not the *violence and savagery* of the fanatic. (2 October 2001)

Then, in a speech that became known by its coda: 'We are at our best when we are boldest', in which he needed to win over a party conference that was potentially hostile because of his position of support for the USA in the proposed war on Iraq:

> ... the purpose is not just to *undermine the government*, but to *undermine Government*, to *destroy the belief* that we can collectively achieve anything, to *drench progress* in cynicism, *to sully the hope* from which energy, action and *change all spring*. (1 October 2002)

And finally in his statement to the House of Commons in February 2003 shortly before the commencement of the Iraq War:

> ... at some point a terrorist group, pursing extremism with no care for human life, will use such weapons, and not just Britain but the world will be *plunged into a living nightmare from which we will struggle long and hard to awake*. (15 February 2003)

The combination of contrast with metaphor occurs in the discourse of other great political speakers such as Churchill and Thatcher. Although it is a rhetorical strategy that many great leaders instinctively draw on when they intend to evoke maximum emotional force, it also has a dangerous pedigree in modern European history and is one that we need to be critically aware of. The heightening of rhetorical tension can lead to an irreversible commitment to certain political positions and this is evidently one of the strategic dangers of Conviction Rhetoric.

9.4.3 Personification

Personification – as we saw in the masterful use by Churchill – is a highly emotive figure of speech because it seeks to represent abstract entities as people. A conflict between ideas can therefore become more persuasive and passionate if it is represented as a conflict between people; personification is therefore an important strategy of Conviction Rhetoric. Blair used personifications extensively when describing the attack on the World Trade Center on September 11, 2001. First the Western way of life is conceived as if it were a person suffering from a blow:

> The atrocities in New York and Washington were the work of evil men. Men who distorted and dishonoured the message of one of the world's great religions and civilisations. Their aim was to stimulate

militant fundamentalism; to separate the United States from its allies; and *to bring our way of life and our economies to their knees.* (13 November 2001)

He then goes on to develop an argument that eventually became the basis for British involvement in the war on Iraq; this was that the West must engage beyond its boundaries in order to prevent further terrorist atrocities:

> Once chaos and strife have got a grip on a region or a country trouble will soon be exported... After all it was a dismal camp in the foothills of Afghanistan that *gave birth to the murderous assault on the sparkling heart* of New York's financial centre. (13 November 2001)

Here both poverty and wealth are conceptualised as if they were people with physical bodies. Finally, this section of the speech is completed with a powerful symbolic reification that evokes a world inhabited by ancient mythological creatures:

> *The dragon's teeth are planted in the fertile soil* of wrongs unrighted, of disputes left to fester for years or even decades, of failed states, of poverty and deprivation. (13 November 2001)

This is not the only instance where the issues that dominated post-September 11 politics – the 'War on Terror' – was conceptualised using personification; consider the following:

> At every stage, we should seek to avoid war. But if the threat cannot be removed peacefully, please let us not fall for the delusion that it can be safely ignored. If we do not confront these *twin menaces of rogue states with Weapons of Mass Destruction and terrorism*, they will not disappear. *They will just feed and grow on our weakness.* (15 February 2003)

The aim of political argument was to encourage public opinion to support a policy of war on Iraq, and this argument was based on the proposition that terrorists were in possession of weapons of mass destruction and the evidence was in the attack on the World Trade Center. The attack on Iraq was based on an assumption that because it had sought to develop weapons it was linked to the attack. In reality the West, and in particular America and Israel, were in control of vast quantities of weapons and the evidence for Iraq having them was dubious. However, for the purpose of arguing for Iraq's culpability, there was an inference that it was a 'rogue state'. Metaphor is used to describe 'rogue states'[2] as animate entities that – like malign offspring – are fed by indecision.

The myth of good and evil that is central to Conviction Rhetoric was sustained by the use of personifications that represent political enemies as if they are monstrous creatures. What distinguishes Blair's use of personification is that it has a very strong negative evaluation – this is in contrast to other metaphor systems such as journey metaphors and creative reification that are more commonly used for positive evaluation. In this respect he differs from Churchill who, as we saw in Table 3.1, generally employed personifications when making positive evaluations.

9.4.4   Neutral reification and the use of phraseology

There were many reifications that could not readily be classified as communicating a positive or a negative evaluation and yet seemed distinctive to Tony Blair's rhetorical style. There are a number of instances of colloquial phrases that indicate a shift to an informal register as in the following:

> But values aren't enough. *The mantle of leadership* comes at a price: the courage to learn and change; to show how values that stand for all ages, can be applied in a way relevant to each age. (2 October 2001)

> But that's the SNP for you – always *letting the Tories in through the back door*. (22 February 2002)

> A Labour party that was transformed from a four times election loser into a *landslide winner*. (22 February 2002)

> Causes like the minimum wage, a Scottish parliament, House of Lords reform, which for 100 years lay *gathering the dust* of accumulated resolutions, now made law and real. (22 February 2002)

These familiar metaphors seem to be highly characteristic of Blair's discourse and their function seems more interpersonal than ideational – that is, they are used to develop a particular relationship of informality with the audience rather than to make significant progress in the development of ideas or of an argument. We should recall that the

---

[2] I discuss the metaphor of 'rogue state' in more detail in Charteris-Black (2009b).

north-eastern constituency of Sedgefield, with a membership of 2000 in 1992, provided Blair with the platform for his leadership campaign; not surprisingly Blair always prided himself in taking an interest in popular pastimes such as following football and going to the pub. Expressions such as *going down the drain* or *landslide winners*, and euphemisms such as *getting in through the back door* or clichés such as *the mantle of leadership* draw on the informal register of pub conversation. In many ways the choice of these expressions is another hallmark of Blair's will to govern because their main purpose was not to polarise opinion to the left or the right, but to create a shared identity with the 'average voter'.

Traditional language wears the guise of common-sense opinion and contrasts with the new chic 'cool' lexicons of the Internet generation. Just as Blair – while espousing the virtues of new technology – apparently remains something of a computer illiterate (cf. Rentoul 2001: 539). The function of these choices is still persuasive, but it is a type of persuasion that works as part of a whole style of discourse aiming to place the speaker as a member of an in-group that includes the audience. We should recall that Blair admired many aspects of Margaret Thatcher; in addition to the firmness and clarity with which she stated her messages, and drew on the *vox populi* when expressing opinions and values. The role of metaphorical phraseology in the discourse of Tony Blair is to link in with these popular values and avoid aloofness. This contrasts with the arcane technical political terms (such as 'compositing') that characterised the discourse of 'Old' Labour.

Blair's skilful use of neutral reification is, then, part of his image as one of the lads – not an aloof or even particularly intellectual thinker – but one who can frame issues in the language of the pub, school staffroom, or the office coffee break. It reflects linguistically the will to govern that characterised Tony Blair and New Labour – and provided a shift in style from the more strident use of metaphor that characterised Blair's Conviction Rhetoric when he was solving world poverty, ending international terrorism or eliminating weapons of mass destruction.

9.5　Summary

In this chapter I have necessarily focused on the most productive types of metaphor employed by Tony Blair. Inevitably there are other domains to which I have given less attention and which may become more explicit with reference to a larger corpus of his speeches. Like Clinton, for example, he shows a predilection for sports metaphors:

We knew: first base was getting the fundamentals in place. (26 September 2000)

However, even here I would suggest there is evidence of other themes that I have identified; for example, in the following apparently sports metaphor, there is evidence of the moral contrast between right and wrong:

> We're standing up for the people we represent, who play by the rules and have a right to expect others to do the same. (2 October 2001)

The rhetorical strategy of demonstrating that he had the right intentions prevails even in sports: Saddam Hussein was a 'cheat' who would never 'play by the rules'. What is perhaps most significant about Tony Blair was his ability to appear to be all things to all people – depending on who he was speaking to at the time. We have seen this chameleon-like tendency in his skilful and unique use of familiar phraseology to communicate the rationality of his policies and how this led to the creation of a myth of himself as the common man – representative of British public opinion.

The findings of this chapter have echoed those for previous ones for both Margaret Thatcher in relation to the discourse of conflict and Bill Clinton in relation to the discourse of rebirth. There was some evocation of Churchill with personifications – but with a different type of evaluation. As with Clinton, GOOD GOVERNING IS CREATING and Blair develops this into GOOD GOVERNING IS DESTROYING when the entity destroyed is negatively evaluated. These underlying concepts combined with strong reliance on MORALITY IS CONFLICT and POLITICS IS ETHICS provided the rhetorical basis for what I have termed Conviction Rhetoric. The visit made by Blair to the USA in January 1993 was highly influential in the content of policy. Blair's increasing separation from the unions paralleled Clinton's attack on 'special interests'. This was a theme in the emergence of New Labour modernisers as they struggled to change the system of voting for party leadership away from the block vote in favour of the 'one man one vote' principle. However, the American influence in the creation of a discourse of legitimisation was rhetorical as well as ideological. Analysis of the metaphors of Conviction Rhetoric has revealed a close similarity between both Blair and Clinton and between them and earlier discourses of European fascism.

More distinctive of Blair – though with its roots in Winston Churchill and Margaret Thatcher – was the integration of a popularist discourse of colloquial phraseology and familiar metaphor – with dramatic, personal statements of moral and ethical beliefs to produce the epic dimension. Describing ethics and morality in the language of conflict created the potential for both Thatcher and Blair to describe actual military conflict in terms of morality and ethics; this formed the basis for the legitimisation of both the Falkland and the Second Gulf wars. Metaphor was at the heart of policy-making – as well as the communication of political issues. If traditional political considerations such as national self-interest had remained at the centre of policy-making, it is unlikely that Blair would have joined a war hatched by the neo-conservatives in America. Conviction Rhetoric served as the moral and ethical basis for action, then played a crucial role in the demonisation of political opponents, but also tied Blair into an irreversible policy that eventually led to both his own downfall and that of his party.

Perhaps the most important political speech he made was the impassioned speech to the House of Commons on 18 March 2003 before the commencement of war with Iraq. In this speech Blair had the difficult rhetorical task of persuading a reluctant House of Commons and general public to support direct military intervention in Iraq. At this point, there was still assumed to be a need for a second resolution in favour of this from the United Nations (one that was subsequently not forthcoming). Having already committed British ground forces to the build-up of the campaign, it was crucial that he did not lose a vote in the House of Commons or he would probably have been forced to resign. It is when faced by a major rhetorical task that Blair integrates a range of rhetorical strategies that it has been necessary to separate for the purpose of analysis.

In spite of the high stakes Blair was keen to employ familiar phraseological expressions such as 'to whet our appetite' – used to refer disdainfully to the diplomatic strategy of Saddam Hussein which he shortly after refers to as 'a diplomatic dance with Saddam'. Here, the colloquial phrases and familiar metaphors pave the way for a whole spate of metaphors with very strong negative evaluations that refer to the two main reasons for military intervention: to put an end to the threat from 'terrorism' and 'weapons of mass destruction'. The threat is represented in terms of metaphors: 'Insecurity *spreads like a contagion*' and 'The purpose of terrorism … sets out *to inflame*, to divide … round the world it now *poisons* the chance of political progress'.

In the last section of the speech a range of metaphors (in italics) interact with other strategies including the question and answer pattern, contrast, reiteration and repetition:

We must face the consequences of the actions we advocate. For me, that means all the dangers of war. But for others, opposed to this course, it means – let us be clear – that the Iraqi people… for them, *the darkness will close back over them again*; and he will be free to take his revenge upon those he must know wish him gone.

And if this House now demands that at this moment, faced with this threat from this regime, that British troops are pulled back, that we turn away at the point of reckoning, and that is what it means – what then? What will Saddam feel? Strengthened beyond measure. What will the other states who tyrannise their people, the terrorists who threaten our existence, what will they take from that? *That the will confronting them is decaying and feeble.* Who will celebrate and who will weep?

Saddam is described as the agent of the forces of darkness and the warning of the dangers of inaction culminates in a series of rhetorical questions. He continues in epic vein:

And if our plea is for America to work with others, to be good as well as powerful allies, will our retreat make them multilateralist? Or will it not rather be the biggest impulse to unilateralism there could ever be. And what of the UN and the future of Iraq and the MEPP, devoid of our influence, *stripped of our insistence*? This House wanted this decision. Well it has it. Those are the choices. And in this dilemma, no choice is perfect, no cause ideal. But on this decision hangs the fate of many things.

The speech then terminates with a set of epic challenges:

Of whether we summon the strength to recognise this global challenge of the 21st century and meet it.
Of the Iraqi people, groaning under years of dictatorship.
Of our armed forces – brave men and women of whom we can feel
proud, whose morale is high and whose purpose is clear.
Of the institutions and alliances that will *shape our world for years to
come.* (18 March 2003)

While metaphors – such as that for darkness and light and the personification 'stripped of our insistence' – provide the frame of the argument, the persuasive effect of Conviction Rhetoric is produced by a rich interaction of figures that include contrast, rhetorical questions, and parallelism. They combine to give the conviction that comes from sounding right.

Blair employs metaphor to demonstrate he has the right intentions and to produce a Conviction Rhetoric to legitimise his policies. The use of demonic metaphors to communicate his perception of political opponents implies that metaphorically his was the party of the angels. Ultimately the danger in describing political situations in the epic language of good and evil is that it implies that the speaker is a moral arbiter. By representing himself as an angel, a man motivated only by altruism, Blair placed enormous pressures on the standards of behaviour of his closest supporters as well as on himself. We saw this on a number of occasions – for example, the resignation of Peter Mandelson and his press secretary Alistair Campbell and media interest in his wife's purchase of two flats in Bristol. New Labour was threatened by public perception of its 'spin doctors' which made it vulnerable to accusations of manipulation and loss of credibility. Morality is not the exclusive preserve of any individual but is a matter for negotiation. The Cabinet resignations of Robin Cook and Clare Short over issues of principle concerning the legitimacy of the Iraq War demonstrated that identifying right intentions is a matter of interpretation. Ultimately, the public made its own choices regarding legitimacy and voted in another Conservative government.

10
George Bush and the Rhetoric of Moral Accounting

10.1 Introduction

In this chapter I focus primarily on the rhetoric of George W. Bush but also compare his use of persuasive language with that of his father, George Bush Senior, who was President from 1989 until 1993. It seemed relevant to compare father and son for a number of reasons: they both represented the Republican Party, they both represented the interests of corporate business and they both initiated American intervention in Iraq. The major difference is that while George Bush Senior led the USA in its new role as the first global superpower, his son led his country in responding to the first major challenge to this status. This was, of course, the largest ever peacetime assault on a civilian population: the September 11th attack on the World Trade Center. The nature of George W. Bush's leadership during this period of national crisis was especially important because of the narrowness of his electoral victory over Al Gore in the highly disputed 2001 elections.

Father and son demonstrated leadership skills in time of war during the military operations that were known respectively as 'Desert Storm' and 'Iraq Freedom'. The two Gulf Wars appear different in that the first was caused by the invasion of Kuwait by Iraq, while the second was a pre-emptive strike by the USA and Britain to prevent Iraq from developing 'weapons of mass destruction'. Evidence of such weapons had largely eluded the United Nations inspectors prior to the war and continued to do so after its termination. However, if one accepts George W. Bush's interpretation of 'Iraq Freedom' as part of a wider 'war on terror' initiated in response to the attack on the World Trade Center on September 11th 2001, then there is less difference between the two wars. Both are then interpreted as responses to acts of aggression – the first against Kuwait and the second against the USA (though there is no evidence of any connection between Iraq and the September 11th attacks). Both were dependent upon some local Arab support and were at least partly motivated by a desire to maintain easy access to the world's largest oil supplies. The similarities between these two major military actions that dominated the presidencies of father and son therefore argue in favour of a comparative approach to their discourse of leadership. Comparison between wars was also part of the political arguments in debates over whether or not to go to war with Iraq; Rohrer (1995) examines the metaphors used by George Bush Senior to conceptualise the political situation in the Persian Gulf in the pre-war period and contrasts the metaphor systems of THE PERSIAN GULF CRISIS IS WORLD WAR II with THE PERSIAN GULF CRISIS IS ANOTHER VIETNAM; as he argues:

> Nowhere else does the adoption of a metaphor system result in as stark a difference in the engendered inferences, because although the 'WWII' metaphor and the mapping of Hitler onto Hussein would result in an imperative to go to war, the 'VIETNAM' metaphor's focus on war as chaotic, unpredictable, and perhaps ultimately unwinnable would reject a decision to go to war in favor of continued sanctions. (Rohrer 1995: 118)

As events turned out, though a moustached tyrant was deposed the war also proved to be unwinnable – showing neither frame as entirely relevant. George W. Bush relied more heavily on a team of speech-writers – Karl Rove, Karen Hughes and David Frum – suggesting an awareness of a need for assistance to compensate for the skills that he lacked. Although the content of his speeches is largely the output of professional speech-writers, his awareness of his need for them was itself a leadership skill. He took their role seriously as one of them testified:

> Bush was an exacting editor. He usually reviewed his speeches early in the morning, directly after his intelligence briefing. He hated repetition and redundancy ... Bush seldom cited statistics when he talked. But he demanded that they be included on the page. (Frum 2003: 48)

However, as I have argued in Chapter 1, given the official status attached to the words of a politician, his own control over what is said (as compared with what has been drafted) and the fact that the speeches can rarely be attributed to any single writer anyway – we should accept politicians as the authors of speeches attributed to them. Bush's close attention to editing implies recognition of his own ultimate accountability and ownership of speeches – even though others made vital contributions.

In this chapter I will first outline how the moral accounting metaphor is central to understanding the rhetoric of the Bush dynasty. In the analysis of metaphors, I will first demonstrate how extensive use of personifications contributed to sounding right in the context of the crisis brought on by 9/11. I will then show how finance and crime metaphors contributed to telling a story that provided a rationale for an aggressive foreign policy because the moral accounting myth argued that it was rooted in having the right intentions.

10.2   The rhetoric of George W. Bush: the moral accounting metaphor

While there are many similarities in language choice between father and son, there were two types of language use that occur with a considerably higher frequency in the discourse of George W. Bush. These are metaphors that draw on the source domains of finance and metaphors of crime and punishment. Finance metaphors are indicated by nonliteral uses of words such as *price, cost, debt*, etc. but also include those that draw on the domain of betting, as in the following:

> Some seem to believe that our politics can afford to be petty because, in a time of peace, *the stakes of our debates* appear small. There is no corner of the Earth distant or dark enough to protect them. However long it takes, their hour of justice will come. Every nation *has a stake* in this cause. (12 September 2002)

Crime and punishment metaphors evoke images from the Wild West in which outlaws and bandits are brought under the control of a governing authority. Soon after the September 11th attack on the World Trade Center George W. Bush made the following comment in response to a question at a press interview:

> Just remember, all I'm doing is remembering when I was kid. I remember that I used to put out there in the old West a 'wanted'

poster. It said, 'Wanted, Dead or Alive'. All I want and America wants is to see them brought to justice. That's what we want. (17 September 2001)

Subsequently he regretted this remark as counter-productive as it brought into focus how images of crime and punishment were to become the defining rhetorical characteristic of his presidency; for example:

Listen, you've just got to know, there's no cave deep enough – there's no cave deep enough – for the *long arm of American justice*. (9 April 2002)

Such metaphors can traced to the rhetoric of his father – for example:

Each of us will measure, within ourselves, the value of this great struggle. *Any cost in lives* is beyond our power to measure. But *the cost of closing* our eyes to aggression is beyond mankind's power to imagine.

The community of nations has resolutely gathered to condemn and *repel lawless aggression*. Saddam Hussein's unprovoked invasion – his ruthless, systematic *rape* of a peaceful neighbor – violated everything the community of nations holds dear. (January 1991)

Crime and punishment and finance represent two topics common to the political communication of father and son: the importance of commercial interests and the need to punish a 'rogue' nation. The difference that September 11th made in American political discourse was that it created a situation in which the USA could with some justification adopt a narrative in which it was the innocent victim of crimes perpetrated by others. Since the September 11th attacks were symbolically on American financial and commercial interests it was quite natural that the domains of ethics and finance should become linked through George W. Bush's concept of a 'war on terror'.[1]

There was evidence from a number of insider sources such as the former treasury secretary Paul O'Neill, Richard Clarke and those interviewed by Bob Woodward that the ousting of Saddam Hussein was the major thrust of Bush's policy from the very beginning of his presidency. As with earlier presidents (most famously Roosevelt's New Deal) the war on terror gave him the moral authority to become a truly heroic

---

[1] I discuss the concept of a 'War on Terror' in Charteris-Black (2004: 39 ff.).

wartime leader, and metaphor provided a powerful rhetorical strategy for overcoming the most literal of events. Indeed George Bush deliberately contrasted literal with metaphoric senses in his speech after the event:

> Terrorist attacks can shake the foundation of our biggest buildings, but they cannot touch the *foundation of America*. These acts shattered steel, but they cannot *dent the steel of American resolve*.

A nation that had been made to look and feel vulnerable needed metaphors of strength to restore its self-confidence. September 11th provided a single definitive event to which he could respond with moderation – as an empathetic leader – or with boldness – as the agent of divine retribution – according to political circumstance. There is evidence that when Bush said 'And an angel still rides in the whirlwind and directs this storm' (first Inaugural, 20 January 2001), he saw himself as this angel and anticipated his role in directing the storm. The war on terror provided a way of telling the story that integrated both an appeal to ethical credibility while simultaneously heightening the emotional appeal to constitute a highly persuasive rhetoric.

The interaction between metaphors from the domains of finance and crime can be understood with reference to a metaphor originating in Johnson (1993) and developed by Lakoff (2002) that is widespread in conceptual systems: the moral accounting metaphor. In this metaphor an increase in well-being is conceptualised as a 'gain' and a decrease in well-being as a 'loss' or a 'cost' so that actions can be described as 'worth it' or 'profitable'. When we refer to actions in such a way we are talking about something qualitative (i.e. well-being) in terms of something measurable (i.e. money). In this WELL-BEING IS WEALTH metaphor, beneficial moral action is described in terms of material gain and harmful immoral action is described in terms of material loss. Because 9/11 was an act of such immorality, its perpetrators incurred a huge moral 'debt' and the remainder of Bush's presidency could be spent in exacting payment for it. The moral accounting metaphor is grounded in basic moral knowledge that we are supposed to pay off our debts. It is effective because the positive evaluation of behaviour that resolves moral debts by settling scores has a historical resonance for many Americans, as it evokes earlier historical periods in American history when powerful beliefs about moral justice have motivated both domestic and international policy. It therefore provided the basis for the communication of ethical legitimacy.

10.3   Metaphor analysis

For George W. Bush I employed a corpus of 40,222 words comprised of the 15 speeches shown in Appendix 15. Many of these speeches can be found at: http://www.whitehouse.gov/vicepresident/. The analysis produced a total of 231 metaphors or approximately one metaphor every 174 words; this was a lower frequency of metaphor than that for the other American politicians examined in this work. The corpus for George Bush Senior was a smaller one of 15,000 words comprised of four major speeches (see Appendix 15). Analysis of the George Bush Senior corpus showed 223 metaphors or one every 67 words. An important comparative finding is that George Bush Senior employed metaphors nearly three times more frequently than his son. The findings of the metaphor analysis are summarised in Appendix 16.

As with other politicians there were problematic issues of classification; for example, the first metaphor in Appendix 16 could equally have been classified as a journey metaphor. Since personifications are based on the concept X IS A PERSON, and a person can also undertake journeys, the issue was whether the metaphor *primarily* brings to mind the image of a person or the action of travelling. In this case it seemed to be the idea THE NATION IS A PERSON that seemed to predominate, although the conceptual metaphor LIFE IS JOURNEY is also active. Of course, such conceptual interactions are not particular to these corpora.

Both George Bush Senior and Junior show a preference for personification over other types of metaphor; the personification THE NATION IS A PERSON is highly productive in their discourse and contributes significantly to their communication of leadership. This is a similar finding to that of similar studies of George Bush Senior by Lakoff (1991) and Rohrer (1995). Reifications and journey and light metaphors are generally popular amongst politicians, and are used by both father and son, while 'story' metaphors seem to be a relatively novel feature that is also common to them. There is certainly evidence of more similarity than dissimilarity in metaphor choices of the Bush dynasty.

10.3.1   Personifications and telling the right story

One immediate parallel between father and son is that they rely heavily on personifications of America to evoke patriotic feelings that are effective in times of national crisis since the idea of the nation has a powerful emotional resonance for many Americans. Both employ the root form

'America' (or any morphological variation) approximately once every 105 words in their respective corpora. Clinton refers to 'America' around once every 98 words while Blair refers to Britain (or any morphological variation of the root form 'Brit') only once every 245 words and Thatcher once every 220 words. The pattern 'America' + verb is often used as a metonym in which 'America' refers to 'the government of America', but it is also used metaphorically by the Bush dynasty and this may be the result of the influence of Churchill's rhetoric on George W. Bush and his speech-writers.

The use of personification carries a strong expressive force because it evokes our feelings and beliefs about people and applies them to feelings and beliefs about abstract political issues. Since the presidency of George W. Bush was dominated by the September 11th attacks, and the subsequent 'war on terror', he looked to Churchill for inspiration and we have seen in Chapter 3 how Churchill had a predilection for personification. Bush uses two major contrasting types of personification: those with a strong positive evaluation that conceptualise the USA as a person who is free and has a personal history, and those with a strong negative evaluation that conceptualise terrorists as lower forms of life such as vermin and parasites. I refer to this second type as 'depersonifications'. Systematic and extensive use of personifications frequently structures the major themes of his speeches.

A very common leadership strategy is to combine the personification A NATION IS A PERSON with one of two metonyms, either LEADER FOR GOVERNMENT or NATION FOR GOVERNMENT. In the speech in which Bush first employed the phrase 'axis of evil' he describes the active response that will be taken to the September 11th attack:

> And all nations should know: *America will do what is necessary* to ensure our nation's security. *We'll be deliberate*, yet time is not on our side. *I will not wait on events*, while dangers gather. *I will not stand by*, as peril draws closer and closer. *The United States of America will not permit* the world's most dangerous regimes to threaten us with the world's most destructive weapons. (Applause) (29 January 2002)

There is a shift from 'America' to 'we' to 'I' to 'the United States of America' as they all refer to the same thing – the government. The equivalence that is established between nation, leader and government is designed to create an impression of unity and common purpose that was necessary to respond to the crisis. This speech was an especially important part of the neo-conservative agenda because a strategy was required at short notice to respond to the unexpected September 11th attacks. Iraq was picked out as a symbol of all states that 'sponsored terrorism' and the term 'axis of evil' presupposed that there was a connection between these states. The speech was the first explicit public statement of a policy that eventually led to the invasion of Iraq in April 2003.

We will recall that the adjective 'evil' played an important part in Tony Blair's Conviction Rhetoric (cf. section 9.2). David Frum – the speech-writer who coined the phrase 'axis of evil' – explained how his choice of the phrase was motivated by the idea of making a connection between various countries and organisations hostile to the USA – such as Iran, Iraq, Hezbollah, al-Qaeda – and the European Fascist movements of the 1930s. He argued that both fundamentalist and Fascist movements shared a common disdain for free inquiry, democracy and rational thought, celebrated death and murder and were obsessively anti-Semitic. As he summarises:

> Indeed Saddam Hussein's Baathist ideology was cobbled together in the 1940s by Arab admirers of Hitler and Mussolini. So there was our link – and our explanation of why we must act: together, the terror states and terror organizations formed an axis of hatred against the United States. The United States could not wait for these dangerous regimes to get deadly weapons and attack us; the United States must strike first and protect the world from them. (Frum 2003: 236)

The 'axis of evil' speech symbolised a coming of age for President Bush because it indicated an end to self-doubt and guilt: what counted most from now on was to fight evil wherever it was found. This was no longer a simple case of national interest but a universal declaration of a war against evil. In this 'war on terror' the USA and its allies represented the forces of good and their enemies, by definition, represented the forces of evil. It was because of this that there was no longer any room for in-between positions – you were either 'for us' or 'against us'. Similarly, Tony Blair used the myth of an epic struggle between good and evil to provide the ethical legitimisation of his policies. It also counterbalanced the myths of rebirth espoused by Clinton and Blair that have been related to European Fascism. It is interesting to note in this highly patriotic speech that personifications based on the metaphor AMERICA IS A PERSON and the metonym NATION FOR GOVERNMENT invariably evoke applause:

History has called America and our allies to action, and it is both our responsibility and our privilege *to fight freedom's fight.* (Applause)

This is not surprising as they represent America as a heroic warrior and as the world leader and defender of universal values:

America will lead by defending liberty and justice because they are right and true and unchanging for all people everywhere. (Applause) (29 January 2002)

The axis of evil speech marked a shift in Bush Junior's rhetoric towards a black and white moral contrast, as in the following where the antonyms 'friend' and 'enemy' are contrasted:

The *United States of America is a friend* to the Afghan people, and we are the friends of almost a billion worldwide who practice the Islamic faith. *The United States of America is an enemy* of those who aid terrorists and of the barbaric criminals who profane a great religion by committing murder in its name. (7 October 2001)

These arguments were introduced to justify an aggressive foreign policy that claimed its legitimacy from having the right intentions:

None of us would ever wish the evil that was done on September the 11th. Yet after America was attacked, it was as if our *entire country looked into a mirror and saw our better selves. We* were reminded that we are citizens, with obligations to each other, to our country, and to history. *We* began to think less of the goods *we* can accumulate, and more about the good *we* can do. For too long our culture has said, 'If it feels good, do it'. Now *America is embracing* a new ethic and a new creed: 'Let's roll'. (Applause) (29 January 2002)

There was nothing new about the claims that America carried the burden of ethical responsibility; for example these occur in George Bush Senior's 1991 State of the Union speech:

For two centuries, America has served the world as an inspiring example of freedom and democracy. For generations, *America has led the struggle* to preserve and extend the blessings of liberty. And today, in a rapidly changing world, *American leadership is indispensable. Americans know that leadership brings burdens, and requires sacrifice.*

Yes, the United States bears a major share of *leadership* in this effort. Among the nations of the world, only the United States of America has had both the *moral standing*, and the means to back it up. We are the only nation on this earth that could assemble the forces of peace.

This is the *burden of leadership* – and the strength that has made America the beacon of freedom in a searching world. (29 January 1991)

And continued right through into the 1992 State of the Union speech:

But we are the United States of America, *the leader of the West* that has become the *leader of the world*. (28 January 1992)

The only significant shift that we find between the two constructions of leadership is that George Bush Senior conceptualised the USA as *separate* from the rest of the world. However, in the discourse of his son the boundary between the rest of the world and the USA dissolved (because of the borderless nature of 'Terror'), leading to a convergence of foreign and domestic policy. Evidence for this is in the extensive use of crime metaphors in relation to international affairs – that I will examine later.

A further personification that Bush Junior employs for adding rhetorical weight is that based on the metaphor HISTORY IS A PERSON. In these metaphors 'history' usually collocates with 'call' as in the following:

History has called America and our allies to action, and it is both our responsibility and our privilege to fight freedom's fight. (Applause) (January 2002)

We did not ask for this mission, yet there is honor *in history's call*. (12 September 2002)

Another common pattern is either with a mental state verb:

History will know that day not only as a day of tragedy, but as a day of decision – when the civilized world was stirred to anger and to action. (11 March 2002)

Or as the subject of the verbs 'record' or 'look back' when making a prediction that a policy will be viewed retrospectively as successful:

History will look back at us, generations will look back at us, and I believe they're going to say, thanks. (9 April 2002)

The effect of this personification is to create a feeling of identity between the political leader and the inevitability of events. It is also reminiscent of Churchill's rhetorical style – consider his use of the personification of history:

> History with its flickering lamp stumbles along the trail of the past, trying to reconstruct its scenes, to revive its echoes, and kindle with pale gleams the passion of former days... Whatever else history may or may not say about these terrible, tremendous years... This alone will stand him in good stead as far as what is called the verdict of history is concerned. (12 November 1940)

The implication of evoking Churchill is to argue that the war in Iraq is conceptually closer to the Second World War than it is to the Vietnam War. It was important to persuade Americans that Saddam Hussein was analogous to a defeated leader, Hitler, rather than to a success-ful one – Ho Chi Minh. As Voss et al. (1992) argue, the Vietnam metaphor was used extensively by both Republicans and Democrats dur-ing the Senate debates over declaration of war in the Gulf. Churchillian personifications create conscious rhetorical associations implying a covert historical analogy that is crucial to the political case being argued.

The impression that particular decisions are part of a predetermined unfolding narrative is also evident in explicit references to the American 'story'. I do not treat these as metaphors but as explicit references to the strategy of framing a mental representation as a narrative. A good example of this is in George W. Bush's first Inaugural speech:

> We have a place, all of us, *in a long story – a story we continue*, but whose end we will not see. *It is the story of a new world* that became a friend and liberator of the old, *a story of a slave-holding society* that became a servant of freedom, the *story of a power* that went into the world to protect but not possess, to defend but not to conquer.

> It is the *American story – a story* of flawed and fallible people, united across the generations by grand and enduring ideals.

> This work continues. *This story goes on.* And an angel still rides in the whirlwind and directs this storm. (20 January 2001)

Here the story that is evoked refers to the Protestant narrative of the Pilgrim Fathers. The rhetorical strategy of telling the right story implies that the narrator will be in control of allocating the roles of hero and villain.

A further personification that was very central to the primary rhetorical objective after September 11th is THE WORLD IS A PERSON. Following the attack on the USA and the decision by the American government to take decisive military action against those associated with this attack, a major aim of Bush's political speeches was to win international support for American action. This conceptual metaphor proved particularly important because it equated the USA as a person with the interests of another person: 'the world'. The following provide some examples of this:

> We are supported by the collective will of the world.

> Every other country is a potential target. And all the world faces the most horrifying prospect of all: These same terrorists are searching for weapons of mass destruction, the tools to turn their hatred into holocaust.

> Before the sun had set, these attacks on the world stood condemned by the world. (12 September 2002)

A favoured collocation is the phrase 'the civilized world': this is a person whose interests are even closer to that of America as shown by the shift from 'civilized world' to 'we' in the following:

> The *civilized world is now responding. We* act to defend ourselves and deliver our children from a future of fear. *We* choose the dignity of life over a culture of death. *We* choose lawful change and civil disagreement over coercion, subversion, and chaos.

The United States of America is constructed as the leader and chief representative of the 'civilized world':

> History will know that day not only as a day of tragedy, but as a day of decision – when the *civilized world was stirred to anger* and to action. And the terrorists will remember September 11th as the day their reckoning began. (11 March 2002)

And on several occasions in the speeches 'America' and 'the civilized world' are referred to as almost synonymous with one another:

> That terrible morning, 19 evil men – the shock troops of a hateful ideology – gave *America and the civilized world* a glimpse of their ambitions. (1 May 2003)

By driving terrorists from place to place, we disrupt the planning and training for further attacks on *America and the civilized world*. (11 March 2002)

Yet on other occasions when speaking to a domestic rather than an international audience the WORLD IS A PERSON metaphor is used rather differently; in some instances the world is conceptualised as an uneducated person who is in need of instruction by the USA:

And then we've got the Peace Corps, and the Peace Corps is a way for Americans to help *teach the world* about the universal values that we hold dear, the true nature of America, which sometimes is distorted around the world. (9 April 2002, Bridgeport, Connecticut)

We may ask ourselves as to what distinction is being drawn when Bush shifts from THE WORLD IS A PERSON metaphor to THE CIVILIZED WORLD IS A CIVILIZED PERSON. The only other qualifiers for 'world' in the corpus are 'Arab' and 'Islamic' as in the following:

And anyone in the world, *including the Arab world*, who works and sacrifices for freedom has a loyal friend in the United States of America. (Applause) (1 May 2003)

America will take the side of brave men and women who advocate these values around the world, *including the Islamic world*, because we have a greater objective than eliminating threats and containing resentment. (29 January 2002)

Here 'Arab' and 'Islamic' are conceptualised as discrete entities that are included within the wider world; however, what is not clear is whether or not they are included or excluded from the 'civilized world'. Indeed other references to the Islamic world imply that they are not (though they have the potential to be):

So we will renew the promise of the Peace Corps, double its volunteers over the next five years – (applause) – and ask it to join a new effort to encourage development and education and opportunity in *the Islamic world*. (Applause) (29 January 2002)

These aspirations are lifting up the peoples of Europe, Asia, Africa and the Americas, and they can lift up all of *the Islamic world*. (12 September 2002)

We can infer from these uses a metaphor such as THE ISLAMIC WORLD
IS A CHILD – in need of education and picking up.

10.3.2 Depersonifications

In direct contrast to conceptualisations of the Islamic world as harmless
and in need of education are personifications that activate a negative
evaluation by conceptualising 'terrorists' in terms of animals, vermin
and insects. These are reminiscent of Tony Blair's monster metaphors
to describe terrorism (cf. Chapter 9). This is a stylistic and conceptual
characteristic of George W. Bush for which there is limited evidence in
his father's speeches. Hunting and animal images were employed early
on in relation to terrorists:

> Initially, the terrorists *may burrow deeper into caves* and other
> entrenched hiding places. (7 October 2001)

> It's an enemy that likes to *hide and burrow* in and their network is
> extensive... But we're going to *smoke them out*. (17 September 2001)

> We will not allow ourselves to be terrorized by somebody who think
> they can hit and *hide in some cage* somewhere... to get them running
> and to find them and to *hunt them down*.

Depersonification is first employed to construct the enemy as non-
human and then as dangerous so that their destruction is necessary
in order to maintain the 'health' of the USA and the rest of the 'civilized world'. This implies a conceptual metaphor: TERRORISTS ARE
DANGEROUS ANIMALS. Clearly, this language is highly emotive and
incites extreme political action. Representing human agents as if they
are dangerous animals implies that they have forsaken any claim to be
treated like human beings, for example with respect to their human
rights under international agreements such as the Geneva Convention.
This is a case of when heightening the emotional appeal, or 'sounding
right', makes the dangerous claim to be thinking right. George Bush
Junior employs an extreme form of rhetoric when referring to perpetrators of terrorism because his metaphors slide down the Great Chain of
Being from hunted animals to 'parasites' in need of total elimination:

> My hope is that all nations will heed our call, and *eliminate the terrorist
> parasites* who threaten their countries and our own. (29 January 2002)

America encourages and expects governments everywhere to help *remove the terrorist parasites* that threaten their own countries and peace of the world. (Applause) (11 March 2002)

They support them and harbor them, and they will find that their welcome guests are *parasites* that will weaken them, and eventually consume them. (12 September 2002)

This implies a further conceptual metaphor TERRORISTS ARE PARA- SITES; another political text in which the word 'parasite' was used with reference to a human topic is Hitler's autobiographical account *Mein Kampf*. In Chapter 11 (entitled 'Nation and Race') Hitler uses cultural stereotypes for animals to refer to the Jews using a shift down the hierarchy of the Great Chain of Being:

... for that reason he was never a nomad, but only and always *a parasite* in the body of other peoples ... His spreading is a typical phe- nomenon for all *parasites*; he always seeks a new feeding ground for his race.

It is also one that is reiterated in various forms through this chapter of *Mein Kampf*:

The Jews' life as a *parasite* in the body of other nations and states explains a characteristic ...

As in Bush's 'axis of evil', Hitler finally shifts to the lowest level of the Great Chain of Being – that associated with evil. Indeed within the Great Chain of Being concept, without evil at the lowest level, good could not exist at a higher one. The shift to the supernatural category is the final stage in Hitler's use of metaphor in *Mein Kampf*:

Here he stops at nothing, and in his vileness he becomes so gigantic that no one need be surprised if among our people the *personification of the devil* as the *symbol of all evil* assumes the living shape of the Jew.

The conceptualisation of an enemy as 'evil' also occurs in the discourse of George Bush Senior:

We are resolute and resourceful. If we can selflessly confront *evil* for the sake of good in a land so far away, then surely we can make this land all it should be. (29 January 1991)

However, it was not one that was developed in his discourse. It was not until a camp was set up at Guantanamo Bay for 'detainees' from the war against the Taliban in Afghanistan that we have the powerful visual evocations of the Nazi concentration camps: humans incarcerated in cage-like structures.

Although depersonification is not uncommon as a rhetorical strategy for powerful evaluations of political opponents as 'enemies', it has been widely criticised in anti-war discourse for the use of inanimate notions such as 'collateral damage' to refer to civilian victims of bombing. I have also shown how it was commonly found (along with rebirth metaphors) in European Fascist discourse of the twentieth century. Evidently, there is a danger when using conceptual metaphors such as TERRORISTS ARE ANIMALS and TERRORISTS ARE PARASITES that they become means of conceptualising policy or 'thinking right' and therefore provide the basis for political action.

It was only by thinking of Jews *as if* they were animals or insects that permitted those in charge of following instructions to implement the policy of the final solution. Similarly in Iraq during the post-'victory' phase, photographic evidence of the physical and sexual degradation of prisoners by their guards appears to have removed any concept of the human rights of prisoners of war.[2] Depersonification is a linguistic strategy for providing the motivation and the moral climate in which such practice can be normalised. Critical metaphor analysis is a means of identifying how discourse contributes to the worst abuses of humanity.

10.3.3   Finance metaphors

Metaphors from the domain of finance occur frequently in the speeches of George W. Bush but less commonly in those of George Bush Senior. They are indicated by words such as 'debt', 'price', 'cost', 'stake', etc. and imply a basic conceptualisation of the relation between individuals and between nations as based on monetary transactions. They are rooted in an underlying concept MORAL ACTIONS ARE FINANCIAL TRANSAC-TIONS and are a very clear illustration of what I have described in the previous chapter as the creation of a marketplace of ethics:

> For every regime that sponsors terror, there is *a price to be paid*. And *it will be paid*. The allies of terror are equally guilty of murder and equally accountable to justice. (12 September 2002)

---

[2] The extent to which degradation of prisoners was a systematic part of official policy is not yet clear.

I suggest that this concept is very similar to Lakoff's (2002) notion of a moral accounting metaphor:[3]

> By this conceptual mechanism, an action of moral import is concep-
> tualized in terms of a financial transaction, with a moral interaction
> being metaphorically equivalent to a financial transaction, one in
> which the books are balanced. Just as literal bookkeeping is vital
> to economic functioning, so moral bookkeeping is vital to social
> functioning. And just as it is important that the financial books be
> balanced, so it is important that the moral books be balanced. (Lakoff
> 2002: 45–6)

Lakoff claims that this moral accounting metaphor is realised in 'basic moral schemes' for fairness such as: moral action is fair distribution. This implies principles such as reciprocation, retribution and restitution because debts have to be repaid to restore the even distribution that existed prior to the debt being incurred. Rohrer (1995: 128) relates this to a metaphor JUSTICE IS A BALANCE that he argues is at the core of much Western moral and legal reasoning. However, this debt payment principle that connects the domains of morality and finance is not restricted to 'Western' culture. The notion of 'blood money' is also found in the Koran and implies that the moral debt that is incurred for some type of unintentional 'wrong' action can be compensated for by a financial payment:

> And it does not behoove a believer to kill a believer except by mistake,
> and whoever kills a believer by mistake, he should free a believing
> slave, and *blood-money* should be paid to his people unless they remit
> it as alms; but if he be from a tribe hostile to you and he is a believer,
> the freeing of a believing slave (suffices), and if he is from a tribe
> between whom and you there is a convenant, the *blood-money* should
> be paid to his people along with the freeing of a believing slave. (The
> Koran: 'The Women' 4.92)

Blood money relieves the moral debtor from the guilt attached to the act that he has committed following the conceptual metaphors MORAL ACTIONS ARE FINANCIAL TRANSACTIONS and JUSTICE IS A BALANCE.

These metaphors are based on the assumption that money is the most valued entity and therefore should form the basis for ethical evaluation.

---

[3] See page 29.

Evidently, then, for Bush *financial* value is equated with *moral* value. We can see this in the following where moral positives and negatives are represented as having a 'price':

> Steadfast in our purpose, we now press on. We have known *freedom's price*. We have shown freedom's power. And in this great conflict, my fellow Americans, we will see freedom's victory. Thank you all. May God bless. (29 January 2002)

> They could attack our allies or attempt to blackmail the United States. In any of these cases, *the price of indifference* would be catastrophic. (29 January 2002)

Following the logic of these concepts, those who behave in a way that is negatively evaluated on the scale of morality incur a metaphoric 'debt' that must literally be 'repaid':

> Shannon, I assure you and all who have lost a loved one that our cause is just, and our country will never *forget the debt we owe* Michael and all who gave their lives for freedom. (29 January 2002)

The notion of the loss of a human life through an act of violence as incurring a debt is one that occurs in both Anglo-Saxon and Arabic culture – so it is potentially a persuasive choice of language in discussing international relations. Within this political myth, the sacrifice that is necessary to achieve political objectives – to make the debtor pay the price that is owed – is conceived as if it were a 'cost' of some sort. There is one instance of this concept in the George Bush Senior corpus:

> Each of us will measure, within ourselves, *the value* of this great struggle. Any *cost in lives is* beyond our power to measure. But the *cost of closing* our eyes to aggression is beyond mankind's power to imagine. (29 January 1991)

Though initiated by the father, it became a theme that was systematically developed in the discourse of the son:

> Since September 11, an entire generation of young Americans has gained new understanding of the *value of freedom*, and *its cost in duty* and in sacrifice.

> Yet, the *cost of inaction* is far greater. (12 September 2002)

Metaphoric representation as a 'cost' implies a degree of obligation: once a consumer has enjoyed the use of a good or service, there is an ethical obligation to pay for it. It also evokes the language of predestination in the ethical discourse of the Bible; for example, in the biblical metaphor the 'wages of sin are death' there is the implication that sin will inevitably lead to death and it is conveyed by a moral accounting metaphor 'wages'. As Lakoff notes, the moral accounting metaphor can be traced in the Judaeo-Christian tradition to the original moral debt that was incurred when Adam and Eve ate the forbidden fruit and were punished by exclusion from paradise. Death is of course the ultimate sacrifice in the attainment of political objectives and even this is conceived as a 'cost':

> We could not have known that bond was about to be proven again in war, and we could not have known its *human cost*. Last month, Sergeant Andrew Russell of the Australian Special Air Service, died in Afghanistan. (11 March 2002)
>
> For the brave Americans who bear the risk, no victory is free from sorrow. This nation fights reluctantly, because we know *the cost* and we dread the days of mourning that always come. (28 January 2003)

Given the importance of financial interests that underlie American neoconservatism, it is not perhaps surprising that when Bush Junior is seeking to persuade regarding ethical choices he draws on the domain of finance. As we saw at the start of section 10.2, political issues and decisions regarding the so-called 'war on terror' are referred to using the gambling metaphor of 'stake':

> Every civilized nation has a part in this struggle, because every civilized nation *has a stake in its outcome*. (11 March 2002)
>
> All free nations *have a stake* in preventing sudden and catastrophic attacks. And we're asking them to join us, and many are doing so. (29 January 2002)

What the betting metaphor emphasises is that political decisions are calculated risks – like the money placed when making a bet – we do not know the outcome beforehand and yet there is no option of not participating in the game. In each of the above examples there is the collocation of every/all with 'stake'. The rhetorical purpose is to persuade all nations to participate in the essentially risk-taking strategy of a pre-emptive strike against Iraq. The metaphor of 'stake' therefore evokes a cost–benefit analysis in which the possible costs of military action are measured against the possible benefits. It contributes to an argument that is claimed to be based on right thinking. The main rhetorical strategy leading up to the war on Iraq was to emphasise the immanence of a strike by the Iraqi forces on a Western target using 'weapons of mass destruction' so that the risks of such a strike exceeded those of embarking on a war. However, the choice of a gambling metaphor was also a rhetorical strategy to communicate the risk element in military combat and to prepare the electorate for the eventuality of the loss of their 'stake'. Since military combats usually entail physical suffering the choice of a gambling metaphor covertly prepares the public to expect that there will be a 'cost' which is the loss of what has been staked.

In much of this work I have argued that metaphor is a primary means of persuasion and legitimisation. Given that financial affairs are also conceived in terms of positive and negative values – of credit and of debit – it can be argued that they are well suited to this purpose. Bush's finance metaphors are direct and to the point, they make no scruples about the basic 'values' equation of ethics with money implied by the conceptual metaphor MORAL ACTIONS ARE FINANCIAL TRANS-ACTIONS. Underlying this point of view, good 'moral' behaviour is conceived in terms of ethical business practice: therefore right actions are profitable. In the same way as his economic policies were designed to make Americans financially prosperous, so his foreign affairs policies were designed to make America morally prosperous.

In historical terms the association between ethical and financial prosperity can be traced to the thesis that underlay the so-called Protestant work ethic: material well-being was a sure indication of divine approval. However, Bush's rhetoric is also addressed to a foreign non-American audience, and there is a need to legitimise actions taken in the American national interest by representing them as in the interests of all nations.

10.3.4   Crime and punishment metaphors

Crime and punishment is fundamental to the moral accounting metaphor and ethical legitimisation because 'When you disobey a legitimate authority, it is moral for you to be punished, to receive something of negative value or have something of positive value taken from you. Moral accounting, then, says that the punishment must fit the crime' (Lakoff 2002: 52). The appeal of the moral accounting metaphor is that it links American cultural values with more universal ethical concepts that associate the domains of finance with crime and punishment such as 'blood money'. These have formed the basis for decisions taken in international courts; for example, the settlement in which the Libyan government has made financial payments to the families of the victims of the Lockerbie bombings. Though metaphors based on crime, punishment and retribution were found in George Bush Senior's discourse, they became much more frequent in the speeches of his son following the September 11th attacks. Lakoff (2002) makes an important distinction between *retribution* when moral books are balanced by a *legitimate* authority and *revenge* when someone takes the law into their own hands. Dominating the perspective of George W. Bush and many Americans following the September 11th attacks was the belief that their country had incurred a huge moral debt which – following the moral accounting metaphor – required an equally large payment in return. It was the size of the debt that warranted the legitimacy of political actions taken to restore moral equality.

Unfortunately, the force of the moral accounting metaphor did not permit a clear distinction between retribution and revenge when applied by George W. Bush. A basic principle of retribution is that punishment is exacted on the actual individuals who are known to have incurred the moral debt following due legal process. However, the 9/11 attacks were undertaken by al-Qaeda rather than by Saddam Hussein. The thinking was that since Saddam Hussein had incurred a moral debt by previous cruel actions against his own people he was therefore an appropriate target for retribution and was eligible to pay America the moral credit it had gained as the victim of the September 11th attacks. It did not seem to matter so much *who* had actually incurred as long as the debt was repaid by somebody! Ultimately this was a case of 'round up the usual suspects'.

Unfortunately, the desire for revenge on an anonymous and invisible abstract noun – 'terrorism' – has led to the deaths of many innocent people with no connection to the original crime. Ironically, the war on Iraq seems have increased the amount of moral debt owed by America and Britain rather than to have repaid it and allowed Islamic extremists to see themselves as moral creditors who are under attack. Another important shift has been that the agent of punishment has shifted from being 'the world' in the discourse of George Bush Senior to 'the USA' in the discourse of his son:

The *community of nations* has resolutely gathered to condemn and repel lawless aggression. Saddam Hussein's unprovoked invasion – his ruthless, systematic rape of a peaceful neighbor – violated everything the community of nations holds dear. *The world* has said this aggression would not stand, and it will not stand. Together, we have resisted the trap of appeasement, cynicism and isolation that gives temptation to tyrants. *The world* has answered Saddam's invasion with 12 United Nations resolutions, starting with a demand for Iraq's immediate and unconditional withdrawal, and backed up by forces from 28 countries of six continents. With few exceptions, *the world now stands as one.* (George Bush Senior, 29 January 1991)

Terror cells and outlaw regimes building weapons of mass destruction are different faces of the same evil. Our security requires that we confront both. And the *United States* military is capable of confronting both. (George W. Bush, 7 October 2002)

We have no intention of imposing our culture. But *America* will always stand firm for the non-negotiable demands of human dignity: the rule of law; limits on the power of the state; respect for women; private property; free speech; equal justice; and religious tolerance. (Applause) . . . (George W. Bush, January 2002)

In the discourse of the father 'the world' is the active agent for punishing criminals while in that of the son it is 'the USA'. This shift reflects the failure of George W. Bush to obtain a United Nations resolution in support of the invasion of Iraq in order to remove Saddam Hussein.

In George W. Bush's speeches crime and punishment metaphors are indicated by the use of words such as 'lawless', 'outlaw', 'wrongdoer' and 'punish' – interestingly none of these words occurred more than once in the George Bush Senior corpus. They are evident in the labelling of actions perceived to be against the interests of the USA as 'lawless' as in the following:

We will defend ourselves and our future against terror and *lawless* violence. (12 September 2002)

At President Shevardnadze's request, the United States is planning to send up to 150 military trainers to prepare Georgian soldiers to reestablish control in this *lawless region*. (11 March 2002)

This nation, in world war and in Cold War, has never permitted the brutal and *lawless* to set history's course. (7 October 2002)

A fundamental rhetorical objective in George W. Bush's use of the moral accounting metaphor was to demonstrate that American foreign policy had the right intentions. This was done by defining the behaviour of those who are opposed to the USA (and, by implication, the world) as illegal and evaluating the actions of his government as restorative forms of justice. Not to punish an illegal action would imply complicity in this action and so punishment itself becomes a form of ethical action. Rohrer (1995) argues that the representation of Iraq as a criminal against a world community by George Bush Senior was part of a SOCIAL CONTRACT metaphor system that was, in turn, projected onto a NEW WORLD ORDER metaphor system. I propose that the representation of the USA as the agent of punishment in the discourse of his son reflects a metonym THE USA STANDS FOR THE WORLD.

Issues of legitimacy depend on perspective and from other perspectives the actions of American governments showed disdain for international law. These included its rejection of the Kyoto treaty on the environment and the invasion of Iraq without obtaining a second resolution from a legitimate international body – the United Nations. The belief that legitimacy is something that the USA defines for itself was also found in the claim for the immunity of Americans from the jurisdiction of the International Court of Human Rights. Similarly, it has been widely noted that Palestine is expected to respect laws passed by the United Nations while little pressure is placed on Israel to do so – apparently because United Nations resolutions are only treated as prerequisites for action when they comply with American foreign policy objectives.

When in international affairs the actions of some governments and leaders are construed as 'crimes' in the discourse of American presidents (as implied by terms such as 'outlaw', 'lawless' and 'punish'), there is the implication that whatever is decided in the USA is globally legitimated. This position was in fact clearly stated soon after the September 11th attacks:

> And we're adjusting our thinking to the new type of enemy. These are terrorists *that have no borders* ... Many world leaders understand that that could have easily – the attack could have easily happened on their land. And they also understand that *this enemy knows no border.* (17 September 2001)

This was a very threatening position because it implies that the USA positioned itself as the sole source of legitimacy in international affairs – able to impose its notions of justice in a world without borders. The conceptual metonym THE USA FOR THE WORLD implied a global hegemony that carried with it non-accountable authority. This implied the ability to capture whoever is labelled 'terrorist' wherever they are, and to impose military solutions in any parts of the world that were deemed 'criminal' because they 'harbour terrorists'. This metonymic association of guilt between terrorists and those who support them is a constant theme in the corpus:

> I also said that if you harbor a terrorist and you feed one, you're just as guilty as the murderers who came to New York City and Washington, D.C. (Applause) (9 April 2002)

The assumption of the ability to identify guilty parties threatened the legitimacy of elected governments because there is no independent forum for deciding what actions constitute either 'terrorism' or 'harbouring terrorism'. For example, the British government could claim that the USA harboured terrorists since some of the funds for the Provisional IRA who undertook bombing campaigns in Britain were collected among the Irish community in New York. Similarly several of the perpetrators of the September 11th attacks were residents of the USA and Germany – and a recent bomber of Stockholm in Sweden had been resident in Britain – so the metaphor of 'harbouring' lacks the type of clear definition that we would expect in legal claims for legitimacy.

Another important phrase from the legal domain is 'outlaw regime'; this is used as a generic term to refer to governments that are perceived as hostile to the USA. Such 'outlaw regimes' are described as being beyond the bounds of morality and – following the moral accounting metaphor – deserving of retribution rather than forgiveness:

> Thousands of dangerous *killers*, schooled in the methods of *murder*, often supported by *outlaw regimes*, are now spread throughout the world like ticking time bombs, set to go off without warning. (12 September 2002)

> Above all, our principles and our security are challenged today by *outlaw groups and regimes that accept no law of morality* and have no limit to their violent ambitions. (12 September 2002)

Bush Senior had also used the notion of 'outlaw':

> We will succeed in the Gulf. And when we do, the world community will have sent an enduring warning to any dictator or despot, present or future, who contemplates *outlaw aggression*. (29 January 1991)

The idea of 'an outlaw regime' matches the invisibility of the 'terrorist' and the act of naming creates political realities. The search for terrorists is driven primarily by fear and the force of ethical accounting is the belief that punishment will restore the moral order. This is because moral crimes have been committed against innocent victims and innocence is fundamental to the moral basis for evaluating political actions as moral.

The term 'innocent' occurs 23 times in the speeches by George W. Bush – as compared with only twice throughout the larger number of speeches by Bill Clinton. Usually the term refers to the victims of the September 11th attack on the World Trade Center as in the following:

> We've experienced the horror of September the 11th. We have seen that those who hate *America* are willing to crash airplanes into buildings full of *innocent* people. Our enemies would be no less willing, in fact, they would be eager, to use biological or chemical, or a nuclear weapon. (7 October 2002)

> America will be better able to respond to any future attacks, to reduce our vulnerability and, most important, prevent the terrorists from taking *innocent American* lives. (25 November 2002)

'Innocent' evokes biblical slaughter when it changes from being an adjective to a noun:

> We remember the cruelty of the murderers and the pain and anguish of the murdered. Every one of *the innocents* who died on September the 11th was the most important person on earth to somebody. Every death extinguished a world.

> No national aspiration, no remembered wrong can ever justify the deliberate murder of *the innocent.* Any government that rejects this principle, trying to pick and choose its terrorist friends, will know the consequences. (11 December 2001)

What is important here is that the identities of the innocent are no longer important but since 'innocents' are an abstract category, it implies that the actual identities of 'criminals' are no longer important either. The war on terror as an abstract concept requires that the victims of terror also become abstractions. This removes the difficult business of *proving* culpability and justifies the incarceration of anyone who is *believed* to be a terrorist or 'to harbor terrorists'. While not metaphors as such, there is a rhetorical motivation which is the creation of a myth in which 'innocent' Americans are contrasted with cruel and violent enemies:

> There can be no peace in a world where differences and grievances become an excuse to target *the innocent* for murder. In fighting terror, we fight for the conditions that will make lasting peace possible. We fight for *lawful* change against *chaotic violence*, for human choice against *coercion and cruelty*, and for the dignity and goodness of every life. (11 March 2002)

Once again the notion of innocence is found in the discourse of the father:

> Most Americans know instinctively why we are in the Gulf. They know we had to stop Saddam now, not later. They know this brutal dictator will do anything, will use any weapon, will commit any outrage, no matter *how many innocents must suffer.* (29 January 1991)

Metaphors of innocence are rhetorically effective for son and father because they provided the warrant for representing the USA as the arbiter of justice and the agent of ethical retribution. If the USA was constructed as the victim of a 'crime', then its intentions would be legitimate. If it were to be claimed that there are victims of terrorism other than the USA then this would reduce the strength of its moral position as both arbiter and instrument of justice. This is why the claims made by the Israeli politicians to be innocent victims of terrorist crimes are not taken up in Bush's speeches: the obligation for the USA to act unilaterally would be weakened if the moral debt incurred was to be shared with other 'innocent' victims.

In his analysis of the language used by George Bush in the First Gulf War Lakoff (1991) argues that there is evidence of the structure of a fairy tale with a hero, a villain, a crime and a victim. In this narrative the hero is also the victim and the villain is the evil perpetrator of a crime. It was Kuwait that was portrayed as an innocent victim in the First Gulf War and the USA as the innocent victim of the Second Gulf War. This shows how the identities given to particular roles in myth-based narratives are under the control of the discourse of American political leaders. It seemed to matter little in this morally based argument that thousands of 'innocents' have been and continue to be killed in Afghanistan and thousands of Iraqi 'innocents' were also killed. It was the representation of America as an innocent victim of a crime that provided the moral basis for the attacks on Afghanistan and Iraq. In this respect the discourse of the moral accounting myth prepared public opinion for the acceptability of military actions that seemed to go beyond what was permitted by international law or natural justice. Instant decisions regarding attribution of guilt and innocence were the characteristic philosophy of the Wild West and appear to be equally prevalent in the shooting of Iraqi civilians in the period after victory has been declared.

Interestingly the myth of innocence also shifted from foreign policy into American domestic policy with the notion of the unemployed as 'innocent' victims of the crime of corporate greed:

> Corporate greed and malfeasance cause *innocent people* to lose their jobs, their savings, and often their confidence in the American system. For the sake of justice, and for the sake of every honest business in America, I have made this my commitment: Corporate misdeeds will be investigated; they will be prosecuted; and they will be punished. (7 January 2003)

The use of the same metaphor of innocence for both foreign and domestic policy encourages the American electorate to shift its conceptual boundaries of the limits of American influence as implied by the conceptual metonym: THE USA FOR THE WORLD. Notions of crime and innocence ultimately provided both the moral rationale for military attacks on those perceived to be associated with the proponents of the September 11th attacks – and provided the basis for the representation of these attacks as justified punishments:

> If they do not refuse, they must understand that all *war criminals* will be pursued and *punished*. If we have to act, we will take every precaution that is possible. (7 October 2002)

Metaphors of crime and punishment are rooted in the notion of legality and in the myth of innocence and guilt that is implied by the moral accounting metaphor. By representing the USA as the innocent victim of a crime, George W. Bush was able to provide the moral basis for acting as judge, jury and executioner in the punishment of those deemed to be guilty. In such a powerful myth there was little onus to provide the usual evidence in support of attributions of guilt and innocence – namely, specific proof that would form the basis for the link between accusation, crime and judgement.

10.4 Summary

In conclusion, we may ask ourselves why the American public was willing to comply with the moral accounting myth of MORAL TRANS-ACTIONS ARE FINANCIAL TRANSACTIONS. One reason may be that having been represented for so long by many political commentators, and other intellectuals such as Noam Chomsky, as the guilty party that had inflicted harm on innocent victims – in Vietnam, Nicaragua, Panama, etc. – American foreign policy had incurred a huge moral debt. Americans were therefore only too willing to believe in a reversal of the ethical scales in which America became the innocent victim of others' aggression since September 11th led to a huge accrual of moral credit. This permitted an aggressive foreign policy in Iraq and Afghanistan to balance the moral accounts. While the motivation of the perpetrators of the September 11th attacks was a settling of the score for previous injustices, most Americans believed that it was a much greater injustice than any that had gone before: a disproportionate response. In just the same way its military intervention in Iraq and Afghanistan are held by the families of victims to be a disproportionate response.

Judgements of complicity and innocence inevitably depend on ideo-logical perspective and angle of viewing; however, the dynamics of the moral accounting metaphor are based on symbolism and political myth. It is the symbolism of the presence of the infidel near the Muslim holy places that is seen as a violation by many Muslims, and in the same way it was the symbolism of the collapse of the World Trade Towers that impacts more forcefully at the mythic level than the actual number of individuals who were maimed or killed. Evidently politicians seek to cre-ate political myths in which their actions are justified as accruing moral credit while those of their opponents incur moral debt. September 11th provided the greatest opportunity since Pearl Harbor for an American president to represent the actions of its enemies as incurring a moral debt that would rightfully be repaid in full – and with interest.

A further reason for the credibility of the moral accounting metaphor was because it was advantageous to represent areas of the world that were not supportive of American values as 'lawless' – in need of 'taming' and 'punishment'. This representation paved the way for a further con-cept THE USA FOR THE WORLD. The imagery of the Wild West was – in the discourse of a Texan president – a historical analogy that evoked nostalgic feelings for a period in their own history when social regulation was imposed on the anarchic codes of those who lived outside the law. It was based in a morality that can be traced back to the Protestant work ethic and the belief that financial transactions could incur moral debts.

Even financial payments such as taxation can be seen as immoral. The tax imposed on tea by the British government sparked off the Boston Tea Party that initiated the American War of Independence. This myth has been revived by Barack Obama's opponents, in response to policies such as health insurance that require taxation, and has inspired them to refer to themselves as 'The Tea Party' movement. Similar myths of guilt and innocence can be traced through the issue of slavery and the treatment of 'First Nation' Americans in the opening up of the American west. Cost–benefit analysis led to the dropping of nuclear bombs on Japan since the cost in Japanese (especially American lives) would be less than the cost of the continuation of war. The moral accounting metaphor is, therefore, deeply rooted in American cultural values and can be drawn on when political conditions create fertile ground for it to flourish. At no time in recent history was this more the case than after the September 11th attacks on the USA.

11
Barack Obama and the Myth of the American Dream

11.1 Introduction

To understand the appeal of Barack Obama it is necessary to consider his symbolic significance as much as the language through which he persuades. This is because he is the living embodiment of the policies he advocates as much as he provides their expressive medium. As a mixed race African American he symbolises the hopes of those who previously struggled to realise the goals of that 'young preacher from Georgia' he referred to when accepting the nomination as Democratic Party candidate. As the child of a single mother, supported by her parents, he has also come to embody how vulnerability arising from family break-up can be overcome by education and perseverance, and how personal hardship can be transformed into a source of strength in political self-representation. As a grass-roots political campaigner who engaged with those in Chicago experiencing socio-economic deprivation, he symbolised the underlying Christian values of self-sacrifice and empathy. It is this combination of *who he is* with *who he has become* that enabled his version of the American Dream to sound as if he was telling the right story. The American Dream was a credible narrative for Obama because his life symbolised it; his life story evoked a response and when myth becomes reality the gods have truly descended to earth.

In this chapter I propose that Obama's rhetorical achievement has been to unify the messianic myth of Martin Luther King – the faith of an oppressed ('black') people in a leader who would take followers out of the biblical land of oppression – with a closely related 'white' myth of the descendants of the Pilgrim Fathers who also sought freedom from religious, political and colonial oppression. Since his ethnic identity and political affiliations were African American, it was vital that he could integrate a 'white' with a 'black' myth. I will first demonstrate how he blends black and white narratives through a detailed analysis of his interpretation of the American Dream myth. I then examine the influence of classical rhetoric in his figures of speech; I will analyse the diversity of these figures and then his creative use of metaphor and its role in structuring speeches. Finally, I will illustrate how the blending of black and white rhetorical features and myths systematically contributed to his ability to sound right.

11.2   Obama and the American Dream

The myth of the American Dream that drives his rhetoric is that most 'American' of all myths, a myth that links individual purpose with the origins of a group identity because it is a story that has appealed to generations of immigrants escaping intolerance, religious, political and economic persecution. What, then, we may ask, is the American Dream? Though it is different for every individual – as Studs Terkel demonstrated in his journey through the USA in the 1970s[1] – their interpretations share certain elements: the American Dream is oriented to *future* states since the metaphor refers to a state of affairs that does not yet exist and combines personal ambition, arising from past experience, with social aspiration. The American Dream is the belief that life can be better than it has been previously and is now; it is the belief that much human suffering is inflicted by other humans and can be eliminated through struggling to achieve ambitions. Above all, the American Dream relates personal and social identity because the dream implies that *any* motivated individual can reach *any* social position, irrespective of their personal, ethnic or social background, including that of the highest office in the land. It is the unifying potential of the American Dream – the merging of the personal narratives with a social story – that makes Obama's rhetoric persuasive.

---

[1] Studs Terkel was an American writer, broadcaster and founding father of oral history. During the 1970s he spent three years travelling around the USA interviewing more than 300 people on their interpretations of 'The American Dream'. He was a strong supporter of Barack Obama though died before his election as President.

It is not surprising that Obama's first published book had 'dreams' in the title: *Barack Obama: Dreams from my Father* (Obama 2007), and in an earlier speech he offers an interpretation of the American Dream:

> It's a simple dream, but it speaks to us so powerfully because it is our dream – one that exists at the very center of the American experience. One that says if you're willing to work hard and take responsibility, then you'll have the chance to reach for something else; for something better. (25 October 2005)

The core notion of the American Dream is future reward for individual effort – or delayed gratification. 'Dream' occurs 35 times in the corpus of speeches I analysed for this chapter, often as a synonym of 'hope', and often in combination with other metaphors such as those based on the concept THE NATION IS A FAMILY:

> It is that promise that has always set this country apart – that through hard work and sacrifice, each of us can pursue our individual dreams but still come together as one American family, to ensure that the next generation can pursue their dreams as well. (28 August 2008)

Here he proposes no inherent conflict between personal ambition and social attainment – that the private good can become the public one. His account of the American Dream emphasises that it is part of a historical myth that traces its origin to the founding document of the Declaration of Independence – the story of a people struggling for freedom from oppression. He also claims that he is personally a symbol of this myth:

> I stand here today, grateful for the diversity of my heritage, aware that my parents' dreams live on in my precious daughters. I stand here knowing that my story is part of the larger American story, that I owe a debt to all of those who came before me, and that, in no other country on earth, is my story even possible. (27 July 2004)

He defines his identity as someone who is living the dream of his parents and who is transmitting this dream to his own children. He continues by alluding to the Declaration of Independence, thereby overcoming any doubt on the part of his audience that he does not identify with the 'white' dreams of those who trace their heritage to the struggle against colonialism, as much as he does with the 'black' 'dreams' of those who fought for their civil rights. By combining appeals based on two different interpretations of the dream by groups who were historically divided he appeals to both white and black aspirations. He is effectively telling two quite different stories as if they were one and the same narrative.

The myth of the American Dream gains its rhetorical strength from resisting analysis; it is a sufficiently vague concept to have multiple interpretations; it can either have the individualist appeal of reward for personal effort, or a social appeal based on shared difficulties experienced by blacks and whites. For Obama the rhetorical value of the myth is because it integrates these differing and sometimes conflicting historical myths, becoming a sort of Everyman myth for Americans; such blending shows in the following:

> A belief that we are connected as one people. If there's a child on the south side of Chicago who can't read, that matters to me, even if it's not my child. If there's a senior citizen somewhere who can't pay for her prescription and has to choose between medicine and the rent, that makes my life poorer, even if it's not my grandmother. If there's an Arab American family being rounded up without benefit of an attorney or due process, that threatens my civil liberties. It's that fundamental belief. I am my brother's keeper, I am my sister's keeper. That makes this country work. It's what allows us to pursue our individual dreams, yet still come together as a single American family. 'E pluribus unum.' Out of many, one. (27 July 2004)

Here he rejects purely individualist interpretations of the American Dream to create an inclusive social narrative that is equally accessible to all Americans. Notice how he includes a reference to an Arab American family, and a child from the south side of Chicago, by implication an African American child, by alluding to a biblical quotation 'I am my brother's keeper' and a Latin saying 'E pluribus unum'– this is a rhetoric that integrates multiple cultural influences. In his announcement of his candidacy for leadership of the Democratic Party the dream is again interpreted as social rather than personal:

> And that is why, in the shadow of the Old State Capitol, where Lincoln once called on a divided house to stand together, where common hopes and common dreams live still, I stand before you today to announce my candidacy for President of the United States. (10 February 2007)

It is the *common* hopes and the dreams of others to which Obama gives as much prominence; fundamental to communicating aspiration is the creation of feelings of unity among disparate individuals: dreams are not private but shared: 'And we will need to remind ourselves, despite all our differences, just how much we share: common hopes, common dreams, a bond that will not break.' This convergence of a leader's aspirations with those of his followers is evident in the first-person plural pronoun in the following:

> We are the ones we've been waiting for. We are the change that we seek. We are the hope of those boys who have little; who've been told that they cannot have what they dream; that they cannot be what they imagine. Yes they can. (5 February 2008)

His own dreams, or hopes, are defined as attainable through realising the dreams of others and this is why he constantly emphasises the *social* potential of the American Dream – even though his definition originates in the traditional interpretation of personal reward for personal effort. Because dreaming is a natural activity, when used as a metaphor it argues for freedom since it implies that others cannot get into our dreams and this makes it a persuasive legitimising strategy because it resists opposition. Logically, it is difficult to reject the idea of dreaming, because it is not clear *what* we would be rejecting in so doing; in this respect the looseness of the concept of the American Dream resists, or blocks what has been referred to as a 'cheater-detection' module (Cosmides 1989, Cosmides and Tooby 1992).

The resistance to critical analysis of the American Dream is precisely what creates the conditions for its rhetorical force – it does not come over as a concept that is threatening since it is open to a wide range of interpretations and because it does not arouse the cheat-detection module. The 'American' component is an appeal backwards in time to a shared sense of history, and though 'dreams' refer to states that do not yet exist they may arise from past experience. Obama uses the figure of the American Dream to relate America's past achievements to future hopes and enables the American Dream to become the basis for acting in the present.

However, Obama also pre-empts alternative analyses of the American Dream by undertaking critical reflection of the idea of 'dreaming'; he does this by indicating that there are situations where the 'dreams' of one social group may conflict with those of another: one group may see the 'dreams' of another as a threat to the realisation of its own dreams.

It is this tension between the aspirations of different social groups that he expresses in the following:

> In fact, a similar anger exists within segments of the white community. Most working- and middle-class white Americans don't feel that they have been particularly privileged by their race. Their experience is the immigrant experience – as far as they're concerned, no one's handed them anything, they've built it from scratch. They've worked hard all their lives, many times only to see their jobs shipped overseas or their pension dumped after a lifetime of labor. They are anxious about their futures, and feel their dreams slipping away; in an era of stagnant wages and global competition, opportunity comes to be seen as a zero sum game, in which your dreams come at my expense. So when they are told to bus their children to a school across town; when they hear that an African American is getting an advantage in landing a good job or a spot in a good college because of an injustice that they themselves never committed; when they're told that their fears about crime in urban neighborhoods are somehow prejudiced, resentment builds over time. (18 March 2008)

Here he directly addresses feelings of disillusionment that can arise among poorer white voters when their 'dreams' have not been satisfied due perhaps to globalisation – he was of course speaking at a time when the expansion of the Chinese economy has been threatening the economic hegemony of the USA. However, this is a prelude to rejecting the notion of 'dreams' competing with each other and bringing to the rhetorical foreground the argument that *all* aspirations can be realised:

> It requires all Americans to realize that your dreams do not have to come at the expense of my dreams; that investing in the health, welfare, and education of black and brown and white children will ultimately help all of America prosper. (18 March 2008)

At the end of the speech he returns to the historical origins of the American Dream myth based on stereotypical definitions of the dream that are founded on hard work and self-sacrifice:

> This time can be different than all the rest. This time we can face down those who say our road is too long; that our climb is too steep; that we can no longer achieve the change that we seek. This is our time to answer the call that so many generations of Americans have

answered before – by insisting that by hard work, and by sacrifice, the American Dream will endure. Thank you, and may God Bless the United States of America. (6 May 2008)

A return in the coda of the speech to the main theme reconciles any potential conflict between the personal and the social; it also links the individual both with others who are alive now, and with their ancestors and descendants. Obama's voicing of spatio-temporal perspectives through the myth of the American Dream in the language of high modality could be described as aspirational discourse. This rhetorical style was entirely consistent throughout the election campaign: there is a single version of the American Dream on offer that emphasises social cohesion. The language of aspiration in which potential followers are exhorted to unite for a common purpose requires the use of metaphor, even though the language after an election may undertake a radical shift of style: as Hillary Clinton noted just before the New Hampshire primary when she quoted Mario Cuomo, the former Governor of New York: 'You campaign in poetry, you govern in prose.'

Obama's rhetorical exploitation of the American Dream is credible both because of its consistency and because his own life symbolised this narrative: if someone from a social and ethnic background not associated with political attainment, someone who had started as a rank outsider to Hillary Clinton in the leadership campaign, and had gone on to win the nomination for the Democratic Party and then the presidency itself – what better proof was there that the American Dream was alive and well? Everything about his comportment sustained this myth: the fact that he looked like a leader – tall and handsome with earlier aspirations to becoming a big time basketball star – his hands-on involvement in his own campaign – from self-authoring speeches to going out and meeting as many people as possible face to face in an era where political analysts had come to believe that the mass media were the only route to conveying effective political messages. Above all he had the one quality that even mythic leaders such as J.F. Kennedy lacked: a powerful, driving and completely irrepressible self-confidence; a belief that he *could* do it; a very clear sense of his own identity and commitment to actually *being* the American Dream as well as talking about it: someone who could talk the talk and walk the walk.

It is well known that Obama has had a very close working relationship with his young speech-writer Jon Favreau. They work collaboratively, with Obama being more closely involved with the production of speech drafts than his predecessor; Favreau's skills were rewarded when he was appointed Director of Speechwriting after Obama's successful presidential campaign. The following gives an idea of the process through which the Inaugural speech was produced:

> The inaugural speech has shuttled between them [Obama and Favreau] four or five times, following an initial hour-long meeting in which the President-elect spoke about his vision for the address, and Favreau took notes on his computer. Favreau then went away and spent weeks on research. His team interviewed historians and speechwriters, studied periods of crisis, and listened to past inaugural orations. When ready, he took up residence in a Starbucks in Washington and wrote the first draft. (Pilkington, E. *The Guardian*, 20 January 2009)

It is worth noting the importance of multiple drafting, brainstorming, historical research and analysis of the relevant speech genre – identifying no doubt the importance of the myth of the American Dream. Obama's rhetorical strategy relied equally on the three artistic appeals of classical rhetoric: ethos, pathos and logos. As with all effective political oratory, an initial legitimising strategy is for the speaker to represent himself as trustworthy and his opponents as untrustworthy; Obama did this through contrasting his position on the war in Iraq with that of his opponents. He opposed the Iraq War from the start, arguing that a government that could embark on such a reckless policy was not legitimate and its other policies could not be trusted:

> When it comes to the war in Iraq, the time for promises and assurances, for waiting and patience, is over. Too many lives have been lost and too many billions have been spent for us to trust the President on another tried and failed policy opposed by generals and experts, Democrats and Republicans, Americans and many of the Iraqis themselves. It is time for us to fundamentally change our policy. It is time to give Iraqis their country back. And it is time to refocus America's efforts on the challenges we face at home and the wider struggle against terror yet to be won. (30 January 2007)

The expression 'It is time' asserts that there is no doubt about what is stated, that it is obvious and self-evident; such expressions can be analysed as instances of epistemic modality that imply certainty on the part of the speaker. But there is also the claim that he is a man who can be trusted. It is this ethical appeal that Obama communicates in statements such as the following:

> I find comfort in the fact that the longer I'm in politics the less nourishing popularity becomes, that a striving for power and rank and fame seems to betray a poverty of ambition, and that I am answerable mainly to the steady gaze of my own conscience. (Obama 2006: 134)

Here there is an inverse relationship between time in politics and the desire for a popularity based on superficial ambitions; there is a contrast between outer values of media success and inner values arising from 'the steady gaze of my own conscience'. This ethical representation of disdain for power implies that political opponents were 'striving for power and fame' and so lack moral credibility. It is therefore not surprising that antithesis is a figure from classical rhetoric that he often employs in legitimising claims, usually by opposing his value system with that of his opponents.

11.3   Classical rhetoric

Classical rhetoric distinguished between two major categories of figurative language: rhetorical tropes and rhetorical schemes. A trope is a figure of speech in which words are used in a sense different from their literal or normal meaning and included figures such as metaphor, metonymy, allusion, periphrasis and hyperbole; by contrast, schemes concern the arrangement or sequencing of words that affect a sentence's structure. Examples of schemes include chiasmus – the reversal of grammatical structures in successive clauses – and parallelism – the use of similar structures in two or more clauses. We might think of tropes as more concerned with lexis and therefore as analysable using lexical semantics, and schemes as more concerned with grammar since they require syntactical change. Both schemes and tropes influence 'meaning' and contribute to persuasive effect. Obama's rhetoric employs the extensive use of both tropes and schemes often in combination with each other. For example, he often contrasts 'Wall Street' with 'Main Street'; this is based on a metonym in which a place stands for the activities that occur there, which in turn stand for the value system on which those activities are based. 'Wall Street', as the location of the Stock Exchange, is a metonym for speculation, and big business values, while 'Main Street', as a location found in the centre of every town, is a metonym for ordinary small town Americans and their small business values:

It's not change when he offers four more years of Bush economic policies that have failed to create well-paying jobs, or insure our workers,
or help Americans afford the skyrocketing cost of college – policies
that have lowered the real incomes of the average American family,
widened the gap between Wall Street and Main Street, and left our
children with a mountain of debt. (3 June 2008)

Here the activities of Wall Street are delegitimised as threats to 'our
children'; quite commonly once the antithesis is created, Obama then
offers his own policies as reconciling differences between the two value
systems:

Let us remember that if this financial crisis taught us anything, it's
that we cannot have a thriving Wall Street while Main Street suffers –
in this country, we rise or fall as one nation; as one people. (15 June
2008)

Put simply, we need tougher negotiators on our side of the table – to
strike bargains that are good *not* just for Wall Street, *but also* for Main
Street. And when I am President, that's what we will do. (16 June
2008)

The use of antithesis is also associated with a style of communication
characterised by a very high level of modality. By simplifying issues
into contrasting positions he is able to represent himself as highly
confident and as someone who will take decisions that overcome conflicts between particular groups in society: a key ethical objective for a
politician is to establish himself as legitimately acting in the interests
of all.

It is in the nature of an appeal based on ethos to imply that the
speaker and audience share the same set of values and Obama states
his own trust in the voting population:

Most of all, I trust the American people's desire to no longer be
defined by our differences. Because no matter where I've been in this
country – whether it was the corn fields of Iowa or the textile mills of
the Carolinas; the streets of San Antonio or the foothills of Georgia –
I've found that while we may have different stories, we hold common
hopes. We may not look the same or come from the same place, but
we want to move in the same direction – towards a better future for
our children and our grandchildren. (6 May 2008)

Here 'trust' is something representing a unifying force that – like the American Dream – crosses spatial divides; this is conveyed through the names of places with geographically dispersed locations.

Obama demonstrates his command of classical rhetoric through effective integration of a range of schemes and tropes and such rhetorical display enhances the emotional appeal of sounding right – frequently at high-impact points in a speech. The following speech ending has parallel structures (in italics and enumerated) and metaphors (in bold):

> And so tomorrow, *as we take* (1) the campaign South and West; *as we learn* (1) that the *struggles of the textile workers* (2) in Spartanburg are not so different than *the plight of the dishwasher* (2) in Las Vegas; that *the hopes of the little girl* (3) who goes to a crumbling school in Dillon are the same as **the dreams** *of the boy* (3) who learns on the streets of L.A.; *we will remember* (4) that there is something happening in America; that we are not as divided as our politics suggests; that *we are one people* (5); *we are one nation* (5); and together, *we will begin* (4) **the next great chapter in the American story** with three words **that will ring** *from coast to coast* (6); *from sea to shining sea* (6) – Yes. We. Can. (8 January 2008)

There are at least six parallel phrases that are of equivalent length and are syntactically equivalent. The primary trope is metaphor. The first two metaphors refer to the story of the American Dream – a national 'story', while the metaphor of 'ring' is an allusion to King's 'let freedom ring' and tells a similar story of aspiration. The parallelism arising from the schemes gives the speech a rhythmic balance that is aesthetically satisfying and, like the movement of tides, sets up expectations that are then fulfilled – culminating in 'Yes. We. Can' – notice the intonational emphasis that comes from treating these three words as separate rather than as a phrase. Delivery is also an essential component of classical rhetoric.

My analysis of Obama's metaphors, that will be described in more detail in the following section, shows that they typically occur in combination with a wide range of schemes – in particular antithesis, parallelism, anaphora, epiphora, isocolon and chiasmus – and also in combination with other tropes such as allusion. An important contribution to his rhetorical success arises from the verbal interaction of metaphor with schemes and other tropes. It is rare to find isolated figures of speech – tropes or schemes – and his rhetoric is characterised by a high density of such features and that prevents the hearer from focusing on any single one of these – they are rhetorically coherent. Figurative clustering has a similar effect to that of myth in inhibiting an analytical response and therefore defying the audience's cheat-detectors; analysis is difficult when rhetorical features are rich and multiplex as in the following (metaphors in bold, metonyms underlined and repetitions in italics):

> ...the same message we had **when we were up** and **when we were down**; the one that can change this country *brick by brick, block by block, calloused hand by calloused hand* – that <u>together</u>, *ordinary* people can do *extraordinary* things; because *we are not a collection of* **Red** <u>States</u> *and* **Blue** <u>States</u>, *we are the United* <u>States</u> *of America;* (3 January 2008)

Various antitheses are juxtaposed: 'up' is contrasted with 'down', 'ordinary' with 'extraordinary', 'red' with 'blue'; note that these antitheses themselves occur in a triplet; there is also a tricolon[2] of syntactically equivalent phrases commencing with 'brick by brick'. There are other repeated words such as 'States'; in addition, two metaphors emphasise contrasts between the Republican and Democratic states and the political allegiances that the colours symbolise. Finally there are the synecdoches 'brick', 'block' and 'hand' that stand for the activity of building that in turn stands for all productive activities. The section ends with a unifying appeal to patriotism and national identity. Rhetorical density and figurative clustering are hallmarks of Obama's style and often occur at salient sections of the speech – the prologues and epilogues – the initial and final parts. This all contributes to the rhetorical means of sounding right.

The importance of timing, rhythm and intensity can all be traced to the black rhetorical tradition (see section 4.3 on Martin Luther King's rhetoric); this black rhetorical style is merged with a classical rhetorical style that comes from features such as anaphora and epiphora (anaphora is repetition of a phrase at the start of a section and epiphora is repetition at the end of a section) as we have seen above in the analysis of 'Yes we can'. The rhythmic effect that arises from the use of tricolons is often for motivational force – particularly when they occur towards the end of a speech; consider the following section from the coda of the Iowa caucus night speech that celebrated a crucial success in his election campaign:

> This was the moment *when we* **tore down barriers** that have divided us for too long (1) – when *we rallied people of all parties* and ages

---

to a common cause (2); when *we finally gave Americans* who'd never <u>participated</u> in politics a reason to stand up and <u>to do so</u> (3).

This was the moment when we finally **beat back** the politics of *fear*, and *doubt*, and *cynicism* (1); the politics where we **tear each other down** instead of **lifting this country up** (2). This was the moment. (3 January 2008)

Triple repetition of the phrase 'this was the moment' frames another tricolon and an isocolon[3] (in italics and numbered); there are also metaphors (in bold) and antitheses (underlined). This is part of a pre-closing sequence that continues with anophora (in italics):

Hope is what I saw in the eyes of the young woman in Cedar Rapids who works the night shift after a full day of college and still can't afford health care for a sister who's ill; a young woman who still believes that this country will give her the chance to live out her dreams.

Hope is what I heard in the voice of the New Hampshire woman who told me that she hasn't been able to breathe since her nephew left for Iraq; who still goes to bed each night praying for his safe return. *Hope is what* led a band of colonists to rise up against an empire; what led the greatest of generations to free a continent and heal a nation; what led young women and young men to sit at lunch counters and brave fire hoses and march through Selma and Montgomery for freedom's cause. (3 January 2008)

This is effective use of a scheme originating in Ancient Greece but with a rhythmic effect that can be traced to African American oratory. But it is the interaction between figures – quite independently of their rhetorical origin – that contributes to his legitimacy by defying the audience's cheat detectors.

There are, then, no holds barred in Obama's rhetoric, commitment to a cause is communicated in the language of high modality, and a sense of certainty permeates his rhetorical style contributing to its coherence. It is important that while particular speeches may be adapted to specific occasions and audiences, there is a more enduring style that creates political identity; part of this is a preparedness to engage in forceful

---

[3] An isocolon is two clauses of similar length.

rhetorical combat – a characteristic that returns oratory to its classical origins where it was employed in judicial and forensic debates as well as political ones. The combative style contrasts with a personality that is characterised by gentleness according to people who have known him well; it is evident in the combination of metaphor with antithesis. Antithesis is a figure in which two positions are juxtaposed: typically in political rhetoric one is represented as legitimate while the other is illegitimate. I will illustrate this with reference to a speech entitled 'Renewing American Competitiveness'. He begins by contrasting an ongoing theme in American foreign policy – isolationism with internationalism (numbers indicate sentences):

> There are some who believe that we must try *to turn back the clock* on this new world; that the only chance to maintain our living standards is *to build a fortress around America*; to stop trading with other countries, *shut down immigration*, and rely on old industries (1). I disagree (2). Not only is it impossible *to turn back the tide of globalization*, but efforts to do so can make us worse off (3). Rather than fear the future, *we must embrace it* (4). (16 June 2008)

Notice how in refuting the isolationist position he treats trade and immigration as equivalent, as if accepting the need for trade in commodities necessarily implies accepting immigration – based on the unspoken premise that labour is a commodity. Metaphor is employed extensively to represent isolationism as a policy based on fear and linked to the past while internationalism is associated with confidence and linked to the future. In the first sentence he puts forward the counterposition: that America should turn isolationist. He explicitly refutes this position in (2) and then introduces his counter-presentation in the third and fourth sentences – arguing both on the grounds of reality about what is possible and on the grounds of utility: economic isolationism would have the opposite effect to the one intended because it would lead to a lowering of living standards. He employs repetition to introduce two metaphors that describe going back in time: 'turn back the clock' and 'turn back the tide'. They represent his opponents' policies as retrograde and backward looking. He also uses a spatial metaphor for separation, 'building a fortress around America', and a personification in (4). The figures of speech contribute to the forming of a logical argument so that the appeal is to logos as well as to pathos – by arousing fears of a counterproductive policy. He then goes on to list a number of historical analogies to provide evidence in support of his policy to

orientate the US towards a positive evaluation of both economic and
technological change:

> But at critical moments of transition like this one, success has also
> depended on national leadership that *moved the country forward* with
> confidence and a common purpose (I). That's what our Founding
> Fathers did after winning independence, when they *tied together* the
> economies of the thirteen states and created the American market (I).
> That's what Lincoln did in the midst of Civil War, when he pushed
> for a transcontinental railroad, incorporated our National Academy
> of Sciences (I), passed the Homestead Act, and created our system
> of land grant colleges (I). That's what FDR did in confronting cap-
> italism's gravest crisis, when *he forged the social safety net*, built the
> Hoover Dam (I), created the Tennessee Valley Authority, and invested
> in an Arsenal of Democracy (I). And that's what Kennedy did in
> the *dark days of the Cold War*, when he *called us to a new frontier*,
> *created the Apollo program*, and *put us on a pathway* to the moon
> (T). (16 June 2008)

It is the supporting evidence provided by these historical analogies that
adds conviction to his arguments; however, this is also done by embed-
ding metaphors within a series of isocolons and a tricolon that I have
indicated this time by using the letters (I) and (T). In describing the policies of Lincoln and FDR there are lists of four actions and I have analysed
these as double isocolons. In line with classical theory, a three-part utter-
ance brings a section to a close as Kennedy's policies are summarised in
a tricolon. There is no tension between the logical mode of building an
argument and the aesthetic mode of how it is expressed. The speech
continues by delegitimising his opponents:

> So there is a clear choice in this election. Instead of reaching for new
> horizons, *George Bush has put us in a hole*, and John McCain's poli-
> cies will keep us there. I want to *take us in a new and better direction*.
> I reject the belief that we should either *shrink from the challenge* of
> globalization, or *fall back on* the same tired and failed approaches
> of the last eight years. It's time for new policies that *create the jobs*
> and opportunities of the future – a competitiveness agenda *built upon*
> education and energy, innovation and infrastructure, fair trade and
> reform. (16 June 2008)

The combative style is enhanced by the containment metaphor of being
in a hole and a return to the antithesis between a fear-based past and a

hope-based future; this is expressed through the syntactic rhythm of parallelism in a series of isocolons. The argument structure here is to refute opponents' policies before putting forward counter-policies based on innovation and competition.

Obama has been likened to the classical orator Cicero and we might wonder why it is that his rhetoric evokes the rhetoric of Ancient Greece more than, say, his predecessor George Bush, or many other American presidents? We have seen from the above analysis that one reason for this is that figures of speech are not employed purely to add colour and interest to his discourse style, or to fit with an ethnically defined rhetorical tradition, but also systematically to develop an argument showing that his policies are based in thinking right. A classical argument structure is to state the position of one's rhetorical opponents – a counter-position – as a prelude to refuting the counter-position and offering a counter-representation; an alternative is to refute the counter-position immediately and then put forward a counter-representation. We have seen in the above analysis that Obama combines both argument structures with a range of figures of speech that were highly valued in classical theory that includes antithesis, tricolons, isocolons, hyperbole and metaphor.

11.4   Metaphor analysis

11.4.1   Overview

A summary of Obama's use of metaphor is found in Appendix 18; it shows a high frequency of metaphors and a wide range of types of metaphor. He uses nearly 10 metaphors every 1000 words; of all the politicians analysed in this work only Ronald Reagan used metaphor as often as this. These metaphors originate from over 20 different source domains including both conventional 'journey' metaphors and personifications, but also less common source domains such as 'sleep', 'reading' and 'fire'. He incorporates types of metaphor based on moral accounting – such as financial metaphors – with those that are well established in American presidential rhetoric such as 'light and darkness', 'landscape' and 'weather' metaphors. Above all, perhaps what is most distinctive about Obama's use of metaphor is that it is novel and creative.

I would like to illustrate how it is creative in two different ways: by using familiar or conventional metaphors for novel metaphor targets and by using novel source domains of metaphor for familiar metaphor targets. First, the metaphor 'harness'[4] was familiar because it had previously occurred in both New Labour rhetoric in Britain and Democratic rhetoric in the USA to represent something potentially problematic as less dangerous because it could be controlled or 'harnessed', so the entities harnessed are negatively evaluated. Obama employs the 'harness' metaphor rather differently to refer to something that offers a solution to a problem and is therefore positively evaluated. An example of this shift from a negative to a positive metaphor target is when the objects of 'harness' are natural energy sources:

> We will *harness* the sun and the winds and the soil to fuel our cars and run our factories. And we will transform our schools and colleges and universities to meet the demands of a new age. All this we can do. And all this we will do. (20 January 2009)

Here the sun and the wind are conceived as sources of power that are offered free by nature – rather as in Brown's description of taxes on the privatised energy companies as a 'windfall tax', something that is usually negatively evaluated, tax, becomes positive evaluated as a gift from nature because windfall apples are those that are blown off the tree. It is not only natural forces that can be harnessed but other energy sources:

> Let's be the generation that finally frees America from the tyranny of oil. We *can harness* homegrown, alternative fuels like ethanol and spur the production of more fuel-efficient cars. (10 February 2007)

There is a contrast between the 'tyranny' of oil – as if dependence on a particular energy source serves metonymically for the corrupt influences that profit from oil – and the moral superiority of other political agents – that are referred to by the 'we' that is the subject of 'harness'. In other cases it is human entities that can be 'harnessed':

> And *we will harness* the ingenuity of farmers and scientists and entrepreneurs to free this nation from the tyranny of oil once and for all. (3 January 2008)

The creative use of the familiar 'harness' metaphor communicates the creativity required to develop new sources of energy: so the meaning is in the content of the message as well as in the rhetorical style.

---

[4] It is a metaphor because it has a more basic sense of securing a horse.

Another familiar metaphor source domain that is used with novel metaphor targets is 'light' as in – 'We'll put government data online and use technology *to shine a light on* spending' (16 June 2008). Here light is linked with the ethical value attached to revealing corruption, based on the concept KNOWING IS SEEING. A highly skilled contrast of metaphoric and literal senses of 'light' occurs towards the end of this speech on economic infrastructure:

> As part of this commitment to infrastructure, we need to upgrade our digital superhighway as well. When I looked at that map of the world mounted on the screen at Google, I was struck at first by the light generated by Internet searches coming from every corner of the earth. But then I was struck by the darkness. Huge chunks of Africa and parts of Asia *where the light of the information revolution has yet to shine*. And then I noticed portions of the United States where the thick cords of light dissolved into a few discrete strands. (16 June 2008)

Here Obama is referring to a visually based method for representing Internet searches on a large electronic map of the world fixed at the Google head office. There is a contrast between the *literal* sense of light and darkness with the *metaphoric* sense whereby light is associated with understanding and knowledge (based on KNOWING IS SEEING); there is also an implied religious sense of light in which light is a biblical metaphor for spiritual enlightenment (Charteris-Black 2004: 185ff.). The implication is that those areas of the United States where the 'thick cords of light dissolved into a few discrete strands' are Republican states that oppose his policies and are associated with both ignorance and spiritual 'darkness'. The exploitation of metaphor and antithesis in metaphors that evoke the Bible is entirely consistent with the claim that religious discourse contributes to his rhetorical style but, since it is implicit, it does not block an appeal to the rationalist views of those who trace their intellectual lineage to the Enlightenment.

Sometimes Obama uses animate metaphors for novel metaphor targets: '*To unleash* the power of the wireless spectrum for our safety and connectivity' (16 June 2008). Here a highly abstract entity such as wireless technology is described as if it were a powerful animal that is under human agency and control – again arguing for the value of technology in solving human problems. Such appeals are likely to attract both contemporary scientific rationalists as well as younger people who feel that technological development is part of their lives.

In other cases Obama combines quite novel metaphors for familiar metaphor targets with the familiar rhetorical purpose of delegitimising opponents; the metaphor of a 'hole' is used with a negative sense of implying an absence of some sort – in particular a spiritual absence as in the following:

> ... the lack of textbooks and computers in schools could be traced to the skewed priorities of politicians a thousand miles away; and that when a child turns to violence, *there's a hole in his heart* no government could ever fill. (10 February 2007)

But the same metaphor is used to refer to his opponents in the following:

> Instead of reaching for new horizons, George Bush *has put us in a hole*, and John McCain's policies will keep us there. (16 June 2008)

A hole is of course a dark place, where no light can reach and clearly implies a negative ethical evaluation:

> I believe in keeping guns out of our inner cities, and that our leaders must say so in the face of the gun manufacturers' lobby – but I also believe that when a gang-banger shoots indiscriminately into a crowd because he feels somebody disrespected him, we've got a moral problem. *There's a hole in that young man's heart* – a hole that the government alone cannot fix. (28 June 2006)

Here the heart is conceptualised as a container that is no longer effective because it has a hole; and since gun violence is analysed as originating in a spiritual 'vacuum', the argument is that the solution to such a problem can only be from spirituality. A metaphor with a similar meaning is 'vessel' as a spiritual 'container' as in the following two examples:

> ... until this black church, on this bright day, seemed *once more a vessel* carrying the story of a people into future generations and into a larger world. (18 March 2008)

> And in time, I came to realize that something was missing as well – that without *a vessel for my beliefs*, without a commitment to a particular community of faith, at some level I would always remain apart, and alone. (28 June 2006)

These metaphors are conceptually the opposite of the 'hole' metaphor – religious faith and in particular institutionalised religion are conceived as a container that offers structure and protection for the individual; the metaphor mappings imply the presence of a 'crew', i.e. others who are in the vessel; it emphasises the importance of sharing the same sense of social purpose that we have seen in the analysis of the American Dream. Spiritual insight might be individual but faith only becomes real when it is also social.

Another quite novel use of metaphor by Obama expresses his commitment to a culture of books and formal learning; in particular the importance he places on history which is metaphorically represented through the metaphor of a book as a source of learning and understanding:

> We are shaped by every language and culture, drawn from every end of this Earth; and because we have tasted the bitter swill of civil war and segregation, and emerged from *that dark chapter* stronger and more united, we cannot help but believe that the old hatreds shall someday pass; (20 January 2009)

Although history as a book is a conventional metaphor originating as a metonym (since we learn about historical events by reading books), the familiar source domain is creatively extended in his use of 'page' in a speech that became known as the 'Turning the Page' speech:

> If you want health care for every American and a world-class education for all our children; if you want energy independence and an end to this war in Iraq; if you believe America is still that last, best hope of Earth, then *it's time to turn the page.* (28 April 2007)

Here the process of change is conceived as turning the pages of a book, implying a sense of progress – with fresh insight coming from each new page. Finally, in one of his most creative metaphors the historical process is itself conceptualised as purposeful and in line with manifest destiny:

> It's the answer that led those who have been told for so long by so many to be cynical, and fearful, and doubtful of what we can achieve *to put their hands on the arc of history and bend it once more toward the hope of a better day.* (4 November 2008)

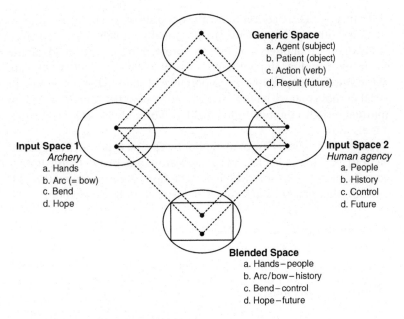

Figure 11.1   Blending analysis of 'bending the arc of history'

Here the concept of history as a bow implies that there is an active change agent – a speaker as archer – who has objectives, a target in space and a future in time: 'better day' again implies a negative evaluation of the current situation. Figure 11.1 shows the vivid metaphor 'bending the arc of history' analysed using blending theory.

There is an extended metaphor with an iconic basis in which the image of an arc evokes the idea of a bow that is bent towards the metaphor target of 'hope'; the elaboration of the metaphor supports Hillary Clinton's claim that campaigning is indeed poetry!

Since his election we have seen much less use of metaphor in his speeches and a far greater emphasis on straight talking – using a distinction originating in classical rhetoric – a 'plain' rather than a 'grand' style characterised by directness, the use of colloquialisms and familiarity. Consider for example the epilogue of the first State of the Union address after his election as President:

You know what else they share? They share a stubborn resilience in the face of adversity. After one of the most difficult years in our history, they remain busy building cars and teaching kids, starting businesses and going back to school. They're coaching Little League and helping their neighbors. One woman wrote to me and said, 'We are strained but hopeful, struggling but encouraged'. It's because of this spirit – this great decency and great strength – that I have never been more hopeful about America's future than I am tonight. Despite our hardships, our union is strong. We do not give up. We do not quit. We do not allow fear or division to break our spirit. In this new decade, it's time the American people get a government that matches their decency; that embodies their strength. And tonight, tonight I'd like to talk about how together we can deliver on that promise. It begins with our economy. (27 January 2010)

Metaphor is notably absent in this speech though we find other rhetorical devices such as the use of quotation from a supporter's letter. The appeal is to moral qualities such as keeping active, social engagement in voluntary activities, decency and strength; and the speech concludes with a very plain statement of the need for economic improvement (reminiscent of Bill Clinton's 'It's the economy stupid'). This is certainly a highly contrasting style to the epilogues of hallmark speeches given during the election campaign that we will examine in the next section. The time for metaphor is primarily when possibilities and aspirations are explored but the long hours of government are often conducted through literal language.

11.4.2 Metaphor and speech structure

As well as the type of metaphors employed by Obama we may also consider how they are employed in his speeches; they are not evenly distributed throughout the speech but occur in clusters at points of high rhetorical impact. This is especially the case in the epilogue or concluding part of campaign speeches, that, according to classical rhetoricians, has a high impact since the last words that the audience hears before taking a decision (in the case of deliberative and forensic oratory) are the most persuasive. The prime artistic appeal for concluding a speech was considered to be pathos; while ethos to establish the relation between speaker and audience is necessary in the prologue, and logos with its appeals based on reason and evidence is essential in the main argument, in the epilogue it is crucial to arouse the emotions. Metaphor is an especially potent resource for doing this, particularly when metaphor clusters involving complex interactions are employed. A good example of this is at the end of his first Inaugural speech:

In the face of our common dangers, in this *winter of our hardship*, let us remember these timeless words. With hope and virtue, *let us brave once more the icy currents, and endure what storms may come.* Let it be said by our children's children that when we were tested we *refused to let this journey end, that we did not turn back nor did we falter; and with eyes fixed on the horizon and God's grace upon us, we carried forth that great gift of freedom and delivered it safely to future generations.* Thank you. God bless you and God bless the United States of America. (20 January 2009)

Here, in contrast to the State of the Union address, there are metaphors from the source domains of weather ('winter', 'storms', etc.), water ('currents') and journeys ('turn back').The first thing to note is that these source domains match the metaphors employed in the speech prologue:

The words have been spoken during *rising tides of prosperity* and the *still waters* of peace. Yet, every so often the oath is taken amidst *gathering clouds and raging storms.* At these moments, America has carried on not simply because of the skill or vision of those in high office, but because we, the People, have remained faithful to the ideals of our forbearers, and true to our founding documents. (20 January 2009)

Water metaphors have been strongly associated in metaphor theory with the expression of emotions (Kövecses 2003) in expressions such as pouring out one's feelings, waves of tears, ripples of feeling, etc. and weather metaphors are conventionally associated with circumstances so that the weather serves as a metonym for the environment in its most general sense: economic and social conditions, as well as physical ones. The point here is that Obama responds to the emotion of fear that is implied by drawing attention to dangers by exhorting courage as an appropriate response to fear. This is a major theme of the speech at the level of pathos. The circularity of the use of metaphor in the prologue and the epilogue has an aesthetic appeal as it brings balance, and returning to a major theme is a characteristic of the musical theory of the coda and therefore contributes to sounding right.

It is interesting to compare this coda with the use of metaphor in his acceptance speech for the Democratic Party nomination:

The men and women who gathered there could've heard many things. They could've heard words of anger and discord. They could've been told to succumb *to the fear and frustration of so many dreams deferred.*

But what the people heard instead – people of every creed and color, from every walk of life – is that in America, our destiny is inextricably linked. *That together, our dreams can be one.*

'We cannot walk alone,' the preacher cried. 'And *as we walk, we must make the pledge that we shall always march ahead. We cannot turn back.'*

America, we *cannot turn back.* Not with so much work to be done. Not with so many children to educate, and so many veterans to care for. Not with an economy *to fix* and *cities to rebuild and farms to save.* Not with so many families to protect and *so many lives to mend.* America, *we cannot turn back. We cannot walk alone.* At this moment, in this election, we must pledge *once more to march into the future.* Let us keep that promise – that American promise – and in the words of Scripture hold firmly, without wavering, to the hope that we confess.

Thank you, and God Bless the United States of America. (28 August 2008)

Here we have extensive use of metaphor in a speech epilogue; there are three primary source domains: sleeping and dreaming – ('dreams deferred'), creation ('rebuild', 'mend') and journeys ('turn back', 'walk alone', 'march', etc.). All of these are oriented to the rhetorical purpose of the speech which is to motivate and inspire; the metaphor target is the American Dream and the creative actions and unity of purpose necessary for success. The epilogue performs the appropriate purpose for an epideictic speech of arousing emotions that are appropriate to an occasion – in this case those of enthusiasm and social effort implied by a journey in the company of others. When we look to the speech prologue again we find metaphors from the same source domains and with similar metaphor targets:

Four years ago, I stood before you and *told you my story* – of the brief union between a young man from Kenya and a young woman from Kansas who weren't well-off or well-known, but shared a belief that in America, their son could achieve whatever he put his mind to.

It is that promise that has always *set this country apart* – that through hard work and sacrifice, each of us can pursue our *individual dreams* but still come together as one American *family,* to ensure that the next generation can pursue *their dreams* as well.

That's why I stand here tonight. Because for two hundred and thirty two years, at each moment when that promise was in jeopardy, ordinary men and women – students and soldiers, farmers and teachers, nurses and janitors – found the courage to keep it alive. (28 August 2008)

He begins with his personal version of the American Dream, and then extends this to its social version with reference to the next generation; this transition draws on the metaphor of the nation as a family, a family that through its efforts sustains a sense of social purpose. Similar rhetorical methods are found in metaphor clusters that characterise the epilogue of the speech in which he announced his candidacy for the presidency; the epilogue commences with a tricolon:

I want *to win that next battle – for justice and opportunity.*

I want *to win that next battle – for better schools, and better jobs, and health care for all.*

I want us *to take up the unfinished business of perfecting our union, and building a better America.*

Then continues with metaphor clusters:

And if you will join *me in this improbable quest,* if *you feel destiny calling,* and see as I see, a *future of endless possibility stretching before us;* if you sense, as I sense, that the time is now to *shake off our slumber, and slough off our fear,* and *make good on the debt we owe past and future generations,* then I'm ready *to take up the cause, and march with you,* and work with you. Together, starting today, let us finish the work that needs to be done, and *usher in a new birth of freedom on this Earth.* (10 February 2007)

There are multiple source domains – war, sleep, moral accounting, journeys, and personifications of 'destiny' and 'freedom'. The figurative interaction is intended to motivate hearers to the actions necessary to bring about the anticipated outcomes, so for example 'war' metaphors imply struggle and effort; sleeping is equated here with inaction rather than dreaming. Metaphor is therefore a central rhetorical figure in creating an aspirational discourse that sounds right as well as expressing the basis for doing right.

11.5 Blending of rhetorical traditions

As well as combining the 'white' and 'black' myths that characterise American political rhetoric, Obama has also embarked on an innovative and largely successful integration of rhetorical traditions by blending the style of African American and classical oratory. At times he makes a direct allusion to the myth of the African American tradition symbolised here by Martin Luther King's use of poetic metaphor:

> We welcomed immigrants to our shores, we opened railroads to the west, we landed a man on the moon, and we heard a King's call to let justice roll down like water, and righteousness like a mighty stream. (10 February 2007)

Here there is a seamless merging of the physical achievements of largely white American pioneers with the legendary 'black' rhetoric of Martin Luther King. The merging of mythic traditions is very evident in the following section that was originally in his autobiography *Dreams of My Father*, but is then quoted in the speech 'A More Perfect Union', indicating its importance to Obama:

> I imagined the stories of ordinary black people merging with the stories of David and Goliath, Moses and Pharaoh, the Christians in the lion's den, Ezekiel's field of dry bones. Those stories – of survival, and freedom, and hope – became our story, my story; the blood that had spilled was our blood, the tears our tears; until this black church, on this bright day, seemed once more a vessel carrying the story of a people into future generations and into a larger world. Our trials and triumphs became at once unique and universal, black and more than black; in chronicling our journey, the stories and songs gave us a means to reclaim memories that we didn't need to feel shame about... memories that all people might study and cherish – and with which we could start to rebuild. (18 March 2008)

Here he explicitly refers to the merging of narratives of black people and white American Christians; there is a biblical metaphor 'vessel carrying the story of a people', and 'chronicling' – a word that implies a written culture – but also reference to the African American oral tradition, 'the stories and songs' that sustained their identity through slavery. He employs the suffering of African Americans and their response to them, as a metonym for *all* human suffering through the phrase 'black and more than black' – eliminating a distinction between 'black' and 'white' suffering. There is explicit reference to the two distinct rhetorical traditions in the content of one of his earlier speeches:

> Obviously, much has to do with charisma and eloquence – that unique ability, rare for most but common among Kennedys, to sum up the hopes and dreams of the most diverse nation on Earth with a simple phrase or sentence; to inspire even the most apathetic observers of American life.

> Part of it is his youth – both the time of life and the state of mind that dared us to hope that even after John was killed; even after we lost King; there would come a younger, energetic Kennedy who could make us believe again. (16 November 2005)

Here qualities such as charisma, youth, eloquence, and rhetorical appeals to the American Dream are represented as being shared by JFK and by King, and he therefore represents a rhetorical tradition of the Democratic Party as having the potential to unify disparate racial groups. The appeal to the idealism of his cause is contrasted with the self-interest of his opponents:

> We have not always lived up to these ideals and we may fail again in the future, but this legacy calls on us to try. And the reason it does – the reason we still hear the echo of not only Bobby's words, but John's and King's and Roosevelt's and Lincoln's before him – is because they stand in such stark contrast to the place in which we find ourselves today. (16 November 2005)

But as well as appealing to a shared set of beliefs, part of member-ship of the same rhetorical tradition is also having a common religious faith:

> But what I am suggesting is this – secularists are wrong when they ask believers to leave their religion at the door before entering into the public square. Frederick Douglass, Abraham Lincoln, Williams Jennings Bryant, Dorothy Day, Martin Luther King – indeed, the majority of great reformers in American history – were not only moti-vated by faith, but repeatedly used religious language to argue for their cause. So to say that men and women should not inject their

'personal morality' into public policy debates is a practical absurdity. Our law is by definition a codification of morality, much of it grounded in the Judeo-Christian tradition. (28 June 2006)

Here the reference to religious language emphasises what black and white rhetorical traditions share and traces this potential for a shared ideology to the idea of 'faith'; he develops the theme of religion as a rhetorical resource in creating political meaning by establishing allegiances that override ethnicity:

Some of the problem is rhetorical: Scrub language of all religious content and we forfeit the imagery and terminology through which millions of Americans understand both their personal morality and social justice. Imagine Lincoln's Second Inaugural Address without reference to 'the judgments of the Lord,' or King's 'I Have a Dream' speech without reference to 'all of God's children.' Their summoning of a higher truth helped inspire what had seemed impossible and move the nation to embrace a common destiny. (Obama 2006: 214)

There is explicit merging of Lincoln's language with that of King through their common grounding in biblical discourse. He then continues:

... the majority of great reformers in American history – not only were motivated by faith but repeatedly used religious language to argue their causes. (ibid.: 218)

Here 'faith' is something that determines both the content of ideology but also the way that it is communicated. In this respect he is making quite explicit what is often implicit in other politicians, such as Blair. By placing himself within a Christian rhetorical tradition he was able – as a person of mixed race – to combine two sources of rhetorical appeal: the black and the white evangelical tradition.

It is the blending of rhetorical traditions of black and white that characterises the most successful formula that eventually became the slogan for his political campaign – 'Yes We Can'. We commenced analysis of this phrase earlier in this chapter, and I will conclude this one with further analysis of this speech from the perspective of blended rhetorical traditions. The repetition of this phrase could be analysed either from the black rhetorical tradition as a call and response routine (see p. 84) or from the classical tradition as anaphora and epiphora – the repetition of a phrase at the start and end of sentences respectively; in the following extract the slogan (underlined) is combined with two other figures from classical rhetoric: parallelism (in italics) and metaphor (in bold):

> <u>Yes we can</u>. (break for cheering) <u>Yes we can</u>. (break for cheering) <u>Yes we can.</u>
>
> *It was a* **creed** written into the founding documents that declared the destiny of a nation.
>
> <u>Yes we can.</u>
>
> *It was* **whispered** by slaves and abolitionists as they **blazed a trail towards freedom through the darkest of nights.**
>
> <u>Yes we can.</u>
>
> *It was sung* by immigrants as they struck out from distant shores and pioneers who pushed westward against an **unforgiving wilderness.**
>
> <u>Yes we can.</u>
>
> *It was* the call of workers who organized; women who reached for the ballot; a President who **chose the moon as our new frontier;** and a King who **took us to the mountaintop and pointed the way to the Promised Land.**
>
> <u>Yes we can</u> to justice and equality. <u>Yes we can</u> to opportunity and prosperity. <u>Yes we can</u> **heal this nation.** <u>Yes we can</u> **repair** this world. <u>Yes we can.</u>
>
> (8 January 2008)

It is not entirely clear whether 'Yes we can' serves as an answer to an implied question (in which case it would be epiphora) or as preceding the actions in the following section (in which case it would be anaphora). The syntactically repeated elements of parallelism (in italics) create structural patterns into which the trope of metaphor can be slotted; the parallelisms introduce a mythic account of American history by integrating the founding fathers (white) with the struggle of slaves (black), the pioneers of the west and the space race (largely white) and the Civil Rights movement (black). The metaphors heighten the appeal to pathos through describing the various examples of the aspirations of whites and blacks, as well as his followers. It is a message that is communicated through both the content of the discourse, but also rhetorically, because of the combination of features from the classical and African American rhetorical traditions. From the classical tradition there is a range of schemes and tropes, while from the African American rhetorical tradition there is the call and response interaction, and the calm to storm delivery; there is the crescendo effect from the decreasing distance between the 'Yes we can's' in the final part of the speech.

The blending of rhetorical traditions is especially convincing because it is consistent, both because it is referred to explicitly by Obama and also because it is inferred from his rhetorical style; above all it is because it comes from a man who can lay claim to both traditions in his DNA. Any potential conflict between the two traditions is reconciled through the emphasis on a shared Christian faith that unites the 'white' and 'black' traditions and evidence for this is in the choice of the word 'creed' in 'Yes we can. It was a *creed* written into the founding documents that declared the destiny of a nation.' It is a return to religious faith that is rhetorically the means for overcoming political and ethnic divisions.

11.6   Conclusion

In this chapter I have proposed that Obama draws on a myth that has high cultural salience in the USA – the myth of the American Dream; he integrates a range of differing personal versions of this story and emphasises its orientation to collective goals. The myth defies analysis and is even more irresistible when coming through someone who symbolises the dream in terms of his personality and demeanour as well as his personal biography. Above all it is a myth to which he is able to ally classical rhetoric with African American rhetoric in what I have described as rhetorical blending; this enacts in language what his own style and existence communicate: an integration of traditions that have at times been in conflict. He is aware of the potential for dreams to collide and draws on Christian imagery as a unifying image for 'white' and 'black' versions of the American Dream.

He draws heavily on the proof of ethos by continually demonstrating that he has the right intentions, and emphasises the dream as a pervasive link between historical experience and future aspiration, so that the myth spans geographical distance and historical time. He sounds right by integrating the voice of Martin Luther King with that of Cicero and classical rhetoric and arouses feelings as much through looking right as sounding right. He also uses metaphor to show that he thinks right as well. I have proposed that there is extensive and complex interaction between rhetorical features – especially metaphor – that defies analysis and is internally coherent, for example in the way that metaphors structure speeches by clustering in prologues and epilogues. As a result, rhetorical choices operate at both the level of individual figures and the text as a whole. I have illustrated the novel use of metaphor in relation both to source and target domains; however, I have also suggested that reliance on metaphor characterises the period prior to his becoming President more than it does his subsequent period in office.

12
Myth, Metaphor and Leadership

12.1 Politicians and metaphor

In the previous chapters through an analysis of rhetoric and metaphor I have developed a theory of how persuasion works in political rhetoric. I have argued that to persuade an audience a politician has to demonstrate that he or she is right; I have then proposed a range of different ways in which we can interpret what it means to be right. A prerequisite of being right is that a politician is interpreted as 'having the right intentions', for without these he or she will have no legitimacy in the first place. Unless their intentions are socially oriented politicians will have no platform upon which to persuade – this is why accusations of corruption undermine the ability to persuade, since a corrupt politician is one who pretends to act in the public interest but in reality acts in the interests of himself or his family. I have claimed persuasion requires 'right thinking' based on appeals to reason; it also requires a politician to 'sound right' through appeals to emotion: persuasion relies on a combination of appeals to the head and to the heart. Through analysis of myth I have also argued that 'telling the right story' is an additional component of successful persuasion. I have noted in passing that with the shift towards visual media 'looking right' has become of increasing importance.

I have tried to demonstrate that analysis of political speeches provides insight into how leadership is communicated and that critical analysis of metaphors provides insight into how rhetoric becomes persuasive. All the politicians analysed in this work make extensive use of metaphor and it is therefore crucial to understand its contribution. It is especially persuasive because it influences evaluation and creates sets of associations that have both emotional meanings but also contain implicit cause and effect arguments. For example, Margaret Thatcher's metaphors associated socialism with negative social phenomena and therefore it became construed as their cause. Metaphor combined with evaluation therefore forms its own psychologically based logic.

A main finding is that metaphor is most effective when interlaced with other figures of speech to become part of a wider system of meaning creation. Strength, determination and the will to govern are communicated by an interaction between metaphor and antithesis or semantic contrast. Myth-based contrasts between good and evil, light and darkness were vital to the rhetoric of Winston Churchill, Martin Luther King, Enoch Powell, Margaret Thatcher and Tony Blair. Reagan's contrast between the possibilities of space exploration and the reality of human destruction formed the basis of his 'intergalactic myth'. Obama contrasted the values of Wall Street with those of Main Street, self-interest and idealism, isolationism and internationalism. The interaction between metaphor and contrast is fundamental to communicating value-based political meaning because of the contrast between the in-groups with whom the politician is allied and the out-groups to whom the politician is opposed.

Political identity relies on highlighting the contrasts between political choices and giving ethical, intellectual and emotional value to them. I also suggest that metaphors are especially effective when combined with other metaphors and that nested metaphors drawing on two or more source domains are likely to be more effective than those that draw on a single source domain because they create multiple arguments. Critical analysis of political language enables us to identify underlying ideologies and myths and thereby to reveal the nature of the value systems on which they are based. By becoming aware of linguistic choices we are also becoming aware of the political choices that they imply and their underlying ethical assumptions.

Style is created through metaphor and without it politicians would lack the hallmarks of charismatic leadership such as passion, energy and conviction. Metaphor choice by a politician is a vital question of leadership style because, like the choice of clothes to look right, it is a way of appealing to others by establishing moral credibility on the basis of shared values. Subliminal communication is based on a search for some form of convergence between the identities and values of leader and follower that is crucial for a power relation to exist. Metaphor is to a politician what sex appeal is to an individual: a covert way of sending out messages of desirability.

In the first part of this final chapter I present a comparative overview of the major findings for the individual politicians analysed, I then summarise the four key rhetorical strategies for persuasion in political rhetoric and demonstrate how metaphor contributes to each of these. These are: establishing the speaker's ethical integrity and moral credibility; heightening the pathos or emotional impact of a speech by sounding right; communicating and explaining political policies by developing political arguments that demonstrate right thinking and forming mental representations known as frames and schemata that contribute to telling the right story.

12.2   Overview of metaphor types in political speeches

Tables 12.1 and 12.2 summarise the findings for the frequency of metaphors in the speeches of British and American politicians respectively. The columns show how often each of the politicians analysed used each type of metaphor and the rows show the frequency of each of the metaphor source domains.

Some metaphor domains are ubiquitous in political speaking while others are restricted to particular politicians. Journey metaphors and personifications were found to be used by all the politicians analysed and accounted for 34 per cent of all the metaphors identified. However, personifications were used statistically more frequently by British politicians while journey metaphors were used more frequently by American politicians. Personifications comprised 19.6 per cent of all the metaphors used by British politicians but only 10 per cent of the American politicians' metaphors, so they were used almost twice as frequently by British politicians when the speeches are grouped together by national background. Conversely, 14.5 per cent of all British politicians' metaphors were journey metaphors compared with 22.4 per cent for American politicians, which means that American politicians use them around one and half times more frequently.

However, consideration of national background may conceal individual variations. For example, personifications were used much more frequently by Churchill than the other British politicians examined, but George W. Bush also used many more personifications than other American politicians; however, he used less than half the number of journey metaphors used by Martin Luther King. Since we know that

Table 12.1   Overview of metaphor types by source domain – British politicians

Source domain	Churchill	Thatcher	Blair	Powell	Total
JOURNEYS	48	26	75	27	176
PERSONIFICATION	144	15	31	48	238*
CREATION			35	11	46
DESTRUCTION			18	5	23
REIFICATION			28	77	105
CONFLICT		53	27	18	98
HEALTH and ILLNESS		24	10	21	55
ANIMALS	15	14	8	14	51*
FIRE	13			4	17
RELIGION/ MORALITY	13	10	6	17	46
LIGHT and DARKNESS	33		5	7	45
FREEDOM and SLAVERY	23		14		37
BUILDINGS	12			6	18
LIFE and DEATH		14	15	2	31
PLANTS		11		17	28
LANDSCAPE	5			13	18
CRIME and PUNISHMENT				6	6
FINANCE			13	9	22
WEATHER	5			5	10
WATER	9			32	41*
SPORTS and GAMES				6	6
COLOUR				5	5
SLEEP				6	6
OTHER	53	21	10		84
TOTAL	373	188	295	356	1,212

*Indicates this source domain is statistically more frequent in British political discourse ($p < 0.0001$).

George W. Bush admired Churchill (and had a bust of him placed in the White House), I suggested in Chapter 10 that his preference for personification arose from the influence of Churchill's style of war rhetoric. Tony Blair also uses them in his demonisation of political opponents in time of war. We may infer from this that the intensity of emotions evoked by war scenarios encourages the use of personification. Personification is a way of making abstract ideological issues meaningful and is therefore a major leadership strategy during times of national crisis, such as war, in both the USA and Britain.

Table 12.2 Overview of metaphor types by source domain – American politicians

Source domain	King	Clinton	Reagan	Bush Senior and Junior	Obama	Total
JOURNEYS	140	76	104	59	85	464*
PERSONIFICATION	18	9	30	110	39	206
CREATION		82	13	35	76	206*
DESTRUCTION		28	15	21	8	72*
REIFICATION	20	8	42	30	31	131
CONFLICT	14	7	35		40	96
HEALTH and ILLNESS	20	6	24		11	61
ANIMALS			4	10	5	19
FIRE		10	8		10	28
RELIGION/ MORALITY		18	13		14	45
LIGHT and DARKNESS	23		20	23	12	78
AMERICAN DREAM					36	36
FREEDOM and SLAVERY	26		8			34
BUILDINGS			20		18	38
LIFE and DEATH		76	4	9	3	92*
PLANTS			22		5	27
LANDSCAPE	26	7	4		6	43
BELL	23					23
CRIME and PUNISHMENT				24		24
FINANCE			10	29	21	60
WEATHER	18	6	11		3	38
WATER		5	13		7	18
STORY				22		22
OTHER	26	21	79	82	17	208
TOTAL	354	359	479	454	447	2,069

*Indicates this source domain is statistically more frequent in American political discourse ($p < 0.0001$).

The case is a bit different with journey metaphors which are used more frequently by American politicians. Part of the explanation is because of historical factors such as the actual journeys undertaken by migrants to get to America, and subsequently migrations within America that have characterised various periods in its history; the space programme also triggered the use of journey metaphors. The British politician who used them the most was Tony Blair. Similarly another metaphor type more strongly associated with American politicians is creation and destruction metaphors, but Tony Blair also used these more than other British politicians.

What this shows us is that there is an interaction between British and American political discourse with implications at the level of metaphor. In some circumstances, such as war rhetoric, an American politician may look for a rhetorical model of metaphor to British political discourse – as Bush did with Churchill for personifications. Conversely in other situations – such as to convey a strong ethical contrast between good and evil – a British politician may look to American political discourse for a metaphor model – as Blair did with Clinton for creation and destruction metaphors. So because the English language is held as a common resource, there can be stylistic shifts of influence in both directions, according to the rhetorical exigencies of the context in which a politician is operating.

Although all politicians demonstrated each of the components of political persuasion for which I have presented evidence, there is perhaps an orientation toward one or more of these rhetorical methods by individual politicians. While running the risk of over-simplification, it may be the case that Churchill and Martin Luther King were primarily persuasive because of their ability to sound right – voice quality and delivery as well as the words that aroused emotions were crucial to their effect. Clinton, Blair and Bush seem to have persuaded primarily through their ability to demonstrate that they had the right intentions, while the remaining politicians analysed – Powell, Reagan, Thatcher and Obama – all in various ways demonstrated the ability to tell the right story through creating highly persuasive myths.

Since journey metaphors are overall the most frequent metaphor type I would like to consider some of the reasons for their importance in political communication and also for their particular attraction for American politicians and those such as Tony Blair who were strongly influenced by them. Journeys involve some type of physical movement from a starting point towards an end point; usually the starting point is in the present and is familiar or known while the destination is in the future and may well not be known. Journey metaphors in political communication typically refer to the predetermined objectives of policy. They imply having a clear idea in the mind of where one would like to be at some point in the future. Therefore journeys imply some type of planned progress and assume a conscious agent who will follow a fixed path toward an imagined goal. Journeys are therefore inherently purposeful. It is this directionality that is important for political leaders who are conscious of the need to appear to have planned intentions. A leader who implied that policies would drift, would take the society nowhere or back to a place where it had already been would be rhetorically unsuccessful.

Lakoff and Johnson (1999: 179) describe our understanding of events and causes in terms of metaphors related to two types of fundamental event-structure metaphors which they describe as the location and object event-structure metaphors. They claim that 'What this mapping does is to allow us to conceptualize events and all aspects of them – actions, causes, changes, stages and purposes, and so forth – in terms of our extensive experience with, and knowledge about, motion in space.' From this perspective journey metaphors comprise what may be summarised as a SOURCE–PATH–GOAL schema. From this general mapping the particular types of submapping for which there is evidence in political speech making are:

Purposes are Destinations
Means are Paths
Difficulties are Impediments to Motion
Long-term, Purposeful Activities are Journeys

We have seen how politicians commonly employ these submappings to produce journey metaphors that persuade their audience of the feasibility of the achievement of political objectives – while at the same time highlighting the need for social unity, effort, etc. in order to attain them.

Alone the abstract spatial notion of purposeful motion towards a predetermined goal using the SOURCE–PATH–GOAL mental model would lack sufficient expressive force to carry great conviction. In addition to this, we also know that journeys can be long or short, that they can be over easy or difficult terrain, up mountains or along level paths, and that they require a mode of travel – foot, horse, cart, car, train, or indeed spaceship. We know that the mode of travel will determine the speed of movement towards the destination. We know that the choice of mode of travel and the nature of the terrain to be traversed will also determine the amount of effort that is required to reach the destination. Space travel has been a particular achievement of American technological aspiration and I have described Ronald Reagan's rhetoric as characterised by intergalactic myths; certainly it is the heroic dimension of space travel – combined also with the historical journeys of migration that were resonant for many Americans – that accounts for the higher frequency of journey metaphors in American political discourse.

We can now begin to appreciate the richness of this source domain: in rhetorical terms it is easy to create a set of contrasts between journeys that are easy because they are over easy terrain with efficient means of transport and those that are difficult for the opposite reasons. The expressive force of the journey metaphors is precisely because of the readiness with which very familiar bodily experience can be integrated into a set of contrasts that serve the basis for a system of evaluation. Consider the experience of finding the way: we know that instruments such as maps and compasses can help us find the way, but also know that human guides are important too. We also know that one of life's worst experiences is getting lost or encountering impediments to movement along our path such as traffic gridlocks or, even more seriously, crashes. Because of this knowledge journey metaphors can represent politicians and their policies as guides, and may systematically be used to give positive evaluations of political leadership and negative evaluations of absence of leadership.

Other metaphor types are restricted to individual politicians; for example, only Winston Churchill and Bill Clinton were found to use fire metaphors; conflict metaphors were used primarily by Margaret Thatcher and Tony Blair. Only Martin Luther King uses the metaphor of a bell (perhaps because of its associations with the church) and water metaphors had a particular attraction for Enoch Powell. These may be considered as rhetorical markers of style differentiation. A number of domains such as health and illness, life and death, the weather, etc. occur in the majority of politicians analysed and if they do not there is nothing to say that a larger sample of their speeches would not show evidence of these types of metaphor.

In the remainder of this chapter I will discuss the primary discourse functions of metaphors that contribute to persuasion in political communication.

12.3   Metaphor and political communication

12.3.1   Establishing the politician's ethos: having the right intentions

Establishing ethos is a prerequisite for persuasion because politicians lack credibility if they are not considered *to have the right intentions*. Unless they communicate an impression of complete self-belief and conviction, politicians lack the tone that is appropriate for political communication because without conviction their rhetoric will sound empty and they will be detected as fraudulent or manipulative. Metaphors when interacting with semantic contrast are a prime means for achieving this; for example, metaphors of light and dark affiliate the speaker and his opponent with good and evil respectively. The analysis has shown a shift from the more outward-looking types of metaphor – personifications of good and evil, journeys towards socially desirable destinations in Churchill – to more explicit claims to ethical qualities. From early on in his political career Barack Obama appealed directly on the basis of his trustworthiness and the lack of trustworthiness of the Republican government of the time. This held a strong ethical appeal to Americans who were sceptical about a largely unpopular and expensive foreign policy based on the invasion and occupation of Iraq. This more explicit statement of ethos reflects a deontic shift toward what I describe as ethical discourse and contributes to persuasion as long as actions correspond with words. But as we saw with Gordon Brown's claim to having a moral compass, it can backfire unless supported by other appeals.

Similarly, when George W. Bush drew on the moral accounting metaphor by describing his actions as repayment of a debt that had been incurred, his rhetorical appeal was to an ethical value system that relied on metaphor to integrate views on politics with views on correct behaviour with money. When Martin Luther King draws on the domain of slavery he was speaking as a black man whose ancestors were slaves and who inherited the moral debt that was their due just as he also inherited the roles of Moses and Jesus. Bill Clinton was able to restore his political image by using metaphor to represent himself as a vulnerable man for whom a moral sense could be reborn because underneath a troubled surface he was (and is) also a good man. Similarly, when Blair used metaphors from the domains of good and evil he implied that he was (and is) an ethical man who appealed to others who shared these values. Only a good man could see that while sometimes GOOD GOVERNMENT IS CREATING (i.e. what is good) at others GOOD GOVERNMENT IS DESTROYING (i.e. what is bad). Metaphor therefore integrates an evaluation of policies with an evaluation of the politician and it is this mirror-like quality that makes them persuasive – the ethical values of audience and politician are reflected in each other.

This view of metaphor as part of a system of meaning that shifts persuasion towards the speaker's value system fits well with a theory of political communication developed by Chilton (2004). This is that the basis for evaluation is spatial proximity to the speaker because the self is the origin of what is true epistemically and what is right deontically:

> Discourse worlds require entities in it to be relativised to the self, the self is the speaker, but the speaker may claim identity with the hearer and third parties, role-players in the discourse worlds are 'positioned' more or less close to 'me' or 'us', the self is positioned at the intersection that is conceptualised not only as 'here' and 'now' but also as 'right' and 'good'. (2004: 204–5)

Metaphors heighten the ethical qualities of the speaker by self-representation as a judge of ethical issues who is ethically close to his audience and shares their intentions; this was especially evident in what I have referred to as the Conviction Rhetoric of Tony Blair but was also present in the self-righteous tone of Margaret Thatcher. Self-representation as a moral arbiter provides the basis for representing those close to the speaker as insiders who share in the ethical virtues of the leader and those who are far from the speaker as outsiders who are excluded from a nest of virtue.

12.3.2 Heightening the pathos: sounding right

Increasing the emotional impact is a vital role for metaphor in a wide range of leadership contexts. These can range from the need to sustain morale during times of national crisis, the need to communicate the emotional investment that political leaders have in their ideas and the need to communicate their empathy with groups who are perceived as weak and deserving of support. The creation of heroes, victims and villains all imply arousal of emotions that are appropriate to the way humans respond to underlying feelings associated with protection of the family, loyalty to the tribe, fear of invasion by an unknown other. We have seen how skilfully politicians as differing in political alignment as Margaret Thatcher, Bill Clinton and George W. Bush have drawn on the most basic emotional drivers: love of life and fear of death, by using metaphors from the domains of life and death, creation and destruction.

We saw from Tables 12.1 and 12.2 that personifications occur in the speeches of all the politicians analysed. The explanation for the high frequency of personifications is relatively easy: nations, political parties, particular systems of political belief (e.g. socialism or democracy) or particular abstract nouns (e.g. freedom, tyranny, progress) become more emotionally arousing by thinking of them as good or bad people. Such personifications have long been the propaganda subjects of the political cartoonist; Victorian editions of the *London Gazette* symbolise the nations of Europe either by caricatures of actual leaders (e.g. Napoleon) or mythical ones (e.g. John Bull) or by images of animals – the Russian bear, the French cockerel, etc. Symbolic figures such as the wandering Jew and the marauding Turk have a long history in expressing emotive responses to particular racial and ethnic groups and personification continues to be a preferred metaphor type in political speeches.

Personifications provide a concrete and accessible framework for the evaluation of abstract political ideologies. They activate emotions originating in pre-existent myths about classes, nations and other social and ethnic groupings, etc. For example, Margaret Thatcher's use of master and servant metaphors was designed to evoke nostalgia for a society based on the British class system. We know that servants work hard for low pay and therefore by describing the state as a servant she implied that it was not necessary to invest highly in it as this would be to treat it as a master. Similarly, representing political abstractions such as freedom and progress, or tyranny and terrorism, creates the myth that nations can be classified as either good or evil – just as we do people. This generates emotionally potent metaphors such as BRITAIN IS A HERO (Churchill).

Such simplification of political issues is a necessary rhetorical characteristic of politicians seeking to provide leadership by evaluating their own decisions as 'right' and those of their opponents as 'wrong'. Leaders who are unsure, or ambiguous, about political issues will not benefit from the positive evaluations that attach to clear and unambiguous statements. Similarly, negative evaluations may be communicated by depersonifications that represent a political opponent as an animal, a parasite, a thing or, worst of all, as an evil being. In this respect personifications provide archetypal political myths because they rely on pre-existent culturally rooted stereotypes to communicate emotionally potent and unambiguous evaluations on an ethical scale of right and wrong.

12.3.3 Communicating and explaining political policies: thinking right

Metaphors are very effective in political communication because they provide cognitively accessible ways of communicating policy through drawing on ways of thinking by analogy. In this way they provide proofs to support the argument (logos). We have seen a number of examples of this, ranging from Margaret Thatcher's communication of constraints on public expenditure with reference to metaphors of the family budget, and Martin Luther King's representation of segregation as either an illness, a prison or as slavery. We have seen how George Bush deliberately drew on Churchill's reifications and personifications in order to argue that the situation in Iraq was similar to that in Europe at the time of Nazism – rather than of Vietnam.

Metaphors may be exploited or manipulated or even reversed in order to communicate a particular political argument. We saw how Margaret Thatcher reversed the Iron Lady metaphor from one that communicated inflexibility and heartlessness to a symbol of strength and self-conviction. We also saw how Tony Blair's metaphor 'I have no reverse gear' was subsequently thrown back at him when he shifted his decision as to whether to allow a referendum on Europe. We have also seen how the conceptual metaphor POLITICS IS CONFLICT was used by both of them in the identification of political opponents. The use of conflict metaphors is very effective as it creates an automatic set of oppositions within a very familiar mental model – that of survival. We know that in conflicts there is an enemy, a territory that is fought for, allies, and an ultimate purpose of victory. Through interacting with semantic relations of contrast, conflict metaphors are effective in constructing national identities, heightening the political spectacle and clarifying political decisions so as to encourage the taking of particular political stances.

Charismatic leadership is communicated through linguistic behaviour and it is by critical analysis of language that we become aware of linguistic choices and the political arguments that they imply. This in turn allows us to evaluate and challenge these arguments. For example, if we can show that a conceptual metaphor such as MORAL TRANSACTIONS ARE FINANCIAL TRANSACTIONS underlies many metaphors in the moral accounting rhetoric of George W. Bush, we are in a position to propose an alternative metaphor frame such as MORAL TRANSACTIONS ARE SPIRITUAL RELATIONSHIPS. Similarly, by identifying the metaphor THE NATION IS A PERSON, we may encourage a less emotive attachment to an anthropomorphic idea of a nation state. Supposing we proposed an alternative conceptual metaphor such as THE NATION IS A MACHINE – one that *imposes* order on its citizens – we may take a less favourable stance towards actions undertaken in the name of the nation. Alternatively, if we substituted metaphors based on the concept THE REGION IS A PERSON, we may develop a political rhetoric that was more favourable towards regions that are struggling for greater recognition of their identity. New metaphors can lead us to fresh perspectives on political issues because metaphor is a very important way of explaining political policy and communicating political arguments.

12.3.4 Communication of ideology by political myth: telling the right story

Leadership is communicated, often unconsciously, through the use of metaphor to legitimise ideology through the creation of myth. It may be that political leaders who are not aware of the covert level of myth are effective speakers precisely because they use metaphors instinctively. However, an understanding of the interconnectedness of metaphor, myth, ideology and persuasion explains how bids for leadership may be successful. If we removed speculative prophecy from the rhetoric of Enoch Powell, the intergalactic myth from Ronald Reagan, the myth of Boudicca from Margaret Thatcher or the myth of the American Dream from Barack Obama we would be depriving them of their most persuasive rhetorical method. This is because their persuasiveness relies on the cumulative expressive effect of the unconscious associations that their metaphors have through the political myths that they create.

Awareness of the subliminal level of political discourse is not restricted to language alone. The subliminal level – by which I mean positive or negative evaluations arising from unconscious associations – may be communicated by other semiotic means; these could include photographs, clothes, political cartoons, political posters and short film excerpts such as those used in party political broadcasts; all these contribute to looking right, which is part of telling a story.

As Barthes (1957) argues, 'The mythical signification ... is never arbitrary; it is always in part motivated, and unavoidably contains some analogy.' By analysing the nature of the analogy on which political myth is based we are identifying what motivates linguistic choice in political speeches. As Barthes (1957: 124) continues: 'A myth is a type of speech which is defined by its intention much more than by its literal sense.' This view of language was at the basis of pragmatics because it develops a theory of communication based on identifying speakers' intentions. The reason for critically analysing metaphor in political speeches is to have a clearer idea of the nature of politicians' intentions – regarding say whether particular social groups will be favoured or otherwise. If political consent is frequently manufactured – a claim for which there is some support given the prevalence of the word 'spin' to refer to acts of verbal deception – then there would seem to be a strong case for unravelling the myths created in political communication.

As we have seen in the previous section, journey metaphors were the only source domain for which I found extensive evidence in each of the politicians analysed. I identified 640 journey metaphors that comprised 20 per cent of all the metaphors used. Why are journey metaphors so central to political speaking? I would suggest that answering this question may take us to the very root of the nature of 'political myth'. In section 12.2 we have seen some of the general characteristics of journeys that make them such an important source of metaphor in political speeches; we have seen that there are prototypical features of all journeys but also optional features that may or may not be activated by the metaphor.

Journeys are therefore a highly expressive source domain for political metaphor because they integrate basic cognitive schematic knowledge of daily experience of movement with other rich and varied knowledge of experiences that only sometimes occur when we go on journeys. I would suggest that their expressive potency for leaders is because they integrate underlying positive experiences of successful arrival at destinations with the knowledge of what can go wrong. However, unlike say health and sickness metaphors, or life and death metaphors where the evaluation is fairly overt because we know health and life are good and that sickness and death are bad, journey metaphors are rhetorically successful because they rely on rich underlying cognitive patterns and on subliminal associations. I would like to take this idea further first by considering the experience of journeys from the point of view of myth and what we might call cultural, historical experience.

In many myths going on long journeys towards some predetermined goal is an established means of taking on the stature of a hero. A very common theme from folk tales around the world is a quest; this is a journey in which the hero encounters various tasks that entail danger and require courage to overcome. The journey is either self-chosen or imposed on a particular individual. Tasks may be finding treasure of some kind (usually guarded by a dragon or other dangerous beast); finding the solution to a riddle (e.g. Rumpelstiltskin), or realising a series of tasks as part of a voyage of adventure. The best example of a self-imposed quest is the search for the Holy Grail that forms a central element in the Arthurian legend. The Grail was supposed to be either the cup used by Jesus at the Last Supper or that was used to catch the drops of blood from Jesus as he hung on the cross. In this legend the more spiritually perfect the Grail hero, the greater the likelihood of his successful completion of the task. The Grail theme – drawing on pagan Celtic mythology as well as Christian and French romantic traditions – is one of the most resonant in medieval spirituality.

In European culture the most influential voyage of adventure is the Greek epic of the Odyssey. Odysseus, King of Ithaca, encounters a series of adventures while travelling home after the Trojan War. These include encountering the lotus-eaters, the Cyclops, the enchantress Circe, the sirens, the clashing monsters Scylla and Charybdis, etc. The character of the hero is vital to his success; Odysseus' qualities of resourcefulness, strength, quick-wittedness and courage have become the benchmark for subsequent heroic travellers. What is important from the present perspective is that journeys are defining activities of core mythical heroes in European culture such as Arthur and Odysseus. The skills that they demonstrate in the pursuit of their quests prove their heroic stature. Is it too improbable to believe that the major reason why politicians draw on journey metaphors is because they wish to inherit the heroic qualities associated with epic heroes? If this were the case then it would explain why journey metaphors occur very frequently in their speeches and why they normally convey highly positive evaluations of the traveller/politician. What is important, then, about journey metaphors is that they provide support for the claim that metaphor provides the crucial link between semi-conscious cultural knowledge of myths and conscious political ideologies. By drawing on deeply rooted cultural schemata politicians are able to represent their beliefs and their policies as heroic tasks and themselves as epic heroes.

I would like to consider another dimension of journeys that accounts for more recent innovations in their use by politicians such as Bill Clinton and Tony Blair when they speak of 'Journeys of renewal' (e.g. State of the Union 1994; Labour Party conference speech 2000). In myth, typically, after death the spirit undertakes a journey or quest to an otherworld. In most European traditions there are three otherworlds: an upperworld for blessed souls, an underworld for the damned and a fairyland populated by supernatural beings. In the Greek myths the souls of the dead were ferried across the River Styx to a neutral underworld governed by Hades. I suggest that the idea of a journey of renewal is intended to activate a deeply rooted and semi-conscious memory that we have of this type of myth. The idea of renewal implies that the policies described are the discovery of something that is already known. It implies that the traveller will benefit from the journey by becoming – in some respect – young again. This type of spiritual quest also evokes other myths in which the traveller seeks some fundamental answer to the problem of death such as a magic potion or an elixir. The idea of a spiritual journey after death is also a covert appeal to the Christian evangelicism that we know is important in the rhetoric of Martin Luther King, Clinton, Blair and Obama.

Finally, in Western culture, journey metaphors also evoke historical memory of journeys that were actually undertaken on this earth for spiritual purposes; these can be classified into two types: the crusade and the pilgrimage. The crusade is related to the mythical notion of a quest as the objective was obtaining something precious – typically papal blessing and a promise of a place in Paradise for those who assisted in the expansion of Christendom. The pilgrimage is a more personal journey of spiritual discovery in which the pilgrim seeks spiritual renewal from a journey to a holy place – usually the birth or burial place of a saint. The pilgrimage was a staged journey undertaken by foot that often was also a form of penance because physical suffering during the journey was a means of purifying the pilgrim of their sins. These journeys have a clear basis in historical experience but also account for the unconscious positive evaluation that is communicated by journey metaphors.

12.4   Summary: myth, magic and power

Recourse to myth and magic by politicians in the discourse of leadership is associated with a sense of the inadequacy of ordinary human skills or rational knowledge to control the world around them. If it is true that myths project powerful, collective emotions of fear and desire, anguish and hope through the situations they depict, then it is not surprising that they should recur in times of crisis and anxiety. However, as Cassirer (1946: 77) argues, there is a vital difference between traditional and modern uses of myth. In traditional societies the makers and users of myth experience it as a revealed reality to which they passively acquiesce. In modern societies myth making – accompanied by slogans, neologisms and semantic distortions – has become an extremely sophisticated, self-conscious activity which makes use of the most advanced techniques available to manufacture consent. A similar issue arises in relation to the charisma of leaders: is it something instinctive and spontaneous or is it something that is skilfully manufactured?

There is perhaps no better way to answer the question than to consider Tony Blair's Labour Party conference speech in September 2003 in Bournemouth in which he addressed a party and a nation the majority of whom public opinion polls had shown to be against a further Gulf

War in Iraq. The main purpose of the conference speech was to unite the party and to restore trust in him and his policies at a time when opinion polls were showing such trust was at an all-time low. It is just such times when the power of metaphor and myth, and of charisma, are most needed to restore the charm of leadership.

There is clear evocation of what Edelman refers to as the Myth of the Conspiratorial Enemy:

> And has lied about it consistently, concealing it for years even under the noses of the UN Inspectors. And I see the terrorism and the trade in WMD growing. And I look at Saddam's country and I see its people in torment ground underfoot by his and his sons' brutality and wickedness.

There is clear identification of the conspiratorial enemy and a suffering people who should be rescued by a hero (notice the use of the first-person pronoun). Evidently, the issues at stake have reached those of an epic struggle in which not to act is more evil than to act, as this in itself will be an invitation to evil. The argument is followed by a statement of heroic conviction:

> You see, I believe the security threat of the 21st century is not countries waging conventional war. I believe that in today's interdependent world the threat is chaos. It is fanaticism defeating reason.

The speaker's personal insecurities take us into a mythical world of an eternal struggle against evil. Blair continues:

> These are my values and yours. They are the key. But the door they must unlock is the door to the future.

In myth, apertures are the means of access to the otherworld and it is therefore natural that keys take on significance as symbols of enabling. Keys were in the charge of powerful deities or specially commissioned supernatural keepers; the Roman God Janus held a key in each hand as he stood at the crossover from the old year to the new, and the Christian heaven is protected by St Peter as its gatekeeper. The one who is entrusted with the keys has power to admit or refuse access to the otherworld, and at the subliminal level Blair represents himself as such an enabling force. He then uses journey metaphors to make a statement of his whole philosophy of leadership in which he represents himself as having progressed from an aspiring to a fully heroic figure:

> And what I learnt that day was not about the far left. It was about leadership.
> Get rid of the false choice: principles or no principles.
> Replace it with the true choice.
> Forward or back
> I can only go one way.
> I've not got a reverse gear.

Here is the clearest evocation of heroic myth in which he is quite explicit in his statement of heroic intent as he invites faith in himself because of his beliefs. As with all travellers who are on a quest, the journey should not be easy and the difficulties of the journey are proportionally related to the gains that are to be attained. The journey metaphor and the qualities of the heroic voyager are then taken up in the coda of the speech:

> This is our challenge.
> To stride forward where we have always previously stumbled.
> To renew in government.
> Steadfast in our values.
> Radical in our methods.
> Open in our politics.
> If we faint in the day of adversity, our strength is small.
> And ours isn't. We have the strength, the maturity, now the experience to do it.
> So let it be done.

This is the voice of the mature traveller who, disdaining shorter or easier journeys, focuses on the spiritual quest. The syntax of 'so let it be done' is an allusion to the Lord's prayer 'Thy will be done'; the rhetoric is heavenly but its implications earthly.

I suggest that the range of rhetorical features of this speech – the use of journey metaphors, myths, personifications and archaic lexical choices – all contribute to persuasion. This is a well-studied speech in which the techniques of persuasion have been analysed and rehearsed to demonstrate that the speaker has the right intentions. This is the rhetoric of a leader who understands, intuitively or through study, how persuasion is realised in political speeches. This is not to question the skill with which it is executed but should invite critical evaluation. The will to govern should not itself legitimise political decisions and an ethical discourse should be accompanied by an ethics of discourse that encourages understanding of how it is we are persuaded by the intentions of others – sometimes in spite of our own conscious awareness. Language – like the siren's song – can possess a magical quality that woos us to disaster against our will. Metaphor and myth provide a soothing narrative that eases the route to power and sometimes defies the critical engagement that this book has sought to encourage.

Appendix 1 Churchill Corpus (25 speeches)

20 January 1940, 'A House of Many Mansions', radio broadcast, London

27 January 1940, 'The First Five Months', Manchester

30 March 1940, 'A Sterner War', radio broadcast, London

13 May 1940, 'Blood, Toil, Tears and Sweat', House of Commons, London

19 May 1940, 'Be Ye Men of Valour', first radio broadcast as Prime Minister, London

4 June 1940, 'We Shall Fight them on the Beaches', House of Commons, London

18 June 1940, 'Their Finest Hour', House of Commons, London

25 June 1940, 'The Fall of France', House of Commons, London

14 July 1940, 'War of the Unknown Warriors', radio broadcast, London

20 August 1940, 'The Few', House of Commons, London

11 September 1940, 'The Crux of the Whole War', radio broadcast, London

12 November 1940, 'Neville Chamberlain', House of Commons, London

8 October 1940, 'Air Raids on London', House of Commons, London

9 November 1940, 'We will never Cease to Strike', Mansion House, London

9 February 1941, 'Give us the Tools and we will Finish the Job', world radio broadcast, London

12 June 1941, 'Until Victory Is Won', St James's Palace, London

16 June 1941, 'The Birth Throes of a Sublime Resolve', radio broadcast to America on receiving an honorary degree at the University of Rochester, New York

29 October 1941, 'Never Give In, Never, Never, Never', Harrow School, Harrow

21 November 1941, 'Parliament in Wartime', House of Commons, London

6 September 1943, 'The Price of Greatness is Responsibility', Harvard

June 1944, 'The Invasion of France', House of Commons, London

8 May 1945, 'The End of the War in Europe', radio broadcast, and House of Commons, London

8 May 1945, 'This is Your Victory', Ministry of Health, London

8 May 1945, 'To V-E Day Crowds', London

5 March 1946, 'Sinews of Peace', Westminster College, Fulton, Missouri

Appendix 2 Churchill's Metaphors Classified by Type/Source Domain

Source domain/type	No.	Example
PERSONIFICATION	144	Communism rots the soul of a nation. (20 January 1940)
JOURNEYS	48	The road to victory may not be so long as we expect. (20 August 1940)
OTHER	37	What a cataract of disaster has poured out. (20 August 1940)
LIGHT/DARKNESS	33	The light of freedom that still burns so brightly in the frozen North. (20 January 1940)
SLAVERY	23	Liberation of the continent from the foulest thralldom into which it has ever been cast. (14 July 1940)
ANIMALS	15	After their very severe mauling on August 17th. (8 October 1940)
FIRE	13	What he has done is to kindle a fire in British hearts,... which will glow long after... (11 September 1940)
BADNESS/EVIL	13	this repository and embodiment of many forms of soul-destroying hatred, this monstrous product of former wrongs and shame. (11 September 1940)
BUILDING/ HOUSES	12	Every one of his colleagues knows he is a tower of strength. (8 October 1940)
WATER	9	...there is a mighty tide of sympathy. (9 February 1941)
MACHINE	7	...by the monstrous force of the Nazi war machine. (14 July 1940)
FAMILY	7	...for the creation of the wider brotherhood of man. (9 November 1940)
WEATHER	5	...However dark may be clouds that overhang our path. (29 October 1941)
LANDSCAPE	5	...subjected to an avalanche of steel and fire. (30 March 1940)
BOOK	2	But here is a chapter of war... (27 January 1940)
TOTAL	385	

Appendix 3 Luther King Corpus (14 speeches)

28 February 1954, 'Rediscovering Lost Values', Detroit, Michigan

5 December 1955, MIA Mass Meeting at Holt Street Baptist Church, Montgomery, Alabama

7 April 1957, 'The Birth of a New Nation', Sermon at Dexter Avenue Baptist Church, Montgomery, Alabama

10 April 1957, 'A Realistic Look at the Question of Progress in the Area of Race Relations', St Louis, Missouri

17 May 1957, 'Give us the Ballot', Address at the Prayer Pilgrimage for Freedom, Washington, DC

November 1957, 'Loving Your Enemies', Sermon at Dexter Avenue Baptist Church, Montgomery, Alabama

16 April 1963, 'Letter from Birmingham Jail', City Jail, Birmingham, Alabama

23 June 1963, Speech at the Great March, Detroit, Michigan

28 August 1963, 'I Have a Dream', Address at March for Jobs and Freedom, Washington, DC

18 September 1963, 'The Eulogy for Martyred Children', 16th Street Baptist Church, Montgomery, Alabama

9 December 1964, Acceptance Speech at Nobel Peace Prize ceremony, Oslo

25 March 1965, 'Our God is Marching on!', Montgomery, Alabama

16 August 1967, 'Where do we go from Here?' Southern Christian Leadership Conference, Atlanta, Georgia

3 April 1968, 'I've Been to the Mountaintop', Mason Temple (Church of God in Christ Headquarters), Memphis, Tennessee

Appendix 4 Luther King's Metaphors Classified by Type/Source Domain

Source domain/ type	No.	Example
JOURNEYS	140	We can't afford to slow up. (*Yes, sir*) The motor is now cranked up. We are moving up the highway of freedom toward the city of equality and we can't afford to slow up because our nation has a date with destiny. We've got to keep moving. We've got to keep moving. (10 April 1957)
LANDSCAPE	26	You have the prodigious hilltops of evil in the wilderness to confront. And, even when you get up to the Promised Land, you have giants in the land. (7 April 1957)
SLAVERY and IMPRISONMENT	26	One hundred years later, the life of the Negro is still sadly crippled by the manacles of segregation and the chains of discrimination. (28 August 1963) If there had not been abolitionists in America, both Negro and white, we might still stand today in the dungeons of slavery. (7 April 1967)
LIGHT	23	It came as a great beacon light of hope to millions of disinherited people throughout the world who had dared only to dream of freedom. (17 May 1957)
BELL	23	Let this affirmation be our ringing cry. (16 August 1967)
REIFICATION	20	Because of the power and influence of the personality of this Christ, he was able to split history into a.d. and b.c. (17 November 1957) But we refuse to believe that the bank of justice is bankrupt. (28 August 1963) The clock of destiny is ticking out, and we must act now before it is too late. (28 August 1963)
ILLNESS	20	These men (the Republicans) so often have a high blood pressure of words and an anemia of deeds. (17 May 1957)

334

Source domain/ type	No.	Example
WEATHER	18	There comes a time when people get tired of being pushed out of the glittering sunlight of life's July and left standing amid the piercing chill of an alpine November. (5 December 1955)
PERSONIFICATION	18	There comes a time when people get tired of being trampled over by the iron feet of oppression. (10 April 1957) But not until the colossus of segregation was challenged in Birmingham did the conscience of America begin to bleed. (25 March 1965)
CONFLICT	14	And another reason that I'm happy to live in this period is that we have been forced to a point where we're going to have to grapple with the problems that men have been trying to grapple with through history. (3 April 1968)
OTHER SOURCE DOMAINS	14	One hundred years later, the Negro lives on a lonely island of poverty in the midst of a vast ocean of material prosperity. (28 August 1963)
MUSIC	6	And somehow the Negro came to see that every man from a bass black to a treble white he is significant on God's keyboard. (10 April 1957)
NIGHT	6	I refuse to accept the view that mankind is so tragically bound to the starless midnight of racism and war that the bright daybreak of peace and brotherhood can never become a reality. (10 December 1964)
TOTAL	354	

Appendix 5 Powell Corpus
(24 speeches)

3 March 1953, Speech on the Royal Titles Bill, London
March 1961, 'Water Tower' Speech
23 April 1961, Churchill Society, London
6 May 1965, 'International Charity: a Sacred Cow', *New Society*
10 December 1965, Speech to Canada Club, Manchester
14 January 1966, Camborne
25 March 1966, Wolverhampton
23 September 1966, York Conservative Association Supper Club
12 December 1966, Wolverhampton
17 February 1967, South Staffordshire branch of the Institute of Marketing, Wolverhampton
9 February 1968, Walsall
17 February 1968, Bowness, Windermere
19 April, 1968, Wolverhampton
20 April 1968, 'Rivers of Blood' Speech, Birmingham
11 May 1968, Chippenham
16 November 1968, London Rotary Club, Eastbourne
30 November 1970, Young Conservatives, Kensington Town Hall
12 February 1971, Association des Chefs d'Enterprises Libres, Lyon
19 June 1971, Doncaster Association Gala, Racecourse, Doncaster
13 July 1971, Monday Club, Painters' Hall, London
13 September 1971, West Ham North and South Conservative Association, London
23 September 1971, Preston and District Chamber of Commerce, Barton, Preston
27 September 1971, Chamber of Commerce, Croydon
22 October 1988, Churchill Society, London

Appendix 6 Powell's Metaphors Classified by Type/Source Domain

Source domain/ type	No.	Example
REIFICATION	77	True, it is also difficult to break out of the net of our own former words, phrases and professions by which we are enmeshed... (14 January 1966)
PERSONIFICATION	48	This incipient perversion of the census machinery derives from the very same general assumption which is pervading and strangling our life and our economy... (19 April 1968)
WATER	32	...will be overwhelmed and swept away if the tide of new immigrants continues to flow... (25 March 1966)
JOURNEYS	27	It is lunacy, yes: but it is a lunacy towards which we are heading by general connivance and with the speed of an express train. (17 February 1968)
HEALTH and ILLNESS	21	This assists our politicians in the necessary process of anaesthetising the British people while they undergo the operation to remove their national sovereignty. (12 February 1971)
CONFLICT	18	Either British entry is a declaration of intent to surrender this country's sovereignty, ... (19 June 1971)
PLANTS	17	This is not the soil of common interest in which lasting goodwill grows... (6 May 1965)
RELIGIONS and MORALITY	17	I prefer, patriotically, to interpret it as the converse and concomitant of our grand national virtue of solidarity, ... (14 January 1966)
ANIMALS	14	To draw attention to those problems and face them in the light of day is wiser than to apply the method of the ostrich which rarely yields a satisfactory result – even to ostriches. (9 February 1968)
LANDSCAPE	13	The reaction to that speech revealed a deep and dangerous gulf in the nation, a gulf which is I fear no narrower today than it was then. (16 November 1968)

CREATION	11	So we today, at the heart of a vanished empire, amid the fragments of demolished glory, seem to find, like one of her own oak trees, standing and growing, the sap still rising from her ancient roots to meet the spring, England herself. (23 April 1961)
FINANCE	9	If that could be demonstrated or even shown to be probable, then many might reasonably think it a gain worth purchasing, even if a high price had to be paid for it. (13 September 1971)
STORY	8	I want to tell you a story, a true story, and a sad story. It is also a cautionary story. Once upon a time there was a greengrocer with one assistant living in Wolverhampton. (17 February 1967)
LIGHT and DARKNESS	7	The outcry which followed illuminated like a lightning flash the gulf between those who do not know or want to know and the rest of the nation. (16 November 1968)
BUILDINGS	6	Otherwise the unity is a facade with nothing more behind it than alliance; and that, of course, we have already in NATO and can have in the future. (19 June 1971)
CRIME	6	It is really an astounding spectacle: the trade unions have clapped the handcuffs on to their own wrists, gone into the dock, and pleaded guilty to causing inflation. (11 May 1968)
SLEEP	6	In the last twelve months, like a heavy sleeper roused at last by an insistent alarm bell, the British have woken up and got to their feet. They have rubbed their eyes and cleared their throat and got ready to speak . . . (19 June 1971)
SPORTS and GAMES	6	And so the merry game goes on, of choking and drowning Britain in a mass of paper planning. (17 February 1968)
COLOUR	5	We have now stood up in the face of the world and told a big, black, bold, brazen lie. (12 December 1966)
WEATHER	5	. . . and with one mighty gust of Homeric wrath were to shout to the politicians and the economic priesthood. (11 May 1968)
DEATH and DESTRUCTION	5	It is like watching a nation busily engaged in heaping up its own funeral pyre. (20 April 1968)
FIRE	4	How dare I stir up trouble and inflame feelings by repeating such a conversation? (20 April 1968)
LIFE and DEATH	2	. . . improving here, modifying there; and then is someone going to come along and put a 'life' upon our handiwork. (March 1961)
TOTAL	364	

Appendix 7   Reagan Corpus (13 speeches)

20 January 1981, First Inaugural Address, Washington, DC
26 January 1982, State of the Union, Washington, DC
8 June 1982, 'The Evil Empire', House of Commons, Westminster, London
25 January 1983, State of the Union, Washington, DC
18 February 1983, 'We will not be Turned back', 10th Annual Conservative Political Association Conference, Washington, DC
25 January 1984, State of the Union, Washington, DC
2 March 1984, 'Our Noble Vision: an Opportunity for All', American Conservative Union, Washington, DC
21 January 1985, Second Inaugural, Washington, DC
6 February 1985, State of the Union, Washington, DC
30 January 1986, 'Forward For Freedom', Conservative Political Action Conference, Washington, DC
4 February 1986, State of the Union, Washington, DC
26 February 1986, Address to the Nation on National Security, Washington, DC
27 January 1987, State of the Union, Washington, DC

Appendix 8   Reagan's Metaphors Classified by Type/Source Domain

Source domain/ type	No.	Example
JOURNEY	104	Now, so there will be no misunderstanding, it is not my intention to do away with government. It is, rather, to make it work – work with us, not over us; to stand by our side, not ride on our back. (20 January 1981)
REIFICATION	42	The constant shrinkage of economic growth combined with the growth of military production is putting a heavy strain on the Soviet people. (8 June 1982)
CONFLICT	35	Above all, we must realize that no arsenal, or no weapon in the arsenals of the world, is so formidable as the will and moral courage of free men and women. It is a weapon our adversaries in today's world do not have. (20 January 1981)
PERSONIFICATION	30	If history teaches anything, it teaches self-delusion in the face of unpleasant facts is folly. (8 June 1982)
HEALTH and IILLNESS	24	No legacy would make me more proud than leaving in place a bipartisan consensus for the cause of world freedom, a consensus that prevents a paralysis of American power from ever occurring again. (25 January 1988)
PLANTS	22	We must cut out more nonessential government spending and root out more waste . . . (26 January 1982)
LIGHT and DARKNESS	20	We have lighted the world with our inventions, gone to the aid of mankind wherever in the world there was a cry for help, journeyed to the moon and safely returned. (21 January 1985)
BUILDINGS	20	Our Founding Fathers prohibited a federal establishment of religion, but there is no evidence that they intended to set up a wall of separation between the state and religious belief itself. (18 February 1983)

(Continued)

Source domain/ type	No.	Example
DESTRUCTION	15	Government can and must provide opportunity, not smother it; foster productivity, not stifle it. (20 January 1981)
CREATION	13	Tax simplification will be a giant step toward unleashing the tremendous pent-up power of our economy. (6 February 1985)
RELIGION and MORALITY	13	Let us now begin a major effort to secure the best – a crusade for freedom that will engage the faith and fortitude of the next generation. (8 June 1982)
WATER	13	...a lighthouse to the ship of state, a source of good judgment and common sense signaling a course to starboard. (30 January 1986)
WEATHER	11	In the face of a climate of falsehood and misinformation, we've promised the world a season of truth, the truth of our great civilized ideas ... (26 January 1982)
FINANCE	10	But all the democracies paid a terrible price for allowing the dictators to underestimate us. (8 June 1982)
FIRE	8	...moral issues only further inflame emotions on both sides and lead ultimately to even more social disruption and disunity. (18 February 1983)
FREEDOM	8	...for the first time in history, government, the people said, was not our master, it is our servant; its only power that which we, the people, allow it to have. (21 January 1985)
LANDSCAPE	4	You know and I know that neither the President nor the Congress can properly oversee this jungle of grants-in-aid; (26 January 1982)
ANIMALS	4	Because that's the way we are, this unique breed we call Americans. (27 January 1987)
LIFE and DEATH	4	The conservative movement is alive and well, and you are giving America a new lease on life. (2 March 1984)
OTHER	79	a revolution of spirit that taps the soul of America, enabling us to summon greater strength than we've ever known; and a revolution that carries beyond our shores the golden promise of human freedom in a world of peace. (6 February 1985)
TOTAL	479	

Appendix 9   Thatcher Corpus (11 speeches)

14 October 1977, Conservative Party Conference, Blackpool
12 October 1978, Conservative Party Conference, Brighton
12 October 1979, Conservative Party Conference, Blackpool
10 October 1980, 'The Lady is not for Turning', Conservative Party Conference, Brighton
16 October 1981, Conservative Party Conference, Blackpool
8 October 1982, Conservative Party Conference, Brighton
14 October 1983, Conservative Party Conference, Blackpool
12 October 1984, Conservative Party Conference, Brighton
11 October 1985, Conservative Party Conference, Blackpool
10 October 1986, Conservative Party Conference, Bournemouth
9 October 1987, Conservative Party Conference, Blackpool

Appendix 10 Thatcher's Metaphors Classified by Type/Source Domain

Source domain/ type	No.	Example
CONFLICT	53	The nation faces what is probably the most testing crisis of our time, the battle between the extremists and the rest. We are fighting, as we have always fought, for the weak as well as for the strong. We are fighting for great and good causes. We are fighting to defend them against the power and might of those who rise up to challenge them. (12 October 1984)
JOURNEYS	26	Our country is weathering stormy waters. We may have different ideas on how best to navigate but we sail the same ocean and in the same ship. (16 October 1981)
HEALTH	24	Three years ago I said we must heal the wounds of a divided nation. I say it again today with even greater urgency. (13 October 1978)
MORALITY/ RELIGION	18	I remember well my nervousness, and pride, as I tried to tell you something of my personal vision and my hopes for our country and our people. (14 October 1977)
LIFE/DEATH	14	So dying industries, soulless planning, municipal Socialism – these deprived the people of the most precious things in life: hope, confidence and belief in themselves. And that sapping of the spirit is at the very heart of urban decay. (9 October 1987)
ANIMALS	14	After years of gnawing and burrowing away in the background they (the extremists) have at last crept out of the woodwork. (10 October 1986)
PLANTS	11	By their fruits shall ye know them. What are the fruits of Socialism? (14 October 1977)

MASTER/ SERVANT	5	That recovery will depend on a decisive rejection of the Labour Party by the people and a renewed acceptance of our basic Conservative belief that the State is the servant not the master of this nation. (14 October 1977)
OTHER	21	We have a duty to make sure that every penny piece we raise in taxation is spent wisely and well. For it is our party which is dedicated to good housekeeping ... (14 October 1983)
TOTAL	186	

Appendix 11 Clinton Corpus (9 speeches)

20 January 1993, First Inaugural Address, Washington, DC
17 February 1993, State of the Union Address, Washington, DC
25 January 1994, State of the Union Address, Washington, DC
24 January 1995, State of the Union Address, Washington, DC
3 January 1996, State of the Union Address, Washington, DC
20 January 1997, Second Inaugural Address, Washington, DC
4 February 1997, State of the Union Address, Washington, DC
27 January 1998, State of the Union Address, Washington, DC
27 January 2000, State of the Union Address, Washington, DC

Appendix 12   Clinton's Metaphors Classified by Type/Source Domain

Source domain/ type	No.	Example
CREATION	82	And the responsibility we now have to shape a world that is more peaceful, more secure, more free. (State of the Union 1999)
JOURNEYS	76	Most Americans live near a community college. The roads that take them there can be paths to a better future. (State of the Union 1997)
LIFE/REBIRTH	68	We must continue to enforce fair lending and fair housing and all civil rights laws, because America will never be complete in its renewal until everyone shares in its bounty. (State of the Union 1993)
DESTRUCTION	28	Above all, how we can repair the damaged bonds in our society and come together behind our common purpose. (State of the Union 1995)
RELIGION	18	Posterity is the world to come, the world for whom we hold our ideals, from whom we have borrowed our planet, and to whom we bear sacred responsibilities. (1993 Inaugural)
FIRE	10	Tonight I ask everyone in this Chamber – and every American – to look into their hearts, spark their hopes, and fire their imaginations. (State of the Union 1993)
PERSONIFICATION	9	I must say that in both years we didn't hear America singing, we heard America shouting. (1995 State of the Union Address)
DEATH	8	...increasing child-support collections from deadbeat parents who have a duty to support their own children. (State of the Union 1998)
REIFICATION	8	On the edge of the new century, economic growth depends as never before on opening up new markets overseas. (State of the Union 1993)
LANDSCAPE	7	From the height of this place and the summit of this century, let us go forth. (1997 Inaugural)

(Continued)

Source domain/type	No.	Example
CONFLICT	7	Tonight I ask that he lead our nation's battle against drugs at home and abroad. (State of the Union 1996)
DAY	6	More than 60 years ago at the dawn of another new era, President Roosevelt told our nation ... (State of the Union 1995)
HEALTH	6	The New Covenant way should shift these resources and decision making from bureaucrats to citizens, injecting choice and competition and individual responsibility into national policy. (State of the Union 1995)
WEATHER	6	And I think we should say to all the people we're trying to represent here, that preparing for a far off storm that may reach our shores is far wiser than ignoring the thunder 'til the clouds are just overhead. (State of the Union 1998)
WATER	5	When Slobodan Milosevic unleashed his terror on Kosovo, Captain John Cherrey was one of the brave airmen who turned the tide. (State of the Union 2000)
OTHER	15	The people of this nation elected us all. They want us to be partners, not partisans. They put us all right here in the same boat. They gave us all oars, and they told us to row. (State of the Union 1997)
TOTAL	359	

Appendix 13 Blair Corpus (14 speeches)

28 September 1999, Labour Party Conference, Bournemouth
26 March 2000, Commons Statement on NHS modernisation, London
26 September 2000, Labour Party Conference, Brighton
11 September 2001, Statement to the House of Commons, London
13 September 2001, Statement to the House of Commons, London
2 October 2001, Labour Party Conference, Brighton
4 October 2001, Statement to the House of Commons, London
12 November 2001, The Lord Mayor's Banquet, London
22 February 2002, Scottish Labour Party Conference Speech, Perth
1 October 2002, Labour Party Conference, Blackpool
7 January 2003, Speech at the Foreign and Commonwealth Office leadership
  conference, London
15 February 2003, Speech at Labour's local government, women's and youth
  conferences, SECC, Glasgow
15 February 2003, Statement to the House of Commons, London
18 March 2003, Statement to the House of Commons on Iraq, London

Appendix 14 Blair's Metaphors Classified by Type/Source Domain

Source domain/ type	No.	Example
JOURNEY METAPHORS	75	There are forks in the road, where which way we take determines the future lives of millions of people. (26 September 2000)
CREATION	35	The health service is one of the great institutions that binds our country together. (22 March 2000)
PERSONIFICATION	31	The SNP committed to taking Scotland out of NATO at a time when the rest of Europe is queuing round the block to get in. (22 February 2002)
OTHER REIFICATIONS	28	The dedication and commitment of our public servants is second to none. But the systems within which they work are often creaking at the seams. (22 February 2002)
CONFLICT METAPHORS	27	So this is a battle of values. Let's have that battle but not amongst ourselves. The real fight is between those who believe in strong public services and those who don't. That's the fight worth having. (2 October 2001)
DESTRUCTION	18	But one illusion has been shattered on 11 September: that we can have the good life irrespective of the rest of the world. (13 November 2001)
LIFE and DEATH	15	And if we wanted to, we could breathe new life into the Middle East Peace Process and we must. (2 October 2001)
FREEDOM and SLAVERY	14	People are born with talent but everywhere it is in chains. (28 September 1999)
FINANCE	13	I call it payment – payment in the currency these people deal in: blood. (2 October 2001)
HEALTH METAPHORS	10	The world has never been more interdependent. Economic and security shocks spread like contagion. (7 January 2003)
ANIMALS	8	... is to enter Iraq to find the weapons, to sniff them out as one member of the European Council put it. (15 February 2003)

RELIGION and MORALITY	6	It is the nation's only hope of salvation. (28 September 1998)
LIGHT and DARKNESS	5	...For them (the Iraqi people), the darkness will close back over them again. (18 March 2003)
OTHER METAPHORS	10	The only Party that spent two years in hibernation in search of a new image and came back as the Addams family. (28 September 1999)
TOTAL	295	

Appendix 15   Bush Corpus (19 speeches)

(i) George Bush Senior corpus (4 speeches)

20 January 1989, Inaugural Speech, The White House
31 January 1990, State of the Union Speech, Washington, DC
29 January 1991, State of the Union Speech, Washington, DC
28 January 1992, State of the Union Speech, Washington, DC

(ii) George Bush Junior corpus (15 speeches)

20 January 2001, Inaugural Address, The White House
7 October 2001, Presidential Address to the Nation, Washington, DC
10 October 2001, Remarks by the President during Announcement at the Federal Bureau of Investigation, FBI Headquarters, Washington, DC
11 December 2001, Remarks by the President at 'The World will always Remember' September 11th ceremony, The White House
29 January 2002, State of the Union Address, Washington, DC
11 March 2002, Remarks by the President on the Six-Month Anniversary of the September 11th Attacks, The White House
4 April 2002, Announcement of President to Send Secretary Powell to Middle East, The Rose Garden
9 April 2002, Remarks by the President on the Citizen Service Act, Klein Auditorium, Bridgeport, Connecticut
12 September 2002, Remarks by the President in Address to the United Nations General Assembly, New York
7 October 2002, Remarks by the President on Iraq Cincinnati Museum Center – Cincinnati Union Terminal, Cincinnati, Ohio
25 November 2002, Remarks by the President on Introducing the Homeland Security Act, Washington, DC
7 January 2003, Remarks made by President Bush on Taking Action to Strengthen America's Economy, Chicago, Illinois
8 January 2003, Remarks by the President on the First Anniversary of the No Child Left Behind Act, The White House
28 January 2003, State of the Union Address, Washington, DC
1 May 2003, Remarks by the President from the USS *Abraham Lincoln* at Sea off the Coast of San Diego, California

Appendix 16 Metaphors of George Bush Junior and Senior

Source domain/ type	Bush Senior	Bush Junior	Example
PERSONIFICATION	60	50	And though our nation has sometimes halted, and sometimes delayed, we must follow no other course. (Bush Junior, 20 January 2001) America is never wholly herself unless she is engaged in high moral principle. We as a people have such a purpose today. It is to make kinder the face of the Nation and gentler the face of the world. (Bush Senior, 20 January 1989)
REIFICATION (INCLUDING CREATION AND DESTRUCTION)	52	43	Through much of the last century, America's faith in freedom and democracy was a rock in a raging sea. Now it is a seed upon the wind, taking root in many nations. (Bush Junior, 20 January 2001) We don't have to wrest justice from the kings. (Bush Senior, 20 January 1989)
JOURNEY	29	30	By directly confronting each of these challenges, we can preserve the hard-won gains our economy has made and advance toward greater prosperity. (Bush Junior, 7 January 2003) But the time is right to move forward on a conventional arms control agreement to move us to more appropriate levels of military forces in Europe... (Bush Senior, 31 January 1990)

352

(Continued)

Source domain/ type	Bush Senior	Bush Junior	Example
FINANCE	3	26	None of these demands were met. And now the Taliban will pay a price. (Bush Junior, 10 October 2001)
CRIME and PUNISHMENT	3	21	If any government sponsors the outlaws and killers of innocents, they have become outlaws and murderers, themselves. (Bush Junior, 7 October 2001)
LIGHT	12	11	Terrorists try to operate in the shadows. They try to hide. But we're going to shine the light of justice on them. (Bush Junior, 10 October 2001, Washington) We can find meaning and reward by serving some purpose higher than ourselves – a shining purpose, the illumination of a thousand points of light. (Bush Senior, 29 January 1991)
ANIMALS	2	8	We will continue to hunt down the terrorists all across the world. Cell by cell, we are disrupting their plans. (Bush Junior, 7 January 2003) American forces had just unleashed Operation Desert Storm. (Bush Senior, 28 January 1992)
OTHER	62	42	In a whirlwind of change and hope and peril, our faith is sure, our resolve is firm, and our union is strong. (Bush Junior, 28 January 2003) The winds of change are with us now. The forces of freedom are united. (Bush Senior, 29 January 1991)
TOTAL	223	231	

Appendix 17   Obama Corpus (19 speeches)

2 October 2002, Speech against the Iraq War, Washington, DC

27 July 2004, Keynote Address, Democratic National Convention

28 June 2006, 'Our Past, Our Future and Vision for America', Address

20 November 2006, 'A Way Forward in Iraq' Remarks, Chicago Council on Global Affairs

25 January 2007, 'The Time has Come for Universal Health Care', Families USA Conference, Washington, DC

30 January 2007, Floor Statement on Iraq War De-escalation Act of 2007

10 February 2007, Declaration of Candidacy, Springfield, Illinois

28 April 2007, 'Turn the Page' Speech, California Democratic National Convention

3 January 2008, Iowa Caucus Night, Des Moines, Iowa

8 January 2008, New Hampshire Primary Night

5 February 2008, 'Super Tuesday', Chicago, Illinois

18 March 2008, 'A More Perfect Union' ('The Race Speech'), Philadelphia

3 June 2008, Final Primary Night, St Paul, Minnesota

15 June 2008, Father's Day, Chicago Illinois

16 June 2008, 'Renewing American Competitiveness', Flint, Michigan

24 July 2008, 'A World that Stands as One', Berlin, Germany

28 August 2008, Acceptance Speech at the Democratic Convention, Denver, Colorado

4 November 2008, Election Night Victory Speech, Grant Park, Illinois

20 January 2009, Inaugural Address, The White House

Appendix 18   Obama's Metaphors Classified by Type/Source Domain

Source domain/ type	No.	Example
JOURNEY	85	We can harness homegrown, alternative fuels like ethanol and spur the production of more fuel-efficient cars. (10 February 2007)
CREATION	76	Together, starting today, let us finish the work that needs to be done, and usher in a new birth of freedom on this Earth. (10 February 2007)
CONFLICT	40	Those are the battles that we need to fight. Those are the battles that we willingly join. The battles against ignorance and intolerance. Corruption and greed. Poverty and despair. (2 October 2002)
PERSONIFICATION	39	Their summoning of a higher truth helped inspire what had seemed impossible, and move the nation to embrace a common destiny. (28 June 2006)
SLEEP	36	It requires all Americans to realize that your dreams do not have to come at the expense of my dreams; (18 March 2008)
REIFICATION	31	That's why we were able to reform a death penalty system that was broken. (10 February 2007)
FINANCE	21	In reaffirming the greatness of our nation, we understand that greatness is never a given. It must be earned. (20 January 2009)
BUILDINGS	18	This is our time – to put our people back to work and open doors of opportunity for our kids. (5 November 2008)
READING	17	It's time to turn the page on health care. (10 February 2007)
RELIGION and MORALITY	14	It was stained by this nation's original sin of slavery. (18 March 2008)
LIGHT and DARKNESS	12	This is the moment when every nation in Europe must have the chance to choose its own tomorrow free from the shadows of yesterday. (24 July 2008)
HEALTH	11	So to say that men and women should not inject their 'personal morality' into public policy debates. (28 June 2006)

FIRE	10	I know that an invasion of Iraq without a clear rationale and without strong international support will only fan the flames of the Middle East, ... (2 October 2002)
DEATH and DESTRUCTION	8	It was the president of the very health industry association that funded the 'Harry and Louise' ads designed to kill the Clinton health care plan in the early nineties. (25 January 2007)
WATER	7	The words have been spoken during rising tides of prosperity and the still waters of peace. (20 January 2009)
LANDSCAPE	6	... tax breaks that mortgage our children's future on a mountain of debt. (5 February 2008)
ANIMALS	5	But for all those who scratched and clawed their way to get a piece of the American Dream, ... (18 March 2008)
PLANTS	5	But I have asserted a firm conviction – a conviction rooted in my faith in God and my faith in the American people. (18 March 2008)
WEATHER	3	Yet, every so often the oath is taken amidst gathering clouds and raging storms. (20 January 2009)
LIFE and RENEWAL	3	Together, starting today, let us finish the work that needs to be done, and usher in a new birth of freedom on this Earth. (10 February 2007)
TOTAL	447	

Bibliography

Abse, L. (2001) *Tony Blair: The Man behind the Smile* (London: Robson Books).

Ahrens, K. (ed.) (2009) *Politics, Gender and Conceptual Metaphor* (Amsterdam and Philadelphia: John Benjamins).

Aristotle, in W.D. Ross (1952) *The Works of Aristotle*, vol. XI *De Poetica*, trans. I. Bywater. *Rhetoric* (Oxford: Clarendon Press).

Atkinson, J. M. (1984) *Our Masters' Voices: the Language and Body Language of Politics* (London: Methuen).

Bakhtin, M. M. (1981) *The Dialogic Imagination: Four Essays*. ed. M. Holquist, trans. C. Emerson and M. Holquist (Austin and London: University of Texas Press).

Barrett, L. (1984) *Gambling with History: Reagan in the White House* (London: Penguin Books).

Barthes, R. (1957) *Mythologies*. Selected and translated by A. Lavers (New York: The Noonday Press).

Beer, A. and de Landtsheer, C. (eds) (2004) *Metaphorical World Politics* (East Lansing, Mich.: Michigan State University).

Billig, M. and MacMillan, K. (2005) 'Metaphor, Idiom and Ideology: the Search for "No Smoking Guns" across Time', *Discourse and Society*, 16(4), 459–80.

Blair, T. (2010) *A Journey* (London: Hutchinson).

Blaney, J.R. and Benoit, W.L. (2001) *The Clinton Scandals and the Politics of Image Restoration* (Westport, Conn.: Praeger Publishers).

Boers, F. (1999) 'When a Bodily Source Domain Becomes Prominent: the Joy of Counting Metaphors in the Socio-Economic Domain', in R.W. Gibbs and G. Steen (eds) *Metaphor in Cognitive Linguistics* (Amsterdam and Philadelphia: John Benjamins), pp. 47–56.

Boyd, R. (1993) 'Metaphor and Theory Change: what is "Metaphor" a Metaphor for?', in A. Ortony (ed.) *Metaphor and Thought*, 2nd edn (Cambridge: CUP), pp. 481–532.

Brown, T. (1988) *JFK: History of an Image* (Bloomington: Indiana University Press).

Bruce, B. (1992) *Images of Power* (London: Kogan Page).

Burns, J.M. (1978) *Leadership* (New York: Harper Row).

Cassirer, E. (1946) *The Myth of the State* (New Haven and London: Yale University Press).

Cameron, L. and Low, G. (eds) (1999) *Researching and Applying Metaphor* (Cambridge: CUP).

Charteris-Black, J. (2004) *Corpus Approaches to Critical Metaphor Analysis* (Basingstoke: Palgrave Macmillan).

Charteris-Black, J. (2006) 'Britain as a Container: Immigration Metaphors in the 2005 Election Campaign', *Discourse and Society* 17(6), 563–82.

Charteris-Black, J. (2007) *The Communication of Leadership: the Design of Leadership Style* (London and New York: Routledge).

Charteris-Black, J. (2009a) 'Metaphor and Gender in British Parliamentary Debates', in K. Ahrens (ed.) *Politics, Gender and Conceptual Metaphor* (Amsterdam and Philadelphia: John Benjamins), pp. 196–234.

Charteris-Black, J. (2009b) 'Metaphor and Political Communication', in A. Musolff and J. Zinken (eds) *Metaphor and Discourse* (Basingstoke and New York: Palgrave Macmillan), pp. 97–115.

Chilton, P. (1996) *Security Metaphors: Cold War Discourse from Containment to Common House* (New York: Peter Lang).

Chilton, P. (2004) *Analysing Political Discourse* (London and New York: Routledge).

Chilton P. and Ilyin, M. (1993) 'Metaphor in Political Discourse: the Case of the "Common European House" ', *Discourse and Society* 4(1), 7–31.

Chilton, P. and Schäffner, C. (2002) *Politics as Text and Talk: Analytic Approaches to Political Discourse* (Amsterdam: John Benjamins).

Clarke, R. (2004) *Against All Enemies: Inside America's War on Terror* (New York: Simon and Schuster).

Cosmides, L. (1989) 'The Logic of Social Exchange: Has Natural Selection Shaped how Humans Reason? Studies with the Wason Selection Task', *Cognition*, 31, 187–276.

Cosmides, L. and Tooby, J. (1992) 'Cognitive Adaptations for Social Exchange', in J. Barkow, L. Cosmides and J. Tooby (eds) *The Adapted Mind: Evolutionary Psychology and the Generation of Culture* (New York: Oxford University Press).

Diggins, J. P. (2007) *Ronald Reagan: Fate, Freedom, and the Making of History* (New York and London: Norton).

Edelman, M. (1977) *Political Language: Words that Succeed and Policies that Fail* (New York: Academic Press).

Edelman, M. (1988) *Constructing the Political Spectacle* (Chicago and London: University of Chicago Press).

El Refaie, E. (2001) 'Metaphors We Discriminate by: Naturalised Themes in Austrian Newspaper Articles about Asylum Seekers', *Journal of Sociolinguistics*, 5(3), 352–71.

Fairclough, N. (1989) *Language and Power* (London and New York: Longman).

Fairclough, N. (1995) *Critical Discourse Analysis: the Critical Study of Language* (London: Longman).

Fairclough, N. (2000) *New Labour, New Language?* (London and New York: Routledge).

Fairclough, N. (2006) *Language and Globalization* (London and New York: Routledge).

Flood, C.G. (1996) *Political Myth: a Theoretical Introduction* (New York and London: Garland).

Frum, D. (2003) *The Right Man: the Surprise Presidency of George W. Bush* (London: Weidenfeld & Nicolson).

Garrow, D.J. (1978) *Protest at Selma: Martin Luther King Jr. and the Voting Rights Act of 1965* (New Haven: Yale University Press).

Garrow, D.J. (1988) *Bearing the Cross: Martin Luther King, Jr. and Southern Christian Leadership Conference* (London: Jonathan Cape).

Geiss, M.L. (1987) *The Language of Politics* (New York: Springer-Verlag).

Goatly, A. (1997) *The Language of Metaphors* (London and New York: Routledge).

Graham, P., Keenan, T. and Dowd, A. (2004) 'A Call to Arms at the End of History: a Discourse-Historical Analysis of George W. Bush's Declaration of War on Terror', *Discourse and Society*, 15(2), 199–221.

Hawkins, B. (2001) 'Ideology, Metaphor and Iconographic Reference', in R. Dirven, R. Frank and C. Ilie (eds) *Language and Ideology*: vol. II *Descriptive Cognitive Approaches* (Amsterdam and Philadelphia: Benjamins), pp. 27–50.

Heffer, S. (1999) *Like the Roman: the Life of Enoch Powell* (London: Phoenix).

Hitler, A. (1969) *Mein Kampf*, with an introduction by D.C. Watt; translated from the German (London: Hutchinson).

Hodge, R. and Kress, G. (1993) *Language as Ideology* (London: Routledge).

Hodgkinson, G. and Leland, C.M. (1999) 'Metaphors in the 1996 Presidential Debates: an Analysis of Themes', in *The Electronic Election: Perspectives on the 1996 Campaign Communication* (New Jersey and London: Lawrence Erlbaum Associates), pp. 149–62.

Hogan, J.J. (1990) 'Reaganomics and Economic Policy', in D.M. Hill, R.A. Moore and P. Williams, *The Reagan Presidency: an Incomplete Revolution?* (Basingstoke: Palgrave Macmillan), pp. 135–60.

Howe, N. (1988) 'Metaphor in Contemporary American Political Discourse', *Metaphor and Symbolic Activity*, 3(2), 87–104.

Hunston, S. and Thompson, G. (eds) (2000) *Evaluation in Text* (Oxford: OUP).

James, R.R. (1973) *Churchill: a Study in Failure 1900–1939* (Harmondsworth: Penguin).

Jamieson, G.H. (1985) *Communication and Persuasion* (London: Croom Helm).

Jansen, S. C. and Sabo, D. (1994) 'The Sport/War Metaphor: Hegemonic Masculinity, the Persian Gulf War, and the New World Order', *Sociology of Sport Journal*, 11, 1–17.

Johnson, K. and Elebash, C. (1988) 'The Contagion from the Right: the Americanization of British Political Advertising', in L.L. Kaid et al. (eds) *New Perspectives on Political Advertising* (Carbondale: Southern Illinois University Press), pp. 293–313.

Johnson, M. (1987) *The Body in the Mind* (Chicago: University of Chicago Press).

Johnson, M. (1993) *Moral Imagination: how Cognitive Science Changes Ethics* (Chicago: University of Chicago Press).

Jones, N. (1996) *Soundbites and Spin Doctors* (London: Cassell).

Jones, N. (1997) *Campaign 97* (London: Indigo).

Jowett, G. and O'Donnell, V. (1992) *Propaganda and Persuasion* (London and Newbury Park: Sage).

Kirkpatrick, B. (ed.) (1992) *Brewer's Concise Dictionary of Phrase and Fable* (London: Cassell).

Koller, V. (2004) *Metaphor and Gender in Business Media Discourse: a Critical Cognitive Study* (Basingstoke: Palgrave Macmillan).

Kövecses, Z. (2003) *Metaphor and Emotion: Language, Culture and Body in Human Feeling* (Cambridge: CUP).

Lakoff, G. (1987) *Women, Fire and Dangerous Things: what Categories Reveal about the Mind* (Chicago and London: University of Chicago Press).

Lakoff, G. (1991) 'The Metaphor System Used to Justify War in the Gulf', *Journal of Urban and Cultural Studies*, 2(1), 59–72.

Lakoff, G. (1993) 'The Contemporary Theory of Metaphor', in A. Ortony (ed.) *Metaphor and Thought*, 2nd edn (Cambridge: CUP), pp. 202–51.

Lakoff, G. (2002) *Moral Politics*, 2nd edn (Chicago and London: University of Chicago Press).

Lakoff, G. and Johnson, M. (1980) *Metaphors We Live By* (Chicago: University of Chicago Press).

Lakoff, G. and Johnson, M. (1999) *Philosophy in the Flesh: Embodied Mind and its Challenge to Western Thought* (New York: Basic Books).

Lakoff, G. and Kövecses, Z. (1987) 'The Cognitive Model of Anger Inherent in American English', in D. Holland and N. Quinn (eds) *Cultural Models in Language and Thought* (New York: CUP), pp. 195–221.

Lakoff, G. and Turner, M. (1989) *More than Cool Reason: a Field Guide to Poetic Metaphor* Chicago (London: University of Chicago Press).

Ling, P. (2002) *Martin Luther King* (London and New York: Routledge).

Lischer, R. (1995) *The Preacher King* (Oxford and New York: OUP).

Louw, B. (1993) 'Irony in the Text or Insincerity in the Writer? – the Diagnostic Potential of Semantic Prosodies', in M. Baker, G. Francis and E. Tognini-Bonelli (eds) *Text and Technology: in Honour of John Sinclair* (Amsterdam: Benjamins), pp. 157–76.

McNair, B. (2003) *An Introduction to Political Communication*, 3rd edn (London and New York: Routledge).

Martin, A. (2000) 'Beyond Exchange: Appraisal Systems in English', in S. Hunston and G. Thompson (eds) *Evaluation in Text* (Oxford: OUP), pp. 142–75.

Medhurst, M., Ivie, R.L., Wander, P. and Scott, R.L. (1990) *Cold War Rhetoric: Strategy, Metaphor, and Ideology* (New York, Westport, Conn. and London: Greenwood Press).

Mervin, D. (1990) *Ronald Reagan and the American Presidency* (Harlow: Longman).

Miller, K.D. (1992) *Voice of Deliverance: the Language of Martin Luther King, Jr. and its Sources* (New York: Free Press).

Mio, J.S. (1997) 'Metaphor and Politics', *Metaphor and Symbol*, 12(2), 113–33.

Musolff, A. (2000a) *Mirror Images of Europe: Metaphors in the Public Debate about Europe in Britain and Germany* (Munich: Iudicium).

Musolff, A. (2000b) 'Maritime Journey Metaphors in British and German Public Discourse: Transport Vessels of International Communication?' *German as a Foreign Language* 3/2000 (Internet journal, cf. URL: http://www.gfl-journal. com).

Musolff, A. (2001) 'Cross-Language Metaphor: Parents and Children, Love, Marriage and Divorce in the European Family', in J. Cotterill and A. Ife (eds) *Language across Boundaries* (London and New York: Continuum), pp. 119–34.

Musolff, A. (2003) 'Metaphor Scenarios in Political Discourse in Britain and Germany', in S. Geideck and L. W. Liebert (eds) *Sinnformeln* (Berlin and New York: Walter de Gruyter), pp. 259–82.

Musolff, A. (2004) *Metaphor and Political Discourse: Analogical Reasoning in Debates about Europe* (London: Palgrave Macmillan).

Musolff, A. (2006) 'Metaphor Scenarios in Public Discourse', *Metaphor and Symbol*, 21(2), 23–38.

Musolff, A. and Zinken, J. (eds) (2009) *Metaphor and Discourse* (Basingstoke and New York: Palgrave Macmillan).

Nash, W. (1989) *Rhetoric: the Wit of Persuasion* (Cambridge: Blackwell).

Oates, S.B. (1994) *Let the Trumpet Sound: the Life of Martin Luther King, Jr* (New York: Harper Perennial).

Obama, B. (2006) *The Audacity of Hope* (New York: Random House).

Obama, B. (2007) *Barack Obama: Dreams from my Father* (Edinburgh: Canongate).

O'Brien, G.V. (2003) 'Indigestible Food, Conquering Hordes, and Waste Materials: Metaphors of Immigrants and the Early Immigration Restriction Debate in the United States', *Metaphor and Symbol*, 18(1), 33–47.

Pancake, A.S. (1993) 'Taken by Storm: the Exploitation of Metaphor in the Persian Gulf War', *Metaphor and Symbolic Activity*, 8, 281–95.

Parry-Giles, S. and Parry-Giles, T. (2002) *Constructing Clinton: Hyperreality and Presidential Image-Making in Postmodern Politics* (New York: Peter Lang).

Ralph, J. (1993) *Northern Protest: Martin Luther King, Jr. Chicago and the Civil Rights Movement* (Cambridge, Mass.: Harvard University Press).

Reagan, R. (with Hubler, R.) (1981) *My Early Years or Where's the Rest of Me?* (London: Sidgwick and Jackson).

Reagan, R. (2011) *My Father at 100* (New York: Viking).

Rentoul, J. (2001) *Tony Blair: Prime Minister* (St. Ives: Time Warner).

Rohrer, T. (1995) 'The Metaphorical Logic of (Political) Rape: the New Wor(l)d Order', *Metaphor and Symbolic Activity*, 10(2), 115–37.

Rose, N. (1999) *Powers of Freedom* (Cambridge: CUP).

Sandikcioglu, E. (2000) 'More Metaphorical Warfare in the Gulf: Orientalist Frames in News Coverage', in A. Barcelona (ed.) *Metaphor and Metonymy at the Crossroads: a Cognitive Perspective* (Berlin and New York: Mouton de Gruyter), pp. 299–320.

Santa Ana, O. (1999) ' "Like an Animal I was Treated": Anti-Immigrant Metaphor in US Public Discourse', *Discourse and Society*, 102, 191–224.

Sauer, C. (1997) 'Echoes from Abroad – Speeches for the Domestic Audience: Queen Beatrix's Address to the Israeli Parliament', in C. Schäffner (ed.) *Analysing Political Speeches* (Clevedon: Multilingual Matters).

Sego, L.P. (2001) 'Philistines, Barbarians, Aliens, et al.: Cognitive Semantics in Political "Otherness" ', in R. Diveren, R. Frank and C. Ilie (eds) *Language and Ideology*, vol. II *Descriptive Cognitive Approaches* (Amsterdam and Philadelphia: Benjamins), pp. 107–16.

Seliger, M. (1976) *Ideology and Politics* (London: Allen & Unwin).

Semino, E. (2008) *Metaphor in Discourse* (Cambridge: CUP).

Semino, E. and Masci, M. (1996) 'Politics of Football: Metaphor in the Discourse of Silvio Berlusconi in Italy', *Discourse and Society*, 7, 243–69.

Shepherd, R. (1997) *Enoch Powell* (London: Pimlico).

Sinclair, J. and Coulthard, M. (1975) *Towards an Analysis of Discourse* (Oxford: OUP).

Sontag, S. (1989) *AIDS and its Metaphors* (London: Allen Lane).

Sopel, J. (1995) *Tony Blair the Moderniser* (London: Michael Joseph).

Sperber, D. (2001) 'An Evolutionary Perspective on Testimony and Argumentation', *Philosophical Topics*, 29, 401–13.

Straehle, C. Weiss, G., Wodak, R., Muntigl, P. and Sedlak, M. (1999) 'Struggle as Metaphor in European Union Discourse on Unemployment', *Discourse and Society*, 10(1), 67–99.

Suskind, R. (2004) *The Price of Loyalty: George W. Bush, the White House and the Education of Paul O'Neill* (New York: Simon and Schuster).

Taylor, A.J.P. (1969) *Churchill: Four Faces and the Man* (London: Allen Lane).

Terkel, S. (1980) *American Dreams: Lost and Found* (New York: Pantheon).

Thornborrow, J. (1993) 'Metaphors of Security: a Comparison of Representation in Defence Discourse in Post-Cold-War France and Britain', *Discourse and Society*, 4(1), 99–119.

Toolan, M. (1988) *Narrative: a Critical Linguistic Introduction* (London and New York: Routledge).

Tsui, A.B.M. (1994) *English Conversation* (Oxford: OUP).

van Dijk, T.A. (1995) 'Discourse Analysis as Ideology Analysis', in C. Schaffner and A. I. Wendon (eds) *Language and Peace* (Aldershot: Dartmouth Publishing), pp. 17–33.

van Dijk, T.A. (1998) *Ideology: a Multidisciplinary Approach* (Newbury Park, Calif.: Sage).

van Dijk, T.A. (2006) 'Discourse and Manipulation', *Discourse and Society*, 17(3), 359–83.

van Dijk, T.A. (2008) *Discourse and Power* (Basingstoke: Palgrave Macmillan).

van Dijk, T.A. (2009) 'Critical Discourse Studies: a Sociocognitive Approach', in R. Wodak and M. Meyer (eds) *Methods of Critical Discourse Analysis* (London: Sage), pp. 62–85.

van Teeflen, T. (1994) 'Racism and Metaphor: the Palestinian–Israeli Conflict in Popular Literature', *Discourse and Society*, 5(3), 381–405.

Voss, J.F., Kennet, J. Wiley, J. and Schooler, T.Y.E. (1992) 'Experts at Debate: the Use of Metaphor in the US Senate Debate on the Gulf Crisis', *Metaphor and Symbolic Activity*, 7, 197–214.

Walton, D. (2007) *Media Argumentation: Dialectic Persuasion and Rhetoric* (Cambridge: CUP).

Wander, P. (1984) 'The Rhetoric of American Foreign Policy', *Quarterly Journal of Speech*, 70(4), 339–61.

White, M. and Herrera, H. (2003) 'Metaphor and Ideology in the Press Coverage of Telecom Corporate Consolidations', in R. Dirven, R. Frank and M. Putz (eds) *Cognitive Models in Language and Thought* (Berlin and New York: Mouton de Gruyter), pp. 277–323.

Wodak, R. and Meyer, M. (eds) (2009) *Methods of Critical Discourse Analysis*, 2nd rev. edn (London: Sage).

Woodward, B. (2004) *Plan of Attack* (New York: Simon and Schuster).

Woodward, J. D. (1990) 'Ideological Images for a Television Age: Ronald Reagan as Party Leader', in D.M. Hill, R.A. Moore and P. Williams, *The Reagan Presidency: an Incomplete Revolution?* (Basingstoke: Macmillan), pp. 115–31.

Young, H. (1993) *One of Us: a Biography of Margaret Thatcher* (London: Pan).

Zinken, J. (2003) 'Ideological Imagination: Intertextual and Correlational Metaphors in Political Discourse', *Discourse and Society*, 14(4), 507–23.

Index of Conceptual Metaphors

AMERICA IS A PERSON, 258

BAD GOVERNING IS DESTROYING, 205
BAD IS DOWN, 99
BRITAIN AND THE USA ARE TRAVELLING COMPANIONS, 69
BRITAIN IS A HERO, 78, 321
BRITAIN IS LIGHT, 78

CIRCUMSTANCES ARE WEATHER, 106
CONFLICT IS BLOOD, 113
CONSERVATIVE POLICIES ARE A MEDICINE, 181, 193
CONSERVATIVE POLICIES ARE UNIMPEDED MOVEMENTS, 179, 193
CONSERVATIVE POLICY IS A LIFE FORCE, 41, 43
CONSERVATISM IS MORAL, 193

DESPAIR IS A VALLEY, 99
DIFFICULTIES ARE IMPEDIMENTS TO MOTION, 317

ETHICAL BEHAVIOUR IS A SHIELD, 78
EUROPE IS A FAMILY, 134

FORWARD MOVEMENT IS GOOD, 99

GERMANY IS DARKNESS, 78
GERMANY IS A VILLAIN, 62
GOD IS LIGHT, 160
GOOD GOVERNING IS CREATING, 205, 221, 238, 241, 247
GOOD IS UP, 99, 161

HAPPY IS UP, 156
HISTORY IS A PERSON, 75, 260
HOPE IS LIGHT, 60, 71, 72, 76, 78

IDEAS ARE LIGHT SOURCES, 71
IMMIGRATION IS INVASION, 125
INDUSTRIAL RELATIONS IS A BATTLE, 171, 172, 193
INFLATION IS AN ENEMY, 170
INTELLIGENCE IS A LIGHT SOURCE, 71
INTENSE FEELING IS HEAT, 75

JUSTICE IS A BALANCE, 267

KNOWING IS SEEING, 297
KNOWLEDGE IS LIGHT, 159, 161

LABOUR/SOCIALISM IS A DEATH FORCE, 193
LABOUR/SOCIALISM IS SINFUL, 193
LABOUR/SOCIALIST POLICIES ARE A DISEASE, 193
LABOUR/SOCIALIST POLICIES ARE IMPEDED MOVEMENTS, 179, 193
LIFE IS A JOURNEY, 45, 47, 66, 75, 95
LIFE IS A STRUGGLE FOR SURVIVAL, 92
LONG-TERM PURPOSEFUL ACTIVITIES ARE JOURNEYS, 234
LOVE IS A JOURNEY, 66

MEANS ARE PATHS, 317
MORAL ACTIONS ARE FINANCIAL TRANSACTIONS, 266, 267, 270
MORALITY IS CONFLICT, 230, 231, 247

NAZISM IS A MONSTER, 64, 78

OPPOSING INFLATION IS A BATTLE, 3

PERMITTING IMMIGRATION IS NATIONAL SUICIDE, 131
POLITICAL IDEOLOGIES ARE ENEMIES, 174
POLITICAL OPPONENTS ARE ENEMIES, 174
POLITICAL STRUGGLE IS A HARSH LANDSCAPE, 97, 107
POLITICS IS CONFLICT, 169, 170ff., 193, 322
POLITICS IS ETHICS, 230, 231, 247
POLITICS IS SPORT, 147
PURPOSEFUL ACTIVITY IS TRAVELLING ALONG A PATH TOWARD
   A DESTINATION, 66
PURPOSES ARE DESTINATIONS, 317

RACIAL EQUALITY IS THE PROMISED LAND, 97
RIGHT ACTION IS A SHIELD, 75

SEGREGATION IS AN ILLNESS, 100
SEGREGATION IS A PRISON, 102, 107
SEGREGATION IS SLAVERY, 102, 103, 107
SOCIAL AND ECONOMIC PROBLEMS ARE ENEMIES, 170
SOCIALISM IS AN IMMORAL PERSON, 185
SPEED IS SUCCESS, 147
STOPPING IS BAD, 99

TERRORISTS ARE DANGEROUS ANIMALS, 264
TERRORISTS ARE PARASITES, 265, 266
THE CIVIL RIGHTS MOVEMENT IS A SPIRITUAL JOURNEY, 89, 93, 107

THE HISTORIC STRUGGLE FOR FREEDOM IS A JOURNEY, 96, 107
THE ISLAMIC WORLD IS A CHILD, 264
THE NATION IS A FAMILY, 191, 282
THE NATION IS A MACHINE, 322
THE NATION IS A PERSON, 55, 64, 77, 78, 256, 322
THE REGION IS A PERSON, 322
THE SECULAR PRESENT IS THE SACRED PAST, 82, 86, 107
THE STATE IS A SERVANT, 190, 193
THE STATE IS THE MASTER, 190, 193
THE WORLD IS A PERSON, 262, 263

UNDERSTANDING IS SEEING, 71, 75, 76, 183

WELL-BEING IS WEALTH, 255

General Index

actor-politicians, 20, 138, 140ff., 144ff.
African Americans, 80, 86, 89, 91
alliteration, 210
American Dream, 38ff., 44, 82, 161, 280ff., 315, 323
anaphora, 291ff., 308
antithesis, 11, 41, 57, 72, 94, 105ff., 167, 193, 289ff., 293, 297, 312
Aristotle, 7, 14, 21, 31, 123
aspirations, 39, 286, 108, 151, 159, 184, 281, 283ff., 304
authoritarian discourse, 233
'Axis of Evil', 26, 257ff.

Bible, the, 23, 77, 269, 297
biblical allusion, 12
Big Society, the, 21, 226
Blair, Tony, 223ff.
  childhood, 224
  communication style, 18, 225ff.
  epic myths, 233
  ethical discourse, 228ff.
  influence of Bush, 258
  influence of Clinton, 215
  influence of Thatcher, 224, 226, 231
  Labour Party conference address 2002, 18ff.
  Labour Party conference address 2003, 38, 326ff.
  speech to the House of Commons, March 2003, 248ff.
blending, rhetorical, 309
blending theory, 48ff., 113, 127ff., 156ff.
blood money, 267ff.
brand, political, 6
Brown, Gordon, 20, 296, 319
Bush, George, Junior, 251ff.
  Hitler and, 265
  influence of Churchill, 52, 257, 261
  moral accounting and, 255ff.
  personifications, use of, 256f.

speech authorship, 252
  see also 'Axis of Evil'; 'War on Terror'
Bush, George Senior, 251ff., 256, 259ff., 265, 271ff.

'call and response', 85, 309
'calm-to-storm delivery', 85, 309
Cameron, David, 20, 21
charisma, 81ff., 109, 137, 200, 306, 312, 322, 326ff.
charity, 117, 132, 134
chiasmus, 10, 57ff., 288
chosen people, 85, 89ff., 92
Christianity, 27, 71, 76, 83, 86, 115, 148, 224, 228, 280, 305ff., 325ff.
Churchill, Winston, 52ff.
  heroic myth and, 54
  use of personifications, 54ff., 61ff.
Civil Rights movement, the, 80, 83ff., 87ff., 93ff., 108
classical rhetoric, 7ff., 18, 124, 288ff., 300ff., 308, 309
Clinton, Bill, 195ff.
Clinton, Hillary, 210, 286, 300
clothes, 166, 312
cognition, 13, 21
  social, 14, 23, 44, 108, 119, 134
cognitive frame, 3, 174
cognitive semantics, 45ff.
coherence, 70, 88, 214, 292
cohesion, 73
conceptual metaphor, 2ff., 24, 29, 35, 41, 45, 47ff.
conflict, 3, 24, 30, 49, 100, 104, 113, 126, 130, 145, 150, 168ff., 177ff., 192ff., 230ff., 247ff., 318, 322
connotation, 40, 196, 227, 240, 242
containers, 111, 161ff., 298ff.
contrast, 6, 16, 18ff., 37, 52, 72ff., 81, 83, 96, 100ff., 110, 125ff., 161, 197ff.
  see also antithesis

Conviction Rhetoric, 10, 142ff.,
148ff., 152, 160, 165ff., 203, 212
critical discourse analysis, 47
critical metaphor analysis, 24, 26ff.,
184
cultural knowledge, 30, 51, 57, 208

death, 18ff., 23, 43, 50, 59, 108, 129,
159ff., 186
delegitimisation, 17ff., 30
deliberative speech, 7
depersonification, 15, 127, 174, 181ff.,
204
dialect, 16
dialogue, reported, 117ff., 146

earth, 149ff.
economics, 36, 111
emotion, 7, 14ff., 21ff., 31, 44, 49, 65,
111, 123ff., 130ff., 134, 145, 159,
172ff., 212, 242, 264, 290, 301ff.,
311ff., 320ff.
emotional coercion, 126, 130
epideictic speech, 8, 303
epilogue, 291, 300ff.
epiphora, 291ff., 308
equivalence, 71, 76, 177, 218, 257
ethics, 229ff., 247ff., 266
ethical discourse, 228ff., 269, 319
ethico-politics, 229, 233
ethos, 7, 14, 18ff., 29, 46, 81, 92,
182ff., 217, 226, 289, 309, 318ff.
evaluation, 3ff., 7, 24, 28, 62, 65ff.,
71ff., 96ff., 101ff., 106, 116ff.,
126ff., 169, 180, 186ff., 201ff.,
207
negative, 65ff., 72, 96, 100, 186ff.,
205, 245, 264, 321
positive, 62, 65ff., 201ff., 216, 236,
238ff., 257, 325
evil, 26ff., 54, 63ff., 71, 115ff., 154ff.,
182, 228ff., 242ff., 258ff., 265,
319
see also 'Axis of Evil'
Evil Empire, 26, 139ff.

faith, 71, 150, 184, 197ff., 299, 306ff.
Fascism, 242, 247, 258
Favreau, Jon, 5, 286ff.

fear, 22ff., 25, 49, 111ff., 120ff., 130,
182, 186, 275, 293ff., 302, 320
film/cinema, 140ff., 151, 154ff., 159,
221, 323
forensic speech, 8, 293
frontier, 149ff., 156
Frum, David, 258

gender, 167
globalisation, 25, 152, 209, 238, 285
Great Chain of Being, 264ff.
Gulf War, 248, 251, 276
guide, 47, 60, 66, 75, 97, 215, 318

hero, 23, 62ff., 78, 82, 111, 126,
136ff., 139ff., 141ff., 146, 151,
159, 169, 196, 199, 201, 210, 259,
317, 320ff., 324ff., 327ff.
everyday heroes, 219ff.
heroic female warrior, 169, 178, 189
heuresis, 8
history, 26, 196, 212, 218, 224, 235,
255
in metaphor, 67, 75, 82, 86, 96, 118,
135, 141, 243, 259ff., 284,
299ff., 308, 315
Hitler, Adolf, 54, 55, 61, 63ff., 77, 252,
258, 261, 265
humour, 2, 15, 46, 160, 162, 190
hyperbole, 46, 55, 57ff., 73, 76, 85ff.,
105, 116, 119, 132, 180, 186

iconography (iconic), 63
ideology, 21ff., 61ff., 65, 89ff., 109ff.,
168ff., 174ff., 178, 184ff., 237ff.,
307, 323
immigration, 13, 24, 49, 109, 112,
115ff., 121, 124ff., 128ff., 162,
293
India, 130ff.
innocence, 87, 275ff.
intention, 13ff., 19ff., 29ff., 43ff.,
49ff., 55ff.
interaction
with audience, 9, 84, 309
of rhetorical strategies, 51, 74ff., 88,
94, 104ff., 167, 249, 255ff., 290,
292, 301, 304, 312
intertextual reference, 94, 106

Iraq War, 49, 230, 243, 287
Iron Curtain, the, 34, 74, 165ff.
Iron Lady, the, 34, 86ff., 302
isocolon, 292, 294ff.
isolationism, 293

Kennedy, John F., 4, 26, 161, 196, 294, 306
King, Martin Luther, 79ff., 212, 218, 280, 305ff., 316, 318ff., 326

leadership, 1ff., 20, 42ff., 46, 151, 183, 185, 203, 225, 246ff., 251ff., 257, 259ff., 311ff.
legitimacy/legitimisation, 19, 26, 33, 111ff., 119ff., 148ff., 228, 240ff., 247ff., 250, 259, 270ff., 292
Lewinsky affair, 195ff., 211
life force, 41ff., 187ff., 210, 240
logos, 7, 14, 15, 287, 293ff., 301ff., 321

Main Street, 288ff.
marching, 88ff.
martyr, 86ff.
maxims, 58
meaning, 31ff., 38ff., 124, 288, 312
media, 3ff. 6, 9ff., 20ff., 86ff., 225
Mein Kampf, 265
memory, 24, 79ff., 111, 176, 326
messianic discourse, 82, 85ff., 87, 106
metalinguistic awareness, 133
metaphor
    clusters, 88, 290ff., 301, 304
    definition of, 31
    interaction effects of, 51, 88, 94, 104ff., 292, 304, 312
    mixed, 74
    'nested', 59, 74ff., 179, 312
    novel, 295ff.
    subliminal effects of, 2, 23, 114, 177, 312, 323, 324
metaphor, types of
    accounting, 29, 253ff., 266ff., 269ff., 322
    animal, 122, 189ff., 264ff., 321
    book, 299
    building, 101ff., 202ff., 238ff., 291

conflict, 3, 30, 49, 92, 104, 126, 130, 168ff., 177ff., 193ff., 199, 230ff., 247ff., 322
creation, 201ff., 237ff., 316
crime and punishment, 270ff.
destruction, 205ff.
family, 29, 134, 191, 282ff., 303ff.
finance, *see* accounting metaphors
gambling, 269ff.
harness, 216, 235ff., 296
health, 101ff., 180ff., 100ff., 324
hunting, 264
journey, 45ff., 60, 66ff., 74ff., 88ff., 95ff., 106ff., 178ff., 198ff., 211ff., 223, 234ff., 302ff., 313, 315ff., 324ff.
landscape, 96ff.
life and death, 63, 187ff., 208ff.
light and darkness, 71ff., 297
master–servant, 190ff., 321
religious, 199, 217ff.
segregation, 100ff.
sports, 146ff., 219ff., 247
transport, 94ff.
metonym, 48ff., 55, 64ff., 113, 176, 257, 273, 277, 288ff., 291, 299, 302, 306
modality, 10, 113, 286ff.
morale, 53, 58, 66, 72, 75, 142, 320
morality/immorality
    moral accounting, 29, 253ff., 266ff., 269ff., 322
    moral conviction, 165, 182
    moral credit, 271, 278
    moral vision, 82, 87
    nurturant parent morality, 29ff., 197
    strict father morality, 29, 197
myth
    'black', 281, 305
    Boudicca, 165ff., 174, 180, 191
    of Britain, 11ff., 41ff., 54ff., 62ff., 71, 76, 78, 109ff., 114ff., 126, 169, 181ff., 191, 257
    Conspiratorial Enemy, 26, 140, 142, 327
    debunking, 221
    definition, 22ff.
    of good and evil, 63, 66ff., 182, 188, 228ff., 245, 258, 312, 319

myth – *continued*
  guilt and innocence, 258, 267, 274,
    277ff.
  heroic, 52ff., 55ff., 62, 64, 77ff.,
    141ff., 151, 174, 189, 193,
    220ff., 259, 276, 325, 328
  historical, 44, 153, 174, 218ff., 282ff.
  intergalactic, 149ff., 155, 163
  messianic, 81ff., 91ff., 107ff., 280
  and magic, 326ff.
  myth making, 38ff.
  political, 24ff., 38ff., 47ff.
  of rebirth/renewal, 115, 150, 152,
    196, 208ff., 240ff.
  romantic, 141ff., 162
  United We Stand, 26, 140
  Valiant Leader, 26, 63, 141ff., 236

narrative, 12, 22, 24ff., 39ff., 60, 81ff.
    90ff., 112, 120ff., 149, 169, 261,
    276, 281, 283, 286
  see also political myth
nationalism, 110
neo-Conservatives, 248, 257
New Labour, 46, 194, 226, 128, 233,
    235, 237ff., 242, 247, 250
Nixon, Richard, 4
non-violence, 104ff.
nostalgia, 190, 212, 219, 321
nuclear weapons, 154

Obama, Barack, 280ff.
optimism, 40, 142ff., 155
Oracle, The, 112ff., 119, 137
oratory, 52ff., 58, 77, 86ff., 287, 292ff.,
    305
'otherness', 168ff.

parallelism, 10, 56, 105, 181, 288, 290,
    295, 308
pathos, 7, 14, 21, 46, 79, 133, 162,
    301ff., 308, 320
performance, 1ff., 2, 7, 8, 20
personification, 54ff., 61ff., 75ff., 78,
    170, 185ff., 190, 243ff., 256ff.
  Blair's use of, 243ff.
  Bush Junior's use of, 256ff.
  Churchill's use of, 54ff.
  Thatcher's use of, 185ff.

persuasion, 13ff., 17ff., 35ff., 43ff., 51,
    311, 313, 316, 318ff., 328
phraseology, 58ff., 117, 227,
    245ff.
polarity/polarisation, 63, 167ff., 182,
    188, 190, 193
  reversal of, 240, 242
political communication, 9, 14, 22,
    160, 225, 316, 318ff.
  see also journey metaphors;
    personification; metaphor,
    subliminal effects of
political debate, 37, 44
political image, 6, 166ff., 319
popular phrases, 112, 116ff.
Powell, Enoch 49, 109ff.
  Powellism, 109ff.
presupposition, 114
problem–solution pattern, 181ff.

racial equality, 97ff.
racial segregation, 80, 100ff.
Reagan, 20, 21, 26, 138ff., 165, 295,
    312, 317
'Reagonomics', 138
reification, 103ff., 199ff.,
    202ff., 205ff., 234, 236ff.,
    241ff., 245ff.
religious discourse, 71, 84, 159, 297
repetition, 10ff., 55ff., 80, 93ff., 105,
    226, 291ff., 307ff.
retribution and revenge, 255, 267,
    271, 274, 276
rhetoric
  classical, 7ff., 18, 288ff., 300, 301,
    308, 309
  combination of rhetorical
    techniques, 12, 41, 49, 51, 94,
    170, 208, 243, 288, 290, 311
  rhetorical intention, 67ff., 82, 142
  rhetorical questions, 11, 55ff., 84,
    249
  rhetorical resonance, 212
  rhetorical strategy, 51, 82, 92, 104,
    112, 200, 212, 235, 243, 255,
    266, 270, 287
  rhetorical tension, 242ff.
  taxis, 8

right
being right, 14, 311
having the right intentions, 14, 19,
29ff., 46, 55, 61, 76ff., 104, 113,
119ff., 167, 180, 195, 221, 247,
250, 259, 311, 316, 318ff.
sounding right, 14ff., 20, 27, 33, 34,
46, 55, 77, 84, 94, 113ff., 116ff.,
167, 264, 290ff., 320ff.
telling the right story, 14ff., 22ff.,
38ff., 55, 68, 120ff., 151, 160,
256, 323ff.
thinking right, 14ff., 117ff., 232,
321ff.
'Rivers of Blood', 44, 49, 112, 118, 122

Saddam Hussein, 230, 232, 247ff.,
254, 258, 271ff.
sarcasm, 12
schema, 14, 25, 49, 64, 140, 156, 179,
188, 205, 325
journey schema, 66, 69ff., 234,
317ff.
schemes, 288, 290
science and technology, 150, 153ff.
semantic field, 48, 156, 240
September 11th/9/11, 48, 251ff.,
271ff.
shining city, 161ff.
slavery, 93ff., 102ff., 118, 305, 319
socialism, 25, 41, 174, 176, 184ff.,
188ff., 312
source domain, 18, 31, 33, 37, 45ff.,
59ff., 61, 66ff., 74ff., 87ff., 99,
128, 156, 159, 201, 234, 295,
302ff., 312, 313ff., 324
sound bites, 9ff., 19ff., 225ff.
SOURCE–PATH–GOAL, 66, 156, 317
Soviet Union, 26, 139, 141ff., 147,
160, 165ff.
spatial concepts, 66, 123, 152ff.,
157ff., 293, 320
speculative prophecy, 112ff.
speech
act/action, 9, 13, 199, 224
authorship, 5ff.
making, 5ff., 75, 317
writers, 5ff., 252, 258, 286
speed, 38, 94ff., 129, 132, 147, 156ff.

spin, 4, 5ff.
spin doctor, 250
Star Wars, 139, 151, 153ff.
style, 1, 8, 20, 312
Blair and, 46, 225ff., 245ff.
classical rhetoric and, 4
Churchill and, 52, 61, 261
Clinton and, 203
King, Martin Luther and, 84,
Obama and, 286, 291ff.
Powell and, 110ff.
Reagan and, 139ff.
Thatcher and, 177ff.
symbols/symbolic action, 1, 138ff.,
148ff., 153, 175ff., 196, 209, 258,
278, 280, 282, 291, 321ff.

target domains, 31, 45, 88ff., 100ff.,
129, 156
Tebbit, Norman, 24, 124
technological revolution/change, 203
television, 4, 20, 86ff., 139ff.,
221, 227
Terkel, Studs, 281
terrorists/terrorism, 232, 264, 274
Thatcher, Margaret, 2ff., 10ff., 23, 25,
35, 40ff., 46, 74, 165ff., 247, 257
compared with Blair, 224ff., 229,
231, 234, 248
Third Way, 194, 242
topoi, 112
trade unions, 119ff., 171ff.
transcendence, 99, 199ff.
tricolon, 291ff., 304
tropes, 288, 290, 308
trust, 1ff., 4, 5ff., 14, 46ff., 51, 183,
219, 287ff., 327

USA, the/America
'America', 211ff., 257
Blair and, 243, 247
Britain and, 69ff., 110, 165
Democrats, 196ff., 203, 205, 208,
211, 226, 237, 261, 280, 286,
291, 296, 302, 306
football and, 148, 219ff.
international law, 273
Iran crisis, 141
Iraq War, 49, 230, 251ff., 276, 287

USA, the/America – *continued*
  politics and, 197ff., 217, 226, 254,
    261, 278ff., 293ff., 316
  popular culture, 146ff.
  race issues, 94
  religion, 218
  Republicans, 4, 39, 103, 140, 197,
    251, 261, 291, 297, 319
  as a 'shining city', 161ff.
  space exploration, 149ff., 153
  strategic defence initiative/'Star
    Wars', 151, 154
  superheroes and, 140, 143ff., 163,
    220, 223
  superpower, 138, 142ff., 151ff., 251,
    262ff., 271ff., 285
  as victim, 276ff.
  War on Terror, 254, 258ff., 271ff.
  see also American Dream; African
    Americans

value system/systems, 3, 44, 187,
  288ff., 312, 319
victim, 63ff., 93, 121ff., 254, 266, 271,
  275ff.
villain, 23, 54, 62ff., 78, 276
voice quality, 3, 84

Wall Street, 288ff.
War on Terror, 244, 254ff., 275
weapons of mass destruction, 49, 244,
  246, 248, 251, 270
Wild West, the, 153, 277
'will to govern' the, 233, 235ff., 240,
  246, 312, 329
world
  hegemony, 152
  Islamic, 263ff.
  New World Order, 273
  otherworld, 325, 327

'Yes we can', 290, 307ff.

CPSIA information can be obtained at www.ICGtesting.com
Printed in the USA
LVOW04s1623030715

444911LV00008B/140/P